Ways *to the* *Sky*

A Historical Guide to North
American Mountaineering

Andy Selters

**AAC
PRESS**

THE AMERICAN
ALPINE BOOK SERIES

Published by:
The American Alpine Club Press
710 Tenth Street, Suite 100
Golden, Colorado 80401
www.americanalpineclub.org

Founded in 1902, the American Alpine Club is dedicated to promoting climbing knowledge, conserving mountain environments and serving the American climbing community. The American Alpine Club Press began publishing in 1902, and publishes such world-renowned titles as The American Alpine Journal and Accidents in North American Mountaineering.

Manufactured in the United States of America.

Project Manager: Lloyd Athearn
Editor: Dougald MacDonald
Consulting Editor: Steve Roper
Layout and Design: Michael Cutter
Cover Design: Michael Cutter
Maps: Martin Gamache
Production Assistance: The Mountaineers Books

Front cover background photo: Jack Durrance rappelling in the Tetons in the 1930s. Photo by Hank Coulter, courtesy Margaret Coulter. Inset photo: Climbers on the summit of Mt. Alberta. North Twin and Mt. Columbia in the background. Photo by Larry Stanier.
Back cover photo: Kim Schmitz on the first winter ascent of the southeast face of Clyde Minaret, High Sierra. Photo by Galen Rowell/Mountain Light.

ISBN: 0-930410-83-1

**THANKS TO THE FOLLOWING
FOR THEIR GENEROUS SUPPORT:**

THE ALPINE CLUB OF CANADA

YVON CHOUINARD

BRADFORD AND BARBARA WASHBURN

PETER MCGANN, M.D.

LLOYD ATHEARN

GREGORY MILLER

CATHY ROSE

Moonset over Mt. Ritter and Banner Peak, Sierra Nevada. PHOTO BY ANDY SELTERS.

Contents

☭ Climbers looking over the peaks of the Ruth Glacier, on the first ascent of the east buttress of Denali. PHOTO BY PETER LEV.

Foreword I

by Peter Croft

NORTH AMERICA IS at once both an almost unbelievably vast arena for mountaineering and, in one way, a surprisingly small one. Its great size is amplified by its diversity. From the volcanoes of steamy hot Mexico to Denali, often described as even colder than any Himalayan giant, peaks of all shapes and sizes are found rising above the desert, rain forest and frozen tundra of this continent. But its giant mass is reduced by the relative ease of crossing the Mexican and Canadian borders, coupled with North Americans' love of the automobile and relatively cheap gas, which allow the huge distances to be traveled routinely. And the use of aircraft, which some bemoan, allows the lifeguard in San Diego to be whisked to a glacial basecamp at the base of, say, Mt. Foraker in just a couple of days. But it wasn't always this way.

The very human history that leads up to this point is a complex one. Its mixed bag of participants from varying backgrounds and isolated climbing communities has meant that often wildly contrary attitudes and techniques have been at work at the same time, sometimes competing but often happily oblivious. And, from first ascents requiring months to lightning-fast single-push ascents with no bivy gear, this appears to be an evolution of more than one species.

Andy Selters has stepped up to the plate to tell this story, and he has done an impressively thorough job. I can imagine him Indiana Jonesing through cobwebbed libraries to find obscure and yellowed journals, and private-eyeing around the continent trying to fit the pieces of the puzzle together. But he has done much more than simply add up the peaks, people and dates involved. Too often histories are reduced to black-and-white arithmetic. Andy has fleshed out even the earliest adventures in living color and allowed us to travel back to feel the climbers' pride and sense their fear. Just as importantly, Andy has explored the motivations, ethics and styles of the characters involved and has allowed his own passion for the peaks to voice concerns over how we climb our mountains and why we must protect them and the spirit of adventure.

Today, the lure of the big-numbered sound bite and the coveted crown of sponsorship are increasingly competing with stylistic and ethical concerns. Some alpinists claim new routes that end far from actual summits; big walls are rappelled, tick-marked with chalk and rehearsed for weeks before the eventual free ascent. To hail climbs such as these as standard-setting without examining and clearly identifying their very divergent styles would be to ignore an intrinsic loss of adventure. Some authors shy away from these subjects, shrugging their literary shoulders as if to say, "It doesn't really matter. Why can't we all just get along?" Well, not to sound neurotic, but on the world stage that's pretty much what Chamberlain said to Hitler back in 1938, and we're damn lucky today that we're not goose-stepping toward our peaks to climb for the Fatherland.

Andy is not some pale-faced urban intellectual whose sense of adventure grows in direct proportion to the distance he keeps between himself and the mountains. He lives at the high doorstep of the Sierra Nevada in eastern California. I suppose some might see this as the middle of nowhere, but, to more than a few of us, it is the center of the universe—Andy never needs to be reminded that he is a climber. And he is the real deal, having ranged all over the world, quietly going for it. Several times I've bragged to him about some area I'd just been into only to be surprised by his sheepish admission that, "Uh, yeah, I've been in there before."

Andy's book has not only introduced me to whole new chunks of history but also helped to fire up recollections of my own. My earliest memories are filled with a yearning for adventure. I remember clearly racing to the corner store to pick up the new *TV Guide*, racing back home and then highlighting every movie that was marked "adventure." Looking back now it was clearly a metaphor for what kind of search my life would become. In a childhood disappointed by narrowly focused sports and stifling rules, it was as if I was waiting for something. I was.

The first climbing trip I ever went on was to the Stikine area in the panhandle of Alaska. This was before I'd ever seen Yosemite or the Canadian Rockies, and I was overwhelmed. Strapping on skis at the high-tide mark, we skinned our way up the North Baird Glacier for five days to reach a basecamp amidst a cluster of unclimbed peaks. The scheduled food drop had not been made and the sugared vitamin pills we were down to did little to reduce our hunger or feeling of exposed isolation. We were seriously discussing the practicalities of skiing out again when we heard the plane. It's funny how quickly one goes from grimly fantasizing about a skeletal death crawl back to civilization to, after a half-dozen chocolate bars, hungrily eyeing the surrounding peaks. I climbed my first first ascent there and experienced snow blindness, like a knife in the eye. And when I slunk, underaged, into an Alaskan bar, it was the first time I visited a foreign land.

The strength and importance of mountaineering in North America lie not only in its remotest corners. They are realized when one immerses oneself in as much of the whole package as one can. I flash back once again to the Waddington Traverse with my best friend Greg Foweraker and Don Serl, the King of the Coast Range. Five days of brilliant knife-edges, huge, spooky crevasses and the highest summits in the range. Five days, long enough for a big pack and clunky boots to feel light and a part of me, and for the deep exposure to go from being intimidating to simply fueling the fire. Flash back again to another time, another place and a different mindset: Slesse Mountain and its elegant northeast buttress. Waking up that morning in Vancouver, the idea popping into my head and then one of those hunched-over-the-wheel-I-can-hardly-wait sort of drives. Next, running for miles up old logging roads through moody, green rainforest under brilliant blue skies. The route itself, long enough to get into the rhythm and getting only better and steeper until I reached the spiky summit. Then, on the descent, the brimming euphoria of continuous movement and solitude that lulled me into dropping my guard on a slime-streaked slab and sent me suddenly flying toward an unthinkable drop-off. And the last-minute snatch at a corkscrewing monkey tail of a cedar branch and the resulting, nick-of-time Tarzan swing to safety. From rock to ice, and from full-fledged expeditions to the spur of the moment, the heart-thumping wonder of each adventure is appreciated best when personal experience compares one to the other.

Good histories like this one are like personal memories. They come pulsing to life, giving us a sense of context, sometimes with a feeling of glorious achievement and sometimes with a cloud of haunting shame. Most importantly, though, they connect us to the passage of time by giving us a big swig of human experience and instilling in us the lasting importance of fighting the good fight.

Foreword II

by Barry Blanchard

ISN'T IT MAGNIFICENT, as a modern mountaineer, to be able to look back down the line of our ascendancy? For me, climbing is simply richer when I know whose steps I am following, which hands found the holds that I hold now. Who were they? Why did they climb up high…searching? What did they find up here?

Yet trying to get a handle on our history can be a little like trying to wrap your arms around an avalanche. There has been so much climbing done, and documented, that it is easy to be overwhelmed and buried. Thank god for the prospecting likes of Andy Selters and the grubstaking of the American and Canadian alpine clubs. Not only has Andy sifted the gems out of several hundred years of North American ascents, he also has identified the themes that have shaped our climbing heritage—named the bends in the river, if you will. Andy traces this flow from its headwaters in the early explorations of North American mountain ranges and through the formation of the various mountaineering clubs and the midcentury current of discovery—both in the lower ranges and among the northern giants—and on into the accelerated run of the first lifestyle climbers of the '60s and the incredibly fast and very good alpinists of the modern era.

Andy points out that over all this history lies the burden and blessing of our wilderness. The mountains of North America are untamed, underpeopled and uncivilized when compared to most other ranges where mountaineering is practiced, and doubly so for the Alps, the birthplace of mountaineering. We have to work very hard to get to, and climb, our mountains. Many of them are more often looked at by grizzly bears than by humans. This land shapes us— we are different from Europeans, we have our own stories, and I am glad to see them come to light through the fine efforts of writers like Andy Selters, Chic Scott (*Pushing the Limits: The Story of Canadian Mountaineering*) and David Roberts (*Escape from Lucania*), to name but a few. I also feel that thanks are owed to the American Alpine Club and the Alpine Club of Canada for their joint publishing effort on this text—BRAVO!

Andy's words will steer you to deeper pools of our story—we are part of a magnificent river that has flown through tens of thousands of days of human striving and search. May you feel some of that the next time you grab a handhold.

Acknowledgments

WHEN I LOOK BACK at who helped make the ED+ odyssey behind this book possible, my first thanks go to Jonathan Waterman, who, while director of publications at the American Alpine Club, handed me a torch that seemed almost impossible to raise high enough. Then I praise the archivists and librarians, from Banff to Jackson Hole and Golden, from Seattle to Portland, Malibu, Yosemite and Boston—their help in walking me down the dusty pathways of history has been vital. As for any writer, my primary job has been to ask the right questions, and in this case the most important answers came from the climbers who made the history. I give thanks to all of them down the decades who took the time to publish their stories. Among the living climbers who opened their minds to my questions, I called on a few repeatedly, especially Bill Pilling, Chic Scott and Peter Croft. Bill is a closet expert on North American mountains, and for Canadian history all roads lead to Chic. Without his generosity and his book *Pushing the Limits* I would still be trying to track down many things Canadian. Peter went beyond my request to share his own stories, as he volunteered to read through the entire manuscript, and from his perspective of everyday intensity he made suggestions throughout.

Many climbers contributed substantial interviews to this book, and it was no small inspiration to keep going after I talked with Yvon Chouinard, Jack Tackle, David Roberts, Jack Roberts, Bradford Washburn, Ken Henderson, Bill Hackett, Jeff Lowe, Michael Kennedy, David Jones, Don Serl, Glen Boles, Rolando Garibotti, Steve House, Galen Rowell, George Lowe, Dan Davis, Henry Barber, Mark Twight, John Clarke, Dave Nettle, John Fischer, Fred Beckey, Glen Dawson, Allen Steck, Doug Robinson, Gray Thompson, Barry Blanchard, Roger Briggs, Greg Lowe and Peter Metcalf.

Dozens of other climbers answered my scores of particular questions and offered other advice, including Stephen Koch, Urmas Franosch, Russell Mitrovich, Jimmy Haden, Jay Smith, Jim Bridwell, Alan Kearney, Larry Stanier, Jack Lewis, Doug Chabot, Richard May, Paul Claus, Kurt Gloyer, Greg Collum, Jim Nelson, Kit Lewis, Bobby Knight, Dee Molenaar, Michael Zanger, Bob MacGowan, Jeff Thomas, Bruce Hendricks, Tom Bennett, Les Wilson, Todd Bibler, Peter Lev, Mark Synnott, John Harlin III, Jane Koski, Neal Beidleman, Greg Horne, Leo Slaggie, Marijke Patterson-Robinson, Mike Sherrick, Jim Logan, Harvey Firestone, Alex Bertulis, Don Gordon, John Bachar, Jim Kanzler, Gil Roberts, Joe Kelsey, Angus Thuermer, Renny Jackson, Tom Hargis, Carl Diedrich, Paul Aubrey, Lou Dawson, Leo Larson, Tom Kimbrough, Chris Jones, Steve Bullock, Eric Beck, Bruce Hendricks, Michael Cohen, Rick Wilcox, Walt Vennum, Steve Larson, Jack Turner, Todd Vogel, Robert Parker, Ed Bernbaum, Paul DegliAngeli, Ed Bergeron, Kevin McLane, Maury McKinney, Brad White, Greg Foweraker, John Thackray, Mike Wood, Warren Harding, Randy Trover, R. J. Secor, Jonathan Waterman, Ed Webster, Marko Prezelj, Todd Calfee, Austin Post, John Baldwin, Charlie Sassara, Alex Bertulis, Laurie Williams, Kevin Steele, Dale Bard, Tom Frost, Don Lauria, Norman Milleron, Jim Ruch, Dan Patitucci, Bob Harrington, Vern Clevenger, John Dittli, Carl Skoog, Claude Fiddler, Chris Bonington, Russ McLean, Leon Blumer, Dave Turner, Dennis Hennek, Doug Scott, Glenn Randall, John Barstow, Mark Houston, Joie

Seagram, Francois Marsigny and Lyle Dean. Without the accumulated centuries of mountaineering that these people knew and shared, this book wouldn't have been much to contemplate.

History buffs Winston Crausaz, Evelio Echevarria, Andy Zdon and Greg Glade provided key help and information at key times. Carol Tonelli and my wife, Carla, supplied translation assistance, and in times of semiconductor desperation, Bruce Horn and Sean Alexander got my Mac back up and running.

Once I had a manuscript, Steve Roper stepped in, and when he applied his impressive and stern command of both English and mountaineering history to my secluded work I watched the text rise to a level I could never have attained on my own. Eventually Dougald MacDonald took up the task of polishing it into a proper product, while the AAC's Lloyd Athearn shepherded the whole project into production. Book publishing is a financially marginal enterprise these days, the more so for a small, part-time organization like the American Alpine Club Press, and I am eternally grateful for the willingness of the AAC, the Alpine Club of Canada and various benefactors to risk sponsoring a book like this.

A very special thanks goes to the many who generously allowed their photographs to be a part of this book. A very deep bow of gratitude goes to Bradford Washburn and Galen Rowell, and to the managers of their archives. Brad's and Galen's images have themselves helped shape North American mountaineering history, and some of them are in this book only out of their personal charity and belief in the value of North American mountaineering.

Introduction

"If you don't look back, the future never happens." –Poet Rita Dove

AMONG THE CONTINENTS, North America boasts mountains as diverse, as grand and nearly as extensive as even Asia's great cordilleras. From the subtropics to the high Arctic, some 15 mountainous regions have beckoned to climbers for many decades. People have climbed in North America through substantial shifts in mountaineering attitudes, styles and methods, and across sweeping changes in civilization. The legacy of ascent here is in many ways overwhelming, but one can still trace an evolution, a heredity that forks through generations and across cultures yet follows a centerline of respect, inspiration and motivation to climb mountain terrain. It's an unfolding story that, at its best, comprises one version of the quest to lift the human spirit.

The vision for this book began with a call from the American Alpine Club to build a series of books that, together, would portray the various legacies of climbing and mountaineering routes in North America—one book for bouldering, another for ski mountaineering, another for rock climbing, another for ice climbing, another for wall climbing. The volume in your hands is the story of original-style mountaineering.

What exactly does this mean? With some struggle, we settled on three broad parameters. The territory would be North America's higher peaks, from Mexico's volcanoes to the far north. This leaves out such terrain as El Capitan and Rocky Mountain waterfalls, not because they don't demand real aspects of mountaineering, but because climbing them doesn't include a quest for the peaks. Second, we chose to focus mostly on climbs that have been done entirely or predominantly "free"—that is, ascents where the climbers needed little or no direct aid from anchors to make progress. Therefore, even though big-wall climbs in, say, Alaska or Baffin Island clearly are a branch of serious mountaineering, such climbs deserve a companion volume. The core heritage of mountaineering is climbing high peaks with the feet and hands, including the use of ice tools. Finally, the primary currency of a mountaineering legacy is its routes, and so the focus for my research was to understand the progression of our mountain routes.

Mountaineers generally seek two types of fruit from their endeavors: experience and accomplishment. Of these, personal experiences might be more important, but a history book is poorly suited to portraying them. Whether it's a predawn start with the moon setting behind a ridge, the satisfaction of a crampon's bite against gravity's pull or the boon of a partnership that clicks smoothly with every pitch, such experiences slake the basic thirst that is mountaineering, yet a history book can only hint at their depth. Accomplishments, on the other hand, become handles that we all use to grasp the lines of history. Great ascents help define a mountaineering era the way a refrain helps define a score, and this book makes use of landmark climbs in this way. Nevertheless, a mountaineering legacy is much more than a sequence of great climbs.

The fiber that ties accomplishments into a meaningful lineage is progress, and this book tries to weave a portrait of North American mountaineering's progression. But what yardstick do we measure with? Younger climbers, for instance, often look down the decades and assume that each new era has brought progressively "better" climbing. Since climbers in 2004 are achieving routes that are technically more difficult than the standards of even 1994, youthful logic tends to assume that climbers way back when must have been mediocre indeed. However, a visit to the steep routes that, for instance, Conrad Kain, Val Fynn or Charles Michael did before World War I cannot fail to elicit respectful surprise from any modern climber. As another example, consider the 1910 first ascent of Denali's north peak. A trio of frontiersmen made this climb using the matériel of a mining outfit, in early April, in a day's roundtrip from a camp almost 9,000 feet below the top. One has to wonder if any but the finest of today's mountaineers would perform as well as any of these pioneers in their day. If we use the subjective yardsticks of tenacity, commitment, heart and even raw skill, it's difficult to see where the forebears left much room for progress.

By the same token, though, some older climbers tend to dismiss the accomplishments of a newer generation. As younger climbers advance their game with new methods, better gear and new types of goals, to a previous generation it can seem as if the adventure, skills, meaning and perhaps even the sanity of mountaineering has been lost. Yet who can blame a younger generation for wanting to forge its own way, just as previous generations did? Climbers progressively take on terrain that their predecessors never imagined. How, for instance, could the famed Canadian guide Edward Feuz ever have dreamed of a climb up the east face of Mt. Assiniboine? Could 1960s expeditionary mountaineer Boyd Everett have comprehended the steep routes and swift style of modern Alaskan ascents?

History shows us that each generation climbs into the uncertainty that it finds exciting, and that each does pretty well at extending the limits of the day. Then, as those climbs start to seem routine, the next generation seeks new ways to the sky—be they unclimbed summits, new routes or established routes climbed in a better style. In this way the measures of accomplishment shift, and directly comparing the climbers of different eras—or even different regions—is like measuring marathoners against sprinters or comparing early pole-vaulters with fiberglass-equipped Olympians. What fosters real progress is always a conceptual breakthrough: a well-planned gamble on a climb that is higher, steeper, longer or in some other way more committing and inspiring. When fresh endeavors prove their merit, the new generation essentially redefines mountaineering. The truest measure of mountaineering progress, then, is the evolution of the idea of mountaineering.

Mountaineering plans evolve, at least in part, within the evolving context of society. For example, compare the Ivy League explorers of the World War II era, who took well-supplied climbing and scientific expeditions to great subarctic summits, with the rock alpinists of the Vietnam-war period, who made low-budget breakthroughs on high granite walls. Both groups practiced mountaineering in the finest sense of the game, yet it can be a stretch for either to appreciate the accomplishments of the other. When you look across such diverse approaches for common ground, you see a perennial spirit that urges us to leave what's normal and comfortable and engage the peaks. That spirit emerges in different forms in every generation. Each generation's legacy is found in the character of its routes and the way they were climbed.

To better anchor the history in this book to the terrain, each chapter features routes that date from that era. I've suggested routes that both embody the given period and, for capable climbers, can be worthy objectives today. I gave added bias to routes that haven't seen as bright a spotlight as our best-known classics. The brief descriptions are designed simply to highlight routes that express our heritage particularly well and to hint at what it takes to climb them. In no way are these mini-portraits designed to substitute for the referenced guidebooks and/or additional research.

In summary, this book seeks answers to two general questions: How did mountaineering get from one decade to the next, and what routes embody that progress?

In North America, mountaineering has always struggled for definition in part because our mainstream culture is distant from the mountains. It's common to label our endeavors as "sport," but this term fits no better than a T-shirt over a down parka. The essence of what mountaineers do is simple and yet elusive, and our challenges are too complex and dangerous to share the themes of gridirons and racetracks. The risky paradoxes of mountaineering are as rich as life in general, and so I prefer the term "life game." Mountaineering is a life game where we climb high terrain by working hard and working well. Only four basic "rules" apply: that we go up of our own will, that we climb under our own power, that we minimize the traces of our passage, and that we come back down.

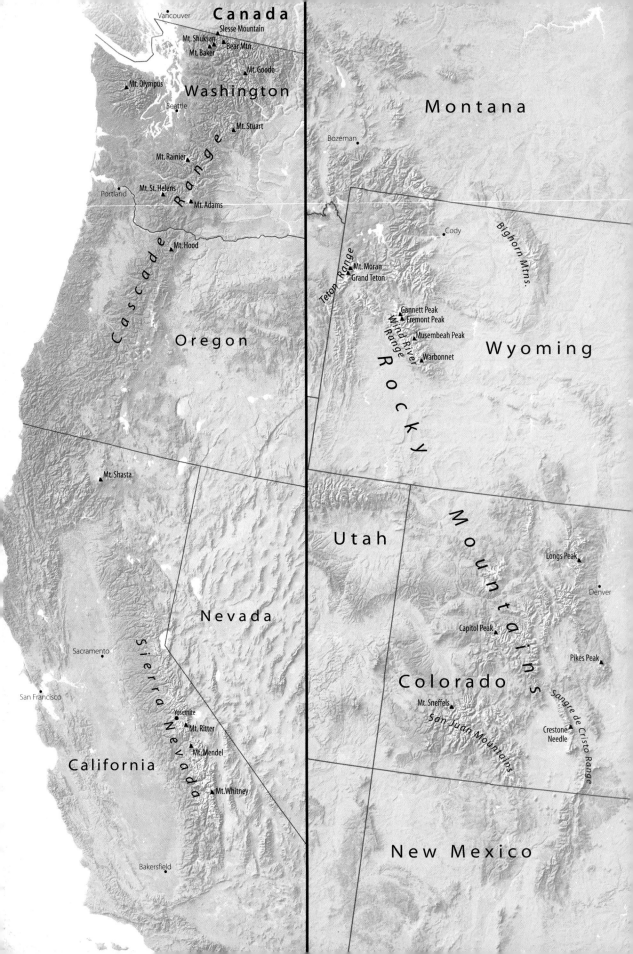

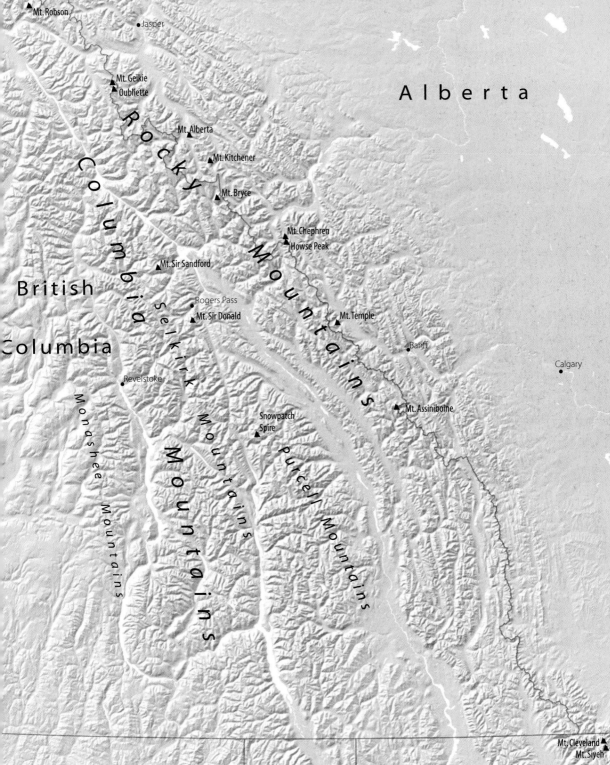

Edmonton

Mt. Robson

Jasper

A l b e r t a

Mt. Geikie
Oubliette

Mt. Alberta

Mt. Kitchener

Mt. Bryce

Mt. Chephren
Howse Peak

Mt. Sir Sandford

Rogers Pass

British

Mt. Sir Donald

Mt. Temple

Banff

Columbia

Calgary

Revelstoke

Mt. Assiniboine

Snowpatch
Spire

Mt. Cleveland
Mt. Siyeh

Washington

Idaho

Montana

Brooks

▲ Shot Tower

Endicott Mtns.   Doonerak ▲

Range

A l a s k a

Mt. Foraker ▲ Denali
▲▲ *Range*
Mt. Hunter ▲ Moose's
Tooth   ▲ Mt. Deborah
▲ Mt. Hayes

Kichatna
Spires

Anchorage ●

Chugach ▲ *Mtns.*
Mt. Marcus ▲
Baker

Mt. Blackburn ▲   *Wrangell*
Mtns.

University ▲
Peak

Yukon

▲ Mt. Lucania
Mt. Saint Elias ▲ ▲ Mt. Logan
▲ Mt. Kennedy

Icefield Ranges

Logan
Mountains

Mt. Fairweather ▲
Mt. Crillon ▲

Devils Thumb ▲

British

Coast

Columbia

Range

Monarch ▲
Mountain

Mt. Waddington ▲ ▲ Mt. Tiedemann
▲ Mt. Queen
Bess

Toba
Inlet

Mt. Tantalus ▲

Vancouver   ▲ Mt. Bardean

Cascades

Period I

Discovery By Summiting

Mountaineering as we know it began in the Alps in the late 18th century, when Europeans started to climb to mountain summits out of curiosity and for the sheer delight and challenge. Progressive Europeans had become enthusiastic about using scientific observation and logic to grasp the natural world, and it was from this optimism about science that the concept of mountaineering emerged. From its inception, mountaineering balanced along a narrow arête between the impractically foolish and the heroically grand.

Other cultures had of course climbed North American mountains before this tradition began, and Chapter 1 starts with an overview of these "pre-mountaineering" ventures. Euro-American climbing began as part of the exploration, conquest and occupation of our continent. Merely traveling through North America's unmapped terrain required significant effort, and climbing the peaks usually was part of a broader excursion. In this era, the greatest ambition naturally focused on the highest summits.

Today we climb many peaks routinely, but reaching the top of a mountain still generates challenge and excitement. We should recall the time when these peaks were remote and untrodden islands in the sky, and no one was quite sure whether going up there was something humans could even get away with.

CHAPTER 1

Mountaineering Takes Shape

When Euro-Americans began to climb the peaks of the North American West, they often found evidence that natives had been there first. Arrowheads and stone shelters testify that native climbers visited the summits, or at least the highest slopes, of significant peaks in the Rocky Mountains, the Sierra Nevada and Mexico. Recent archaeological evidence from 57 peaks in the American Rockies and Mexico shows that Neolithic peoples visited the tops of prominent peaks long before the development of historic cultures.

For the most part, the evidence for native climbs is so scant that it barely allows us to speculate on their goals. Some ascents probably included a practical aspect, such as hunting bighorn sheep, and every tribe probably had a spiritual sense of the mountains—they felt that mountains transcended the familiar lowlands and thereby embodied powerful forces. We can see this in the myths and legends that tribes ascribed to the peaks, some of which portrayed the mountains as demigods who helped in original creation, provided refuge from floods, or played roles in morality lessons. For many tribes, these legends still have meaning today.

Some peoples who lived near impressive mountains developed fearful or humble respect for the peaks. The Koyukon of interior Alaska, for example, would speak about Denali—or even in the direction of Denali—only with a hushed voice. Many natives believed that to set foot on a high peak would be a serious insult, possibly with catastrophic consequences.

In contrast, tribes on the east side of the Rocky Mountains used mountains for vision quests. The seekers would climb to high points, put themselves through privations to connect with the great spirits, and receive messages that would help guide their lives. For the Crow, especially, a high and austere ascent made a quest more powerful. Other native climbers include the Inuit of Baffin Island, who have climbed peaks into the present day, though how many and in what contexts we don't know.

Vision quests may have led to the construction of North America's most famous high artifact, the shelter-ring of stones known as the Enclosure, atop the west buttress of the Grand Teton, 490 cliffy feet below the main summit. In Colorado, Araphoe men reached the summit of Longs Peak, a 14,259-foot-high

☾ Artist's interpretation of James Stevenson and Nathaniel Langford on top of the Grand Teton. Artwork appeared in *Scribner's Monthly*. COURTESY ANGUS THUERMER.

mountain with steep flanks that would rebuff a number of early American attempts. The natives climbed to this broad summit to catch eagles for ceremonial feathers, tethering a coyote carcass as bait and hiding in fissures nearby.

The premier Cascade volcano, Mt. Rainier, understandably had an important role for peoples of this area, and natives may have climbed it. Sluiskin, the Yakama Indian who guided the first documented ascent party to the base, said his grandfather had reached the crater rim. Sluiskin gave a description reminiscent of the old Gibraltar Ledges route, including a possible reference to the summit steam vents—a "fiery lake"—within the crater.

The Squallyamish of the Puget Sound area had a legend in which a strong, successful man went to the top of Tahoma (Mt. Rainier) in search of *hiaqua*, the wealth of seashell-wampum. After many trials, he indeed found on the summit a deep well of *hiaqua*. Gathering as much as he could, he began the descent, but the angry spirit of the mountain flung lightning at him and forced him to toss away the treasure. Humbled, he returned to his campfire and faithful wife, and from then on he lived with a grace that served his people well.

Some of the most interesting tales of pre-European mountaineering come from the conquerors of Mexico. The Aztecs, like most Native Americans, believed that spirits inhabited all landforms, and that high mountains were the abode or even the embodiment of particularly powerful deities. Many of the Aztec's notorious ritual sacrifices were offered to the peaks and carried out atop lower summits.

A 17th-century Spanish chronicle recorded an Aztec account of an ascent of Popocatépetl in 1296. Drought gripped the Aztec lands and a prince named Chalchiuhtzin climbed to the 17,930-foot-high summit and whipped himself in a penitent request for rain. Other chronicles record that, about 1448, the Aztec emperor Montezuma I sent 10 men to climb Popocatépetl to find out why the mountain smoked. The men reached the crater, but only two survived to tell the tale. Oral tradition also

The Enclosure, on the top of the west buttress of the Grand Teton, as it stood in the 1930s. PHOTO COURTESY JACKSON HOLE HISTORICAL SOCIETY AND MUSEUM.

held that, around the year 1175, natives even climbed 18,620-foot-high Citlaltépetl, the highest peak in Mexico and the third-highest on the continent. In 1983, climbers found Toltec artifacts near the 17,159-foot summit of Iztaccíhuatl, suggesting that natives likely climbed this peak as well.

First European Ascents

Spanish conquistadors became the first Europeans to discover and climb high peaks in North America. In 1519, when Hernando Cortés and his small army marched from the coast toward the Aztec capital, Popocatépetl was spewing smoke and ash. Aztecs told him that to climb it was suicidal. Cortés saw this as an opportunity to impress the natives with his men's prowess, and he dispatched Diego de Ordáz to lead a group to the summit. In the face of volcanic fury, they may have succeeded or at least come quite close. How much this ascent fueled Montezuma II's fear of the Spaniards and the success of their

Popocatépetl from the north. PHOTO BY ANDY SELTERS.

invading army we can't say, but it is one of the world's few climbs that may have played a role in the course of civilization.

Soon after the climb, de Ordáz and Cortés contested for power, and even though King Carlos recognized de Ordáz for the ascent, the senior Cortés claimed his rival didn't make it. Thus started a legacy of first-ascent controversies that would be renewed on most of North America's prominent peaks.

A few decades later, British explorers seeking the Northwest Passage to the Pacific became the first Europeans to report sightings of North America's arctic mountains. Martin Frobisher and John Davis led excursions along the island that would later be named for the arctic explorer William Baffin.

The first known Anglo to climb a North American summit was Darby Field. In 1642 he made a two-week excursion from Massachusetts to the high point of the White Mountains in New Hampshire, the noble peak later named for George Washington. Field hoped to get a better view over the countryside and to reach shiny stones that glistened from the summit. He convinced two Abenaki natives to lead him to the base, but their fear of the treeless heights kept them from going higher. On top, the shiny rock turned out to be humble schist.

Alpine Roots

During the Middle Ages, Europeans developed disdain for their mountains, an attitude that might be called anti-sacred. People wrote of the peaks as demonic realms of perpetual winter, and travelers typically averted their eyes from alpine views. As late as 1708, a prominent doctor and authority on the Alps was refining a classification of the evil dragons thought to inhabit the peaks.

By the mid-1700s, however, scientific, geographic and mathematical discoveries had inspired progressives to refute superstitious assumptions about nature. The Enlightenment period rose as intellectuals argued that truth-seekers must give free rein to curiosity and depend on direct observations and logical analysis.

This Enlightenment spirit spawned fresh

Spanish colonial buildings of Mexico City, with Popocatépetl in the background. PHOTO BY ANDY SELTERS.

and adventurous interest in mountains, and in the 1760s a couple of different men initiated the notion to climb to the top of 15,771-foot Mont Blanc, the highest point in the Alps. The main protagonist was a scientist who hoped to get barometric readings from the top, and he offered a reward to the peak's first climbers. Reacting to this incentive, as well as to their own inspiration, village doctor Michel-Gabriel Paccard and his porter, Jacques Balmat, climbed to Mont Blanc's summit in 1786. The mountaineering tradition now looks to this climb as its seminal ascent.

Over the ensuing decades, occasional eccentric tourists and scientists repeated the climb of Mont Blanc, but it would be 50 years before more than a few would follow.

Explorers and Soldiers

It was during the Enlightenment that Europeans first saw the mountains of the North American West. The first were trappers who worked the Rocky Mountains starting in the 1730s. In the following decades European interest in the unknown continent and the possibility of discovering the mythical Northwest Passage led such naval explorers as Vitus Bering, Jean Francois de Galaup (the Earl of La Pérouse), Alessandro Malaspina, James Cook and George Vancouver to cruise the western coast. These sailors spied many high peaks from the water. Malaspina and Cook both measured Mt. St. Elias at over 17,500 feet. La Pérouse wrote of what we know as southern Alaska: "Its scenery has no parallel, and I doubt whether the lofty mountains and deep valleys of the Alps and Pyrenees afford so tremendous yet so picturesque a spectacle, well deserving the attention of the curious, were it not placed at the extremity of the earth." Vancouver's explorations in the early 1790s bestowed names on the primary Cascade peaks.

Vast distances kept most of the world from understanding the West in more than mythical terms. For instance, when President Thomas Jefferson assigned Meriwether Lewis to lead an expedition to the Pacific in 1804, he told Lewis that the natural law of symmetry meant the storied Rocky Mountains must be similar to the Appalachian chain in the

The Earl of La Pérouse, an early explorer of North America's western coast. COURTESY ED STUHL COLLECTION.

George Vancouver's ship *Discovery* in Puget Sound, 1792. PAINTING BY S. F. COOMBS. MSCUA UNIVERSITY OF WASHINGTON LIBRARIES, ACC# TRA507.

East, and so the portage across the continental divide would take no more than half a day. When they reached the Rockies, their crossing exacted a week of overland toil.

In Mexico, in 1804, the explorer Alexander von Humboldt measured the heights of the giant volcanoes, and his hasty and distant appraisal of Citlaltépetl placed it about 350 feet lower than Popocatépetl. (It is actually nearly 500 feet higher.) Humboldt's reputation was unassailable, however, and throughout most of the 19th century knowledgeable geographers believed that either Mt. St. Elias or Popocatépetl was the highest peak in North America.

Farther north, David Thompson brought the extent of the northern Rockies into general understanding between 1807 and 1811. A British explorer working for the fur-trading North West Company, Thompson traveled twice with his wife and their growing brood

of children across the range, once north and once south of the Columbia Icefields. His final product was a 10-foot-tall map of the vast Columbia and Athabasca drainages, and this proved to be the most useful chart of the region throughout the 19th century.

In the 1820s, British botanist-explorer David Douglas was commissioned to scout the vegetation and general resource potential of the Fraser and Columbia river basins. On his way back, following Thompson's route to Athabasca Pass, he climbed a nearby peak and named it Mt. Brown. Back in London, Douglas relied on a previous miscalculation of the region's general elevation and told the Royal Geographic Society that the peak he had climbed was 17,000 feet high. He compounded this error with a claim that it was the highest known peak in North America, even though he'd likely seen higher peaks himself. Douglas' claims persisted for some 70 years before mountaineers understood that the Canadian Rockies, spectacular though they may be, reached no such heights.

For later explorers, climbing the high Western peaks took on strategic and emblematic value. American soldiers climbed certain summits to add validity and grandeur to the claims of their country, as well as to gain viewpoints over Mexican territory. In 1820, 1833 and 1842, U.S. military teams climbed, respectively, Pikes Peak and two prominent summits in the Wind River Range. John Fremont was the leader of the 1842 expedition, and the 13,745-foot peak his team climbed is named for him.

In 1838, four Belgians made the first confirmed ascent of Citlaltépetl in Mexico. Henri Galleoti and Augusto B. Ghiesbreght were explorers commissioned by their government to study the natural history of central Mexico, and Jean-Jules Linden and Nicolas Funk joined them for this ascent. They climbed the now-standard Jamapa Glacier "over some steep fields of snow so hard that at every step we slipped, with much danger of tumbling some hundred yards below," Galleoti reported. "We thought that our youth would keep us going better than our spirits."

Nearby Iztaccíhuatl wouldn't be climbed until 1889. Surveyors and others made earnest attempts starting in the 1850s, but all were turned back by icy slopes. Finally, in November 1889, a German and a British diplomat teamed up and succeeded via the Ayaloco Glacier. At the summit, however, they found a bottle with a note in it from James de Salís, a Swiss resident who had made numerous attempts over five years and had left his mark on top just five days earlier.

"A Flowing Exhilaration of Spirits"

Back in Europe, mountains had become objects of veneration. Commerce and nationalism were soaring to new heights—especially in Britain—but the accompanying repression and pollution was beating down bodies and spirits. People started to look to the mountains for fresh air, both literally and figuratively. The new cultural movement known as Romanticism included an admiration for wild places and mountains as havens

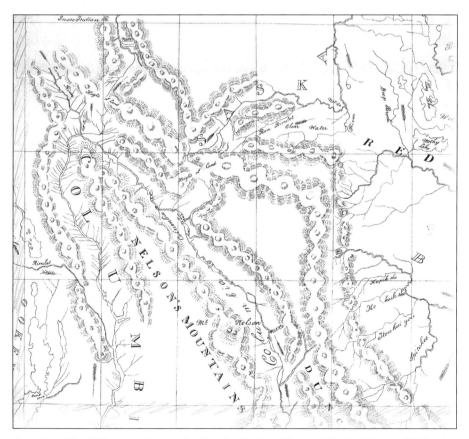

A section of David Thompson's map, showing the "Big Bend" in the Columbia River and "Nelson's Mountains," which we now call the Columbia Mountains.

Dawn over Citlaltépetl, from Popocatépetl. PHOTO BY ANDY SELTERS.

for rejuvenation. Albert Smith, a leading mountain aficionado, wrote that high upon Mont Blanc,

> *The consciousness of success...the pure transparent air, the excitement attached to the very position in which we found ourselves, and the strange bewildering novelty of the surrounding scenery, produced a flowing exhilaration of spirits that I had never before experienced.*

As Romantic yearning blended with Enlightenment curiosity, a general recipe for mountaineering started to brew, especially among the British. Alpinism soon expanded from the realm of a few explorers into a thrilling holiday tonic for the middle class. Vacationing climbers recruited alpine herdsmen and hunters as guides. Gentlemen vied to be the first to reach unclimbed summits, and ascents of such steep-sided peaks as the Wetterhorn (1854) and the Matterhorn (1865) inspired devotees with the notion that, with bold effort, incredible summits could be attained.

This new, athletic form of mountain appreciation did not develop without controversy. Hard-core Romantics such as John Ruskin mistrusted all things technical, and he accused some climbers of impiously reducing the majestic peaks to "racecourses" and "soaped poles in a bear garden which

you set yourself to climb and slide down again with 'shrieks of delight.'" Many also accused climbers of irresponsible risk-taking. When four of the men descending from the first ascent of the Matterhorn fell to their deaths, charges of rashness rose to the throne of Queen Victoria. *The Times* (of London) called such alpinists "dilettantes of suicide."

Treading the fine line between recklessness and heroism, alpinists succeeded in building their game into a noble tradition. The core alpine experience became day climbs ("tours") based out of lodges or huts, following the ropes of hired peasant-guides, usually along ridgeline routes. During the second half of the 19th century, guides and their clients developed proficient methods, special tools and a whole milieu of ethics and aesthetics. As mountaineering expanded around the world, these became the standard by which all mountaineering experiences and accomplishments would be gauged.

Some of the American gentry traveled across the Atlantic to take part in alpine tours. Well-to-do Yankees also began to vacation at new luxury hotels in the Green and White mountains of New England, and in the Adirondacks of New York, and the more vigorous would hike to the tops of various summits. Around Boston, these experiences inspired the formation of the Appalachian Mountain Club (AMC) in 1873.

Les grands Mulets
Ascension au Mont Blanc.

Artist's dramatization of an early climbing scene in the Alps, on Mont Blanc. COURTESY HENRY S. HALL, JR. AMERICAN ALPINE CLUB LIBRARY.

Mt. Rainier from the southwest. In 1857 Kautz reached the crater rim from the right, gaining the head of the long, slender glacier that now bears his name. The 1870 Stevens-Van Trump ascent started up a similar way, then climbed ledges on Gibraltar Rock, the prominent crag below the right skyline. PHOTO BY AUSTIN POST, U.S. GEOLOGICAL SURVEY.

The Cascade Frontier

Out in the Pacific Northwest, a few migrants occasionally took time off from subjugating the natives and having their way with the local timber, fish, minerals and grasslands to climb the surrounding peaks. As Seattle, Portland, Victoria and other frontier outposts grew into small cities, the nearby Cascade volcanoes attracted some of the West's first citizen mountaineers—those who climbed simply for adventure, without any official responsibility. In the 1850s, such pioneers climbed to the summits (or nearly to the top) of Shasta, St. Helens, Hood, Adams and Rainier, even though they had little or no experience in alpine methods.

These doughty pioneers found that dense forests and steep canyons with crashing rivers often made getting to the base of the peaks at least as debilitating as the climbing. They often described their relief at rising above the reach of mosquitoes and brush to ascend the glacial slopes. On the snow, however, the unprotected climbers often paid for their ascents with sunburn and snow blindness.

A few ascents climbed into the realm of fairly serious mountaineering. A. C. Isaacs and party, for example, made a near ascent of Mt. Shasta in winter conditions on March 26, 1856. A year later, Lt. August Kautz led a private party to try Mt. Rainier. They had no idea how to judge the scale of the peak or the effects of foreshortening, and from a high camp at treeline Kautz was confident the summit was only three hours away. Freezing cold, burning sun and thin air took an unexpected toll the next day, and all but Kautz turned around. At 6 p.m. he reached the crater rim and realized that his life would be in jeopardy if he didn't head back down.

In 1862, Victoria, British Columbia, attracted the first immigrant experienced in the

Mt. Baker from the north. Coleman's route climbed the glacier to the col right of the peak and continued to the top near the right skyline. PHOTO BY KEVIN MCLANE.

Alps, artist Edmund T. Coleman. A charter member of Britain's Alpine Club, Coleman was looking for a fresh start, for he had spent his inheritance and he felt the Alps were getting crowded. A man of learning and high society, Coleman sighed with self-imposed "solitude and exile" in the new land, where people were obsessed with practical matters and didn't share his "visionary" aspirations.

Coleman's new home had a view of unclimbed Mt. Baker. His first efforts to reach it foundered in huge logjams on the Skagit River and the Koma Indians' refusal to let him pass. In 1868, Coleman and three partners approached Baker via the Nooksack River drainage and paid two Nooksack men to escort him to the base. Thomas Stratton took the lead on the peak, cutting steps with Coleman's ice axe up the final headwall. Coleman, who compared the peak to the Jungfrau, was the first mountaineer in the Western Hemisphere to climb with a real ice axe and primitive crampons (called "creepers").

Two years later Coleman joined U.S. Gen. Hazard Stevens and prospector Philemon Beecher Van Trump to try Mt. Rainier, which probably had not had a complete ascent. Coleman was 47 years old and he lumbered under a pack that included a botanical press and sketching materials. Stevens and Van Trump packed lean and soon left Coleman behind in the forest. Their Yakama guide

Sluiskin pointed them toward what would be called the Gibraltar Ledges route. The pair reached the crater rim at 5 p.m. and then persevered west to the highest point. With neither bivouac gear nor enough daylight to descend, they faced a struggle to survive. Luckily, they found ice caves hissing with volcanic steam, and in one of these they lasted the night, tormented both by scalding and by frostnip. Their route would be the demanding *voie normale* up Rainier until 1936, when a key ledge on Gibraltar Rock fell away.

Edmund Coleman's drawing "The Cornice" portrays Thomas Stratton cutting steps up the final headwall of Mt. Baker. ARTWORK FROM *HARPER'S NEW MONTHLY MAGAZINE*, NOV. 1869. COURTESY UNIVERSITY OF WASHINGTON LIBRARIES, REF.#8682.

Aspirants work through the forest en route to Mt. Adams, ca. 1911. MSCUA UNIVERSITY OF WASHINGTON LIBRARIES, NEG# UW23417z.

As the coastal cities grew, Cascade climbs became popular events where large parties followed established routes, everyone marching closely in the footsteps of a leader, braced for the slopes with various sorts of staffs or axes. Fascination with the great Cascade volcanoes led to some novel events. For the Fourth of July in 1870, Civil War veteran Perry Vickers had the idea to "illuminate" Mt. Hood. He built a nighttime fire high on the peak to create a spectacle for people below— the bonfire site is now known as Illumination Saddle. Vickers tried to get support for a giant illumination that would be visible from Portland, some 50 miles away, but potential backers doubted that anyone could survive a night in the thin, cold air on the summit. Three years later, however, Vickers set off flares from the summit, and on July 4, 1887, another party torched a huge blaze of "red fire" (probably strontium nitrate powder), a sight plainly visible from Portland.

Someone then came up with the idea of carrying Army heliographs, or signal mirrors,

to the summits. Climbers organized to haul these 19-pound devices simultaneously to the tops of Baker, Rainier, Adams, Hood and Diamond Peak, and to relay Morse code through the skies. On July 10, 1895, the teams atop Hood and Adams successfully flashed messages 58 miles to each other across the Columbia River Valley. Unfortunately, smoke

Climbers on the summit of Mt. Adams, July 10, 1895, with heliographs to signal compatriots on the summit of Mt. Hood. PHOTO COURTESY THE MAZAMAS, ACC. #VM1993.008.

Climbers on Rainier's Gibraltar Ledges Route, ca. 1922. PHOTO MSCUA UNIVERSITY OF WASHINGTON LIBRARIES, COLLECTION #341, BOX25, ALBUM 60.

Climbers reaching the summit of Mt. Hood on the final slope of *Cooper Spur*, July 19, 1894. PHOTO COURTESY THE MAZAMAS, ACC. #VM1993.008.

from forest fires obscured communication between the other peaks.

On the north side of Mt. Hood, Scotsman David Rose Cooper opened a resort, and a primary attraction for his guests was to climb the volcano by a long east-side route. Two of Cooper's associates, Will and Doug Langille, opened a direct route to the top in 1891. With some 1,000 feet of slope sustained at nearly 40 degrees, *Cooper Spur* was the most serious snow and ice climb yet done in America. They also found it prone to sun-induced avalanches. Eventually Cooper's men would fix a long, fat hand line to the route to secure tourist ascents. In the fall of 1892, Will Langille and G. W. Graham wove a new route up Hood's north flanks, calling it the *Sunshine Route*.

Early Sierra Climbs

Out of view of urban centers, California's Sierra Nevada initially attracted few citizen mountaineers; government survey teams generally were the first to climb in these mountains. California organized the state's official survey under Josiah Whitney, directing him to point the way to additional mineral wealth. But Whitney's crew spent much of the summer of 1864 stretching its mandate to explore the High Sierra. These escapades unearthed the likelihood that the Sierra held the highest summits in the United States.

Yale graduate Clarence King made it his aim to climb the highest of all, which had been christened Mt. Whitney. In 1871, on a determined dereliction of his survey duties (by then in Colorado), King thought he had succeeded. But his summit day was cloudy, and a year later a local sheriff found King's marker on nearby Mt. Langley. Finally, in 1873, the first known ascent of the highest peak in the continental United States—at 14,496 feet—fell to Charles Begole, Albert Johnson and John Lucas, a local trio calling themselves "The Fishermen."

John Muir also made his way to the Sierra. This vagabond Scotsman felt to his bones that climbing mountains presented not a trial of hardships but rather an opportunity for rejuvenation. He wrote, famously:

> *Climb the mountains and get their good tidings. Nature's peace will flow into you as sunshine flows into trees. The Winds will blow their own freshness into you, and the storms their energy, while cares will drop off like autumn leaves.*

We also remember Muir for writing, "Who wouldn't be a mountaineer! Up here all the world's prizes seem nothing." Muir would become America's most enduring spokesman for wild nature.

Muir made broad tours of Sierra terrain, stretching some bread, tea, matches and a billy into multiday journeys. His keen eye and sharp deductions woke geologists to the role glaciers had in shaping Western mountains, and he made a number of the continent's first steep and rocky ascents. Muir's climb of Mt. Whitney in late autumn 1873, after the Fishermen ascent, negotiated "by direct course" a chute through the peak's intimidating eastern front. Muir later guided other parties up this exposed climb—now known as the *Mountaineer's Route*—but cautioned that "soft and succulent people should go the mule way."

Mountaineering's Dual Goals

Both Muir and King wrote essays and books that enthralled the American gentry back East, and these helped place Sierra mountaineering among the new Western legends, along with Indian battles and giant trees. Today the writings of these two men serve as classic illustrations of the dual aspects of mountaineering.

King wrote of intrepid adventures in the great outback, of pressing on through terrain that he had declared "utterly impossible." His

Clarence King flanked by two of his associates on 1860s surveys in the High Sierra, James Gardiner (left) and Richard Cotter. COURTESY THE BANCROFT LIBRARY, UNIVERSITY OF CALIFORNIA, BERKELEY.

primary motivation seems to have been success—as when he described his goal as, "but one, to reach the highest peak in the range." However, King also looked beyond summit conquests to show how climbing adventure could promote higher values, such as courage and trust.

In one tale, "The Descent of Mt. Tyndall," the climax came when King followed a difficult lead by his partner, Richard Cotter. King tied into the rope Cotter lowered to him but resolved to climb without weighting the cord. Using "every pound of strength and atom of will," King reached Cotter's stance, only to find him "sitting upon a smooth roof-like slope, where the least pull would have dragged him over the brink." King said he had "never known an act of such real, profound

courage" as when Cotter tied his own life to his partner's efforts.

Although we know that King dramatized and sometimes grossly exaggerated his exploits, he gave voice to people's expectation that the challenges of mountaineering would lift men to higher moral ground. Subsequent climbers would hold up such character building as the premier benefit of mountaineering.

Muir, by comparison, described climbing as if he were being carried upward by the joy of a mystical experience. One has to read between his ebullient lines to know that he endured hunger, cold bivouacs and exposed climbing. His essay based on his first ascent of Mt. Ritter is a classic account of meeting the mountaineering challenge. At one point, he describes himself paralyzed with fear at a precarious passage, "unable to move hand or foot either up or down....

John Muir in the early 1900s. COURTESY HENRY S. HALL, JR. AMERICAN ALPINE CLUB LIBRARY.

> *My doom appeared fixed.... But this terrible eclipse lasted only a moment, when life blazed forth again with preternatural clearness.... The other self, bygone experiences, Instinct, or Guardian Angel—call it what you will—came forward and assumed control. Then my trembling muscles became firm again, every rift and flaw in the rock was seen as through a microscope, and my limbs moved with a positiveness and precision with which I seemed to have nothing at all to do. Had I been born aloft upon wings, my deliverance could not have been more complete.*

King, the man of accomplishments, saw mountains as a natural venue for achievement, and for him climbing was a way to extend oneself to the utmost. Muir, the seeker of experience, emphasized that, "going to the mountains is going home." Truth be told, Muir on occasion displayed an element of competitive pride, and King could describe the peaks in adoring terms. Their primary tendencies, however, speak to the twin streams of accomplishment and experience that run throughout mountaineering history, sometimes united and sometimes in diverging currents.

A Technical Siege

By 1860, Yosemite Valley had become one of the West's most alluring marvels. Bold men scouted the huge knuckle of Half Dome for potential ascents, but Josiah Whitney dismissed thoughts of climbing the bald monolith, saying it was "perfectly inaccessible, being probably the only one of all the prominent points about the Yosemite which never has been, and never will be, trodden by human foot."

Undaunted, blacksmith and trail builder George Anderson began a variety of attempts to climb Half Dome. One time he dressed in burlap coated in sticky pitch and tried to squirm up the smooth granite. Then, over the summer of 1875, Anderson made a Herculean effort that must have built his blacksmithing arms into terrifying proportions. He used a hammer and a half-inch hand drill to bore holes six inches deep into the granite, and into each hole he drove an iron rod. Standing on this, he drilled the next hole. From the high point of each day's effort he strung a rope down the 45-degree slabs, and finally he reached the top.

Half Dome from the northwest. George Anderson's first ascent route was just around the left skyline. PHOTO BY ANDY SELTERS.

Except for an ascent of France's Mont Aiguille in 1492, no one had ever climbed a peak in such a manner. Anderson's tactics were too exotic to generate the controversy that would have erupted had he engineered a route like this even 50 years later.

Early Rocky Mountain Climbs

As in California, the first documented ascents of many Rocky Mountain summits also fell to government surveyors. Most of these climbs, while crucial to the mapping of the West, were routine challenges. Two dominant peaks, however, inspired committing efforts.

Artist's interpretation of James Stevenson's party viewing the Grand Teton from the west. Artwork appeared in *Scribner's Monthly*. COURTESY ANGUS THUERMER.

Early tourist-mountaineers had tried to climb Longs Peak beginning around 1860, but slabby cliffs repeatedly turned climbers away. Two men probably found a way to the top in 1865, but credit for the first certain Caucasian ascent goes to an 1868 party led by John Wesley Powell, a one-armed Civil War veteran and the government's most observant and adventurous Western explorer. Powell's route required four days of rough backcountry travel, including the probable first ascent of two 13,000-foot peaks along the way. The night before their ascent of Longs, L. W. Keplinger, a student in the party, climbed the Class 3 chute that proved to be the key to the summit. A newspaper account remarked that the toughest section "required great caution and coolness, and infinite labor to make headway, life often depending upon a grasp of the fingers in a crevice that would hardly admit them."

With the completion of the transcontinental railroad across southern Wyoming in 1869, two government-backed teams arrived to map the American Rockies systematically: the Hayden Survey, commissioned by Congress, and an Army survey designed and led by Lt. George Wheeler. Members of the Hayden survey, led by Captain James Stevenson, laid plans in 1872 to climb the Grand Teton, the "lord of the empyrean," which they called Mt. Hayden. Scanning this huge, craggy thumb from the west, Stevenson's partner Nathaniel Langford wrote:

> I tried to calculate the risks of our contemplated clamber, and I began to regard as impossible the attainment of its top; and yet, as an achievement as well as for the expansive and magnificent view to be obtained from it as for any renown it might give, it seemed to me to be worthy of the greatest risks and strongest efforts.

Stevenson and Langford, a bank examiner and the first superintendent of Yellowstone National Park, persevered around cliffs and over ice sheets, and they may have succeeded in making the first ascent of the peak, which Langford described (inaccurately) as "more abrupt" than the Matterhorn. Americans read Langford's tale of the perilous climb in the popular *Scribner's Monthly*. Later, however, climbers would find reason to doubt they reached the summit (see Chapter 4).

STEVENSON IN PERIL.

Artist's dramatization of a slip by James Stevenson during his claimed first ascent of the Grand Teton. Artwork appeared in *Harper's New Monthly Magazine*. COURTESY ANGUS THUERMER.

In Colorado, the Wheeler and Hayden teams scrambled up dozens of high peaks, and the images of Hayden photographer William Henry Jackson and painter Thomas Moran gave the world a grand portrait of the magnificent but inhospitable American West. Hayden concluded that no one would need to survey Colorado after him, since the high, arid state "will never support so dense a population that a more detailed survey will be required."

By the 1880s, Estes Park became the Rockies' first resort to attract mountaineers, with as many as 20 parties a year vying to climb Longs Peak. Rev. Elkanah Lamb started guiding parties to that summit for $5 per day. The man of the cloth wrote that, "If they would not pay for spiritual guidance, I compelled them to divide for material elevation."

New England's Alpine

Although the highest summit in New England reaches only to 6,288 feet and the region holds no glaciers, ferocious weather made the Presidential Range of New Hampshire's White Mountains one of the early centers of North American mountaineering challenge. Near the end of the 19th century, serious mountaineers began to explore these peaks in winter.

Herschel Parker, a professor of electrical engineering at Columbia University, was the most avid of a small group that made repeated winter ascents of Mt. Washington. As he put it, "One of the chief attractions of the Great Range in winter is...the opportunity for real alpine work." Winter climbers at this time improvised candle lanterns for predawn travel, snowshoes for use below treeline, and creepers and an alpenstock for icy, wind-blasted slopes. Parker made his first of 11 winter ascents of Mt. Washington in 1890, and twice he climbed via the steep headwall of Tuckerman Ravine.

In the last week of 1895, Parker and R. C. Larrabee left a hut in the col southwest of Mt. Madison at 8:15 a.m. and crossed the summits of Adams, Jefferson and Clay to arrive atop Mt. Washington about 1 p.m. The weather was fine, and despite icy slopes the

Mt. Washington with Tuckerman Ravine on the left and Huntington Ravine on the right. PHOTOGRAPH #2478
© BRADFORD WASHBURN. COURTESY PANOPTICON GALLERY, WALTHAM, MA.

two made their way down the far side of Mt. Washington without mishap. They continued over several other peaks and were caught by nightfall on Mt. Clinton, but the moon guided them down to Crawford Notch. Parker was essentially correct in saying this was "the first time that a complete traverse of the Great Range had been made in winter," and, except for Mt. Madison, they did it in a single day. In 1918, Willard Hellburn and Henry Chamberlain included Mt. Madison when they did a complete traverse of the Presidential Range, taking 13 hours.

Summary

As the 19th century came to a close, mountaineers of two generally different lineages were climbing American summits: Westerners in the Cascades and the Sierra, and Easterners in the Colorado Rockies and in New England. Both groups enjoyed climbing as a strenuous sort of leisure. The relatively isolated Westerners figured out their own ways to climb, while the Easterners followed alpine traditions. The latter would take part in the coming rush for the "real alps" of North America, the Rocky Mountains of Canada.

SUGGESTED ROUTES
FROM THIS PERIOD

IZTACCÍHUATL (17,159 feet/5,230 meters)
Ayaloco Glacier

The three great volcanoes of central Mexico peren-nially attract climbers seeking high altitude with modest technical challenges during stable winter weather. Since the mid-1990s, however, "El Popo" has been erupting and climbing it is prohibited. To climb Citlaltépetl (El Pico de Orizaba), the third-highest peak in North America, most visiting climbers follow the Jamapa Glacier on its northern flank.

The most interesting of the three peaks is Iztaccíhuatl (The Sleeping Woman). Long inactive, this multiconed, north-south volcanic ridge stretches for at least four miles above 16,000 feet. The highest cone is *El Pecho* (The Breast) at 17,159 feet. Steep faces and pocket glaciers cling to either flank of Izta, offering a variety of routes. The first certain ascent was on the west side, up the Ayaloco Glacier. While this is not the standard route to the top, it is popular. Like all glaciers at subtropical latitudes, this one is diminishing rapidly due to global warming, and if current trends continue it will be gone within a few decades.

Approach: Acclimatization is the first require-ment, and most will want to start this process with a couple of days in Mexico City at 7,800 feet. From there you drive east through the town of Amecameca and up to the Paseo de Cortés, the pass between Izta and Popo. Consider it mandatory to acclimatize here, spending at least a couple of days camping and hiking from 12,000 to 14,000 feet. The Ayaloco Glacier route begins from the road-end north of the pass, at a spot called La Joya, at 13,100 feet.

Iztaccíhuatl as seen from Popocatépetl, from the south. PHOTO BY ANDY SELTERS

Climber on the Ayaloco Glacier, Iztaccíhuatl. PHOTO BY ANDY SELTERS.

Mt. Ritter from the east. Muir's north face route is on the right skyline. PHOTO BY ANDY SELTERS.

Route: Traversing grassy spurs and ravines, you gain some 2,600 feet en route to the glacier. At 15,400 feet there is a small hut that can serve as a temporary shelter, but a perch this high with no water is not a good campsite. The main technical challenge of the route is the glacier, which is only moderately steep but often icy, especially after December. Good crampon technique is a must. Once you reach the summit ridge, the next rise to the north is Izta's highest point.

Descend by retracing this route or follow the summit ridge (*Arista del Sol*) south over rocky *Las Rodillas* (The Knees) and then drop west and return to the road head.

First Confirmed Ascent: James de Salís, November 1889

Difficulty: PD+, AI 2, 4,000 feet

Guidebook: *Mexico's Volcanoes: A Climbing Guide*

MT. RITTER (13,157 feet/4,010 meters)
North Face

The graceful crest of Mt. Ritter, with its sister summit Banner Peak, stands well above the other mountains southeast of Yosemite National Park. Ritter is the namesake of a spiny subrange of the Sierra, part of the divide between forks of the San Joaquin River. The Ritter Range's metamorphic rock is hard and firm, but loose rocks are common.

Approach: From Mammoth Mountain Ski Area take a mandatory $7 shuttle over Minaret Summit to Agnew Meadows. Shuttle hours are from 7 a.m. to 7 p.m., making it inconvenient (or worse) for the return trip. From the trailhead, most climbers backpack in a few miles and camp at one of the lakes east of Ritter.

Route: Gain the Banner-Ritter col (12,000 feet) and climb Ritter's north snowfield. In late summer and fall this apron can be a skating rink of hard ice. Then climb the rock above (some will want a belay). The angle eases after a couple of hundred feet, followed by enjoyable scrambling to the top. Descend the south snowfield, aiming southeast toward a chute through cliffs. Easy ground leads to benches above the lakes below. It will be helpful to scout a route through these benches before your ascent.

A climber at the top of Mt. Monroe before dawn on a winter traverse of the Presidential Range. The route ahead is visible to the southwest, including Mts. Eisenhower and Jackson. PHOTO BY MARK CARROLL.

First Ascent: John Muir, October 1872
Difficulty: PD, Class 4, AI 2-3, 1,300 feet
Guidebooks: *The High Sierra; Sierra Classics*
Permit: A permit from Inyo National Forest is required for an overnight stay in the Ansel Adams Wilderness.

PRESIDENTIAL RANGE (6,288 feet/1,917 meters) Winter Traverse

Even though these peaks are only 5,000 to 6,000 feet high, they have winter conditions consistently harsher than most any other mountains in the Lower 48. On an average February day atop Mt. Washington, temperatures will be in the single digits (F), the humidity will be about 60 percent, the wind will average over 40 miles per hour, and visibility will be mediocre. On bad days, the cold, wind and white-out can be as brutal as a wicked May day on Denali. Almost everyone does the traverse from north to south, to take in the highest of the nine peaks at the start of a good weather window. Depending where you start, the traverse covers from 19 to 23 miles and about 7,500 feet of ascent and descent.

Snowshoes, crampons and an ice axe—and experience with their use—are all mandatory. Fit climbers who pick a day with good conditions can do the traverse in 12 to 14 hours, but most take

three days. None of the huts along the route is open, so a full winter-camping kit is necessary.

Approach: Start with one of a variety of trails that climb south from Highway 2. The fastest and most popular path to the peaks is Valley Way, which leaves from an outpost called Appalachia. After a long, woodsy climb, find a leeward campsite at tree-line south of the Madison-Adams Col. Many bag Mt. Madison the night before starting the traverse.

Route: Start the skyline tour from the Madison-Adams Col, climbing over Adams, down to Edmands Col and up to Mt. Jefferson. The slopes of Jefferson can be the trickiest of the route, with ice and/or avalanche hazard. Up to this point it's not too hard to bail north, if necessary, to tent sites at The Perch or to a shelter operated by the Randolph Mountain Club at Gray Knob. Once you're past Edmands Col and atop Jefferson, the route is continuously exposed and most of your escape options to the east or west involve extensive trail breaking.

Continue south over Mt. Clay and up to Mt. Washington (the weather station here is NOT open to climbers), and then turn southeast down the Crawford Path. Ideally you'll make it over Monroe and Franklin to camp below treeline around Mt. Eisenhower. From there it's a few hours' trip to Crawford Notch and Highway 302.

Full moon over the north side of Mt. Hood as viewed from Cloud Cap. The *Sunshine Route* is marked, and *Cooper Spur* is the left skyline. PHOTO BY LLOYD ATHEARN.

First Ascent: Herschel Parker and R. C. Larrabee; December 1895; Including Mt. Madison: Willard Hellburn and Henry Chamberlain, 1918

Difficulty: D, AI 2

Guidebook: *AMC White Mountain Guide*

MT. HOOD (11,235 feet/3,424 meters)
Sunshine Route

On a clear afternoon, Mt. Hood's majestic cone reigns over Portland—one reason it is probably the most commonly climbed major summit in North America. Combine this popularity with the dynamic hazards of an isolated, steep mountain, and you have the formula for many accidents. The original southern route sees the most traffic, while the north-side routes present relative solitude with just a bit more challenge. The *Sunshine Route* is the most likely to have good early-summer conditions.

Approach: From the town of Hood River, drive up the northern base of Hood to park below Cloud Cap Inn, near timberline at 5,900 feet. Snow might block the upper stretch of road into late spring and early summer. Fit climbers who find good conditions can complete an ascent from here in a day.

Route: Take the trail that leads onto lower *Cooper Spur*, where you can scout the best way to drop west and cross the Eliot Glacier. From the glacier, climb onto the rise known as Snow Dome, and again scout the way between crevasses ahead. Climb in a rising traverse around Horseshoe Rock to the skyline, and follow this upper stretch of Cathedral Ridge to the summit. The most secure descent is by the same route. *Cooper Spur* is a quick descent option, but is wise only during optimum conditions. Some arrange a car shuttle and descend to the south.

First Ascent: Will Langille and G. W. Graham, September 1892

Difficulty: PD+, 4,000 feet

Guidebook: *Oregon High*

Permit: A free, self-issued wilderness permit is required for camping. A "Northwest Forest Pass" ($5 per day or $30 per season) is required for parking.

CHAPTER 2

The Pure Canadian Outback

Canadians expanded their western frontier, they confronted mountains much more rugged and extensive than their American counterparts. No enterprising soldiers or vagabonds would even reach the base of the Canadian peaks before the mid-19th century, much less claim major summits. Not until a railroad punched through did mountaineers learn what western Canada held. With this inroad came a trickle and then a steady stream of climbers skilled in alpine traditions, and before long the "Canadian Alps" were a premier destination for international mountaineers. As they sought out these wilderness peaks, alpinists played a leading role in the region's exploration and mapping.

Rails into Wilderness

The developments that would bring the world to Canadian mountains began around 1871, when politicians in Ottawa called for a railroad link to entice British Columbia and its gold mines and timber into their four-year-old federation. Surveyors started scouting train routes through the ranges, but even with help from Indian guides—who barely knew the rugged canyons themselves—it was 11 years before they could delineate a way through the Rockies and Columbia Mountains.

The first trains of the Canadian Pacific Railway (CPR) chugged over Kicking Horse and Rogers passes (through, respectively, the Rockies and the Selkirks) in 1886. Soon after that, CPR began to advertise first-class tourist service through this uninhabited outback. The company marketed the mountains as embodying all the glories of the European Alps, plus the wonder of untracked wilderness. As historian R. W. Sandford wrote,

A Canadian Pacific Railway train heading out from Glacier House. VAUX COLLECTION, WHYTE MUSEUM OF THE CANADIAN ROCKIES, ACC.# V653/P5.

◖ Edward Feuz in action. COURTESY HENRY S. HALL, JR. AMERICAN ALPINE CLUB LIBRARY.

Rev. William Spotswood Green's drawing "The Cornice" of himself and Rev. Henry Swanzy approaching the summit of Mt. Bonney. FROM GREEN'S BOOK, *AMONG THE SELKIRK GLACIERS.*

"Almost overnight the lone land of the West, with its stupendous peaks and roaring rivers, became a symbol of the purity of experience Victorian poets had celebrated." To avoid having to haul kitchen and dining cars up and down the steep Selkirk grades, the railroad company built a comfortable hotel three miles west of Rogers Pass, which they called Glacier House for its view of the Great Glacier (later named the Illecillewaet Glacier).

A year after those first trains passed, surveyors based at Field made Canada's first recorded big-mountain climb, with a long, difficult day to the top of Mt. Stephen. The next year, 1888, Glacier House entertained its first British alpinists, a trio led by Rev. William Spotswood Green. They warmed up on Terminal Peak and next went to Mt. Bonney. Carrying a surveyor's plane table, they wrestled through alders and met a grizzly during the approach. During the climb of Bonney they suffered a hailstorm, an avalanche and the munching of their rope by a "snafflehound" (a marmot or pika). When their food ran out, the men ate tea leaves. On Bonney's summit, Green wrote, "The foremost thought in our minds was, 'What about the getting down!'" A "rope-down" (descending by hand line) eased the way. On his way back home, Green described this bully adventure to the Appalachian Mountain Club (AMC), and in London the Royal Geographical Society absorbed his tales of a whole league of real alpine peaks with icy ridges and impressive glaciers.

Rev. William Spotswood Green, who led the first climbing expedition to the mountains of Canada. COURTESY WHYTE MUSEUM OF THE CANADIAN ROCKIES.

By this time, the important summits in the Alps had all been claimed for 20 years or more, and so leading alpinists were traveling to more exotic ranges, such as the Caucasus and the New Zealand Alps. Green's tales added Canada to the list of exciting new destinations. In 1890, another British climber, Harold Topham, began a Selkirk tour with ascents of Mt. Donkin and Mt. Fox. During this same time, two Swiss Alpine Club (SAC) members, Emil Huber and Carl Sulzer, sought the prize of the Rogers Pass area, the striking pyramid of Mt. Sir Donald. From a camp at

Charles Fay, the patriarch of North America's original mountaineering community and founder of the Appalachian Mountain Club. WHYTE MUSEUM OF THE CANADIAN ROCKIES, ACC.# AC OP/802.

Phillip Abbot's portrait, from the journal *Appalachia*.

treeline, they started up the southwest face and swiftly made the summit, where, "Shortly after 10 a loud SAC yodel echoed into the blue sky over the mighty glaciers."

As its luxury wilderness-tourism business grew, the CPR built other plush lodges at Banff and Laggan (Lake Louise). By the turn of the century, a few thousand people came

each summer for comfortable adventure holidays. J. Garnier de L'Estoille, a visiting French climber, wrote, "Don't hesitate, go straight to Glacier House—remain there one long week and after you will be in the finest condition to meet the awful life again."

Charles Fay, president of the AMC and the dean of American mountaineering, started bringing club members to this area in 1895. Philip Abbot, the brightest young talent of American climbing, led AMC members up the first ascent of Mt. Rogers, north of Rogers Pass. As many later aspirants to Canadian summits would find, a long, brushy approach made for an extended day. On their return from the peak they found no place to bivouac, so they thrashed through alders until they straggled into Glacier House at dawn. "We did our own work, and fairly earned for ourselves what measure of success we had," Abbot wrote. "There is a fascination in this which outweighs all aesthetic considerations whatever."

Tragedy and the First Guides
After climbing Mt. Rogers, Abbot and partners returned to Laggan to attempt the first ascent of prominent Mt. Lefroy, but their bid failed. The next year, 1896, Abbot and other AMC members returned to Lefroy. The steep, firm snow was at the limit of their abilities, and Abbot had to cut many steps with his ice axe. Where possible he led the party onto rock, but the loose stone offered little security. Within a few hundred feet of the top, Abbot unroped to scout the route above. As Charles Thompson later wrote, "Five, ten, fifteen minutes passed. In the impressive silence came the dull thud of a falling body, faint and rattling at first, heavy and crashing as it came bounding nearer." To their horror, Abbot came tumbling down with holds that had broken off; he fell 1,600 feet to his death.

This accident shocked everyone involved with Canadian mountaineering. As with the Matterhorn tragedy, social guardians shouted accusations of irresponsibility. Even the CPR had to defend the image it had built by promoting mountain tourism.

With the reputation of alpinism in Canada

The climbing team that would avenge the death of Philip Abbot and make the first ascent of Mt. Lefroy. Left to right: Charles Thompson, Charles Fay, unknown, Harold Dixon (seated), unknown, unknown (behind), John Norman Collie (with pipe), Herschel Parker and Peter Sarbach. PHOTO COURTESY WHYTE MUSEUM OF THE CANADIAN ROCKIES, ACC. # V653 NG4-278.

at stake, Fay wrote to his AMC membership: "Thus closed the saddest episode in the history of our Club…. It occurs at the very dawn of a new era of genuine alpine climbing…. Shall the incipient movement cease…? We…have no sympathy with such a conclusion." Fay and Abbot's British friend Harold B. Dixon decided to avenge the tragedy the following year with a team of blue-ribbon climbers. These included John Norman Collie, Dixon's Swiss guide Peter Sarbach (a companion of Whymper's on early Matterhorn attempts) and Herschel Parker. All nine climbers summited Mt. Lefroy on the anniversary of Abbot's death. The ascent initiated in North America a universal pattern of mountaineering tragedies: Committed

climbers confront despondency with the conviction that careful and optimistic determination must win the day.

Obviously Canadian mountains had to be taken seriously, and climbers soon began to employ that most critical aid of the alpine tradition: professional guides. This was the period when Alfred Mummery and other fine climbers were experimenting with going guideless in the Alps, and Abbot himself had advocated guideless mountaineering as making for "a fair and even tussle with Nature." But most vacationing climbers believed in following skilled servants who made their living by guiding climbs.

In 1899, Canadian Pacific began to import Swiss guides, installing them at Laggan and at

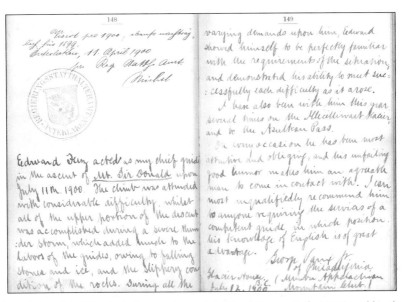

Pages from Edouard Feuz Sr.'s *Führerbuch* documenting a July 11, 1900, ascent of Mt. Sir Donald in the Selkirks. Each guide owned one of these leather-bound books, where clients would leave references for prospective clients to review the guide's performance. This ascent, done with George Vaux Jr. of Philadelphia and co-guide Karl Schluneggar, was the third ascent of the peak, and the route, which differed slightly from the original route, became the standard route from Glacier House. COURTESY HENRY S. HALL, JR. AMERICAN ALPINE CLUB LIBRARY.

Glacier House. Most hailed from Interlaken, where they had learned to guide in the steps of their fathers and grandfathers, and where they already had a union. Although these men were thrilled to visit a new continent and to climb new peaks, they still worked under the thumb of a domineering tour and hotel corporation, and they gained only a modest improvement in their pay and social standing. The railroad paid them subsistence wages and required them to entertain the media, travel in Swiss folk costumes, and do menial work when not engaged with guests.

With this system in place, climbing activity accelerated dramatically. Such guides as Edouard Feuz (sometimes spelled Edward), his son Edward Jr., Christian Häsler Sr. and Jr., Rudolph Aemmer and brothers Hans and Christian Kaufmann could analyze an unclimbed route, lead steep rock and boiler-plate ice, steer the rope over gendarmes to protect the team, decide when to encourage and when to discourage the *Herren* and *Frauen*, and all the while keep a courteous bearing and a pipe in their teeth. British and American clients such as Charles Fay, Albert

and Elizabeth MacCarthy, Joseph Hickson, Gertrude Benham, Alexander McCoubrey and Dr. J. Monroe Thorington returned to Canada over many seasons to book their favorite guides. Even the aristocracy dabbled in guided climbs, as, for instance, when William Randolph Hearst Jr., Leopold Amery or Roger Berens and his bride—newlywed heirs to the Hudson's Bay Company—roped up in the Rockies. Naturally, the most exciting goal was to claim the first ascent of a prominent peak. Guide Edward Feuz Jr. eventually would lead the most first ascents, with 78 in the Rockies and Columbia Mountains.

Each day was a crucial test for a guide, for any mishap was utterly his responsibility and the unstated consequence for any significant oversight was an ended career or worse. However, the custom in Europe and in Canada was that the primary credit for climbs went to the client. For these reasons, guides held back from dramatic initiatives and bold leads. A few of the day's most avid clients might have had more bravado (and, in some cases, more sheer climbing ability) than the men they hired. Nevertheless, the early guides

Edouard Feuz Sr. and Christian Häsler. PHOTO VAUX COLLECTION, WHYTE MUSEUM OF THE CANADIAN ROCKIES, ACC.# V653 NG4-278.

Edward Feuz Jr., arguably the era's most prolific guide. PHOTO BY BYRON HARMON, COURTESY WHYTE MUSEUM OF THE CANADIAN ROCKIES, ACC.# NA71-3707.

deserve mountaineering's highest regard. Over many hundreds of climbs, with clients from stumbling novices to experts, often on unknown routes, Canada's immigrant, pre-World War II guides led the first ascents of virtually all the prominent peaks in the Canadian Alps, and with an essentially perfect safety record. Without them, many ascents might have been decades in coming, and with likely many more mishaps.

Alpinists' Early Methods

Today we often judge climbers by their technical abilities, but in the days before pitons and effective belaying, the emphasis was on a lead climber's judgment, confident manner, ability to assess the mountain and the team, and mastery of the methods of the day. At the start of steep terrain, the two to four members of a rope team would tie in along a hemp or manila rope 60 to 100 feet long. While everyone climbed together, the leader carried a few coils in his hand. On rock, he wove some safety into the group's progress by loop-

ing this slack around gendarmes and over projections. When the terrain steepened even more he would hurry onto a solid stance, brace himself, and pull in the rope hand over hand (or, later in this period, over a shoulder or around the chest) as the others came up. Guides still use these techniques today on "classic" terrain, referring to it as "short-roping." Short, severe sections called for one climber to offer his shoulder or even his head for the leader to step up on—a technique called *courte-échelle* (literally "short ladder").

Descents were handled similarly, with the leader going first on easy ground, arranging the rope as practicable. On steeper ground he came down last, directing the team and running the rope over projections. For very steep descents, teams arranged a "rope-down" by looping the rope over a knob for everyone to lower himself hand over hand.

On snow and ice, early climbers carried an alpenstock, a shoulder-high staff tipped with a spike. Plunged into the snow, this would provide a brace. Later models had an adze for chopping steps. By the time guides began working in Canada, they and practiced amateurs used a shorter, belly-high ice axe with a specially designed pick and adze. Wielding one of these, a strong leader could chop stair-steps even in steep, hard ice. As on rock, the leader progressed while his followers held the rope and stood fast as best they could, plunging their axe shafts into the snow or stabbing in their picks where the surface was firm.

Nailed boot soles were a crucial part of the outfit in Canada, for both rock and snow. These had hobs (spikes) for the center of the sole and molar-shaped cleats for the edges; the finest nails came from Switzerland. The nails made ankle-high boots quite heavy, but, compared with leather soles, their grip and durability made them worth the weight. Every climber carried spare nails and learned how to replace them. (Only a few pioneers in the American West were familiar with boot nails, and into the 1920s most climbed in leather soles.)

During this era some progressive climbers around the continent used "creepers," or primitive crampons. These helped reduce the need for cutting steps in frozen snow, but on hard ice they were disdained because the spikes hindered balance and required deeper steps to be cut.

As a safety system, these early methods were adequate to catch a slip or to reassure a nervous follower. A leader, however, was fully aware that nobody could catch his falls—aware, in fact, that any fall of his would probably pull off the whole team. Thus the maxim was "the leader does not fall." The best leaders were impressively efficient in their ropework, but their main sources of security were confident movement and a focus on managing the team's morale. The safeguards of old alpinism were mostly psychological, backed up by modest technical means, yet they worked surprisingly well. Even though climbers steadily

Christian Häsler and Ernest Feuz guiding a young client on the steep crags of Mt. McGill in the Canadian Rockies. PHOTO BY BYRON HARMON, COURTESY WHYTE MUSEUM OF THE CANADIAN ROCKIES, ACC#V263/NA71-1339.

An early attempt to climb Mt. Sir Sandford. COURTESY HENRY S. HALL, JR. AMERICAN ALPINE CLUB LIBRARY.

pushed the limits of "justifiable risk," accidents were rare. By the first years of the 1910s, daring climbers in Canada and the Sierra Nevada were venturing well out onto the razor's edge of vertical terrain, where most climbers today would not hesitate to deploy anchored belays.

Canada's Golden Age

It took about a decade after Rev. Green's pioneering Selkirk visit before interest among European alpine circles escalated from curiosity to competition. But from about 1898 until World War I, the Canadian Alps became one of the world's prime destinations for alpinism. Peaks accessible in a day or overnight from Laggan and Glacier House all were claimed within a few years, so anyone interested in first ascents subsequently had to mount at least a small expedition. In the Rockies, climbers went out with trains of pack stock, and between slapping mosquitoes, riding through rivers, clambering over deadfall, surmounting high passes, eating bacon, beans, bannock and cowboy coffee, and sleeping under oiled canvas, the tourist-climbers had much to write home about.

Women joined some of the early Canadian climbs, and though none would lead climbs until later, women often outnumbered men on AMC excursions. Georgia Engelhard and Kate Gardiner were known to challenge the fitness of their guides.

Decorum at this time insisted that mountaineers come back with more than just stories of daring—they had to show responsible enterprise, namely the pursuit of science. Thus, climbers often lugged survey tools and cameras to the summits to make panoramas and maps. Refined society also expected discourse about the summit, including an aesthetic evaluation of the peak's prominence and the view it commanded. Through such descriptions of summit experiences, we can mark how the attitudes of climbers evolved from wilderness-as-hardship to exploration-with-enthusiasm.

David Douglas, for instance, had written of Mt. Brown back in 1827: "The view from the summit is of too awful a cast to afford pleasure. Nothing can be seen...except mountains towering above each other, rugged beyond description."

Sixty-eight years later, Philip Abbot showed more appreciation, but even he wished for a few more outposts of civilization. Of the prospect from Mt. Hector, he wrote that the wild grandeur was indeed "boundless and complete," but for this it was still "monotonous" and "not beautiful."

As backcountry travel became more familiar and the limits of Rockies exploration seemed to be in sight, pioneering climbers began to understand that they were partaking in a precious opportunity. J. Norman Collie, writing of his first ascent of Mt. Athabasca in 1898, effused,

> The view that lay before us in the evening light was one that does not often fall to the lot of modern mountaineers. A new world was spread at our feet; to the westward stretched a vast ice-field probably never before seen by human eye, and surrounded by entirely unknown, unnamed and unclimbed peaks.

When Collie, Hugh Stutfield and Hermann Woolley looked upon the Columbia Icefield and its ring of great peaks, this was probably the most exciting discovery of the period. They found that one of the summits, The Dome (now known as Snow Dome), was the triple-divide apex of the continent—the point where the watersheds of the Pacific, Atlantic and Arctic oceans meet.

Collie was a pioneer of X–ray technology and a man brimming with adventurous intelligence. In the Alps and the Himalaya, he had partnered with Alfred Mummery, the world's foremost climber of this period. Stutfield was a prominent scholar and gentleman as well, yet the two of them grew to love the wild Rockies, where "a tent and an outfit always afford an easy means of escape from that over-civilization which, as some of us think, is already sufficiently burdensome in our home surroundings."

Despite occasionally being forced to hunt for a goat or bighorn for food, these gentle-

A section of John Norman Collie's map of the "Columbia Icefields, from *Climbs and Explorations in the Canadian Rockies.*"

men enjoyed "absolute freedom from all the taint of the vulgar or the commonplace, and the sense of mystery and of awe at the unknown—things which are gone for ever from the high mountain ranges of Europe."

A New Matterhorn

As the full scope and grandeur of the Canadian Rockies became known, gentlemanly efforts to claim the big summits gathered into a competitive rush. The most obvious summit awaiting history's pen was Mt. Assiniboine, a peak whose northeastern aspect recalls the Matterhorn. In 1899, a guideless team retreated after holding a bad fall. More failed attempts amplified the peak's reputation, and by 1901 people realized that whoever stood atop 11,869-foot Assiniboine would claim the highest summit yet climbed in Canada.

Canadian Pacific saw a publicity opportunity and pronounced Assiniboine "North America's Matterhorn." The railroad recruited

Edward Whymper, the celebrity of the Matterhorn first ascent, to attempt it. The railroad gave Whymper carte blanche to climb as he wished in Canada, and ensured that no competing parties would climb near Assiniboine during his trip. But Whymper was in his 60s, quite taken with liquor, and uninterested in a challenging climb. Many who met him tell of an arrogant man distressed with the legacy of the Matterhorn tragedy, and the few easy climbs he undertook seem to have been distractions from an insolent bender.

James Outram, another British Alpine Club member, joined Whymper for a couple of excursions. Whymper then offered to pay Outram to take up the torch of Assiniboine. Whymper's packer, Bill Peyto, was more than happy to escort Outram to the peak. Outram took the advice of another packer, Tom Wilson, and approached from the south instead of the oft-attempted north ridge. Following guides Christian Häsler and Christian Bören, he reached the top. To the consternation of the guides, Outram showed his appetite for adventure by insisting they descend via the north ridge, and the client led his guides down without incident. Overall, the climb was a notch easier than that of the Matterhorn.

Now Canadian Pacific made James Outram its hero, and he rode their bankroll of rail tickets, guides and publicity into a gentleman's rivalry with J. Norman Collie. In 1902, both men had on their agenda three big peaks to the north: Forbes, Bryce and Columbia. Collie softened a possible confrontation by suggesting that Outram join his team heading for Forbes. Collie was delayed, however, and so Outram took off with guide Christian Kaufmann and hustled up the North Saskatchewan River and across the Columbia Icefield to the top of Mt. Columbia. He and Kaufmann then raced back to meet up with Collie, and, following Kaufmann and

his brother Hans, the party of seven succeeded along the exposed, loose shale of Mt. Forbes' southwest ridge.

Outram and Christian Kaufmann kept up their blazing pace and headed back north for Mt. Bryce. This triple-summited giant presented an enigma, for the only apparent way to the highest, western crown was via a long, demanding ridge over two other summits. Outram and Kaufmann by now formed a confident partnership. Kaufmann launched up a cliff band at the foot of the first summit with some wide stemming, pulling away loose holds with care. When the 60-foot rope ran out, he was still 20 feet from a stance, so Outram started climbing too. With their lives both depending on their unbelayed moves, they successfully reached the ridgecrest.

It was almost noon before they gained the first summit. There, Kaufmann made it clear that to continue would mean being benighted.

Mt. Assiniboine from the southwest. The first ascent route followed the ridge from lower left to upper right, then worked left to a chute leading to the top. PHOTO BY GLEN BOLES.

Members of the first team up Mt. Freshfield. Guide Christian Kaufmann at far right. PHOTO BY J. NORMAN COLLIE, COURTESY WHYTE MUSEUM OF THE CANADIAN ROCKIES.

James Outram. PHOTO COURTESY WHYTE MUSEUM OF THE CANADIAN ROCKIES.

On the first ascent of Mt. Forbes. COURTESY WHYTE MUSEUM OF THE CANADIAN ROCKIES, ACC#V364/36.

Outram insisted they keep going, and they completed the long traverse around the central summit and finally topped the main west peak. They had to reverse their route to get down, and when they made it back to the top of the initial cliff darkness was total. Facing either a frigid bivouac or a terrifying downclimb in the dark, they chose the downclimb. Neither man fell and they stumbled back to camp by 1 a.m. They had accomplished Canada's most committing climb to date, and the most aggressive season yet on the continent.

Selkirk Expeditions

Selkirk peaks reigned over canyons too steep and densely forested for pack stock, so climbers looking for summits had to go for it on foot. Moreover, guides wouldn't tote more than the 30 pounds explicit in their contracts, and so for any extended excursion a guide would use up more provisions than he would carry. For these reasons, the Selkirk peaks beyond the Rogers Pass vicinity inspired some of the world's first multiday mountaineering expeditions where climbers carried everything on their own backs.

Three Americans were the primary enthusiasts for these demanding trips: Boston lawyer and business manager Howard Palmer, botany professor Frederic Butters and retired banker Edward Holway. From 1908 until 1925, these three ventured into some of the remotest parts of the Selkirks, including the Purity, Dawson and Battle ranges. They climbed as many summits as practicable and made maps and geological observations. Palmer commented on the pleasures of going guideless: "One was absolutely free to do as his mood prompted.... There was no responsibility to 'make' such and such a climb on such and such a day. Above all, there was nobody to grumble at a failure or to criticize one."

These three naturally aspired to climb the commanding peak of the northern Selkirks, Mt. Sir Sandford. Surveyor Arthur Wheeler had certified it as easily the highest Selkirk

Mt. Sir Sandford from the north. PHOTO BY DAVID P. JONES.

summit, but few others had even glimpsed it, and the first party to approach Sir Sandford had suffered a harsh lesson in the serious nature of pioneering in this country.

In 1907, American students Merkle Jacobs and Edward Heacock were ferrying supplies through the woods up the Gold River Valley when a boulder rolled onto Jacobs' leg and broke his femur. It took Heacock four days of running to reach a doctor who by chance was in the area and return with him. The bone was reset, but the terrain was too rough for Jacobs to be moved, so he had to stay put until the bone could heal. It would be at least six weeks. Heacock and Merkle's brother Bob supplied the encampment, but on one journey, with the Gold River surging with snowmelt, their canoe overturned and Ed Heacock disappeared. Eventually Jacobs recovered enough to be helped out, and by the end of the year he could walk.

Starting in 1908, Howard Palmer made nearly annual journeys to try Sir Sandford. These trips were notable for clouds of mos-quitoes and "stumbling through pools of water up to our knees, fording shallow streams, falling into rotten stumps, and, of course, grabbing prickly devils' club for support.... At each halt relief from our tormen-tors could only be obtained by waving a leafy branch continuously." After two expeditions, Palmer and partners had worked the approach from the railroad down to seven days. The third and fourth trips saw them turn back repeatedly from halfway up the peak's north ramparts, in the face of sus-tained steep ice, cold weather or deep, ava-lanche-prone snow. During 1911, George Culver led another attempt on Sir Sandford, via the east ridge. He brought guides Rudolph Aemmer and Edward Feuz Jr., and had this team not run short of supplies they might have beaten Palmer to "his" peak.

Culver's competition persuaded Palmer and Holway to hire the same two guides the following year. On the north ridge, Aemmer surpassed the previous high points by chop-ping steps under a threatening serac wall. He

Howard Palmer and Allen Carpé. COURTESY HENRY S. HALL, JR. AMERICAN ALPINE CLUB LIBRARY.

SUGGESTED ROUTES
FROM THIS PERIOD

MT. BRYCE (11,506 feet/3,507 meters**)**
Northeast Ridge

Mt. Bryce is an outlier west of the Columbia Icefields, partly famous for its enormous, 7,500-foot north face. (This major ice climb was first done in 1972.) The northeast ridge that James Outram and Christian Kaufmann climbed remains a challenge and one of the finest skyline routes on the continent. In 1971, three Canadians were the first to climb the ridge in its entirety, following the crest over all three summits.

Approach: Outram and Kaufmann began their day from Cinema Lake, about three miles east of the start of the northeast ridge; most parties now start from a bivouac at the base of the ridge. Two main approaches reach this spot. The classic and more scenic hike starts at the Icefields Parkway, heads up the lower Saskatchewan Glacier, and turns south via Castleguard Meadows and Thompson Pass. This takes one and a half to two days. The new approach begins with a 75-mile drive from Golden, B.C., past Kinbasket Lake and up the valleys of the Bush River and Rice Brook Creek to the east side of the peak. It is important to check locally on logging road conditions, but, depending how far the road is drivable, it can take less than a day to reach the base of the ridge. Some climbers bring a mountain bike to ride past any gated closures.

Route: The crux 25-meter rock pitch at the base of the ridge is rated 5.6. Easier mixed climbing then continues to the east summit. Either climb over the top of the central summit via its spectacular mixed and corniced ridge, or traverse on a glacial bench to the south to reach the main summit more quickly. At the final col you face the route's main elevation gain, up a moderately steep snow and ice arête with a few more rock steps. The 1971 party found an icy spine between rock prows, and the variety of terrain forced them to take their crampons on and off 13 times during the day. To descend, retrace the route, taking the bench around the central summit.

led a second crux on the corniced summit ridge, where the guides teamed up to pull and push Palmer over the impasse. They made the top, and, as Palmer wrote,

> *Thus fell the haughty monarch.... The veil of primeval obscurity has been torn from this obstinate mountain and its surroundings, the region has been mapped, and the chief peaks, glaciers and streams named. If the work has not always proved easy, the rewards have been out of all proportion.*

In the winter of 1910 an avalanche killed almost 60 people near Rogers Pass, and by 1916 the CPR had circumvented the pass with a tunnel. Since the Great Glacier had receded almost out of view of the hotel, tourists were less interested in the area. In 1925 Glacier House closed, and for over 30 years few climbers visited the Selkirks.

Mt. Bryce from the north-northeast. PHOTO BY DON BEERS.

First Ascent: Christian Kaufmann and James Outram, July 1902; Including central summit: Glen Boles, Don Forest and Murray Toft, 1971; First winter ascent: G. Golvach and J. McKay, February 1991

Difficulty: D-/D+ (depending whether central summit is included), 5.6, AI 2

Guidebook: *Selected Alpine Climbs in the Canadian Rockies*

MT. SIR SANDFORD (11,555 feet/3,522 meters)
Northwest Ridge

Mt. Sir Sandford towers in height and mass over all the otherwise impressive peaks within the Big Bend of the Columbia River. During the peak's second ascent, in 1946, an American team found excellent névé on the slope of Howard Palmer's original attempts. They climbed a chute they called The Hourglass, which avoids Aemmer's dangerous traverse—modern ice-climbing standards make this the route of choice.

Approach: The Alpine Club of Canada's Great Cairn Hut at 6,200 feet provides a base for an ascent. Palmer's old approach is overgrown, and the most direct walk to this hut starts from Swan Creek, just above the shore of Kinbasket Lake. Two or three long days over three cols will bring you to the hut. Most parties choose to fly to Great Cairn by helicopter, arranged in either Revelstoke or Golden.

Don Forest climbing on the main peak of Mt. Bryce, during the first continuous ascent of the northeast ridge. PHOTO BY GLEN BOLES.

Mt. Assiniboine from the north. PHOTO BY BARRY BLANCHARD.

The northwest ridge of Mt. Sir Sandford. PHOTO BY DAVID P. JONES.

Route: Climb up the glacier tongue that pours off the col between Sir Sandford and Ravelin Mountain. Below the col, veer up and left on an ice ramp toward an icefall, then climb back right for 300 meters, up Palmer's "Long Slope," to the crest of the northwest ridge. At a rock spur turn left and climb The Hourglass, a long rope length of 45-degree ice. The angle of the ridge eases until its intersection with the summit ridge, where steep snow and cornices might require an occasional belay. Descend by retracing the route.

First Ascent: Rudolph Aemmer, Edward Feuz, Howard Palmer and Edward Holway, June 1912; Hourglass Variation: Charles Haworth, Donald Hubbard, Sterling Hendricks, Samuel Moore and Arnold Wexler, July 1946

   Difficulty: AD, AI 2, 4,500 feet
   Guidebook: *Selkirks North*

MT. ASSINIBOINE (11,870 feet/3,618 meters)
North Ridge

The dominant summit in the southern Canadian Rockies attracts at least a few score climbers a year. The peak is named for the native people of this area.

Outram's descent line, the north ridge, has become the most popular ascent route, and it is a good introduction to moderate challenges in the range.

   Approach: The R. C. Hind Hut near the north side of Assiniboine is the logical base for ascents. Getting there requires a 12-mile hike on good trails from a branch of the Spray Lakes Road out of Canmore. Many hike to the hut in a day, while others choose to break up the hike with a night at cabins, a lodge or a campsite near Lake Magog. Another option is to ride in or send your gear on a helicopter to Lake Magog. Other climbers ride mountain bikes up the trail.

   Route: From the Hind Hut, Assiniboine's north ridge is the left-hand skyline. Easy ground leads a good thousand feet up the lower ridge. As it steepens, aim up and right onto the north face, heading for a passage through the looming band of red cliffs. Then veer back to the ridge and continue to the second crux, the Grey Band. Again, work slightly right to a moderate passage (5.5). Near the summit, cornices often require care. Descend by retracing the route.

   First Ascent: Christian Häsler, Christian Kaufmann and W. Douglas, July 1903 (first descended by Kaufmann, Christian Bören and James Outram, 1901); First winter ascent: Don Gardner, Eckhardt Grassman and Chic Scott, December 1967

   Difficulty: AD, 5.5, 3,500 feet
   Guidebook: *Selected Alpine Climbs in the Canadian Rockies*

CHAPTER 3

Pioneer Alaskan Expeditions

While most North American climbers focused on alpine-scale peaks, far to the north whole worlds of super-mountains waited, essentially unvisited. These snowbound massifs rose to such scale over such vast glaciers, and were so distant from any outpost of civilization, that they demanded a whole new order of mountaineering. Into the 1870s, Euro-Americans had only a vague, maritime acquaintance with the Alaskan peaks, but around the turn of the 20th century a variety of explorers initiated attempts to climb the subarctic giants.

In 1867, right after the United States purchased Alaska, surveyor George Davidson led the territory's first recorded climb, reaching the top of Makushin, a 6,680-foot-high volcano in the Aleutian chain. A dozen years later, John Muir explored southeast Alaska with missionaries and natives. He revealed Glacier Bay to the world (in the 90 years since George Vancouver's visit, glaciers had receded from the outer coast and exposed the embayment), trekked up the Stikine River Canyon, and climbed a hill named Glenora Peak, where he exalted the glacier-draped valley around him as "a hundred Yosemites."

During the following decades, many Western nations looked to expand their frontiers of geographic knowledge. With sponsorship from scientific societies, government agencies, media companies and wealthy patrons, explorers sailed, rode, mushed and marched to the poles, Tibet, the Himalaya and Alaska. These trips were organized along military models and aimed to glorify the sponsoring nations and cultures. To Alaska also came a few brazen bootstrap teams—intrepid pioneers who depended mostly on pluck and determination to climb at the edge of the known world.

The North's Highest Peak?

The first Alaskan objective of this age was the tremendous peak that towers over the coast, Mt. St. Elias. Until Angelo Heilprin accurately surveyed Citlaltépetl in 1889, geographers had good reason to suspect that St. Elias was the highest peak on the continent. Highest or not, no one doubted that climbing this giant would require far more effort, commitment and resources than any Alp or Mexican volcano. But it took a number of trials for people to understand the true magnitude of the challenge.

Up to this time, most wilderness expeditions depended on hunting game and cooking

☾ Italians hauling a sledge en route to Mt. St. Elias, 1897. PHOTO BY VITTORIO SELLA, COURTESY FONDAZIONE SELLA.

Italians on the summit of Mt. St. Elias, 1897. PHOTO BY VITTORIO SELLA, COURTESY FONDAZIONE SELLA.

with firewood along the way. But the sea of glaciers surrounding St. Elias would require a party to be completely self-contained for weeks. Moreover, the crevassed glaciers and mountain slopes precluded using dogs or horses to haul loads, so all the necessary supplies would have to be transported by manpower. The setting and scale of St. Elias made it a blend of Himalayan and polar challenges.

Between 1886 and 1891, four well-supported teams approached the peak. Each found that wet, stormy weather and the unstable glacier surface transformed simple operations into hours of daily toil. The second team, sponsored by New York media companies, reached about 11,000 feet on the southwest ridge, just below the satellite now known as Haydon Peak. However, as they looked over at the main mass of St. Elias, they saw huge, steep, icy slopes far beyond their means to climb.

Geologist, geographer and mountaineer Israel Russell led the third and fourth expeditions to St. Elias. During the first, he made a determined solo summit bid and endured

stormy days without food or water. He also glimpsed, to the northeast, a massif he correctly guessed might be even higher than St. Elias. He named it for Sir William Logan, founder of Canada's Geologic Survey. During his second trip, in 1891, Russell followed the Newton Glacier and discovered the only practicable route up St. Elias for climbers of this era: the north ridge. He and his partners might have succeeded except for an overambitious plan to summit from a camp about 10,000 feet below the top. Subsequent Alaskan expeditions would owe much to Russell's pioneering, not only in geography but also in basic essentials such as improved sunglasses and equipment for cooking and camping on glaciers.

In 1896, a man with extensive resources contacted Russell to ask about St. Elias. This was His Royal Highness Luigi Amadeo Giussepe Maria Ferdinando Francesco, Prince of Savoia, Duke of the Italian principality of Abruzzi. The duke was an amateur alpinist who had climbed with Alfred Mummery on the first ascent of the Zmütt

Ridge on the Matterhorn. His relatively new nation was struggling with regionalism, debt and political infighting, and it seems mountain excursions offered the duke some peace from the stress of his primary duties. His superiors eventually agreed to support his St. Elias expedition in the hope that a heroic success might help inspire the patriotism of their people.

Russell advised the duke that St. Elias was a polar-type challenge and that alpine skills would be useless. The duke, however, foresaw the value of alpinism as well as polar perseverance, and he made the core of his team five of the finest guides from Courmayeur, the famed village on the south side of Mont Blanc. To document the story, his team also included a surveyor, a writer and a photographer.

The duke knew he had to find a level of compromise between adequate supplies and overburdening the team. His men sealed crackers, soup cubes, chocolate, compressed beef, bacon, rum, condensed milk and the like into tin drums; each 53-pound can would supply one day's rations for the 10-man team. In the days before rubber or foam sleeping pads, insulation from the snow presented a real challenge, so the duke commissioned custom, iron folding cots, each weighing four pounds. The team packed both of the standard mountain tents of the era: Whymper tents weighing 33 pounds each and efficient Mummery tents that weighed 14 pounds. Notwithstanding their best efforts to trim weight, they unloaded more than 3,000 pounds of gear and supplies near the mouth of Icy Bay in late June of 1897. This burden would have to be lugged over more than 60 miles of complex glacial terrain.

To aid in this march, the duke had hired nine Seattle students and workmen as porters, and at tidewater he hired some native Tlingits to carry loads across the moraines. Once on the vast bed of the Malaspina Glacier, the 10 Italians alone dragged four sledges with payloads of 750 pounds. As they gained elevation onto the Seward and Newton glaciers, the frequent rain turned into snowfall and the going

became slow and sloppy. Philipo de Phillippi, the author on the expedition, wrote that, "We sunk to our waists, patiently seeking our route among a labyrinth of ice blocks, over insecure ice bridges, amid the deafening roar of the avalanches and the crash of falling stones." It took them 36 days to reach St. Elias' north col. His Royal Highness led the team masterfully; he often broke trail and found the route himself, and occasionally even helped with the freighting.

The Italians decided that success would depend on making their high camp at the north col, and they carried two and a half days of supplies to that 12,500-foot saddle. Good weather held, and the next day, July 30, 1897, they started toward the top at midnight. Above 16,500 feet, all began to gasp in the thin air. The guides had experienced higher altitudes in the Andes, but found they suffered even more here, and so they were the first to discover that high altitudes in the far north cause more distress than in the tropics. (Later geographers would document a general compression of the atmosphere around the poles, making for thinner air at a given elevation.) At noon all 10 reached the summit, at 18,005 feet. They could clearly see Mt. Logan, 28 miles away, although their account doesn't acknowledge that this peak looked higher than St. Elias.

The Duke of Abruzzi, on the trip to Mt. St. Elias. PHOTO BY VITTORIO SELLA, COURTESY FONDAZIONE SELLA.

Italian camp at about 7,500 feet on the Newton Glacier, 1897. Their route climbed to Russell Col, visible behind, and up and left to the summit along the skyline (north) ridge. PHOTO BY VITTORIO SELLA, COURTESY FONDAZIONE SELLA.

They arrived back at the coast 57 days after they had started, on the exact day the Duke of Abruzzi had planned. This climb, the first of a number he would lead around the world, was the world's first expeditionary success on a major mountain, and it came off with barely a glitch.

The True Highest

While the duke was planning his expedition, a few newspapers reported that prospectors in interior Alaska had found a mountain they measured at roughly 20,000 feet. Decades and even centuries before, seafaring explorers probably had seen the peak, and inland natives knew it as Denali ("the High One"). But the mountain did not make it onto U.S. maps until W. A. Dickey, a gold prospector and Princeton *cum laude*, named the peak for William McKinley, an 1896 presidential candidate who favored gold as the nation's monetary standard. (The U.S. Geological Survey officially adopted the name Mt. McKinley, but since the 1970s momentum has built to call the mountain Denali again—this book uses both names interchangeably.)

In 1903, Judge James Wickersham led the first attempt on Mt. McKinley and reached only 8,100 feet, below the northwest buttress. The Fairbanks magistrate admitted to being completely overwhelmed by the vast prospects above. Later that year, explorer Frederick Cook, outfitted with sponsorship from *Harper's* magazine, led a team to the route Wickersham had attempted. Cook reached 10,900 feet on the northwest buttress but still had a very long way to go when he retreated, "thwarted by an insurmountable wall." Cook circled around Mt. Foraker and McKinley, and astutely foretold the challenges of climbing the latter peak:

> *The prospective conqueror of America's culminating peak will be amply rewarded, but he must be prepared to withstand the tortures of the torrids, the discomfort of the North Pole seeker, combined with the hardships of the Matterhorn ascent multiplied many times.*

Cook's primary ambition was beating Robert Peary and others to the North Pole—still the period's ultimate exploration prize—and he decided that climbing Mt. McKinley would help gain the necessary publicity and backing for his polar quest. In 1906 Cook

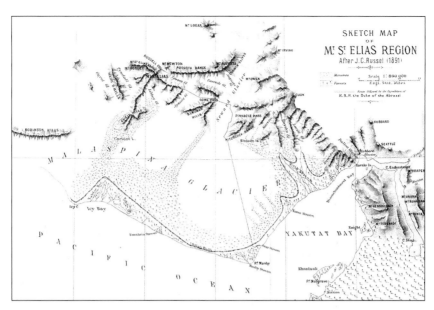

Section of the Duke of Abruzzi's map of the Mt. St. Elias area, showing the Italian route. Based on Israel Russell's original cartography, from *The Ascent of Mt. St. Elias.*

returned to Denali with the sponsorship of a wealthy patron. He also collected two of North America's finest mountaineers, Herschel Parker and Belmore Browne. As he had before, Cook approached the mountain from the south, and after many trials the group barely reached a viewpoint above the Tokositna Glacier. They returned to the lowlands, where Cook was to guide his patron, Henry Disston, on a hunting trip. When Disston could not make it, Cook convinced packer Ed Barrille to scout up the Ruth Glacier with him. He told Browne not to bother coming along, as they would do no climbing.

When the pair returned just two weeks later, Cook announced to the incredulous Browne that he and Barrille had summited McKinley. Back in New York, his claim brought him a hero's welcome, and his North Pole plans found enthusiastic support.

The following year, 1907, two expeditions tried to follow Cook's route, with Browne and Parker leading one and John Rusk of the Mazamas (see Chapter 4) heading the other. They all returned certain that Cook had not climbed past the incredible walls they saw— and certainly not in just two weeks. Moreover,

Parker and Browne tracked Cook's photographic trail to a small knob with a vista that precisely matched the photo Cook claimed to have taken from the summit. He had obviously fabricated the ascent, and his claims never would have gained credence except that East Coast sponsors, media, fans and even geographers were utterly ignorant of the super-alpine terrain around Denali, and were eager to crown a hero. Cook supporters continued to argue that their man should be given the benefit of the doubt, and the controversy continued for decades, consuming many times more energy and time than Cook and Barrille had spent on their jaunt.

Two years later, Cook persevered through an epic North Pole expedition and again claimed success. This time, Peary's sponsors helped orchestrate questions about Cook's claims, and the worldwide wave of doubt soon reached Fairbanks, where it energized local conviction that Cook's McKinley climb was a hoax. In a boisterous saloon, 51-year-old Tom Lloyd boasted that an Alaskan would be the first to summit McKinley, and he bet two cents that he could do it. Three saloonkeepers each offered a $500 incentive, and the so-called Sourdough Expedition had its grubstake.

A Mazama camp on the Ruth Glacier, during the 1907 expedition that attempted to trace the route of Frederick Cook to the summit of Mt. McKinley. To the right is Mt. Dan Beard, and Mt. McKinley's summit is in the distance. PHOTO BY FRED H. KISER, COURTESY OF THE MAZAMAS, NEG. #A347, ACC#VM1993.031.

Lloyd was not in prime fitness, but he gathered three of the strongest men he knew: Charlie McGonagall, Billy Taylor and Pete Anderson. All four knew how to operate in snow and bitter cold, and they agreed it would be best to approach the mountain in winter. They reasoned that traveling on snow with dogsleds would make for much easier going than slogging across muddy tundra with loaded horses, or, worse, packboards on their backs. They also predicted that crevassed glaciers would offer better travel conditions when they were covered by winter snow. The Sourdoughs planned to climb from the north, because they had been told of fairly gentle slopes on that aspect above 12,000 feet and McGonagall had already noticed a key pass to the northern glacier. They planned to leave in late December and take dogsleds as high as possible. To warm their tent, they brought a sheet-metal woodstove, and they dragged a 14-foot-long spruce trunk to erect on the summit as proof they had made it.

Starting up "Wall Street" (the Muldrow) Glacier, they packed a snowshoe trail into the dry snow and then led the dogs and sleds up the firm track. Although the crevasses were frighteningly deep, the men felt they didn't need ropes to cross the snow bridges because each carried a long pole, expecting that it would bridge any gap they might fall into. Luckily the snow held and this method was never tested. On icy slopes they hewed steps with a wood axe or coal shovel, and higher up they strapped on creepers. Plenty of wool socks inside knee-high "mukluks" of thick leather kept their feet warm.

Their strategy was to establish a trail to a high camp at about 10,900 feet, stock it with supplies, and then prepare a long ladder of steps into a basin at 14,600 feet. They all gave 43-year-old Pete Anderson credit as the strongest of the team. On April 3, 1910, Anderson, Taylor and McGonagall, dragging the pole by hand line, crossed the basin and climbed toward the north summit via a couloir steeper than 40 degrees. While McGonagall planted and guyed the pole atop the ridgecrest, the other two continued to the top of the north peak at 19,470 feet. Had they planned to reach the higher south summit, it seems likely they could have climbed it, but from below they thought the northern dome looked higher, and that their pole would be more evident there.

The three summiters returned to their mining work at Kantishna, leaving Lloyd to tell the world of the climb. Unfortunately, Lloyd broadcast that he and the others had summited both peaks. There was no hope of spotting the pole from distant Fairbanks, and the climbers had no photographs to prove their story. Thus, for some years, doubt shrouded the claims of the whole expedition.

Decades Ahead of Her Time

During the summer of 1911, another scrappy, self-supported and unlikely climber challenged the seventh-highest peak in the north, 16,390-foot Mt. Blackburn. The leader of this expedition had climbed peaks around the world, including Chimborazo, Mont Blanc and a few in the Canadian Rockies, generally with guides. Remarkably for the day, this leading climber was a woman.

Dora Keen entered adulthood with an intensive, all-women's education from Bryn Mawr. When she reached her late 30s she bucked social norms and took to traveling and climbing on her own. She came to Alaska as a frontier tourist, but when she saw Mt. Blackburn towering far above the Copper River, with a possible route to the top, she mounted a two-week attempt. The glacial approach took too long, however, and so she retreated with plans to return the next year.

The following April, Keen hired seven Alaskan prospectors and a dog musher and began a month-long expedition. They proceeded with the savvy of northern mountaineers attuned to life on snow. Low on the Kennicott Glacier, they traveled between 3:30 a.m. and 10 a.m., before the day's warmth would soften the snow. Afternoon heat released daily avalanches from the 10,000-foot-high southeast face, so they took care to camp on spurs that diverted the cavalcades of snow and ice. At 8,700 feet, they decided their route was too dangerous to climb with big loads, so it was time to go light and fast. They packed a minimum of sleeping gear, dry food and candles to melt snow for water. At 12,400 feet they bivouacked in snow shelters (Keen in a private shelter), but awoke to a raging storm and decided to retreat.

Most of her assistants then left the expedition, but Keen wouldn't give up, and George Handy and Bill Lang stuck with her. After a long wait for good weather, they began again. When mushy snow portended danger by noon, they bivouacked under an ice wall, again with only candles for fuel. Keen wrote that the afternoon avalanches rained around, "as if the American Falls at Niagara were suddenly overwhelming us." Pushing on for four more days

The Sourdough team at a photographer's studio in Fairbanks. Standing from left to right: Charlie McGonagall, Pete Anderson and Billy Taylor. Tom Lloyd is seated. COURTESY HENRY S. HALL, JR. AMERICAN ALPINE CLUB LIBRARY.

and three more spare bivouacs, Keen and Handy reached the top on May 19. Four years later these two pioneers would marry.

It later turned out that Keen and Handy may not have reached the highest point on Blackburn's broad summit dome, but their savvy, lightweight tactics and calculated risk-taking were characteristics of expeditions not seen again for decades.

The Peak of Peaks

The highest point in North America still was unvisited, and Belmore Browne, Herschel Parker and Merle LeVoy decided to make another attempt. They saw the wisdom of traveling in winter, and early in 1912 they started mushing from Seward. After gaining the Sourdoughs' northern glacier, they established the highest camps yet in North America, at 15,000 and 16,000 feet. In the thin air, they had

Mt. Blackburn from the southwest. Dora Keen's ascent climbed the glacier in profile, below the right skyline.
PHOTOGRAPH #571 © BRADFORD WASHBURN. COURTESY PANOPTICON GALLERY, WALTHAM, MA.

a hard time digesting thier high-fat pemmi-can, but on June 29 they pressed for the top. As they drew near, a fierce squall came up from the southwest. When they crested the summit ridge at 20,100 feet, Browne "saw a sight that will haunt me to my dying day. The slope above was no longer steep!" They only had to hike 200 yards up a trivial grade to reach the summit, but the storm in their faces was too much and they had to retreat. Back in camp they tried to recuperate, but with little food they could stomach they only grew weaker. Nonetheless, they made another attempt. This time the weather held, but they were too weak to press on and they dejectedly gave up. This decision probably saved their lives—one day after they exited McGonagall Pass a great earthquake shook tremendous avalanches all over their route.

The first complete ascent of Mt. McKinley fell the next year to a team organized by

Hudson Stuck, the Episcopal archdeacon of the territory. At 50, Stuck was far from the fittest climber, but he recruited two very strong Alaskans: Harry Karstens, a miner and explorer who would later become the first superintendent of Mt. McKinley National Park, and Walter Harper, a 21-year-old half-Koyukon Athabascan and half-Irishman who worked with Stuck's congregation as a trans-lator and assistant. Stuck also signed up Robert Tatum, a 21-year-old adventurer from Tennessee, to climb and handle the cooking, and Johnny Fredson, a teenage Athabascan who would manage their basecamp.

Stuck's team found that the 1912 earth-quake had strewn ice blocks all over the Muldrow Glacier, making for challenging trav-el. As they climbed higher, Stuck marveled at the huge, almost unknown faces around him—walls that would have dwarfed most of the world's best-known mountains: "We were

Mount McKinley, 1912

On June 29, 1912, Belmore Browne, Professor Her-
[sch]el C. Parker, and Merle LaVoy made a desperate
[atte]mpt to reach the top of Mount McKinley from their
[16,]000-foot camp, despite feeling very badly from the
[foo]d that they had been eating. The "Pemmican" that they
[ha]d made from Dall Sheep meat had too much fat in it,
[so] they simply couldn't digest it above about 15,000
[fee]t. On their first attempt at the summit, they had to quit
[only] about two hundred yards below the top, in a raging
[tem]pest of blowing snow, although the skies were cloudless.
   A second attempt, on July 1, fizzled out at an alt-
[itud]e of about 18,000 feet—as they were so exhausted,
[fro]m climbing all-out on their first try, that they could go
[no] further—even though the weather on that second
[day] was both windless and cloudless.
   This superb photograph, taken during their second
[atte]mpt, was taken by LaVoy, with Professor Parker in
[the] foreground and Belmore Browne in the lead. Compare
[wi]th Brad Washburn's aerial photograph 7260, which was
[tak]en many years later—as well as with his small 1942
[pho]tograph, taken on the US Army Alaskan Test Expedition.
[On] that climb, Bob Bates and Terris Moore reached the
[sum]mit at 4:10 PM on a gorgeous, windless, cloudless
[afte]rnoon—to be speedily followed by Brad Washburn
[and] Einar Nilsson. Almost on the top, on the descent,
[Bra]d took a small picture of Bates and Moore, exactly
[wh]ere he believed that Belmore's team had quit, almost
[exa]ctly 30 years before !!!— When BW showed this

Herschel Parker (in front) and Belmore Brown near the summit of Mt. McKinley in 1912, on their second attempt.
PHOTO BY MERLE LEVOY, COURTESY OF BRADFORD WASHBURN, HENRY S. HALL, JR. AMERICAN ALPINE CLUB LIBRARY.

within 'the hall of the mountain king' indeed; kings nameless here, in this multitude of lofty summits, but that elsewhere in the world have each one his name and story."

The team's familiarity with arctic travel and methodical planning of food, clothing and shelter allowed them to work hard day after day. As Stuck wrote, "To roam over glaciers and scramble up peaks free and untrammeled is mountaineering in the Alps. Put a forty-pound pack on a man's back with the knowledge that tomorrow he must go down for another, and you have mountaineering in Alaska." They depended heavily on relatively lean pemmi-can from game they shot themselves. At nearly 18,000 feet they made their highest camp, and at that altitude all but Harper suffered from headaches, lassitude and an inability to sleep.

On summit day, June 7, 1913, Harper set the pace and carried the precious atmos-pheric instruments. On the way up he looked to the north peak and, a couple of miles away, spotted the Sourdoughs' spruce pole, finally confirming their ascent. Stuck collapsed as he joined his three partners at the summit of the continent (20,320 feet), but then stood and led them all in a Latin chorus of *Te Deum*, giving praise to God. Stuck later wrote:

> *Only those who have for long years cherished a great and almost inordinate desire, and have had that desire gratified to the limit of their expectation, can enter into the deep thankfulness and content that filled the heart upon the descent of this mountain.... A privileged commun-ion with the high places of earth had been granted.*

So Many Mountains
During this same summer of 1913, survey teams working to delineate the Alaska-Canada border came to the Icefield (St. Elias) Ranges. An 1825 agreement had summarized the border along the Alaska panhandle as the

Section of the 1913 American-Canadian Boundary Commission's map of the area around Mt. Logan.
COURTESY HENRY S. HALL, JR. AMERICAN ALPINE CLUB LIBRARY

supposed single crest of a line of mountains. The surveyors found that the terrain was much more complex than any such imaginary spine, and the Logan-St. Elias area forced them to accept a 60-mile gap in their charts. Nevertheless, they did some impressive climbing, most notably when A. C. Baldwin led a team to 13,500 feet on Mt. St. Elias, below the northwest ridge. One of the highest of the many peaks they summited was 13,440-foot Mt. Natazhat. These surveyors also confirmed Mt. Logan as the second-highest peak on the continent, at 19,850 feet (now surveyed at 19,550 feet).

After the ascent of Denali, no one came to Alaska to climb for many years. Although countless major peaks awaited ascents—and even discovery—potential sponsors were uninterested. And these mountains were so distant and demanding that no more bootstrap expeditions would climb in Alaska until society and technology had advanced to change the game.

Mt. St. Elias from the north. The 1913 Boundary Survey party climbed the sunlit glacier to about 13,500 feet.
PHOTOGRAPH #1983 © BRADFORD WASHBURN. COURTESY PANOPTICON GALLERY, WALTHAM, MA.

Denali from the north. The Muldrow Glacier is the large glacier to the right. PHOTOGRAPH #3220 © BRADFORD WASHBURN. COURTESY PANOPTICON GALLERY, WALTHAM, MA.

SUGGESTED ROUTES
FROM THIS PERIOD

Over the decades, Mt. St. Elias' original Newton Glacier/North Ridge Route was climbed occasionally, but starting in the 1970s the glaciers around St. Elias began to break up and access to Russell Col became unacceptably dangerous. Warming trends also have made Dora Keen's unrepeated south-face route on Mt. Blackburn even more dangerous than when she climbed it. Thus, only one route from this period is recommended.

DENALI (20,320 feet/6,194 meters)
Muldrow Glacier

This is still the classic way to reach the top of the continent. Air support to the north side of Denali is not allowed, so most teams arrange to have the bulk of their supplies ferried from Kantishna onto the Muldrow by dogsled in February or March. Then they hike in during May or June to reach the cache and start their climb.

Approach: The trip starts from near Wonder Lake, at 2,100 feet, with a 19-mile hike to McGonagall Pass. The first challenge is to ford the wide, multichanneled waters of the McKinley River. This is an icy, sometimes dangerous wade that is best attempted in the morning, when snowmelt is reduced. Descend from McGonagall Pass to the Muldrow.

Route: In the middle reaches of the Muldrow Glacier, numerous big crevasses and two icefalls must be circumvented. Weak snow bridges can make this the most hazardous terrain on the route. At about 10,500 feet, avoid the Harper Icefall by climbing to the narrow crest of Karstens Ridge. This butts into Browne's Tower, where you veer back into the upper basin and onto the Harper Glacier. Browne, Stuck and subsequent parties climbed to the south peak directly from here, but in 1947 Bradford Washburn's party climbed via a camp at Denali Pass. Now most parties follow this route, which has the advantage of a view to the west and south, where most storms come from. Plan at least three weeks for the expedition.

First Ascent: North peak: Pete Anderson, Charlie McGonagall and Billy Taylor, April 1910; Main peak: Walter Harper, Harry Karstens, Hudson Stuck and Robert Tatum, June 1913

Difficulty: D-, 15,000 feet

Guidebooks: *High Alaska; Denali: A Climbing Guide*

Permits: A permit to climb Denali must be obtained from the National Park Service in Talkeetna. There is a peak fee of $150 per person, and registration must be submitted at least 60 days in advance. To arrange for dogsled services, contact Denali Wilderness Enterprises, Box 378, Healy, AK 99743.

CHAPTER 4

The Rise of Clubs

Around the turn of the 20th century, many factors coalesced to send a wave of middle-class people into North America's mountains. The United States and Canada had entered their industrial age and, just as in Europe, an echo of disillusionment and longing for nature and discovery swept over the population. Leading citizens bemoaned a society going flabby without the exertions of frontier life, and exercise regimens including bicycling and hiking grew into prescribed fads. One-and-a-half-day weekends and summer vacations became common just as a growing road network made mountain areas more accessible. In short, more people were ready and able to go where only explorers and well-heeled tourists had roamed a decade before.

All over the continent this evolution led to the formation of mountain clubs. For people from many segments of society, these clubs became indispensable gateways to the mountains. The Appalachian Mountain Club had been in full swing since 1873, and now almost every region organized a club or two:

the Sierra Club (1892), the Mazamas (1894), the Rocky Mountain Club (1896), the American Alpine Club (1902), the Alpine Club of Canada (1906), the Mountaineers (1907), the Vancouver Mountaineering Club (1907), the Colorado Mountain Club (supplanting the Rocky Mountain Club in 1912) and the Club de Exploraciones de México (1922).

In almost every case, these clubs were founded by a few mountain enthusiasts who envisioned improving society with the fitness and character fortification that seemed inherent to mountaineering. The founders also hoped enthusiasts would help defend the mountains from industrial encroachment. For aspiring mountaineers, joining a club gave access to travel, gear, partners, training and information. The clubs were a natural arm of the turn-of-the-century Progressive movement, which believed in strengthening civic institutions.

Most of these clubs held annual, two- to four-week summer outings in prime summiting areas. A few experienced climbers and naturalists would lead as many as a couple of hundred participants on hikes and peak climbs. Compared with individual expeditions, these group outings had to be managed for general safety and efficiency as well as adventure. In the 1916 *Appalachia*, Allen H.

⟳ Part of the Mazamas founding party on the summit of Mt. Hood on July 19, 1894. PHOTO COURTESY OF THE MAZAMAS COLLECTION, BY B.C. TOWNE, ACC.# VM1993.008.

Bent wrote of such club ascents: "When there is serious climbing to be done military discipline prevails and, as a result, large numbers have been able to climb our highest mountains."

Mountaineering clubs outpaced broader society in encouraging women to participate. Nowhere on the continent could women yet vote, but females comprised about half the membership of the Mountaineers and the Alpine Club of Canada, among others, from their inception. By comparison, the original (British) Alpine Club did not admit women until the 1970s. To be sure, men still led most climbs and meetings.

Clubs had to balance the ambitions of their enthusiastic tigers with the need to train and oversee less experienced members. Each club handled this challenge differently, and their methods had lasting effects on mountaineering progress in each region.

The Grand Teton Reclaimed

In the Tetons, local lore held that the 1872 surveyors Langford and Stevenson had not really reached the summit of the Grand Teton. The most vociferous objections came from William Owen, a Jackson summer resident and surveyor. Owen scoffed at the fanciful descriptions in Langford's magazine

account—such things as ice sheets and bighorn sheep near the top—and he felt certain that the pair had turned back at the Enclosure. Starting in 1891, Owen made a number of attempts at the "real" first ascent, but the cliffs above the Enclosure turned him back. Word of these attempts reached Denver's new Rocky Mountain Club, and the club invited Owen to join their man, Rev. Frank Spalding, for an attempt in 1898. Owen reinforced the team with two other locals, John Shive and Frank Petersen.

When Spalding arrived, Owen led the party up fairly easy ground to the Enclosure, and then Spalding took the lead. He solved the now-famous "Belly Roll" and "Crawl" problems and negotiated the final chimneys without much trouble. On the summit, finding no previous record of an ascent, the team planted the colors of Spalding's club and carved their names into a stone.

Back in the valley, Owen started a lifelong campaign to establish his claim to the Grand Teton's first ascent. Frank Spalding, on the other hand, soon changed his mind and accepted Nathaniel Langford's word that he and Stevenson had succeeded by the same route. Scholars and aficionados have spent countless hours poring over the subtle details of this controversy, and while there are real

Historic insignias of climbing organizations in North America. Clockwise from top left: Alpine Club of Canada, Sierra Club, Appalachian Mountain Club, The Mountaineers, British Columbia Mountaineering Club, The Mazamas, Harvard Mountaineering Club. COURTESY HENRY S. HALL, JR. AMERICAN ALPINE CLUB LIBRARY.

SPALDING   ASCENDING THE GLACIER TO GRAND TETON

Billy Owen, John Shive, Frank Petersen and Thomas Cooper climbing the (then much snowier) slopes below the Lower Saddle, en route to their ascent of the Grand Teton. Cooper halted at the Lower Saddle. PHOTOGRAPH BY FRANK SPALDING, COURTESY COLORADO MOUNTAIN CLUB.

Members of the 1898 Grand Teton party return through "The Crawl" (known for years as "the Cooning Place") on their way down from the summit. PHOTO BY FRANK SPALDING, COURTESY COLORADO MOUNTAIN CLUB.

reasons to doubt the 1872 climb, it seems unlikely that conclusive facts will ever surface. Thus it seems fair to give Langford and Stevenson the benefit of that doubt.

A few months after the Spalding-Owen climb, Army Capt. Charles Kieffer wrote a letter to Owen saying that he and soldiers Logan Newell and John Rhyan had climbed the Grand Teton in 1893. No other information about Kieffer's climb has been found, and so his letter adds a third layer of mystery to the Grand Teton's first ascent.

Early Sierra Club Climbs

Founded by John Muir and others in 1892, the Sierra Club was the first West Coast mountain club. Among the members, a group of professors from the San Francisco area, including Bolton Brown, Joseph N. LeConte and Helen Gompertz, was especially active in exploring the barely known reaches of the Sierra.

John Shive, Frank Spalding and Frank Petersen on the summit of the Grand Teton, 1898. PHOTO BY BILLY OWEN, COURTESY COLORADO MOUNTAIN CLUB.

In 1901 the club initiated its annual High Trips, and among the scores of unclimbed summits they sought out, none were more mysterious, intimidating and enticing than the legendary Palisades. LeConte had seen this "forbidding array of jagged spires" from a distance, and in 1903 he and three companions branched off from the club outing to make an attempt.

From the southwest base, they confirmed that North Palisade was the highest tower. They climbed a rocky chute and aimed for a col—later to be called the U-Notch—but found no reasonable way to get there. They satisfied themselves with making the first ascent of nearby Mt. Sill and trundling blocks off the northeast side of the crest to the Palisade Glacier. The next day they tried again and this time exited the rocky chute via ledges below the notch. LeConte found a chimney that led upward around apparent impasses, and he, James Moffitt and James Hutchinson reached the 14,242-foot summit.

The Mazamas

The beacon of Mt. Hood had long drawn Portland residents to the mountains, and in 1887 a group of them formed the Oregon Alpine Club. However, the serious climbers among them were frustrated to see this club settle into unadventurous tourism. In 1894, led by Will Steel, the climbers formed their own club, the Mazamas. To emphasize that theirs was a climbing club, they held their founding meeting on Mt. Hood's summit. At 11,235 feet, 155 men and 38 women signed a charter with the requirement that prospective members would have to climb "a snow peak on which there is at least one living glacier and the top of which cannot be reached by any other means than on foot."

After a 1906 Mazama outing to Mt. Baker, two Seattle members of the party, W. Montelius Price, a businessman, and Asahel Curtis, a landscape photographer, claimed the first ascent of nearby Mt. Shuksan. (Hermit-pioneer Joe Morovitz had probably climbed Shuksan in 1897, but he left no proof.) During this excursion, Price and Curtis decided that Seattle needed its own Mazamas auxiliary. The next summer, the Seattle Mazamas decided to climb Mt. Olympus, the highest summit of the Olympic Mountains. A reputation for exceedingly

The 1906 Mazama party, led by Fred Kiser, on the summit of Mt. Baker. From left to right: Charles Forsyth, L. S. Hildebrandt, Martin Wanlich, Fred Kiser and C. M. Williams. PHOTO COURTESY THE MAZAMAS, TAKEN BY ASAHEL CURTIS., ACC.# VM1993.026.

Mazamas on their 1906 outing, working through crevasses on the Mazama Glacier on their way to the top of Mt. Baker. PHOTO COURTESY THE MAZAMAS, KISER PHOTO CO. #3151, ACC.# VM1993.026-N82.

dense forest persuaded the club to hire a trail crew to prepare an approach up the Elwha River early in the season. Although the cost to each participant was $40—almost two weeks' wages—65 eager members signed up for the expedition.

However, as the departure date approached, Belmore Browne, Walter Clarke and Herschel Parker came to the area, collected some of the Mazamas trail crew, and climbed Mt. Olympus on July 17, 1907. The club was furious that these high-profile climbers had jumped their claim, but they decided to proceed with their trip anyway. On August 13, 11 Mazamas climbed the central peak of Olympus' three summits and found the register of the Parker party. They continued to the west peak and found to their excitement that it stood about 30 feet higher than the central summit—and there was no record of an ascent. Thus the Seattle Mazamas won their claim to Mt. Olympus.

The Mountaineers

After this climb, the Seattle group renamed itself the Mountaineers, and the next year they elected as president the man who

George Meany leading a sunrise Protestant service at a Mountaineers outing in Spray Park, at Mt. Rainier. PHOTO COURTESY MSCUA, UNIVERSITY OF WASHINGTON LIBRARIES, MOUNTAINEERS ARCHIVE, NEG.# UW 23416Z.

A group of Mountaineers scouting the way to the summit of Mt. Olympus in 1913. PHOTO COURTESY MSCUA, UNIVERSITY OF WASHINGTON LIBRARIES, MOUNTAINEERS ARCHIVE, NEG.# UW 23418Z.

would set the club's style for decades to come. George Meany, dean of the University of Washington's history department, brought a militaristic culture to the club. Under Meany, a bugler always signaled the day's events, including any retreat from a climb. Sundays in the mountains started with Meany leading Protestant services. During his 27 years as the charismatic marshal of the club, scores of initiates were instilled with respect for the mountains, God and the Mountaineers.

All three West Coast clubs had a high percentage of female members, and at this tender stage of gender integration it was crucial to avoid even an impression of scandalous commingling. Unmarried men and women always had separate tent areas. Women were allowed to wear skirts "not much below the knee," which supposedly allowed them to see their feet. Under the revealing skirt they had to wear wool knickers called "bloomers."

Mazama party on Mt. Hood's *Sunshine Route*, July 17, 1927, moments before the fall that injured nine and killed one. PHOTO BY HERMANN, NEG.#312, ACC.# VM1994.001.

The Mountaineers' lead climbers had no experience in up-to-date alpine techniques, so they concocted homegrown methods for shepherding dozens of novices. Parties were divided into "companies" of about a dozen, assigned "captains" and "staff officers," and marched across the glaciers in formation. Out of fear that tying people together might precipitate group falls, everyone climbed unroped. An officer or two would travel below his moving company, ready to stop any fall with a flying tackle. Ropes were carried to fix as hand lines over steep sections and to fish out anyone who fell into a crevasse. Amazingly, there were no fatal accidents during the decades when the club used these methods..

Portland's Mazamas, on the other hand, roped its members together. The first disaster to strike a North American climbing club occurred during a Mazamas climb of Mt. Hood's *Sunshine Route* in 1927, when one member slipped and pulled off the entire party. Many were injured and one climber died from being impaled on his ice axe.

In 1914, the Mountaineers built a lodge one mile from the railroad line at Snoqualmie

A Mountaineers group in 1911 (possibly below Goat Rocks). A captain has just saved a falling member with a tackle. PHOTO COURTESY MSCUA, UNIVERSITY OF WASHINGTON LIBRARIES, MOUNTAINEERS ARCHIVE, NEG.# UW 23420Z.

Seattle Mountaineers on The Tooth, near Snoqualmie Pass, in 1927. From the top: Larry Byangton (?), Paul Shorrock, William Maxwell and an unidentified man. PHOTO COURTESY MSCUA, UNIVERSITY OF WASHINGTON LIBRARIES, MOUNTAINEERS ARCHIVE, NEG.# UW 23423Z.

Arthur Oliver Wheeler. PHOTO COURTESY WHYTE MUSEUM OF THE CANADIAN ROCKIES, ACC.# NA66-299.

Pass, and this encouraged climbing on the smaller, craggy peaks in this area. To inspire members, the club gave medallions to those who climbed any of 10 designated Snoqualmie-area summits. By the 1920s the club also started awarding special honors to those who climbed all six of the club's landmark summits: Olympus, Baker, Rainier, Glacier Peak, Adams and St. Helens. The club and its goals essentially came to define mountaineering in the Cascades.

A Nation of Mountaineers

The Alpine Club of Canada arose out of the frustrations of Arthur Oliver Wheeler, a government surveyor who had mapped many Canadian mountains. Wheeler bemoaned the fact that British and American climbers, with their Swiss guides, were gathering all of the first ascents of Canadian peaks while Canadians barely knew what marvels their mountains held. During 1901 and 1902, Wheeler crossed paths with a variety of foreign luminaries, including Charles Fay, James Outram and Edward Whymper, and these acquaintances helped inspire him to form a Canadian club.

Wheeler's quest drew little attention until 1905, when he sent letters to Canadian newspapers extolling the need for a mountain club but also allowing that it might be expedient to simply form a Canadian branch of the American Alpine Club. A staff writer at the Winnipeg *Free Press* assailed Wheeler's

The original members of the Alpine Club of Canada outside of their founding meeting in Winnipeg. Dignitaries include A. O. Wheeler, third from the left in the front row, Elizabeth Parker next to him, and Arthur Coleman holding the ice axe. PHOTO COURTESY WHYTE MUSEUM OF THE CANADIAN ROCKIES, ACC. # AC OP-369.

suggestion as a form of surrender and proclaimed that Canada needed its own organization. The writer was Elizabeth Parker, wife of Herschel Parker. Though Mrs. Parker would never climb herself, she had very strong ideas about what sort of nation Canada should be. She and Wheeler organized the founding meeting of the Alpine Club of Canada (ACC) in March 1906 in Winnipeg. In the club's founding essay, newly elected Secretary Elizabeth Parker penned a manifesto for North American mountaineering. She and Wheeler believed that industrialization was making society "effete" and "unbalanced," and that, "Among other corrections none is more effective than this of the exercise of the mountain craft…. We ought to become a nation of mountaineers, loving our mountains with the patriot's passion."

The more who could take up this passion the better, Parker believed, and she disparaged elite concerns that the masses would debase the mountains. The real hazard to mountaineering, she asserted, would come from commercial interests, "the monster,

Elizabeth Parker, from the *Canadian Alpine Journal*, 1938. COURTESY WHYTE MUSEUM OF THE CANADIAN ROCKIES, ALPINE CLUB OF CANADA COLLECTION.

Mammon." Americans and Europeans were building roads, cog railways and cable cars to summits—on Pikes Peak and Mt. Washington, for instance—and plans were rumbling for tourist conveyances to the summits of Hood, Shasta and other peaks. The ACC, she wrote, would "set a face of flint

Members dining at the ACC's first outing at Yoho, in 1906. Elizabeth Parker and A. O. Wheeler at the right. COURTESY WHYTE MUSEUM OF THE CANADIAN ROCKIES, ACC.# AC OP-369.

against" such developments. President Wheeler added that the club's activities would "produce men and women of moral greatness."

If the new club's bugle sounded an almost religious note, its leaders made no apologies. Parker quoted the poet Robert Browning to suggest that mountains generate religious experiences, "which fools call Nature and I call God." The club motto would be *Sic itur ad astra* ("This way to the stars.") Among the early ACC members, seven percent were ministers.

He Who Must be Obeyed
Wheeler's sense of mission permitted him to enlist Mammon in the cause, and he sought commercial and public underwriting for the ACC's wilderness mountaineering camps. Arguing that the nation needed moun-taineers and that climbing would enhance railroad tourism, he persuaded the Dominion of Alberta to foot much of the cost for the club's first camp, and he got Canadian Pacific Railway to loan a cook and two Swiss guides. Thus, just four months after the club's March 1906 founding meeting, a mass of novices coalesced in the Yoho Valley, camped and ate in style, and took mountaineering instruction from Edward and Gottfried Feuz. Forty-four climbers "graduated" from this camp, includ-

Alpine Club of Canada members descending the Yoho Glacier in 1914. Note the wood axe for chopping steps. PHOTO BY BYRON HARMON, COURTESY WHYTE MUSEUM OF THE CANADIAN ROCKIES, ACC#V263 NA71-5970.

ing 15 women. Soon afterward the club named two of the peaks it had climbed President and Vice-President, honoring the railroad executives who supported the club's operations. The mutually beneficial triangle of railroad, mountaineering and tourism would continue for many years.

Wheeler's powerful personality also would dominate the club for decades. Described as a "benevolent dictator," Wheeler made it his business to direct who would climb what and when, and he personally enforced camp rules. Anyone straying beyond camp boundary lines had to notify him with their reasons and the planned return time. Even AMC doyen Charles Fay was almost banished after overlooking this fiat. The 1913 *Canadian Alpine Journal* (*CAJ*), which Wheeler himself edited, captioned his photo "He who must be obeyed." He served as ACC president from 1906 to 1910, director from 1910 to 1926, editor of the *CAJ* from 1907 to 1927, and honorary president from 1926 until his death in 1945.

In 1909, Wheeler answered the letter of a nearly starving Austrian guide named Conrad Kain and offered the young man $2 per summer day, plus another $2 for each day of guiding, to work for the ACC. Though he would often pine for home, Kain felt "certain that Canada is better for a workman; he has freer course and better opportunity." Kain was pleased to find that, in Canada, "Every climber, male or female, carries [packs] for himself. It is one of the best qualities they have! In Canada the guide is never looked upon as a beast of burden, as one so commonly sees him in the Austrian mountains." Kain became one of Canada's favorite and most skilled guides.

Like the American clubs, the ACC pioneered the inclusion of women in mountaineering. In camp, women had to wear skirts over their bloomers, but once out of view from camp they were required to stash skirts and climb in bloomers because billowy hems posed a hazard.

Besides initiating novices into mountaineering, the ACC aimed for the first ascents of prominent peaks. The club's initial effort was to assist the American Alpine Club in sponsoring Herschel Parker and Belmore Browne on their 1912 attempt on Mt. McKinley. Closer to home, the obvious goal was Mt. Robson.

The Robson Saga

Although few Canadians had seen 12,972-foot Mt. Robson, it was known to be the highest peak in the Canadian Rockies. Many still think of Robson as Canada's premier

Conrad Kain, photographed by Byron Harmon. COURTESY WHYTE MUSEUM OF THE CANADIAN ROCKIES, ACC.# NA66-408.

mountain, and the story of its first ascent has been the nation's most enduring mountaineering enigma.

At the ACC's 1906 camp in Yoho, Wheeler encouraged veteran explorer and geologist Arthur P. Coleman to organize an attempt on Robson. The following summer, Coleman

Mt. Robson from the south. The Emperor Ridge is the left skyline, and the high cirque on the left was where Kinney and Phillips climbed. The hanging glacier on the right is where Kain descended after the first ascent. PHOTO BY ANDY SELTERS.

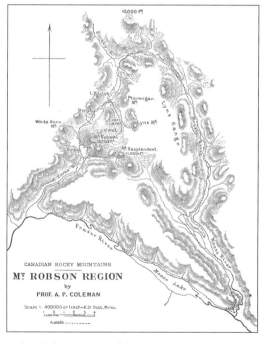

Arthur Coleman's map of the Mt. Robson area, from *The Canadian Rockies, New and Old Trails."*

recruited his brother Lucius and Rev. George Kinney, a bold young man who had raised some eyebrows by climbing alone to the top of Mt. Stephen. No roads led to Robson, and the three men spent some 39 days in 1907 just working out the 260-mile approach.

The same team returned in 1908, and Kinney, climbing alone, pioneered a way up difficult snow-choked chimneys and across ledges to the lower spine of what we now call the Emperor Ridge. A storm seemed to be gathering and he retreated. After a final joint foray to the base of the northeast face, the team returned home and began planning a third expedition for the next year.

Feeling the immensity of Robson under his feet seemed to light an obsessive fire in Kinney. It had become clear to him that a Robson success would be an alpine achievement well beyond anything yet done in North America. Arthur Coleman, however, was an explorer more than an alpinist, and at age 56 he had little stomach for steep ground. As the

Curly Phillips on Mt. Robson. PHOTO BY GEORGE KINNEY, COURTESY WHYTE MUSEUM OF THE CANADIAN ROCKIES.

1909 season approached, Kinney heard that a strong British party with a Swiss guide would be heading for Robson. Kinney borrowed some money and bolted to beat the British, leaving the Colemans in the lurch. The reverend hoped to find a partner en route, and at an outpost near Jasper he met Donald "Curly" Phillips. An experienced horse packer, Phillips was plucky and fit, and he agreed to try Robson as his very first climb.

It was a lean expedition. Indian dogs swiped much of Kinney's food and some mishap bent his rifle. They chased down marmots and grouse, and carried firewood up the mountain's west flank to heat tea and stews. Kinney led with his ice axe and nailed boots, while Phillips followed in his leather-soled wrangling boots, bracing himself against the snow with a stout stick. While descending from their second try, Kinney scouted to the south and saw that a ledge led to the southwest bowl, offering "a long slope of snow clear to Mt. Robson's highest pinnacle." With this discovery, Kinney gained "confidence of ultimate success."

On August 12 they bivouacked on a ledge at about 10,500 feet. The next day mists swarmed over the peak, but the clouds never delivered more than a minor squall and their shade helped keep the bowl from melting into a theater of avalanches. Kinney led an upward traverse, and, after "floundering through...treacherous masses" of rimed snow, the pair "stood at last on the very summit of Mt. Robson." At the nearest rocks, "a few hundred feet below the peak," Kinney cached a Canadian flag and a record of their travails.

Officially, the ACC hailed the climb as a great accomplishment. Kinney repaid his borrowed money with speaking engagements, and the *CAJ* ran the article that Kinney and Phillips jointly authored. Privately, however, Wheeler, Coleman and other influential members called Kinney rash and irresponsible for taking a novice up a route prone to avalanches. Wheeler and others also may have doubted the veracity of the ascent. And Wheeler had found other ambitions for Robson.

In 1911, Wheeler led a survey of the Robson area. His party included Kinney, Phillips and Conrad Kain. Despite extended spells of fair weather, Wheeler did not allow any of the party to climb. Frustrated, Kain snuck out of camp and made the first ascent of Whitehorn Mountain, and later he led photographer Byron Harmon on an unauthorized first ascent of Resplendent Mountain. Wheeler

The Grand Trunk Northern Railway unloading passengers near Yellowhead Pass for the 1913 ACC climbing camp at Mt. Robson. PHOTO BY P. L. TAIT, COURTESY WHYTE MUSEUM OF THE CANADIAN ROCKIES.

raged over these challenges to his authority, and he didn't recognize Kain for climbing Whitehorn until Walter Schauffelberger's party found Kain's cached register two years later. It became apparent that Wheeler was planning a major Robson event for 1913, and he wanted to save the area's first ascents for members of that expedition.

Return to Robson

Wheeler used his organizational skills and political connections to build the 1913 Robson camp into a great extravaganza. He gathered sponsorship from the federal and provincial governments, and from the new Grand Trunk Northern Railway. The tracks of this second railroad line had just reached over Yellowhead Pass, near Robson. Wheeler got the railway to dispatch a special run of

☾ Conrad Kain belaying two clients over a gendarme on an ascent of Resplendent Mountain in 1913. PHOTO BY BYRON HARMON, COURTESY WHYTE MUSEUM OF THE CANADIAN ROCKIES, ACC#V263 NA71-5998.

luxury cars to carry the party within a few miles of the basecamp. A circle of mountaineering dignitaries would take part, and Curly Phillips would be in charge of the packing. Kinney, ostensibly Robson's greatest hero, would not attend.

The crowning event would be Conrad Kain leading William W. Foster and Albert H. MacCarthy up Mt. Robson, via a route Kain had scouted from Resplendent. Foster was a deputy minister for the government of British Columbia, and his rising career promised that the ACC would have a good friend in high circles. MacCarthy was a New Jersey banker, a retired captain in the U.S. Navy, and a prominent member of the American Alpine Club.

On July 31, 1913, Kain, Foster and MacCarthy headed for the northeast face of snow and ice that now bears Kain's name. With one hand braced on the slope and the other wielding his axe, Kain whacked steps up 1,200 feet of 45-degree ice and snow to reach the east ridge. He continued to lead up the difficult ridgecrest, and near the top he

confronted a maze of steep walls and terraces. Finally, in the late afternoon, Kain
turned to his charges and announced,
"Gentlemen, that's so far as I can take you."
He recalled that "only 15 minutes were
allowed us on the summit, 10 of pure pleasure and five of teeth chattering."

Knowing that steep ground and afternoon
avalanches would make it foolish to descend
the same route, Kain led the team down the
unvisited south face of the mountain to a
shivering open bivouac. Seracs calved off and
thundered nearby, and Kain noted, "If that
goes on it will spoil my night's rest." At dawn
they continued down under those seracs and
finished the descent. This was certainly the
most difficult ascent to date in North
America, demanding skill and tenacity of the
highest international standards.

Back in camp, Foster told the admiring
camp the details of their ascent. Then,
according to Elizabeth Parker's article in
Scribner's magazine, Curly Phillips came up
to him and said that, four years before, "We
didn't get up that last dome." Foster asked
where the packer and Kinney had halted, and
Phillips replied that the final dome was 60 or
70 feet high. None of this was announced to
the camp at large, but the ACC position quietly changed. In the next *CAJ*, Kain confirmed
that Phillips had told him he and Kinney did
not climb the final dome "because the danger
was too great." Wheeler declared that the
1913 ascent was "the first complete ascent of
Mt. Robson."

So rebuffed, George Kinney left mountaineering and returned to serving as a minister in remote parts of British Columbia. He
maintained until his death in 1961 that he
and Phillips had made the top, and by the
1990s historians had come to feel that he
might have been right. For one thing, no
Robson climber has ever found a final summit "dome" that would present any difficulty. Second, contemporaries including
Conrad Kain, Albert MacCarthy and Edward
Feuz all privately believed Kinney. Others
are said to have believed that Wheeler
cooked up the story to elevate the status of
the 1913 climb. Some suspected that Curly

Phillips might have complied with a con-
spiracy instigated by Wheeler to suppress
the 1909 ascent—a suspicion that grew
when the ACC contracted with Phillips so
steadily after 1913 that he virtually became
the club's official packer.

The final twist in this saga started when
historian Chic Scott unearthed the fact that,
in 1959, four Harvard climbers high on
Robson came across a deteriorating can con-
taining the flag and note that Kinney had
stashed. It was not generally known where
they found this cache until 2000, when
Scott's publisher, Gillean Daffern, tracked
down one of the Harvard climbers, Leo
Slaggie. The can was a few hundred feet
below the Emperor Ridge and well west of
the top, Slaggie said. This is far from any
descent route from the summit, but it is consistent with a descent from a high point
along the Emperor Ridge. Kinney's description of his summit view mentions that he
looked directly "down a sheer precipice that
reached to the glacier at the foot of Berg
Lake," a view consistent with a point along
the Emperor Ridge. Thus, this seems to have
been the high point of the 1909 climb.

Since clouds whipped over the mountain
that day, Kinney and Phillips might not have
seen that higher ground rose to the east. It's
also possible that, along this cockscomb
ridge of big, snowy "gargoyles," Phillips might
have glimpsed an unclimbable gendarme 60
or 70 feet higher. Even if they did not reach
the true summit, they indisputably made a
very impressive, rough-and-ready ascent of
some of the most sustained and intimidating
terrain yet climbed.

Days after the Kain ascent, Wheeler anoint-
ed a second team to try another route on
Robson, the striking southwest or
"Wishbone" arête. The lead climber was
Swiss businessman and guide Walter
Schauffelberger. In just 14 hours,
Schauffelberger led Harley Prouty and Basil
Darling up nearly 7,000 feet of icy rock and
snowy gargoyles. Within 400 feet of the top a
squall turned into a ferocious storm, and in
the face of driving snow, hail and lightning
they had to retreat to a bivouac. Many later

Charles Fay, William Foster and Oliver Wheeler, probably in the Selkirks. COURTESY HENRY S. HALL, JR. AMERICAN ALPINE CLUB LIBRARY.

climbers looking for a Robson route safe from avalanches would try this arête, but for decades none would climb so efficiently nor come close to this team's high point.

During the Great War

After the 1913 camp, Arthur Wheeler proposed that the ACC next raise its sights to Canada's highest peak, distant Mt. Logan. But then Canada became embroiled in the European war. In October 1914, Canadian troops shipped off and club activity virtually stopped. During these dark years many peaks of the Rockies were named for war heroes and heroines, including Clemenceau, Kitchener, Joffre, Edith Cavell, Brussels and Sir Douglas (Haig).

In 1914 and 1916, retired officer Albert MacCarthy returned to Canada with his wife, Elizabeth, also a keen climber. Wheeler made Kain available as a guide, and in 1914 the trio climbed Mt. Farnham, the highest peak of the southern Purcells. In 1916 they started their campaign with a scouting hike under Mt. Louis, a striking blade of limestone north of Banff. Probing Louis' lower slabs, Kain and MacCarthy suddenly found themselves in position for a summit bid. They climbed around the southeast corner and entered a long, deep chimney. This provided a final struggle, but to their own surprise the two men soon stood on top. Back in the valley, Kain called, "Ye Gods, Mr. MacCarthy, just look at that—they never will believe we climbed it."

With John Vincent, the three then went to the "Nunatak Peaks" of the southern Purcells. Wheeler and Kain had sighted these granitic towers while surveying in 1909, and Kain described them as "very much like Chamonix aiguilles" rising from beautiful glaciers. Though no steeper and substantially smaller than the mountains of the Rockies, these peaks were smooth spires with scant holds for nailed boots. Kain relished the challenge, saying, "On peaks of the Rockies, where the stone formation is rotten, such places would be difficult and dangerous, but when every hold is solid difficulties are welcome and met with a smile."

Mt. Louis from the southeast. Kain and MacCarthy started by traversing up the shaded east face, then turned onto the sunlit face to work up chutes and ribs to a strenuous chimney leading to the top. PHOTO BY GLEN BOLES.

Elizabeth MacCarthy rappelling off the crux gendarme on Bugaboo Spire. PHOTO BY ALBERT MACCARTHY, COURTESY WHYTE MUSEUM OF THE CANADIAN ROCKIES, ALPINE CLUB OF CANADA COLLECTION.

The south ridge of Nunatak Three presented Kain with a particularly steep and smooth gendarme. He had no anchors and the lives of all four depended on his "vacuum grip." After spending an hour and a half to climb 70 feet, Kain locked his fingers into a slanting crack about two inches wide and reached easier ground. During their descent they employed the latest method for steep rappelling: Wrap a couple of turns of the rope around one ankle, pinch the strands between the feet, hold tight to the strands above, and slide down.

MacCarthy termed Nunatak Three a "bugaboo," applying the name of a nearby creek where miners had a particularly tough time extracting gold. Subsequent climbers would call it Bugaboo Spire, and Nunatak One came to be called North Howser Tower.

Vancouver Mountaineers

In the same spirit as Seattle and Portland climbers, Vancouver citizens pioneered climbs in the mountains just beyond their city limits. In 1907, the new Vancouver Mountain Club forged a way to the top of Mt. Garibaldi, the long-dormant volcano that looks over Howe Sound.

As in the Selkirks, steep, heavily vegetated canyons in the coastal mountains precluded any use of pack stock, but determined members fought their way to the alpine country. Between 1910 and 1914, Basil Darling led some very tough approaches and exposed,

➲   A modern climber on Conrad Kain's route to the top of Bugaboo Spire. The crux pitch goes up the white rock on the next tier above the climber. PHOTO BY CHRIS ATKINSON.

steep climbs near Howe Sound, reaching the tops of Sky Pilot, Serratus Mountain and Red Tusk. He also led the first ascents of Golden Ears and Cathedral Mountain east of Vancouver.

Perhaps the most notable of Darling's climbs was on Mt. Tantalus, the highest non-volcano of the region. His party started from sea level with a struggle across the mouth of the Squamish River, followed by a 4,000-foot climb through dense bush to a steep, broken glacier. Finally they worked up steep and complex rock to the 8,540-foot summit.

In 1912, Tom Fyles, a British expatriate, joined the Vancouver club, which by then was known as the British Columbia Mountain Club (BCMC). As a postman, Fyles walked for work as well as for pleasure. He was so fit and enthusiastic that one member said, "Fyles *was* the club. He led every trip."

In 1916, Tom Fyles led his brother across the first traverse of Serratus Mountain, a prominent peak in the Tantalus Range. The two encountered steep fourth- and fifth-class terrain along the long, jagged east ridge. Another alluring challenge was Mt. Judge Howay, a double peak visible from Vancouver yet accessible only after a multiday excursion. On his fourth attempt, in 1921, Fyles and two others got lucky with the weather and succeeded on a steep, rocky route to the higher northwest summit.

Teton Satellites

Not until after the war did climbers start to make serious attempts on the secondary summits in the Tetons. Yellowstone National Park Superintendent Horace Albright wanted to gather public support for expanding the park to include the Tetons, and in 1918 he invited American Alpine Club members (who then totaled only 18) to come climb at government expense.

LeRoy Jeffers answered this invitation the next summer and headed toward Mt. Moran, the impressive northern bastion of the range. Jeffers climbed a gully to access the narrow northeast ridge, and after some very exposed climbing he made it over the lower north summit. He continued toward the main sum-

mit, but a fierce storm of sleet and lightning pushed him back.

Three years later, Dr. Legrand Hardy, Ben Rich and Bennett McNulty climbed directly up to the higher, south summit of Moran via the Skillet Glacier. They climbed with "short, tough sticks...and two short auto shovels." Other prominent Teton summits remained unclimbed for some time. Not until 1923 would Coloradan Albert Ellingwood and partners finally make the first ascents of the Middle and South Tetons.

Canada's Highest

In the 1920s, the world-famous quest for Mt. Everest reinvigorated club efforts. Mallory and Irvine's story inspired Henry Hall and Osgood Field to found the Harvard Mountaineering Club, which would become the most successful climbing club on the continent. Hall would be the club's patriarch for decades, overseeing the development of an astonishing percentage of America's finest mountaineers.

In Canada, the Everest attempts helped spur the ACC to mount its long-postponed quest to climb Mt. Logan. In these days, before the debilitating effects of Himalayan altitudes were well known, Logan's remote, extensive glaciers and high latitude made some wonder if the Canadian giant might be more demanding than Everest. Logan would present more vertical relief than Everest, a 12-mile summit plateau to cross and a subarctic climate.

William Foster was now a distinguished Great War veteran and the president of the ACC. In November 1923, he selected as leader of the Logan climb his partner on Robson, the American Albert MacCarthy. Though he would turn 49 during the expedition, MacCarthy was still a dynamo and tough as leather. His assignment was a logistical challenge of the first order, and he would command every aspect of it with dogged, hard-edged authority.

Notes and a photograph from 1913 boundary surveyors suggested that a western approach, from the outpost of McCarthy, Alaska, might deliver one to a "trench" cutting

Sledging en route to Mt. Logan on the 1925 first ascent. COURTESY HENRY S. HALL, JR. AMERICAN ALPINE CLUB LIBRARY.

up to Logan's vast summit plateau. In 1924, MacCarthy scouted the area and found it would be 140 miles to the base of Logan—86 miles by glacier. Leaving nothing to chance, he planned to assault the mountain with about six times more time and supplies than the Duke of Abruzzi took to climb Mt. St. Elias, starting with a preliminary expedition just to stock the basecamp. This supply expedition would carry 10 tons of freight, not quite half of which would be cached for the climbing team. To make use of sleds that could be dragged by horses and dogs, they would travel in the winter and would employ local Alaskans.

The supply operation alone became a two-month ordeal. As they sledged through the Chitina River Valley, temperatures plunged to 50 degrees below zero, river ice collapsed around them, and harnesses froze to the horses. The many trials made the effort "twice as hard as anyone had calculated it would be," MacCarthy said. The tonnage was delivered, but MacCarthy and his main partner, 50-year-old miner and Yukon pioneer

Andy Taylor, didn't return to town until April 26. They had just 11 days to recover before meeting their climbing partners: Frederick Lambart, the deputy leader and a veteran of the 1913 boundary survey, William Foster and four relatively youthful members of the American Alpine Club—Allen Carpé, Henry Hall, R. M. Morgan and Norman Read. They had decided to go guideless.

Even with the cached loads waiting, the climbers shouldered 75 to 100 pounds on their packboards for the walk to the foot of the "trench." Next they had to skirt an icefall, and it took the eight men 11 ferries to establish a ton of gear and supplies at a higher camp, at about 10,000 feet. This warehouse included the latest equipment: rubber air mattresses, 24-pound, down-filled bedrolls and sturdy tents with steel poles. Three of the group's innovations would become standard items on expeditions for decades: the single-pole, pyramidal Logan Tent, willow wands to mark a route for foul-weather travel, and a dense mass of flour, molasses, eggs, dried fruit and other ingredients baked into "Logan bread." Carpé wrote that the dreary toil of heaving so much cargo wore down their bodies, and the "awful loneliness of these great ranges" eroded their morale.

MacCarthy whipped them upward, and on at least one instance team members questioned his judgment. Five men had gone down from a camp at the edge of the plateau at 18,500 feet to get more supplies, and as they returned a storm pummeled them. The five started to retreat, but MacCarthy appeared in the mist from the higher camp and ordered them to persevere. They obeyed, but when they finally regained the upper camp at 9 p.m. Morgan's feet were frozen. The next day, Hall volunteered to help him off the mountain.

The rest of the team worked for two more days to position themselves for a summit bid. They went for the top on June 23, burdened with an impressive load of 60 pounds of bivouac gear each. Glad for crampons on the wind-hardened snow, they finally stood at Logan's highest summit in gloomy twilight. "We were foolishly happy in the success of our venture, and we thought that our troubles were at an end," MacCarthy wrote later. But as they started their descent, a storm swamped the team, and by midnight they were too weak to go on. With their mitts and snowshoes they dug a bivouac hovel.

In the morning they pushed on in a whiteout, and in the gloom MacCarthy, Carpé and Foster lost their way. These three spent a second night out, but they made it back to camp on the 25th. They rested for a day before starting the two-week trek toward civilization. On the way back they suffered through more storms and watched Lambart's frostbitten feet slough skin off to the bones. They stepped off the ice to see lupines and hummingbirds along the Chitina River, and Carpé later wrote, "Perhaps you would have to spend two months on the ice and snow as we did to know the poignant joy of these simple things." The editor of Britain's *Alpine Journal* would declare, "Greater hardships have probably never been experienced in any mountaineering expedition."

Summary

Clubs continued to be a vital force for bringing novices into mountaineering and for environmental conservation. But once the summits in their territory had been climbed, most of the prominent clubs failed to support

The 1925 Mt. Logan team below the Chitina Glacier. From left to right: Norman Read, Allen Carpé, William Foster, Albert MacCarthy, Henry Hall, Andy Taylor, Robert Morgan and Frederick Lambart. COURTESY HENRY S. HALL, JR. AMERICAN ALPINE CLUB LIBRARY.

Camp en route to Mt. Logan, 1925. COURTESY HENRY S. HALL, JR. AMERICAN ALPINE CLUB LIBRARY.

Members of the 1925 Mt. Logan expedition carrying loads through the icefall in the King Trench, below the north face of King Peak. COURTESY HENRY S. HALL, JR. AMERICAN ALPINE CLUB LIBRARY.

Members of the 1925 Mt. Logan expedition resting at "Prospector's Pass" during the stormy descent from the summit. COURTESY WHYTE MUSEUM OF THE CANADIAN ROCKIES.

younger climbers looking for new adventure. Club-sponsored expeditions would claim one more major first ascent—Mt. Fairweather—but the heyday of mountaineering clubs as institutions to support leading mountaineers was passing. A new generation of climbers would find challenges either on their own or within the few clubs that geared themselves to more serious mountaineering.

![Suggested Routes logo]

SUGGESTED ROUTES
FROM THIS PERIOD

MT. ROBSON (12,972 feet/3,954 meters)
Kain Face

Mt. Robson dominates its surroundings like few mountains can, and few routes besides Kain's remain such serious challenges so many decades after their first ascent. A Harvard team finally repeated Conrad Kain's northeast face route in 1953, and with today's ice climbing standards this makes a serious but not-too-technical route for capable climbers.

Approach: The excursion starts with a stiff hike; most make a camp after 10 miles at Berg Lake, then

Looking at Mt. Robson from the northeast, from just above the Robson-Resplendent col. PHOTO BY GLEN BOLES.

use a second day to reach a high camp somewhere on the Robson Glacier. The most advantageous camp is in the 10,000-foot-high basin near the Dome, an area that puts you in good position to get up the face early, before morning heat might loosen avalanches on the face. In any case, the old direct route to this basin is now broken by a dangerous icefall, and wise parties first climb to the Robson-Resplendent Col (9,500 feet), and then traverse to the basin above the icefall.

Route: Kain's 1,500-foot ice face, plastered to the east ridge, averages a bit steeper than 45 degrees. Judging its surface condition is a crucial element of this climb. From its top, traverse the east ridge and continue up the snow and ice of the peak's east face. Near the top you'll have to work over "The Roof," a bergschrund-like formation that frequently requires locating a steep snow ramp to break through overhangs. When the typical cloud cap covers the summit, it can be very difficult to find a way through this section. Most now descend by the same route, taking care that the day has not brought dangerously warm conditions to the face.

First Ascent: Conrad Kain, Albert MacCarthy and William Foster, July 1913

Difficulty: D, AI 3, 5,000 feet from upper Robson Glacier.

Guidebook: *Selected Alpine Climbs in the Canadian Rockies*

MT. OLYMPUS (7,965 feet/2,428 meters)
Blue Glacier

The highest glacier-draped crags of the Olympic Peninsula make for a grand backcountry outing. While the technical challenges are modest, climbers need to be capable in glacier travel and routefinding skills.

Approach: Start with a 17-mile trail up the Hoh River Valley to a basecamp at Glacier Meadows, at 4,200 feet. The snout of the Blue Glacier is not far to the south.

Route: Climb up the Blue Glacier from its toe or, if snow coverage is light and the complex crevasses are open, stay on the east moraine and gain the glacier higher up. Then climb up to the western cirque of the Blue Glacier to reach the Snow Dome. From there you have two main options. The original route goes through a notch and into the central cirque of the Blue Glacier. There you cut south to the West

Approach: Most people arrange for a floatplane landing at Lake Lovelywater or a helicopter drop at Red Tit Col. An ACC cabin is available at the lake by reservation.

Route: From Lake Lovelywater, climb 1,100 feet over the crest of the range at the Ionia-Serratus Col, then traverse an easy glacier under Red Tit Col and continue along the west side of the south ridge of Mt. Tantalus' sister peak, Mt. Dione. Cross to the east side of Dione and traverse easy snow and rock to the north edge of Dione. From there you make a short descent into a couloir, then traverse a spectacular tower called Witches Tooth, and then rappel into the Darling Couloir. Fourth-class rock then traverses upward to the summit of Tantalus. The best way to return is by a lower route across Tantalus' east face leading to a rappel into a couloir. Scramble on ledges back up to the east face of Mt. Dione. All in all, this is a very long roundtrip from Lake Lovelywater.

First Ascent: Basil Darling, J. Davies and A. Morkill, 1911; Via Red Tit Col: A. Parke and K. Winter, 1962

Difficulty: AD+, Class 4, over 5,000 feet of gain from Lake Lovelywater

Guidebook: *Alpine Select*

Mt. Olympus from the northeast. PHOTO BY AUSTIN POST, U.S. GEOLOGICAL SURVEY

Summit, where a steep snow pitch and some third-class scrambling lead to the top. Those who want to climb directly to the higher West Summit from the Snow Dome will find the climbing only slightly more difficult. You can also head for the West Summit's west ridge, a 5.3 route that was first done in 1964. In any case, take care to not get caught in a whiteout that could block visibility for your descent.

First Ascent: Mazamas party, August 1907

Difficulty: PD

Guidebook: *Climber's Guide to the Olympic Mountains*

Permit: There are fees to enter Olympic National Park and for a backcountry camping permit.

MT. TANTALUS (8,540 feet/2,603 meters)
Southeast Spur

The Tantalus Range is a beautiful spine of granite, old volcanics and glaciers west of Squamish, British Columbia. Early BCMC members named it for the tantalizing skyline it presented from the Squamish-Garibaldi area. The first-ascent team attacked the east face of the highest peak directly, but now climbers traverse from the south to join that route on the main peak.

Mt. Tantalus from the east. PHOTO BY KEVIN MCLANE.

MT. MORAN (12,605 feet/3,842 meters)
Northeast Ridge

If not for the Grand Teton some six miles to the south, massive Mt. Moran might be the most famous peak in Wyoming. The massif rises some 5,800 feet above the nearby plain to a flat, 15-acre summit area. Its northeast ridge is a big, well-defined spine of solid rock that demands endurance and classic mountaineering skills. Most climbers now follow the complete ridge, including the Great Gendarme, as pioneered by Colorado mountaineers in 1924.

Approach: Until 1953, climbers drove to Moran on a road that ran to the north end of Leigh Lake, but noisy motorcycles prompted park authorities to close this road. Now Mt. Moran is the most remote major peak in the Tetons, and most people will need three days to climb this route. One can minimize the hike by starting for the peak by water—either canoe or kayak to the north end of Leigh Lake or hire a motorboat across Jackson Lake (6,772 feet). From either shore, head up toward the Skillet Glacier, tracing game trails and whacking bush. At about 8,400 feet, the slope leading right to the northeast ridge opens up. You can either camp near the stream coming down from the Skillet Glacier or climb to the more traditional and scenic campsites at the ridge just below the Great Gendarme, where snowmelt can usually be found.

Route: Pass the Great Gendarme on the right, and then follow the exposed ridgecrest, with only occasional variance, toward the main peak. Traverse left into a chimney—the crux of the route—that leads to the north summit. A scenic quarter-mile hike along a narrow ridge leads to the main summit plateau. Descend by the same route.

First Ascent: From above Great Gendarme: LeRoy Jeffers, August 1919; Via complete ridge: Albert Ellingwood and Carl Blaurock, August 1924

Difficulty: PD, 5.4, 3,000 feet from ridgeline bivouac

Guidebook: *A Climber's Guide to the Teton Range*

Permit: A fee is required to enter Grand Teton National Park, and backcountry camping requires a free permit.

Mt. Moran from the northeast. AERIAL PHOTO BY LEIGH ORTENBURGER.

Period II
Adventure Revitalized

In every mountain range, sooner or later the original vision of simply reaching the summits becomes stale. Alpine summits became fairly routine by the 1870s, and by the 1920s in North America there was the same sense that reaching a summit might be a fine personal achievement, but, in the familiar ranges at least, nothing extraordinary.

Out of this sense of familiarity, a new generation soon developed a new mountaineering vision. Younger climbers added the goal of getting to summits via steep, challenging terrain, by way of a peak's bolder architecture. This budding vision spread across North America as technical methods for climbing steep terrain drifted over from Europe. New techniques and equipment prompted climbers to chose *routes* as their operative goals—the ridges, faces and couloirs that their predecessors hadn't even imagined as possible. We can characterize this shift as the transition from exploratory mountaineering to technical mountaineering.

Even as technical mountaineering developed on North America's more familiar mountains, however, many of the greatest peaks in North America remained unexplored—whole ranges had not yet been seen by Euro-Americans. In these remote cordilleras, a second generation of exploratory mountaineers renewed the tradition of summiting and surveying. Thus, between the world wars, North American mountaineering split into two somewhat distinct circles of climbers looking for different sorts of challenges and operating in different parts of the continent.

Both groups climbed in the post-World War I context. For most nations involved, the Great War spanned more than four of the most horrible years in history, and it dragged whole cultures into deep disillusionment. The social contract between ruling elites and the general public cracked, and from this time on tradition would be held in suspicion and individuals began to demand more rights and autonomy. This was the formative period for the modern era, and the shock waves that shifted social foundations also changed the way people looked at adventure and mountaineering.

For Canada, the war brought nearly as much agony as it did to the European nations. Even though (or perhaps because) Canadian loyalty to Europe had grown a bit musty, an unfair proportion of Canadian men was sent beyond the front lines as shock troops, and thousands were killed or maimed. For this and a variety of other morose reasons, many young Canadians lost faith in the noble aims espoused by their elders, including the genteel form of mountaineering.

The senior guardians of the Alpine Club of Canada aggravated this generation gap by redoubling their emphasis on the goals and methods of their pioneers. As they re-sang the refrain that mountaineering was a noble path to virtuous character, potential recruits turned a deaf ear. By the 1920s, the average age of ACC members was a mature 44. Moreover, the Canadian

Alps no longer attracted leading European climbers. Europeans' own post-war agonies limited their ability to travel, and exciting new routes in their own Alps kept them busy. With a few notable exceptions, Canadian climbing became moribund for decades.

By contrast, although the United States saw many youths cut down during its 19 months in the war, America's fewer losses and her powerful, pivotal role allowed a heady sense of victory. After the armistice, opportunities for personal freedom in America quickly expanded. Labor and women's rights, along with longer weekends and summer vacations, helped feed a mushrooming sense of opportunity. The automobile and the expanding network of roads were tailor-made for individuals with some means, and more than one climbing community collected around a partner with a car. Mass marketing and vacation time expanded leisure interests, including a taste for competitive sports. The same social forces, however, also brought slums, careening markets, corruption and a broader sense of anxiety and cynicism. With all of the transformations that we associate with the Roaring '20s, the very concept of personal adventure also grew. Previously unacceptable risk-taking of all sorts gained a broad validity. For those with a curiosity for the mountains, this new age generated both the impetus to dream and the means to go.

Recall that the primary generation of exploratory mountaineers had set out under the scrutiny, sanction and sponsorship of society's aristocracy. Climbers of this tradition returned to institutions in London, New York and other urban centers with achievements of scientific interest to their peers, sponsors and overseers. By comparison, the new technical mountaineers would neither seek nor attract much social support. No longer did Americans wonder what lay beyond the Mississippi, and the technical routes that now attracted climbers were barely comprehensible to the gentry or the general public. Mountaineering exploits would rarely make the pages of even a local newspaper—and even then they were in the context of stunts.

What seemed to be lost in this transition was what traditionalists called "the Spirit of Wonder" or "the essence of Romance." Indeed, from this period onward, mountaineering writers would rarely venture into Romantic raptures or noble proclamations in the style of John Muir or Elizabeth Parker. Their accounts mostly focused on topographic and technical factors. Personal experience became a silent force, something alluded to but no longer a matter of public concern—in fact a matter of public mystery. For nearly the rest of the century, when some great climbing achievement or tragedy attracted the public's attention, the encounter would inevitably inspire one question: "Why?"

Yet, compared with their predecessors, the new mountaineers would take on more exacting and intimidating terrain, and they would do it without guides and often without even club support. Just as revolutionary, more than a couple of the new climbers would be unchaperoned women. The new climbers were pioneers in the spirit of individualism budding across North America, and the only thing they wanted or would get from society was the freedom to climb the routes that so inspired them.

CHAPTER 5

Frontiers of Verticality

Even before the turn of the 20th century, a few North Americans ventured onto steep, exposed ground—what we would call technical mountaineering. The Canadian guides and a few of their charges were quite proficient, of course, but there were other bold amateurs as well. Early on, for example, the friendly weather and firm rock in California's Sierra inspired daring explorations.

In 1896, Stanford professor Bolton Brown made an extraordinary climb to the top of Mt. Clarence King, a remote granite steeple. Brown committed to some exposed, delicate moves and then ascended the final pinnacle by pulling on a rope he'd knotted and wedged into a fist-sized crack. Climbers today rate this pitch exposed 5.7 or 5.8. Commenting on his apparent foolishness, Brown characterized well the attraction of steep climbing:

> *When every foothold and handhold must be separately found and judged...I, at any rate, grow quite ecstatically careful—the intense nervous stimulus and tension, combined with the absolute steadiness and poise required, being exactly one of the chief delights of the sport. I am sure several men with pike-poles could not have got me off that ridge.*

Within a few years of this climb, Charles Michael, a man with a similar high spirit, took a position as the assistant postmaster in Yosemite Valley. According to Sierra Club member Owen L. Williams, Michael "made ascents of practically everything in the Valley that does not require pitons," often with his

Charles Michael in the Sierra. PHOTO BY ENID MICHAEL, COURTESY YOSEMITE MUSEUM.

Rudolph Aemmer, Edward Feuz Jr., Val Fynn and Basil Gordon on a pinnacle at Abbott Pass in 1911. COURTESY WHYTE MUSEUM OF THE CANADIAN ROCKIES, ACC# V200 PA44-86.

wife, Enid. During summer holidays Charles and Enid toured the High Sierra with a couple of pack mules. Charles would climb up impressive towers, using his rope only to help himself back down. Modern climbers still speak with respect for his remarkable routes (now rated fifth class) up such unclimbed peaks as Red Kaweah (1912), Devils Crag #1 (1913) and Michael Minaret (1923).

Amateurs in Canada

Each time Edouard Feuz guided Mt. Sir Donald, he looked over to the peak's striking northwest edge and thought that, with a competent client, he could make a spectacular climb up that blade in the sky. When German Ernest Tewes showed up late in the 1903 season, Feuz proposed this climb. Along with a second guide, Christian Bören, Feuz and Tewes found firm, angular quartzite that lured them like a ladder into exhilarating heights. A few hundred feet below the top, they escaped from the knife-

edge and took the upper west face to reach the summit by early afternoon. Tewes would write, "The new route can scarcely become popular. The difficulties are so manifold and intense, the climbing from the first to the last moment so expert, that the expedition can stand side by side with the most arduous expedition in the Alps."

The most advanced amateur of this time in North America was Val Fynn. A Russian-born Irishman, Fynn had climbed some 50 new routes in the Alps. He immigrated to St. Louis with his electrical engineering skills and took long, productive climbing holidays in Canada. In 1909, with Arthur Bartleet, he finished the northwest arête of Mt. Sir Donald straight to the top. He also climbed a new route on the east face of Mt. Louis. After Fynn married, he started sharing the lead more with guides, especially Rudolph Aemmer. Fynn and Aemmer completed the second north-south traverse of Mt. Victoria's long, serrated summit ridge, and the pair made a

Mt. Sir Donald from the northwest. The northwest arête faces the camera, and the north face (climbed in 1961) is on the left. PHOTO BY NORMAN CLYDE.

The frontispiece photo of Mt. Alberta that lured the first ascent party. FROM THE ORIGINAL CLIMBING GUIDE TO THE CANADIAN ROCKIES.

groundbreaking attempt on Mt. Temple's big, complex east ridge.

In 1922, at age 52, Fynn and Aemmer made one of the most challenging ascents of this decade, a direct route to Mt. Victoria's south summit. Starting from Lake Louise at midnight, the two attained a glacial bench at the base of Victoria's 1,600-foot northeast face before 6 a.m. Most of the face rears up as ice and snow, and, after chopping a few hundred hard-won and insecure steps, the two aimed for rock islands as much as possible. As the day's warmth softened the surface they had to chop even deeper to get secure steps, but eventually they won the top.

Two years later, Fynn joined Cyril Wates and Malcolm Geddes to make the first ascent of the king peak of the Ramparts Group in the northern Rockies, Mt. Geikie. Wates had retreated from Geikie's steep walls several times, but Fynn's talent made the difference. The trio followed a rocky couloir slashing up

the southeast face. Then they made a difficult ascent along the northeast ridge to the top, where Fynn led up a "steep and narrow crack...by wedging stones into it [for holds]."

In Europe, the post-war generation of climbers was finding the commitment and means to climb intimidating alpine faces, and these higher standards made their first appearance in North America in 1925. Mt. Alberta was the most dramatic peak yet unclimbed in the Rockies. The first Canadian Rockies guidebook (1921), compiled by American J. Monroe Thorington, had a taunting frontispiece photo of Alberta captioned "A Formidable Unclimbed Peak of the Range." Conrad Kain and Val Fynn had been among the suitors for Alberta, but foul weather and forest fires, respectively, kept each from even setting their boots onto the castle of stone.

Thorington's book reached the royal court of Japan, a nation which a decade before had formed an alpine club on the British model. Yuko Maki, the aide-de-camp to Japan's crown prince, had proved his abilities with the first ascent of the dramatic east arête of the Eiger. This inspired him to start looking for something to attempt in the Himalaya. But when the Marquis Mori Tatsu Hosokawa saw the frontispiece photo of Alberta, he suggested that Maki lead an expedition to this worthy objective.

Maki assembled five of his countrymen and engaged two crack guides from Switzerland, Heinrich Fuhrer (not the well-known immigrant-guide of the same name) and Hans Kohler, as well as skilled amateur Jean Weber. After careful scrutiny of the peak's southeast face, they found what proved to be the only feasible route for this era.

The team needed all the pitons they brought, and Fuhrer was tested to near the limits of his considerable abilities. Describing the loose rock, Weber wrote that "every gripp [sic] had the tendency to remain in the hand." It was afternoon before they confronted the steep, dark band that guards the top of the peak, and the only viable way was at an overhang. Here they resorted to a double

courte echelle, described by Weber (with his original spelling intact):

> *On the very edge of the bottomless abyss Mr. Hayakawa stood facing the wall on the narrow ledge, then Kohler mounted him and ankered his legs around his horses shoulders and tried to catch with his hand a firm gripp on a not too solid hold; after this Fuhrer [wearing felt-soled Kletterschue] climbed with the push of someone over both and could just reach the borde of the exposed balcony. Fortunately was he sceptical to gripps he was feeling and he begann a thoroughly cleaning anxiously watched by the rest who gave rope alittle by little as he proceeded and ankering ourselves to imaginary holds in case that terrible thing should happen none dare to think of…. At least gave the tension away to joy when Fuhrer disappeared above the precipice and he declared from unseen spaces better conditions ahead. The progress of the rest to get up was rather slow since each one hung for an instance in the air until he was able to grasp some rocks which mostly just yielded with the result of experiencing a choking sensation connectet with the dropping back into airy spaces.*

Everyone made it onto the summit ridge, where the challenges included cornices and a gap 60 feet deep. They made the top, left an ice axe as proof, and returned to an uncomfortable bivouac on the ridge. Everest veteran Frank Smythe would later fail on Mt. Alberta and conclude, "I can only say of Alberta that I know of no Alpine peak so difficult by its easiest route, and but one or two Alpine routes to compare with the pitiless limestone slabs with no belays and few resting places."

Summit note left by the party making the first ascent of Mt. Alberta. Photo by John Oberlin, on the second ascent in 1948. COURTESY WHYTE MUSEUM OF THE CANADIAN ROCKIES, ALPINE CLUB OF CANADA COLLECTION.

America's Rockies

In Colorado, William S. Cooper, John Hubbard, Percy Hagerman and others climbed many daring routes before World

War I. Hagerman led the first ascent of Capitol Peak in the Elk Mountains in 1909, straddling the now-famous Knife Ridge. Between 1904 and 1908, Cooper and Hubbard climbed numerous peaks in the Grenadier-Needle areas. Cooper quit, however, when doctors told him, with the medical caution of the previous century, that his heart couldn't take so much exertion. He went on to help lead the effort to create Glacier Bay National Monument.

A few years later, like Val Fynn in Canada, Albert Ellingwood began leading climbs of a whole new standard. Ellingwood was the rare Westerner of this time to earn a Rhodes scholarship to Oxford. In Britain, local climbers taught him modern crag climbing techniques, and he learned alpine climbing in Switzerland. The Brits had pitons by this time, but they emphasized that the finest climbing depended on them as little as possible. Ellingwood understood that a new chapter in American mountaineering was waiting to be written, and that progress would mean looking beyond mere summits to the challenges of getting there. "Difficulty has a charm that is irresistible to many," he would write, and, "The enthusiastic alpinist is completely happy only if his skill is severely taxed."

Ellingwood returned to the United States in 1914 to teach political science and to spend summers mountaineering around the West. He climbed new rock routes in various American ranges, including a productive trip with Carl Blaurock to the Sierra. Often he partnered with Eleanor Davis, an outstanding climber who, with Ellingwood, made the first female ascent of the Grand Teton in 1923.

In 1916, Ellingwood and Davis joined a Colorado Mountain Club outing to the Crestones, the last 14,000-foot summits in the Rockies still unclimbed. Ellingwood and Davis outlasted others in the party to complete a traverse of both Crestone Peak and Crestone Needle. They found the conglomerate rock to be well featured with sound cobbles, and Ellingwood deployed a belay rope with a savvy not yet seen south of Canada. During their descent, they marveled at how

Albert Ellingwood on the Grand Teton. COURTESY JACKSON HOLE HISTORICAL SOCIETY AND MUSEUM.

the northeast side of Crestone Needle swooped down for almost 2,000 feet in a continuous prow.

Ellingwood's ascents inspired other CMC aficionados to climb exciting new routes, especially Carl Blaurock and Hermann Buhl. Buhl (not the famous Austrian who would climb Nanga Parbat) had emigrated from Germany after the war, and from his homeland he imported ice axes and boot nails, gear previously unknown to the region. Blaurock, a Denver native, partnered with Bill Ervin to be the first to climb all of Colorado's 14,000-foot peaks, completing them by 1923. In 1924, Blaurock, Buhl and Buhl's wife joined Ellingwood for probably the first technical climbing expedition to the remote core of the

Wind River Range. They made the first ascent of Mt. Helen by its craggy east ridge and then climbed an icy chute up Fremont Peak's northwest ridge.

That north edge of Crestone Needle stuck in Ellingwood and Davis' minds as one of the greatest pieces of alpine architecture in Colorado, and nine years after their original visit they returned with Stephen Hart and Marion Warner to climb it. Things went smoothly for the first 1,000 feet, but then, Ellingwood wrote, a ferocious hailstorm "began to turn the landscape white."

> *The rocks were cold and every nook and cranny held all the hail it would contain.... Our best chance was a long, thin crack that shot up to the right of the arête.... It was slow work. The rock was slippery and each step and handhold had to be swept clear of hail.... It is not altogether desirable that four people should be strung out on a rope along a hundred feet of such a crack, all more or less dependent on such attachment to the rock as can be secured by a single hand and foot.... Four busy hours expended on four hundred feet!*

The northeast face of Crestone Needle. Ellingwood's route traversed in from the right and followed the central prow to the summit. PHOTO BY STEVE ROPER.

Ellingwood continued to lead upward without any pitons yet bolstered by confidence that he "never failed to find an anchor where I could hold a thousand pounds without difficulty if necessary." The crack they climbed is now rated 5.7, and the ascent became a landmark of the period.

In wry testimony to the new approach to mountain climbing, Ellingwood recalled the Middle Age conundrum of how many angels might sit on the point of a needle: "I would adapt it and propound: From how many angles can the Needle's point be reached?"

Icy New England

On the East Coast, dedicated climbers started climbing steeper ground in the White Mountains in winter, in the tradition of Herschel Parker's search for alpine conditions. In February 1902, an unknown climber from an AMC team left steps revealing the first winter ascent of the headwall of Mt. Washington's Huntington Ravine, via a steep, snowy chute. Three winters later, another AMC party climbed the Great Gulf cirque of Mt. Washington. Icy snow forced slow step cutting, and after dark they luckily found their way to the summit hut to survive the night. Not until 1910, when George Flagg led a climb along the north edge of Pinnacle Ridge, did anyone climb the crags of Mt. Washington in summer.

Around 1916, Boston-area climbers were among the first on the continent to look for challenge not only on exalted high terrain but also on local bluffs. John Case, a man with a solid alpine background, initiated climbs on various outcrops around the city. Staid AMC leaders criticized these "acrobatics" and wouldn't accept accounts of such climbing in their journal. Willard Hellburn was another Boston crag activist, and in 1919 he took his

Huntington Ravine on the eastern flanks of Mt. Washington. *Odell's Gully* is on the far left. *Central Gully* is the snow line in the middle. *Pinnacle Gully* diagonals up to the left from the base of *Central Gully*, behind the rock buttress. PHOTO BY ED WEBSTER.

skills to Maine's greatest peak, Katahdin. He led the Chimney, a route declared impossible back in 1855, and four years later Hellburn and his wife, Margaret, repeated the Chimney in winter, finding that deep snow actually made the climbing easier.

"Alpine conditions" were the goal for traditional New England mountaineers, and ideally that meant hard snow, a fairly malleable surface. Even in the Alps, summer ice was a medium exclusively for skilled climbers—and then only for modest stretches. Winter's glassy water ice suggested only skating, never climbing. (John Muir may have been the first to climb frozen waterfall ice when, in the 1870s, he nicked his way up a cone of ice cauliflowers at the base of Upper Yosemite Falls.) But the new generation of New England climbers would break through these limitations.

The first foray onto Mt. Washington's solid water ice came in 1927, when John Holden and Nathaniel Goodrich of Dartmouth climbed the *Central Gully*, one of the easiest of six chutes that hold ice on Huntington

Ravine's headwall. The next year, Noel Odell, the man who had last seen Mallory and Irvine, started a guest professorship in geology at Harvard, and during his first New England winter Odell led Jack Hurd, Lincoln O'Brien and Robert Underhill up one of Huntington's more sustained ice gullies. This so astonished the AMC that its journal summarized the future of climbing in Huntington Ravine this way: "Apparently nothing remains to be done."

Yet others knew that to the right of Odell's Gully waited what seemed to be the ultimate ice climb, the "Fall of the Maiden's Tears," the gully below Pinnacle Ridge. In winter this cascade froze into an 800-foot-high flow of crystalline, blue-green intimidation. Could a sane person with just an axe and nailed boots consider climbing it? On a rink-hard sheet of ice like this, there was no way a belayer could hold a fall.

Early the following winter, two teams tried it. First came Yale brothers William and Alan Willcox, with Julian Whittlesey. Then, in April, Underhill and O'Brien attempted the gully.

Both teams took a good part of the day to climb a single pitch. Although the angle eased above, they retreated with the realization that they couldn't finish before darkness. After their retreat, Underhill and O'Brien climbed another gully (later called *Damnation*) with a steeper crux than Pinnacle but much less ice overall. In January 1930, Whittlesey came back with William Willcox, who was wearing crampons, but the tight crampon straps brought on frostbite, and they retreated again. A month later Whittlesey returned a third time, with Sam Scovill. This time Whittlesey hewed steps at a furious pace, leading the entire route. Their success had nothing to do with improved gear, methods or conditions—Whittlesey simply gathered the tenacity to climb all day up ground that most climbers might take on only for short sections.

Pinnacle Gully was the first and only technical climb either Whittlesey or Scovill would ever complete, yet their route remained the most serious testpiece of North American winter ice climbing into the 1960s. Bill House and Alan Willcox finally made the second ascent in 1934, and they took two days, retreating for the night and then reclimbing their chopped steps the next day. It wasn't until the fifth ascent, in 1948, that another party completed *Pinnacle Gully* in a single day.

The Piton: European Roots

In the late 1920s, some American climbers began to use pitons, the simple iron anchors that redefined climbing and came to rival the ice axe as a symbol of mountaineering. When Americans started hammering in pitons, they imported a methodology and ethic that had been worked out in the Alps.

In the limestone peaks and sandstone towers of the eastern Alps, Austrian, German and Italian climbers were scaling routes unimaginably steep by North American standards, pulling on fingertip holds and stepping up onto tiny edges as early as the 1890s. They had developed special shoes soled with felt or rope; in some cases they climbed barefoot. They also developed the basic protection

Henry Barber and Guy Waterman getting set to climb *Pinnacle Gully*, on the 60th anniversary of the route's first ascent. Waterman is wearing the same pack that Julian Whittlesey used during his historic climb.
COURTESY HENRY BARBER.

system that is still in use today. When the leader wanted to keep going where a fall seemed possible, he hammered a piton into a crack, clipped the rope through a carabiner attached to the piton, and proceeded while his partner fed the rope. A nearby piton gave the confidence ("indirect aid") to climb through difficult sections. These and other new techniques spread across the Alps, including a better rappel method—the body-wrap arrangement invented by German Hans Dülfer.

Many British climbers railed against using pitons. To them, the essence of climbing was to generate character and judgment by utilizing only one's grip and stance on the native rock structure, and the climbing experience was at its best when a team moved from stance to stance in nimble alertness, guiding the rope over projections and encouraging and cautioning each other. They believed that an exacting and positive attitude should win the day or else discretion should hail retreat. Yet what was the ethical basis to prohibit pitons? In *Mountaincraft*, the period's English-language mountaineering bible, Geoffrey Winthrop Young laid out the problem:

> *If a spike may be legitimately stuck in a sole, why not in a rock? If an axe may be carried for ice, why not a hammer for rock? The more we examine, the less we are able to draw any satisfying line between aids which contribute only to our safety and aids which by securing our safety contribute also to our success.... Logically, there is nowhere we can draw the line. On the other hand, if we do not, our grandest cliffs may someday present the appearance of pin cushions, vying with the 'prickly porcupine' and a new generation will be using electric drills and pulleys for their pegs and cords.*

As each new edition of *Mountaincraft* was published from 1921 to 1949, Young's manual gradually evolved to accept and encourage limited piton use.

When stories from the eastern Alps revealed that some were using pitons not just as backups but also as "direct aid"—holding onto them or even attaching short ladders for progress—the feared decay of climbing into rote engineering seemed at hand. Anglo-Germanic rivalries helped divide the camps. However, progressive climbers understood that, while pitons could indeed be a crutch, they also could be used judiciously to move onto otherwise unapproachable terrain. By the 1920s, piton-aided ascents of big, steep routes were energizing and redefining alpinism. What came to pass was a middle way based on the abilities of leading climbers: Pitons were deemed acceptable when they advanced good technique, and unacceptable when they substituted for poor technique. This "occasional piton" ethic was the model that came to America.

Early Piton Routes

Paul and Joe Stettner were craftsmen who, in the mid-1920s, had fled from growing rightist politics in Germany and immigrated to Chicago. They had enjoyed many climbs in Austria, and in 1927 they decided to make a climbing trip to the Rockies. They mail-ordered hardware and felt-soled shoes from their homeland, and in September they took off on motorcycles for Colorado—a week-long ride. A guide there refused to sell them a climbing rope, saying the season was too late and the climbing too dangerous. The Stettners decided to make do with a sisal (agave) utility rope from a hardware store.

Five years earlier, Princeton professor James Alexander had climbed a route up the lower east face of Longs Peak. He stemmed up a watercourse and balanced across a cat-walk to Broadway Ledge, possibly completing the first technical route on this wall. (A Swiss

Joe Stettner at the start of the *Stettner Ledges* route on Longs Peak (ca. 1942). PHOTO BY BOB ORMES. COURTESY THE STETTNER COLLECTION.

Joe (left) and Paul Stettner at the Timberline Cabin on Longs Peak around the time of their September 1927 first ascent of the *Stettner Ledges* route. PHOTO COURTESY THE STETTNER COLLECTION.

man, Werner Zimmerman, may have climbed a similar route in 1919.)

The Stettner brothers went to the same face but chose a line to the right of *Alexander's Chimney.* They jammed up steep, sustained corners and pulled their way up small flakes. Paul led the whole way, while Joe followed with a pack heavy with their nailed boots. At one point Paul had to undercling a flake and place three pitons in close succession; his strength gave way and he took what may be the continent's first leader fall. After five hours of the hardest climbing they'd ever done, they finished a direct, 800-foot line up the face and then connected with *Kiener's Route* to reach the top. Their pitches—now rated a fairly sustained 5.8—set a new technical standard in North America. For years the few who knew of the "Austrian Route" spoke of it in a context of unattainable daring and

mystique. The Stettner brothers later pioneered other outstanding routes in the Rockies, including, in 1933, the comparably difficult north face of Lone Eagle Peak.

Two Harvard men—Kenneth Henderson and especially Robert Underhill—took the lead in spreading piton-aided mountaineering across America. Both had learned to climb in the Alps following the ropes of guides, and then had decided to take the leap of leading themselves. Underhill wrote, "When you do guideless climbs in Switzerland you like to fancy yourself a guide, so you get yourself a guide-size ice axe, a great big heavy one, with a handle about a yard long. We had exaggerated ice axes to make sure it seemed we were so damned good."

As a philosophy professor at Harvard, Underhill was able to get more free time than

The east face of Longs Peak. The Stettners' route climbed the lower, lichen-streaked wall, then traversed right to chutes leading to the summit. PHOTO BY ED WEBSTER.

his favorite partner, Henderson, who worked as a financial analyst. In 1929, these two visited Jackson Hole and promptly climbed a 4,000-foot prow that had stymied at least seven previous attempts: the Grand Teton's east ridge. Other parties had been blocked at the first big gendarme, the Molar Tooth. But with some crafty downclimbing and a rappel, Underhill and Henderson worked around the north side of the Tooth to a gully. They climbed this until they met a headwall, where they switched from nailed boots to tennis shoes. Placing a couple of pitons on ground now rated 5.7, they moved readily over slabs and up a chimney. The route continued up rock and ice that Henderson called "the finest kind of climbing" and which he deemed comparable to contemporary classics in Switzerland.

In print, Henderson cautioned Americans that the new route was quite difficult, but privately both he and Underhill knew that greater challenges could soon be won. Over the next weeks and subsequent seasons these two completed many other new climbs together, especially in the Wind Rivers and Tetons.

During this time, Francis Farquhar (another Harvard graduate) became active in the Sierra Club. This club had gathered a bevy of talented young climbers bursting with energy for the Sierra peaks, but none of them knew how to use ropes. They were scrambling up and down steep rock with no aids except tennis shoes, shoulder stands and bravado, and older club members were concerned that accidents might soon be coming. Farquhar met with Underhill at the Harvard Mountaineering Club's 1930 summer outing

Ken Henderson and Robert Underhill at Billy Owen's house in Jackson Hole, soon after returning from their first ascent of the Grand Teton's east ridge. COURTESY KEN HENDERSON COLLECTION.

Ken Henderson "roping down" from the first ascent of Mt. Owen, 1930. COURTESY JACKSON HOLE HISTORICAL SOCIETY AND MUSEUM, ACC.# 58.0356.001.

in the Selkirks, and he invited Underhill to write an article on rope work for the *Sierra Club Bulletin* and to visit the Sierra and teach the methods.

Two Weeks in the Tetons

On his way west in July 1931, Underhill stopped in the Tetons to storm up five dramatic new routes in less than two weeks. First, he joined geologist and park ranger Fritiof Fryxell to traverse Nez Percé east to west. Next, he and Fryxell made the first ascent of the Middle Teton's north ridge.

Underhill and Fryxell then snuck off to the most formidable wall in the range, the north side of the Grand Teton. They went in secret, so a potential retreat wouldn't tip off any others that the time for this intimidating wall might be at hand. They aimed for the west edge of the big face and, dodging rockfall, they found a surprisingly quick way to the top of the Grandstand, a big step on this chilly prow. The first belayed pitches went

well, but in a wet chimney on the steepest part of the arête both climbers were stymied. Finally Underhill stood in nailed boots on Fryxell's head and drove in a piton. At Fryxell's behest, he stepped onto this piton and then tapped in another and stepped on it too. Above, they found challenging but easier climbing to the top, and the north ridge, one of the most classic technical routes in the country, was theirs.

After that, with ranger Phil Smith and another Harvard man, Francis Truslow, Underhill led another new route, up the Grand Teton's southeast ridge. In a chimney there he made some of the most difficult moves of his life, partly by hooking the pick of his ice axe over rock flakes.

That same day, July 15, 1931, a green, 17-year-old local completed another remarkable route. Glenn Exum had heard from his friend Paul Petzoldt (who was guiding clients on the original route the same day) about the possibility of climbing the Grand Teton's

Robert Underhill toproping on a crag near Boston, 1929. COURTESY BRIAN UNDERHILL.

Norman Clyde

Underhill continued west to meet the Sierra Club group, where his cultured manners contrasted with the gruff crust of the most legendary climber on the Pacific seaboard, Norman Clyde.

In 1925, Clyde had summited 48 Sierra peaks, half of them first ascents. The year after that he climbed 60, and his career was just beginning. Clyde had been a happily married schoolteacher until his wife died of tuberculosis in 1918. Then he moved to Independence, a hamlet right below the eastern walls of the Sierra, and started teaching there. In 1928, Clyde went to break up some youthful Halloween pranksters and fired shots into their escaping car. No one was hurt, but the school board fired Clyde. He retreated into the mountains essentially full-time, getting by with frugality, caretaking of cabins, guiding, writing and borrowing.

With the Sierra backcountry his true home, Clyde marched into basecamps lugging packs weighing over 100 pounds with items for every contingency. "The pack that walked like a man" included literary epics in the original Greek, cast-iron pans, boot anvils and revolvers. The latter he carried "for collecting purposes," and, he told friends, in case an accident someday called for a self-administered dose of euthanasia. He especially loved the Palisades, and during one spring there he climbed Temple Crag 30 days in a row. The Sierra Club recruited him to guide during their annual summer outings, as well as to lead excursions to the Rockies. Clyde had seen Swiss guides' rope work on a trip to Canada, and when Underhill arrived the club expected Clyde to contribute to the professor's teachings. However, as one who usually climbed alone, Clyde's best advice was, "Always keep three points of contact to the rock."

Underhill led practice in rope techniques around Tuolumne Meadows. Then Farquhar led Underhill, Clyde, Bestor Robinson, Lewis Clark and teenagers Glen Dawson and Jules Eichorn on a drive south to the Palisades. There they climbed Temple Crag and linked a cockscomb traverse from North Palisade to Starlight Peak. The next day, despite a pattern

south buttress from a prominent ramp halfway up. Exum was intrigued, but since he had no appropriate boots he borrowed Petzoldt's oversized and leather-cleated football shoes. Alone and without a rope, Exum walked up the ramp and found that it ended at a gap at the arête's crest, high above the talus. After considering the gap and the consequences of a misstep, he turned back once and then returned to look again. After advancing and hesitating seven times, he saw a boulder he might latch on to, but he would have to jump to reach it. He leaned out from small holds and jumped. Hugging the boulder, he realized, "There was only one way to go and that was up." Exum continued up the smooth and exhilarating arête that soon bore his name, and the ascent made him an instant hero. Jack Durrance (see Chapter 7) would write that, "Nowhere in the history of mountaineering has anyone received as much acclaim and notoriety for 20 feet of climbing as Glenn did."

Norman Clyde. COURTESY NORMAN CLYDE COLLECTION.

Climbers on the east face of Mt. Whitney, possibly on the first ascent. PHOTO BY NORMAN CLYDE.

of afternoon thunderstorms, the group went for the last unclimbed pinnacle of the Palisade spine. The terrain proved very steep, and the 20-foot summit block presented a serious problem, now rated at unprotected 5.8. They took turns climbing it as clouds gathered, and as Eichorn was about to make his ascent a lightning bolt hit, leaving him momentarily dazed. In the teeth of thunder, lightning and pelting hail, Clyde led everyone down a different route via ledges, steps cut in ice and rappels. They named the spire Thunderbolt Peak, and when it was later measured at over 14,000 feet, it gained the reputation of being the toughest 14'er in the United States.

Farquhar had been nudging Underhill to take on the steepest face on the Sierra's highest summit: Mt. Whitney's east face. The four best climbers—Underhill, Clyde, Dawson and Eichorn—chose this as their next target. At 9:30 a.m., they left the lake at Whitney's base, wearing tennis shoes and anticipating a tough climb. By quarter past noon they stood

on top, having placed just one piton. All four were pleased but underwhelmed—Underhill called the route "The Big Bluff."

A year after this landmark tour across the West, Robert Underhill married the finest woman climber in America, Miriam O'Brien. She had taken to rock mountaineering like a horse to running, often leading climbs herself. After their marriage, the Underhills turned to exploratory and technical mountaineering on pack trips in Idaho and Montana. He later summed up his climbing by saying, "I thought mountains were damn good things."

A Sierra icon, Clyde would continue to climb into the 1960s. Jules Eichorn would write, "For me, there can never be a human being so completely in tune with his chosen environment—the mountains—as Norman Clyde."

Dynamic Belays

Eichorn and Dawson were excited to realize they could climb as steep rock as their mentors did, and more swiftly. They'd learned that a rope and pitons were helpful for tackling

Glen Dawson, Robert Underhill, Jules Eichorn and Norman Clyde on the summit of Mt. Whitney after making the first ascent of the east face. COURTESY NORMAN CLYDE COLLECTION.

tough sections, but these aids were not revolutionary—at least not yet. Underhill himself reckoned that the best Italian hemp rope would break if a leader fell from more than about eight feet above a piton. A leader's real security still lay in his or her stance, grip and fluid motion on the rock, and by keeping within the limits of gymnastic security and rock quality.

A couple of years after his tour with Underhill, Dawson and others repeated Whitney's east face and then downclimbed the route as well. This fad of downclimbing challenging routes caught on in the Tetons, too, and it shows the fascination with steep mountain architecture. In March 1932, Eichorn joined with Richard Leonard and Bestor Robinson to form the Cragmont Climbing Club, a group focused on the small outcrops around Berkeley. This group would evolve into the Rock Climbing Section of the Sierra Club (RCS). Leonard was not content with the notion that falling was unacceptable, and he set out to improve belay methods. After studying British climbing texts, he and his buddies practiced using the rope to catch heavy sacks tossed off the cliffs. Leonard found that the European methods of running the belay rope over a shoulder or around the chest were bound to fail with a hard fall. His tests showed that feeding the rope around the hips offered much greater resistance.

Leonard then brought to the fore an even more valuable technique: the dynamic belay. By letting the force of a fall pull the rope through gloved hands before bringing the climber to a slow stop, he learned he could dissipate the force of the fall and ease the impact on the rope, anchor, belayer and climber. Few, if any, climbers had thought to practice holding falls before, and most climbers would go their entire careers without falling. But soon the Cragmont guys were taking 15-foot test plummets with their trusted buddies holding the rope. With their new confidence in an anchored and skilled belay-

Jules Eichorn belaying a partner to the top of "The Milk Bottle," the summit block of Starlight Peak in the Palisades. PHOTO BY NORMAN CLYDE.

er, the Californians' attitude shifted from Geoffrey Winthrop Young's "the leader does not fall," to Leonard's, "It is still not good for a leader to fall; but if he does, this much is certain: the rope *must* run, and the belayer *must not* be pulled off."

Armed with equipment imported from Europe at dear cost, and ready to risk short falls, the Cragmont climbers initiated direct aid on Yosemite towers and traveled to vertiginous cliffs around the continent. They proudly accepted the label "rock engineers," a moniker that traditionalists applied derisively.

In southern California, Glen Dawson was the star climber, leading routes that are now rated up to 5.8, often with sparse protection. On Mt. Whitney's east face, Dawson had noticed that a direct prow to the right looked like a more exciting climb, probably with more solid rock. In 1937 he led a party up that east buttress, using four pitons along the way. Dawson pulled through steep and delicate moves now rated 5.7 and named the route *Sunshine-Peewee*, inspired by his fondness for warm, high-altitude rock and a big block that protrudes from the prow. Two weeks later, Arthur Johnson and Bill Rice repeated the route, needing only the first two pitons, and then downclimbed the route as well.

In 1935 and 1936, Glen Dawson traveled to Austria and Germany, where he sampled a very high level of rock climbing and became familiar with the Willo Welzenbach six-tier system of difficulty ratings. At Dawson's suggestion, the Sierra Club adopted a similar set of grades:

Class 1: *Rock climbing experience unnecessary.*
Class 2: *Ropes should be available.*
Class 3: *Ropes should be used.*
Class 4: *Belays should be used—consecutive climbing.* [One climber moving at a time.]
Class 5: *Pitons should be available.*
Class 6: *More difficult than fifth class. As yet undefined.*

Proficient Sierrans gradually came to describe the higher ratings in a way that can be paraphrased, "If we climbed without the rope, it was Class 3, and if we used the rope it was Class 4. If we placed pitons above the belay it was Class 5, and if we used the pitons for direct aid it was Class 6." This rating system eventually was adopted across the continent.

Colorado Mountain Club members Barbara Buchtel, Forrest Greenfield, Louis Hough, Henry Buchtel and Dwight Lavender on top of Colorado's Wetterhorn, 1929. PHOTO COURTESY COLORADO MOUNTAIN CLUB.

San Juan Mountaineers

In the late 1920s, a group in southwestern Colorado started making some of the first new climbs in the San Juan Mountains since the 19th-century surveys, and they formed a club they called the San Juan Mountaineers. Their prime mover was Dwight Lavender. He grew up in Denver but became fascinated by the San Juans during summer stays at his family's ranch. While attending college at Stanford in California, Lavender forged "San Juan Pitons," which had a hook that could be hammered closed around the rope, avoiding the need for expensive and heavy steel carabiners.

One of the main challenges the group aspired to was the north face of Mt. Sneffels. In 1931 and 1932, Lavender and others climbed couloirs on either side of this face, and by 1933 they figured they were ready to try the rock wall directly. The first few pitches were the steepest. Disaster almost struck

Carl Blaurock (left) and others on the summit of Crestone Needle, 1920. PHOTO COURTESY COLORADO MOUNTAIN CLUB.

when Lavender went to pendulum under an overhang and his belayer above was not yet prepared. Melvin Griffiths felt the rope almost pull him off, and as it slipped over his shoulder he barely dug in his heels and held on. Soon the climbing eased, and by sunset the party stood on top of the 1,200-foot face. Also this year, Lavender and Carleton Long made the first ascent of Jagged Mountain, a castle of granitic spires that still challenges climbers. Sadly, soon after Lavender finished college, he contracted polio and died at age 23.

Through the 1930s, Carl Blaurock and the Colorado Mountain Club continued to put up technical routes in Colorado, perhaps most notably the steep and insecure north face of Capitol Peak.

Cascadians Cut Loose

In America's Northwest, well into the 1930s, climbers rarely ventured beyond sanctioned club ascents. Occasional visiting alpinists generated a stir, but the locals took little personal inspiration from these ascents. For instance, when French skiers in 1922 made the first winter ascent of Mt. Rainier, the visiting masters were admired but not emulated. Hans Fuhrer, a guide from Grindelwald, immigrated to Portland, and between 1915 and 1925 he led over 250 ascents of Mt. Hood and Mt. Rainier, including (with his brother and fellow guide Heinrich) one of the period's only new routes, a chute on the south side of Mt. Rainier. Yet no one attempted to learn from Fuhrer's example.

Although morning snow conditions on Cascade peaks often make for ideal cramponing, local climbers shunned "creepers" as dangerous, and only by 1927—after an accident—were Rainier guides reluctantly allowed to wear them. In general, a conservative stagnation had developed in this area, not unlike that within the Alpine Club of Canada. Although climbers on Baker and Rainier looked east and north to a sea of rugged summits, the peaks of the North Cascades remained virtually unexplored.

Joseph Hazard was a progressive Mountaineer who tried to prod his club into recognizing climbers' need to grow. In the

1917 club annual he wrote, "No longer are we at the mercy of the accident of a three-week's vacation. We have at our command an amazing variety of activities that may be contracted into the few swift hours from Saturday to Monday morning.... Many are frankly interested in first ascents, in speed records, in endurance tests."

Yet the Mountaineers' leadership had so thoroughly assumed the role of gatekeepers to the Cascades that upstarts who began to climb apart from official trips were labeled "outlaw climbers." This conservatism included disallowing pitons and deliberately *not* teaching technique to younger climbers. The Mountaineers' venerable president, Edward Meany, and other leaders believed that lessons involving risk had to be learned in the manner of the pioneers, over years of outings. Simmering discontent came to a boil over management of the Mountaineers' clubhouse at Snoqualmie Pass. This lodge made a nice weekend basecamp, but it needed continuing support and club leaders steadfastly required that all climbers going *anywhere* in the Cascades register and pay a fee at the clubhouse. For some members, this attempt to place the club bureaucracy ahead of the mountains' call was the last straw.

Hermann Ulrichs had joined the Mountaineers after moving to Seattle in the late 1920s, and he became the first prominent renegade. Ulrichs had grown up climbing in the Sierra, often alone. On a Boy Scouts trip, at age 19, he upset his leaders by splitting off from the group and making the third ascent of North Palisade, by the direct ridge that had turned away the first-ascent party. Two years later, he made the first ascent of Bear Creek Spire. He later climbed in the Canadian Alps, including a lone ascent of Mt. Sir Donald. In 1927 he climbed Mt. Lefroy and descended past a guided party with a spectacular glissade. A day later, one of the clients, Malcolm Geddes, tried to glissade the same slope and fell to his death. Some heaped blame on Ulrichs, and indeed he was nagged with guilt.

In the Cascades, Ulrichs started making "outlaw ascents" in 1932, following only crude maps and his nose for peaks. In 1933 he finally quit the Mountaineers, saying, "I looked at the various maps of the Cascades, and there seemed to me more interesting places than Snoqualmie Pass." By 1934 he wrote that "19 new cairns have had to be built" on summits he reached, including Mt. Maude, Silver Star Mountain (actually a second ascent) and the east peak of Mt. Buckner.

New Routes on Rainier

In the fall of 1934, 35 other young "outlaws" formed a subgroup of the Mountaineers. At the core of their insurgency was the desire to acquire and disseminate techniques for steep climbing. Chief of acquisition and dissemination was Wolf Bauer, a young German immigrant who obtained mountaineering texts from his friends in Germany. After practicing what he read, Bauer shared the techniques of rock and ice climbing and rappelling, and soon his students Lloyd Anderson and Jack Hossack were teaching as well.

Bauer wanted to climb the north side of Mt. Rainier, and the *Ptarmigan* (northwest) *Ridge* looked like the best possibility, although the route had turned back a variety of parties. The ridge presented a couple of thousand feet of steep climbing, with some rock and much ice where dozens of steps had to be cut. At this time, Cascade climbers thought it best to attempt a route like this in the late season, when firm snow and ice conditions ensured minimal avalanche danger and solid footing. Late in the summer of 1934, Hans Grage joined Bauer, and they found a way through the rock walls up to the moderate ground below Liberty Cap. But Grage was a smoker who was pushed to his limit, and with the hour late they turned back. It became clear to Bauer that a team needed more time.

In September the next year, he and Jack Hossack carried bivouac sacks and a stove onto the ridge. Although they moved slower with their burdens, they reached a reasonably comfortable spot atop the headwall where they shivered through the night. The next day they finished the route to the summit.

Three weeks later, after a couple of inches of autumn snow had coated the mountain's

hard mantle, Jim Borrow, Arnie Campbell and Ome Daiber set out to climb the central prow of Rainier's north wall. This cleaver now is known as *Liberty Ridge*, but at the time it wasn't distinguished from the Willis Wall, the infamous aspect of Rainier where active serac walls release avalanches by the ton. Park rangers tried to forbid the climbers from approaching the area, but Daiber was an experienced Cascade climber and rescuer known to the park superintendent, and a phone call got them authorization.

Daiber was an engineer, and with his eye for efficiency he proposed a gamble that few climbers would have taken at the time on such a route—and, in fact, few take even today. From the 6,000-foot-high base of the route, they left their sleeping bags and extra supplies behind and planned to climb fast, with only one bivouac. During their one night they would huddle around candles in a silk tent. They knew that a storm would put them in serious danger, but they decided that at any hint of foul weather they could retreat.

The heavily crevassed glacier slowed their first day, but even though they didn't get on the ridge until 3 p.m. they chopped steps up 30- to 45-degree slopes to a bivouac almost halfway up the route, on a pumice shelf at 11,000 feet. They suffered that night about as they expected, and the next day icy slopes and thin air slowed their progress. When a crevasse wall blocked the way, Campbell and Borrow lifted the diminutive Daiber in their arms so he could jump the gap. By the light of their carbide lamps, they reached the top in time for a second, even colder bivouac, and then descended the next day. They had completed the most classic route on Rainier, and, as Campbell later wrote, "It never entered my mind that the climb would mean anything to anyone except the three of us. It was just the most fun climb of my life."

In the remote North Cascades, the peak that taunted the young renegades most was Mt. Goode. Failed attempts by at least three experienced teams—including one by Hermann Ulrichs and Dan O'Brien—had lifted Goode's reputation. Bauer and Hossack collected some of the 1936 class of student climbers,

Mt. Goode from the northwest. The first ascent route climbed near the right skyline. PHOTO BY JOHN DITTLI.

George MacGowan, O. Phillip Dickert and Joe Holwax, and started toward the peak by taking a ferry up Lake Chelan. A Canadian party was also on the boat, and it turned out they were aiming for Goode as well. Bauer's team kept their intentions quiet. Bauer had a car ready at the far end of the lake, and with this they beat the Canadians to the peak. Near the top, Bauer led the ice-glazed squeeze chimney that had stymied previous climbers, continuing to bridge between its walls even as they flared to five feet apart. With some deft piton protection, a rope tossed over a knob to ascend with prusik knots and then a fingertip traverse, he found a way to the top. The young climbers and the new technical methods had proven their mettle.

On the same day, a trio of the Mountaineers' old guard—Forest Farr, Norval Grigg and Don Blair—broke the norms by going to Dome Peak, another remote Cascade spire that had denied previous forays. The trio donned tennis shoes to ascend a granite chimney that curved to the top. Two months after this, Dickert, Hossack and MacGowan made the first climbing foray into the virtually unknown peaks at the head of the Skagit River, the northern Picket Range. There they climbed a glacier to the top of a remote crown of crags and named it Mt. Challenger.

The next year, a group of ambitious Boy Scouts split away from their troop, in a spirit similar to the outlaw Mountaineers. Teenagers Calder Bressler, Ralph Clough, Bill Cox and Tom Myers founded the Ptarmigan Mountaineering Club and acquired as best they could the ways and means of technical climbing. In 1938 they laid out a plan to tour a whole region and climb as many peaks as possible. The Ptarmigans chose the terrain between the Suiattle and Cascade rivers. They climbed both summits of Dome Peak, and in the ensuing week they topped about a dozen mostly unclimbed mountains. On one particularly long day they climbed Spider Mountain, Mt. Formidable, Magic Mountain and distant Johannesburg Mountain. On their last climbing day they summited three peaks north of Cascade Pass: Sahale Mountain, Boston Peak and Mt. Buckner.

Summary

These early decades of individualistic climbing broke substantial social, technical and geographic ground. Climbers of this period gave to subsequent generations the inspiration and blueprint for self-sufficient backcountry adventures on technical mountain routes. Yet few at the time believed steep climbing could advance much farther. Miriam Underhill, one of the most innovative climbers of the day, remarked that the limits of rock climbing with indirect aids were almost certainly being reached in the 1930s. None could have imagined the steep routes that were to come.

SUGGESTED ROUTES
FROM THIS PERIOD

MT. WHITNEY (14,495 feet/4,418 meters)
Sunshine-Peewee Route (East Buttress)
This is the most classic route to the highest summit
in the Lower 48. Fit climbers do this route in a summer day from the car, but it's normal to plan for a
multiday trip, and many parties spend an
unplanned night on the peak.

Approach: From the trailhead at 8,400 feet, the
hike up the North Fork of Lone Pine Creek is less
than five miles, but the steep climber's path includes
some exposed ledges, and it's a stout 4,300 feet of
vertical gain to Iceberg ("East Face") Lake. From there
you scramble to a notch between two towers where
the East Face route heads up a ramp to the left. The
Sunshine-Pewee Route starts up the right-hand tower.

Route: Begin with strenuous work up a roughly
defined corner. Thin cracks split superb rock on the
next tier; keep going up easier corners and slabs.
About two-thirds of the way up, you pass to the
right of a jutting block, the "Peewee," for which
Dawson named the route. Veer left into a right-fac-
ing corner system that takes you to blocky ground
below the summit. Descend by the 1873 Muir route,
which can be icy.

First Ascent: Glen Dawson, Muir Dawson, Richard
Jones, Bob Brinton and Howard Koster, September
1937
Difficulty: AD+, 5.7, 1,500 feet
Guidebooks: *The High Sierra*; *Climbing California's
High Sierra*; *The Good, The Great and The Awesome.*
Permits: A permit for overnight camping must be
obtained from the Inyo National Forest; reservations
are recommended.

MT. WASHINGTON (6,288 feet/1,917 meters)
Pinnacle Gully
While modern ice gear may seem to make light
work of a route rarely steeper than 45 degrees, every
winter climb on Mt. Washington must be taken seriously. Even on the best days, winter weather here

The east face of Mt. Whitney. The *Sunshine-Peewee
Route* starts behind the tower at lower right, and then
follows the sunlit skyline. PHOTO BY ANDY SELTERS.

John and Kathy Drew climbing *Pinnacle Gully* in 1980.
PHOTO BY ED WEBSTER.

The southeast face of Mt. Geikie. PHOTO BY GLEN BOLES.

often means temperatures of 0°F with high winds and high humidity. Moreover, the techniques to climb vertical ice don't necessarily transfer to efficient passage on 30- to 60-degree water ice.

Approach: From Pinkham Notch (2,030 feet), the Huntington Ravine headwall is about a two-hour hike up a well-packed trail.

Route: *Pinnacle Gully* is the obvious thick flow of beautiful blue-green ice under the right side of Pinnacle Ridge. The first pitch is the steepest—up to almost 60 degrees—and a total of four to five rope lengths finishes the route. A variety of descent routes are possible, and your choice will depend on the weather, snow conditions and time left in the day.

First Ascent: Julian Whittlesey and Sam Scovill, February 1930

Grade: AD+, AI 3, 1,000 feet

Guidebook: *An Ice Climber's Guide to Northern New England*

MT. GEIKIE (10,728 feet/3,270 meters)
Southeast Face

Mt. Geikie ("Geekee," named for a Scottish geologist) is one of the greatest obscure mountains on the continent, and its easiest route is a challenging, big-scale exercise in classic rock mountaineering. Nowadays, most parties avoid the bad rock and ridgeline complications of the first-ascent route and take a direct variation. (Lawrence Grassi and A. W. Drinnan pioneered this variation during the second ascent of the peak, in 1926.) For pre-World War II climbers, this was a coveted testpiece, and even now it's a challenge to get up and down this route without a bivouac.

Approach: Starting from outside Jasper, the hike to the south side of Geikie takes a full day or more. You also can arrange a helicopter ride from Valemount, B.C., to Geikie Meadows, just over a mile from the peak.

Route: From Geikie Meadows, climb to the Blue Inkwell, a small tarn hidden under the face. The obvious couloir ascends up and right from there, and you follow it for about 1,000 feet of easy gain until prominent ledges let you exit left. From there the route will test your routefinding and Class 3-5 rock climbing skills for another 3,700 feet, as you work left up ledges and a vague chute system near the center of the face, and then take ledges left again to work onto the summit ridge. Generally the rock is fairly firm quartzite, and it is most reliable where it is steepest. Descent is by the same route.

First Ascent: Via east ridge: Val Fynn, Malcolm Geddes and Cyril Wates, July 1924; Direct southeast face: Lawrence Grassi and A. W. Drinnan, August 1926

Difficulty: D-, 5.5, 5,000 feet

Guidebook: *Selected Alpine Climbs in the Canadian Rockies*

Permits: A fee is required to enter Jasper National Park, and a free permit is required for backcountry camping. It's also recommended to register your climb with park wardens before the climb, and to confirm your safe return.

MT. RAINIER (14,410 feet/ 4,392 meters)
Ptarmigan Ridge

Mt. Rainier holds reasonable claim to being the premier mountain in the Lower 48. The giant volcano dominates the Cascade region, and more of America's Himalayan climbers trace their roots to Rainier than to any other peak. There are about 35 distinct lines, with numerous variations, and every aspect has excellent routes. *Liberty Ridge* is the most alluring and sustained feature on the peak, but *Ptarmigan Ridge* is a route just as worthy and, in some ways, more interesting. Compared to its more famous neighboring spur, this broad northwest ridge presents some pitches that are more technical. It also has notable but manageable objective hazards.

Approach: From the trailhead at Mowich Lake (4,929 feet), hike for about three miles on a good trail to Spray Park, then turn south to start hiking up the lower reaches of Ptarmigan Ridge. A long uphill march brings you to a spectacular bivouac site just past a point at 10,300 feet, a grandstand below the main show of the ridge.

Route: On the first ascent, when there was more snow and ice and when seracs above were more stable, Bauer and Hossack climbed ramps through the cliffs ahead. Nowadays, climbers hike down and west—making fast time in this area threatened by seracs—to circumvent the cliffs. Turn the cliffs, cross a bergschrund and climb a 40-degree snow and ice slope. In warm temperatures, rockfall can be a danger here, but prudent parties find little or none. Aim

Mt. Rainier from the northwest. *Ptarmigan Ridge* is marked, *Liberty Ridge* is the prominent spur in the face to the left, and *Curtis Ridge* is near the left skyline. PHOTO BY AUSTIN POST, U.S. GEOLOGICAL SURVEY.

for a 50-degree chute that leads to the highest rock band. The best way to clear this upper obstacle is to climb right on ice and rock to reach a very short, nearly vertical chute that cuts up to the icecap. Crevassed but moderately angled glacier slopes lead to the top of Liberty Cap. Rainier's highest point is Columbia Crest, two-thirds of a mile farther southeast. The best descent is to traverse the peak and go down either the Emmons or Ingraham route; either way will require a car shuttle.

Difficulty: D, AI 2-3, Class 4, 4,000 feet

First Ascent: Wolf Bauer and Jack Hossack, September 1935; Western start: Gene and Bill Prater, July 1959 (second ascent of route)

Guidebooks: *Cascade Alpine Guide (Columbia River to Stevens Pass); Mount Rainier: A Climbing Guide; Climbing Mt. Rainier*

Permits: A fee is required for entering Mt. Rainier National Park, and a free wilderness camping permit is required for overnight stays. Climbers must purchase a $30 pass, good for one calendar year.

CHAPTER 6

The New Explorers

Even as progressive climbers in America's Lower 48 shifted their focus to technical routes, most of the continent's greatest peaks were not just unclimbed but completely unexplored. To these remote peaks in Alaska, the Yukon and British Columbia went a new generation of exploratory mountaineers. Like their predecessors, these climbers had to make long approaches through difficult wilderness, map the terrain, and ferry supplies to the base before even tackling their climbs.

Among the wildest peaks in North America were the mountains along British Columbia's coast. The progression of pioneers and railroads across the province had come to an abrupt end in 1863, when Chilcotin Indians massacred an entire party working on a road. When the next attempt to open a trans-province route was swept away in a flood in 1874, would-be developers gave up and the region was relegated to *terra incognita*. Since it was assumed that British Columbia's mountain ranges diminished in size from east to west, no one guessed that worthwhile peaks lay near the coast. Into the 1920s, the

best map of the coastal region was based on the old trail projects, and it showed just three summits over 10,000 feet and no glaciers—even though glaciers had been glimpsed.

In truth, this difficult country hid some of the most sensational mountains in North America. The highest and most glaciated peaks in Canada south of the Yukon ultimately were revealed by one of the most remarkable couples in mountaineering history.

Mystery Mountain

Phyllis James started climbing with the British Columbia Mountain Club (BCMC) at age 11, in 1909, from her home in Vancouver. During World War I she worked as a nurse, and into her care came Don Munday with a battle wound to his arm. Don started joining her on BCMC outings, their respect for each other grew, and they married and spent their honeymoon in the Mt. Robson area. In 1924, during a second trip to Robson, Phyllis became the first woman to climb the great peak. Edward Feuz Jr., her guide, asserted that she was "as strong as any man." Don would write that the relationship he and his wife shared made them "more than the sum of our parts."

In June 1925, as the Mundays looked north from the summit of Mt. Arrowsmith on

☾ Don and Bert Munday packing in to Mt. Waddington in 1928. PHOTO BY PHYLLIS MUNDAY, COURTESY WHYTE MUSEUM OF THE CANADIAN ROCKIES, ACC. 414, BOX1/7 #19.

Don and Bert Munday at a camp en route to Mt. Waddington, 1928. PHOTO BY PHYLLIS MUNDAY, COURTESY WHYTE MUSEUM OF THE CANADIAN ROCKIES, ACC. 414, BOX5/7 #62.

Vancouver Island, they got a hint of high peaks among the clouds in the distance. Three months later, from a viewpoint above Bute Inlet, they glimpsed a peak far grander than any mountain imagined in this region. Don wrote of that electric moment, "It was the far-off finger of destiny beckoning." They called the peak Mystery Mountain.

The Mundays had no illusion about how arduous it would be to reach Mystery Mountain. They essentially had no money to spare, Don suffered from his war wound, Phyllis had premature arthritis, and they had to put their daughter Edith in the care of others when they left home. Yet they would spend nine arduous seasons exploring and trying to climb Mystery Mountain. They fashioned most of their own equipment, including a small boat (the *Edidonphyl*) to motor from Vancouver to the head of Bute or Knight inlet. Hiking from tidewater, they took stern pleasure in penetrating some of the most severe brush and woods imaginable, crawling under enormous deadfall, wading swamps and escaping floods, enduring mosquito swarms, and literally fighting off grizzlies.

Phyllis Munday packing in to Mt. Waddington. COURTESY HENRY S. HALL, JR. AMERICAN ALPINE CLUB LIBRARY.

Crossing Tumult Creek en route to Mt. Waddington. PHOTO BY PHYLLIS MUNDAY, COURTESY WHYTE MUSEUM OF THE CANADIAN ROCKIES, ACC. 414, BOX 3/7 #90.

Between clearing paths and triple-ferrying supplies, it generally took them at least a couple of weeks to reach one of the glaciers. Don asserted that "the man who cannot pack...not less than half his body weight...all day through rough country hardly qualifies as being fully fitted to tackle the Coast Range."

Don acquired some surveying skills, and he measured Mystery Mountain at over 13,000 feet. Many scoffed at this claim, and Arthur Wheeler denied that any coastal peak could exceed Mt. Robson—until he saw the survey data and calculated the height himself. After much discussion, the Mundays and Canada's Geographic Board agreed that the big peak should be named after Alfred Waddington, the man who had initiated the road across the range in the 1860s.

In 1926 and '27, the Mundays made high camps on the glaciers with only tarps and firewood for camping gear. They found a workable approach to the peak in 1927, but were chased off near the top by a terrific thunderstorm. In 1928 they invested in a stove, and this freed them to make a higher camp. With Don's brother Bert, they succeeded in climbing Mystery Mountain's northwest summit. Across a gap they marveled at the preposterous main summit. Though it stood just 60 feet higher, the unapproachable blade of rimeplastered gneiss and schist was, as Don put it, "an incredible nightmarish thing that must be seen to be believed, and then it is hard to believe.… Plates and plumes and festoons of ice 'feathers' many feet thick draped even vertical rocks."

Henry Hall devoured Don Munday's journal articles on Waddington, and in 1931 and 1932 he scouted an inland approach to the peak. Then, in July 1933, he hired the continent's most prolific guide, Hans Fuhrer, for an expedition to the area. Hall chanced to meet the Mundays in Vancouver on his way to the peak, and he invited them to join him. The climbers followed Fuhrer on an impressive 6,500-foot day of difficult ice and rock

Phyllis and Don Munday looking at Mt. Waddington across the Franklin Glacier, from the southwest. COURTESY WHYTE MUSEUM OF THE CANADIAN ROCKIES, ACC. 414, BOX 5/7 #21/27/54.

climbing to the first ascent of 12,323-foot Mt. Combatant. They bivouacked on this summit, where they had a close view of the north side of Waddington, the only face the Mundays hadn't studied. They eyed a thin possibility for a route, and the next year the same four veterans returned and repeated the ascent of Waddington's northwest summit. Then they traversed to the north face of the main peak, and the master climber Fuhrer made a short foray up rimed, vertical rock. With only a handful of pitons, however, he knew he could not climb such a tower.

After their return, the team suggested that the best hope for climbing Waddington was for some very capable rock climbers to get lucky with a long spell of sunny weather, when they might try the steeper south face after the ice plumes had melted away. The Mundays and Hall gave up their own hopes of climbing Waddington.

Instead, they set their sights on some of the hundreds of other peaks they had spied in the Coast Mountains. Farther north, east of Bella Coola, 11,722-foot Monarch Mountain captivated Hall. In June 1934, Hall and Ernest Feuz circumnavigated this peak in 50 hours, traveling 35 miles and climbing 12,000 vertical

Don Munday cutting steps across the Franklin Glacier, 1928. PHOTO BY PHYLLIS MUNDAY, COURTESY WHYTE MUSEUM OF THE CANADIAN ROCKIES, ACC. 414, BOX5/7 #49.

Rudimentary 1920s map of the southwest section of British Columbia, with Don Munday's notation on the location of "Mystery Mountain." COURTESY WHYTE MUSEUM OF THE CANADIAN ROCKIES, ACC. 414, BOX 4/7 #1.

Michael Down on the east ridge of Monarch Mountain. PHOTO BY DON SERL.

feet. Hall and Fuhrer returned to climb Monarch in 1936. The bergschrund almost stopped them, and Hall described their struggle with a 10-foot overhang of snow: "Finally Hans, from my shoulder, got a hold with both ice axes and pulled himself up three feet, handed down one axe with which I pushed him up another four feet, and finally reached the underlying ice twenty feet above." They persevered through continuously steep snow and a final rock section to reach the highest peak between Waddington and the Fairweather Range.

Hall and the Mundays continued to collaborate into the 1940s. Together they climbed Mt. Silverthrone, northwest of Waddington, and in 1942 they made the first ascent of Mt. Queen Bess, a stunning fin of ice and granite southeast of Waddington. Looking back on her many excursions, Phyllis wrote:

> When my old body is finished, and dies, my soul will come to a place like this…. It will travel all over the glaciers, which I love so dearly, and the sparkling snow fields, the deep blue crevasses and shining seracs—and the steep snow ridges and rock faces—and finally, with all the world at my feet, to sit exalted on my summit to just look, and look, and love it, deep, deep, down in my soul.

Munday party on the Corridor Glacier, below the south flank of Mt. Waddington. PHOTO BY PHYLLIS MUNDAY, COURTESY WHYTE MUSEUM OF THE CANADIAN ROCKIES, ACC. 414, BOX 4/7 #101/17.

Mt. Queen Bess. PHOTO BY PETER JORDAN.

Mt. Waddington from the southeast, probably taken on the first ascent of Mt. Munday in 1930. PHOTO BY PHYLLIS MUNDAY, COURTESY WHYTE MUSEUM OF THE CANADIAN ROCKIES, ACC. 414, BOX 5/7 #8.

↻ Monarch Mountain from the east. The first ascent route followed the ridge facing the camera. PHOTO BY DON SERL.

These expeditions inspired a variety of BCMC members to venture deeper into the dramatic coastal mountains. In 1927, Mills Winram, Fred Parkes and Stan Henderson climbed Slesse Mountain, a spectacular granite tooth just north of the border. Tom Fyles, still the prime force of the BCMC, led Munday-esque explorations around the heads of the Lillooet and Toba rivers in 1932 and 1933, and he inspired a young rock climbing protégé, Alec Dalgleish, whose prowess would later lead the club to follow the Mundays' suggestion for climbing Waddington's south face.

Wilderness Ranges Farther South

Although America had long since pushed its frontier to the Pacific, scores of peaks were yet unclimbed, and America's pioneer technical climbers began exploring ranges that had been bypassed earlier. In 1923, Norman Clyde went to Glacier National Park and climbed 38 peaks, 10 of them first ascents. The following year he helped lead a Sierra Club outing to this region, and a large group made the first ascent of Mt. Cleveland, the highest peak in the park.

Albert Ellingwood returned to the Wind River Range in 1926 and made the first ascents of what would be named Ellingwood Peak and Sacagawea. Ken Henderson, Robert Underhill and Henry Hall pioneered a number of peaks in the northern Wind Rivers in 1929, as well as a new route on the icy north face of Gannett Peak.

Sierran Bestor Robinson instigated, in 1932, an excursion to the highest peak in Baja California, Cerro de la Encantada, known locally as El Picacho del Diablo. With him came Norman Clyde, Glen Dawson, Nathan Clark, Richard Jones and Walter Brem. After a couple of days' approach with burros, they reached the west rim of deep Cañon Diablo and saw 10,154-foot Picacho's twin summits to the south. They planned "a day's climb" via the southwest ridge, but the ridge turned out to be more complex and rugged than they'd imagined—requiring belays and rappels—and at dark they were still short of the summit. Desperate for water, they descended for

Henry Hall, pioneer of many wilderness ranges, including the Coast Mountains. PHOTO #57-4274 © BRADFORD WASHBURN. COURTESY PANOPTICON GALLERY, WALTHAM, MA.

1,000 feet before finding a pool. The next day they finally made the top and then descended some 4,000 feet into Cañon Diablo before they could find a way to climb back to the rim. Later they learned that an American cartographer, Donald McLain, had climbed the peak in 1911 via a long backpacking scramble directly up Cañon Diablo.

During this period, Southern California climbers first ascended the tremendous north chute of Mt. San Jacinto, near Palm Springs. Climbing from 3,000 feet to 10,804 feet, the Snow Creek drainage snakes up what is arguably the biggest continuous scarp in the Lower 48. It is thought that Stewart White and Floyd Vernoy made this climb in 1931, and that White pioneered the now-classic winter ascent in 1937.

The Shrinking Wilderness

Mountaineers in the 1930s began to gain a worrisome perspective on the American landscape, as wild mountain areas became islands of quiet beauty in a sprawl of urban din and resource extraction. Most mountain clubs were active in trying to keep their region's mountains free from industrial development, and a number of mountaineers became leaders in wilderness preservation.

Plant physiologist Bob Marshall started climbing peaks in the Adirondacks at a young age, and by the time he was 23 he had reached 42 of the 46 Adirondack summits over 4,000 feet. Independently wealthy, he started taking trips in 1929 to the remote Brooks Range in Alaska. There he scrambled up peaks and looked over magical worlds unimagined by society. One peak in particular, 7,610-foot Doonerak, became Marshall's repeated target, but he never did find a way up its rocky tip.

In 1930, Marshall published an essay, "The Problem of the Wilderness," which eloquently laid out how Western man's proclivity to exploit wilderness paradoxically left him longing for wild places. He felt that adventures like climbing were crucial to human life; in fact, he wrote, "Life without the chance for such exertions would be for many persons a dreary game, scarcely bearable in its horrible banality." He quoted the great pacifist Bertrand Russell: "Many men would cease to desire war if they had opportunities to risk their lives in Alpine climbing." In 1935, Marshall and a group of like-minded men founded The Wilderness Society.

David Brower, another pioneering environmentalist, started visiting the Sierra Nevada as a boy, and in 1934 he and Hervey Voge toured nearly the whole length of its higher reaches, summiting whatever unclimbed peaks looked good, including the steep and loose Devils Crags. They joined Norman Clyde and others at various stages of this long, carefree summer, leaving little notebook registers on each new summit.

During World War II, Brower served with the 10th Mountain Division in Europe, where he despaired at the roads, ski chalets and power lines that had, in his mind, "killed" the Alps. Before he even returned home, Brower started writing articles that warned against making American mountains too accommodating to tourists or resource extraction. After the war, he became America's premier environmental leader.

Harvard Men Go North

Starting in the late 1920s, individuals from Harvard College practically took over the first ascent business in North America's big mountains. Under Henry Hall's leadership, the Harvard Mountaineering Club gave underclassmen ready access to the inspiration, maps and partners for expeditions all over the continent.

In the Canadian Rockies, although the most prominent peaks had all been climbed, dozens more worthwhile objectives remained untouched—and whole subranges had yet to see a climber. In 1927, Alfred J. Ostheimer, a 19-year-old Harvard student, went on a peak spree unprecedented in Canada.

Ostheimer started by hiring a capable crew, including Hans Fuhrer and Jean Weber as guides, Curly Phillips as packer and three other men as porters to supply high camps. Between June 22 and August 23, he and his entourage toured the Columbia, Chaba and Clemenceau icefields, and they climbed 36 peaks—27 of them first ascents. On one endurance push, he and Fuhrer tried to mop up the main peaks of the Columbia Icefield in a single sweep. At 1 a.m. they left the Athabasca River. A morning storm forced them to huddle, but soon they climbed North Twin, and by sunset they were the first to stand on Mt. Stutfield. Into the night they continued, singing to keep up their momentum. They made the first ascent of Mt. Kitchener at midnight, and through the wee hours they continued, reaching the top of Snow Dome at dawn. They planned to detour to Mt. Columbia, but another storm sent them down the Columbia Glacier to collapse in camp by noon. In about 35 hours they had covered over 30 miles with about 10,000 feet of elevation gain and loss.

Alaska and the Yukon Territory still held one of the world's greatest realms of unexplored mountains. In fact, only four of the biggest summits had been climbed or even attempted, and whole regions remained blank on the maps.

The first "secondary" giant to draw climbers was Mt. Fairweather, the huge, multiridged pyramid that towers to 15,320 feet

Hans Fuhrer, one of the most prolific guides in North American history. COURTESY HENRY S. HALL, JR. AMERICAN ALPINE CLUB LIBRARY.

only 15 miles from the open ocean north of Glacier Bay. As on the Duke of Abruzzi's expedition to St. Elias, all loads would have to be ferried by men, but the Fairweather expeditions would have no hired help. In 1926, William Ladd, a New York physician, teamed with Allen Carpé and Andy Taylor for the first attempt, less than a year after the latter two endured Mt. Logan. They chartered a small boat from Juneau and approached the mountain's west ridge. Difficult climbing and their overextended line of supplies forced a retreat from 9,200 feet.

In 1930, two expeditions went to Alaskan peaks. Taylor, Carpé and young Harvard graduate Terris Moore crossed from McCarthy to the north side of the Wrangell-St. Elias area. They made the first ascent of Mt. Bona, a 16,421-foot massif of glaciers, via the northwest ridge. Meanwhile, a young group of Harvard undergraduates tried for Fairweather. This expedition foundered in a long approach north from Lituya Bay and reached only 6,700 feet on Fairweather's west ridge. Their leader was a sophomore named Bradford Washburn.

The following year, Ladd, Carpé, Taylor and Moore returned to Fairweather. After a five-week approach from Lituya Bay, the climbers finally got a good view of the peak and saw that one of Fairweather's southeast ridges offered more hope than the west ridge. Though much of this new spur was fairly steep, excellent snow conditions in the early mornings allowed them to place their only camp a full 4,000 feet above the glacier, at 9,000 feet. On June 3 the foursome almost made the 15,320-foot summit, but hard ice and a sudden storm forced a retreat. With supplies and time running low, Ladd and Taylor graciously decided they would descend and free up food and fuel for the two younger climbers.

Late on June 7 the weather finally cleared, and at 10 p.m. Carpé and Moore started out. They wore crampons over their rubber-soled "shoe–pacs" and carried a steel tent pole to use as a flag staff to signal their partners from the top. They made their way past newly formed cornices and 55- to 60-degree snow and ice slopes, and in impressive style they completed the first technically demanding Alaskan ascent. Carpé noted that on this and all the northern peaks he had climbed, his aneroid indicated air pressures akin to summits 2,000 to 3,000 feet higher, confirming anecdotal evidence that mountains at higher latitudes reach into thinner air than those of similar elevations at temperate and tropical latitudes.

The next year, 1932, Carpé was commissioned to set up scientific equipment on Mt. McKinley to study cosmic rays. His first assistants were Edward Beckwith and young Teton climber Theodore Koven. They became the first climbers to enjoy the thrill and convenience of arriving at an Alaskan peak by ski plane, as pilot Joe Crosson put them onto the Muldrow Glacier at 5,700 feet. Crosson's take-off failed, however, and not until the next day did he get back in the air, with Beckwith aboard. Tragically, Carpé was cavalier about traveling unroped across the Muldrow's crevasse bridges, and he fell into a slot and was never found. When Koven tried to rescue him, he fell into a different crevasse, managed to climb out, but died from his injuries.

During this same season, Bradford Washburn focused his sights on the Fairweather Peninsula's second great peak, Mt. Crillon. This mountain would dominate his focus for three seasons.

Washburn had started climbing as a teenager on tours in the Alps, where he told his guides he wanted them to prepare him for Alaska. When he entered Harvard, he wrote a book on his alpine experiences and used his return from that to buy a car that made the New England mountains more accessible. When Mt. Crillon called, he wrote a book on his Fairweather trip and then took out a life insurance policy that he used as collateral for a loan. In college he studied surveying, photography and cartography. He researched the methodology of supply logistics, and, using waxed canvas bags, adapted the Duke of Abruzzi's system of packing food into one-day rations. Washburn saw great peaks essentially as fields of study waiting to be mapped, photographed and understood to the nth degree—and, of course, to be climbed.

The Depression came down hard in the fall of 1932, and by the time Washburn and Robert Bates graduated next spring America's optimism had imploded into a mire of uncertainty and unrest. Their commencement speaker, Harvard President A. Lawrence Lowell, told them they were graduating "into a world uneasy and distressed, but for that very reason needing sound thinking, broad sympathies and above all courage."

It seems that mountain forays provided something of a postgraduate education in just such characteristics for this era's Harvard climbers. Along with becoming professionals who contributed at high levels of society, these men made mountaineering expeditions the lodestones of their personal lives. Bates would become a professor and authority in

Mt. Crillon from the south. The first ascent crossed the glacier in the foreground, climbed through a gap at right, and gained the right-hand skyline. PHOTO #57-1852 © BRADFORD WASHBURN. COURTESY PANOPTICON GALLERY, WALTHAM, MA.

English and the humanities, Charles Houston a doctor and a medical researcher, and Adams Carter a linguist. Terris Moore, an earlier graduate, came to head the Boston Museum of Science and then the University of Alaska. Washburn would succeed Moore at the Boston museum. All led or joined important expeditions to Alaska, the Himalaya and the Andes. Climbing historians would refer to these men as "the Harvard Five."

Crillon, Foraker and Lucania

Soon after that 1933 graduation, Washburn, Bates, Houston, Carter and three glaciologists landed near the sea at Crillon Lake and made a long journey across glaciers onto Crillon's east ridge. Unfortunately, just a few hundred feet from the top, deep powder snow brought their efforts to a halt. The following June, Washburn led a third attempt, and with firm snow conditions up high he and Carter were able to enjoy a beautiful summit.

In comparison to the pioneers in the Tetons and Sierra, these men were inexperienced at technical climbing. Bates made his first rappel on Mt. Crillon in 1933, and none of them thought pitons had more than an occasional role in climbing. But Crillon had taught them how to live and climb on great, snowy and sometimes steep Alaskan mountains like none before them. On Crillon, Bates would recall, "We had the wonderful feeling of youth that whatever happens we can deal with it."

While his friends were climbing Crillon, 20-year-old Charlie Houston was gearing up to lead the first expedition to Mt. Foraker (known to Athabascans as Sultana, Denali's wife). At 17,004 feet, Foraker is the continent's sixth-highest peak. Houston and four companions started with horse packer Carl Anderson from McKinley Park, and in four days the expedition reached the northwest side of the peak. The mountain's northwest ridge looked like the best route, and they decided that Anderson, Charles Storey and Houston's father, Oscar, would work from below to supply camps while Charlie, Graham Brown and Chychelle Waterston pushed the route above.

The 1933 Crillon team (left to right): Charlie Houston, Bob Bates, Bill Child, Brad Washburn, Walt Everett and Ad Carter. PHOTO #57-1667 © BRADFORD WASHBURN. COURTESY PANOPTICON GALLERY, WALTHAM, MA.

The narrow ridge presented a number of challenging sections, and a delicate bergschrund forced the leader to haul his pack. The team placed its highest camp at about 13,700 feet, and on a stormy August 6 they climbed all the way to the north summit and returned to camp. When the weather cleared four days later, they returned to climb the south summit, just in case it might be higher—it proved to be about 200 feet lower. This jaunt gave the climbers the first-ever view of the Kahiltna Glacier, the potential southwest approach to Denali.

The next year, 1935, attention turned to the tremendous unmapped peaks and glaciers north and east of the St. Elias and Logan massifs. Among the prizes there were the two highest unclimbed peaks on the continent: 17,150-foot Mt. Lucania and its sister peak, 16,644-foot Mt. Steele. Bradford Washburn wanted to climb Lucania, but William Ladd asked him to defer to Walter Wood of the American Geographic Society, who was already mounting an effort. Wood approached from the east, from Kluane Lake,

where the only way to Lucania is over the top of Steele. Guide Hans Fuhrer led Wood, his brother Harrison and Joseph Fobes up Steele's 9,000-foot-high east ridge. The snow on the uncorniced ridge was in good nick, but the angle was unrelenting, offering no suitable place for a camp. At 4:30 p.m., after a very long day, they reached the top of Steele. When they looked along the extensive ridge connecting to Lucania, they knew that it was far beyond their reach. In *Life* magazine, Wood's editor proclaimed Lucania to be unclimbable.

Earlier in the same season, Washburn led the first survey through the unknown core of the Icefield Ranges, south of Lucania. He started in February with a brutally cold, open-door photographic flight over the area, and he found that high peaks and glaciers extended much farther east than anyone had expected. Based on the aerial photographs he developed on-site, Washburn arranged to land a team on a previously unknown east-draining glacial system some 60 miles long, which they named the Lowell Glacier. His team included Bob Bates, Andy Taylor, Adams Carter, Ome Daiber and two assistants. By dogsled, ski, raft and mostly on foot, they mapped over 5,000 square miles of giant mountains and vast glaciers.

When Washburn heard that Wood had failed to climb Lucania, he laid plans for a 1936 expedition. The key to climbing the "impossible" peak, he believed, would be to land a ski plane at the southern foot of Lucania. Washburn contacted pilot Bob Reeve of Valdez, who had equipped his Fairchild with skis made out of a steel saloon counter in order to supply miners in winter. In spring, coastal Valdez had no snow for takeoffs with skis, so Reeve launched from mudflats at low tide. Temperatures were unusually warm, and when Reeve touched down onto the Walsh Glacier with his first two passengers, the plane mired into hip-

deep slush. Only after three days could Reeve force a hair-raising takeoff, leaving Washburn and Bob Bates with a long, uncertain hike back to civilization.

The two men decided to follow Wood's route back to Kluane Lake, over the top of Mt. Steele. They climbed to the Lucania-Steele col, and, what the heck, took a two-day side trip over to the top of Lucania. Then they trimmed their packs to 50 pounds and headed over Steele. From Steele's base they faced a march of over 70 miles, starting with the Steele Glacier. As they arrived into lower country it seemed their epic was nearly over, but they found the Donjek River far too swift to cross, and they had to hike miles upstream to cross the Donjek Glacier. With their supplies about gone they desperately half-swam across part of the icy outflow of the glacier. The hungry march came to a thankful end when they bumped into a packer just west of Kluane Lake.

During the following years, Washburn planned expeditions to big, snowy peaks in "secondary" ranges of Alaska. In 1938, he and future Himalayan doyen Norman Dhyrenfurth co-led the first climbing trip into the Chugach Range. They stuck out weeks of storm to make the first ascent of 13,250-foot Mt. St. Agnes (now known as Mt. Marcus Baker), the highest peak in the range. Then Washburn went to the Wrangell Mountains to join Terris Moore for the first ascent of Mt. Sanford, getting lucky with great snow conditions for a ski run down.

On the 1933 attempt at Mt. Crillon, Charlie Houston (top, right) prepares to climb over Bob Bates in order to clear the bergschrund and access the upper glacier and the main peak. Ad Carter follows. PHOTO #57-1605 © BRADFORD WASHBURN. COURTESY PANOPTICON GALLERY, WALTHAM, MA.

Bob Reeve's Fairchild mired in the slush on the Walsh Glacier, below Mt. Lucania. PHOTO #57-2125 © BRADFORD WASHBURN. COURTESY PANOPTICON GALLERY, WALTHAM, MA.

Mt. Lucania (left) and Mt. Steele as viewed from the east. Washburn and Bates climbed from the left to the col between them, summited Lucania, and started their long hike out to Kluane Lake by descending the ridge on Steele at lower right. PHOTO #1328 © BRADFORD WASHBURN. COURTESY PANOPTICON GALLERY, WALTHAM, MA.

In 1940, Washburn led a party of eight (including his wife, Barbara) on the first ascent of Mt. Bertha, the third peak to be climbed in the Fairweather Range, adjacent to Mt. Crillon. This climb started from Hugh Miller Inlet, 20 miles east of Bertha, with dogsled and air support. The roundtrip took about a month, and on Bertha's northeast ridge they employed fixed ropes for carrying loads over some of the steepest terrain of Washburn's career.

During all of these trips, Washburn gathered detailed geographic data and high-quality aerial photographs. He was becoming a one-man repository of topographic information and climbing possibilities for the greatest peaks of the continent.

Clouds of War

Farther east, Walter Wood was playing a similar role in the high peaks of the Icefield Ranges. His surveyor's education in Switzerland had landed him a leading position with the American Geographic Society. After being scooped by Washburn on Lucania, Wood made airplane access and supply the core of his planning. In 1941, Wood arranged to try both 15,885-foot Mt. Wood (named for a Canadian officer) and 14,787-foot Mt. Walsh with his wife and a

Bob Bates and Bradford Washburn on the summit of Mt. Lucania. PHOTO #57-2256 © BRADFORD WASHBURN. COURTESY PANOPTICON GALLERY, WALTHAM, MA.

team including Robert Bates and U.S. Army Capt. Albert Jackman. With Europe at war, the military foresaw the possibility that American troops would need to fight in remote, cold

Nearing the summit on Mt. Hayes. PHOTO #57-4260 © BRADFORD WASHBURN. COURTESY PANOPTICON GALLERY, WALTHAM, MA.

Walter Wood and Robert Bates on the summit of Mt. Walsh. PHOTO WALTER WOOD COLLECTION, COURTESY ARCTIC INSTITUTE OF NORTH AMERICA.

mountains, and they wanted Jackman to learn what he could about high-mountain clothing, rations and airdrop methods. Wood used a plane not only to establish basecamp but also to drop supplies at pre-selected campsites up to and over 10,000 feet. On the broad ridges of both peaks, the airdrops landed well, allowing the climbers to carry light packs and arrive at their campsites to waiting plywood boxes of ample supplies. They made successful ascents of both Wood and Walsh.

In June of that year, Henry Hall and Brad Washburn planned a go at 13,832-foot Mt. Hayes, the highest peak of the Hayes Range,

135 miles east-northeast of Denali. Two previous attempts had failed. Just two weeks after hatching their plans, Hall and Washburn shared a basecamp at 4,900 feet below the north ridge of Mt. Hayes with Barbara Washburn, Sterling Hendricks, Benjamin Ferris and William Shand. Also with them was Lt. Robin Montgomery, a U.S. Army observer who watched as nearly a ton of supplies parachuted onto basecamp from a DC–3. Washburn calculated that these air conveyances cost a fraction of the price to hire a pack train.

The climbers lugged supplies to a chain of depots along the ridge but established only two camps. July storms added fresh, cold snow, making trail breaking a steady chore, but the team preferred that to icy slopes. From a 9,500-foot-high notch, all but Henry Hall summited on August 1 above a sea of clouds. Afterward, Hendricks, Ferris and Shand climbed a nearby peak, later named Mt. Moffitt, the second-highest peak in the Hayes Range.

It had been a hurried, three-week jaunt to the mountains. Of their return, Washburn wrote that, "With regret we...headed westward once more to Fairbanks and the land of plenty." Four months later, the "land of plenty" would be under siege and rationing supplies, as America joined the Second World War.

⬤ SUGGESTED ROUTES
FROM THIS PERIOD

MT. HAYES (13,832 feet/ 4,216 meters)
North Ridge

Among the countless striking ridges on Alaskan peaks, Mt. Hayes' north ridge stands out as a classic, graceful spine of medium scale—by Alaska standards, which translates as a substantial challenge. After climbing this route in the 1980s, Alaska veteran Geof Radford wrote, "When you read of an ascent done 45 years before, with heavy gear, 10-point crampons and step chopping, there is a tendency to suppose that it can't be that 'hard' by modern standards. This is a mistake."

The Hayes Range is an extension of the Alaska Range, and these mountains stand well inland—continental enough to be beyond the reach of the heaviest punch of coastal fronts, but hammered from the northwest by arctic storms.

Mt. Hayes from the northwest. The north ridge rises from the left. PHOTO #2948 © BRADFORD WASHBURN. COURTESY PANOPTICON GALLERY, WALTHAM, MA.

Approach: At this time, there is no air service available from Fairbanks, so most parties either approach on skis in the spring or fly with a pilot from Talkeetna, preferably to land on the Hayes Glacier not far from the base of the route.

Route: Hayes' north ridge rises nearly 9,000 feet in about five horizontal miles. Since the first ascent, large crevasses have split the lower sections of the ridge, adding some routefinding and technical challenges. A typical party will place two camps on the ridge, and the notch at 9,500 feet still makes an excellent spot for the highest camp. With the advantage of lightweight gear and luck with firm conditions, modern teams climb the ridge alpine style, but seracs, crevasses, cornices, steep drifts and ice and snow of all qualities present challenge after challenge. Above the north shoulder at 12,500 feet, the ridge is horizontal but very narrow and often sprouts double cornices. Descent is by the same route.

First Ascent: Brad and Barbara Washburn, Sterling Hendricks, Benjamin Ferris and William Shand, July 1941

Difficulty: TD, 9,000 feet

MONARCH MOUNTAIN
(11,722 feet/3,573 meters)
East Ridge

Monarch indeed of the central Coast Mountains, this peak has become modestly popular, by regional standards, because of its prominence, wild surroundings and moderately challenging terrain.

Approach: The simplest way to Monarch is to hire a helicopter from Hagensborg, near Bella Coola. An excellent basecamp and landing site are found at a rock island in the Horseshoe Glacier, at about 7,500 feet. A cheaper alternative is to arrange a floatplane to land at Success Lake; it's a moderate day's walk from the lake to basecamp, and supplies can be airdropped to the camp. Strong parties can climb the route in a very long day from basecamp, but it's more common to use one of the excellent bivouac sites on the route.

Route: Climb through an easy icefall to Horseshoe Glacier's upper basin, then head up moderately steep snow and ice slopes to gain the east ridge at about 9,600 feet. Moderate rock steps along the crest lead to the glacier hanging across the upper ridge. If possible, climb the lower

Monarch Mountain from the northeast. The east ridge is the left skyline. PHOTO BY DON SERL.

bergschrund and trend south to a snow and ice chute that leads to the summit crags. If the lower 'schrund is impassable, bypass it to the north, climb an icy chute to the north ridge, and follow that for a few pitches to the top. Descend the same route.

First Ascent: Hans Fuhrer and Henry Hall, July 1936

Difficulty: AD+, AI 2, Class 4, 4,000 feet

PICACHO DEL DIABLO
(10,154 feet/3,095 meters)
Pinnacle Ridge

"Cerro de la Encantada" is the crest of an enormous escarpment that dominates the spine of northern Baja California. Many will be surprised to learn that this ridge at latitude 31 degrees gets plastered with snow and ice in winter. Groups looking for a rugged and enchanting backpack approach the peak via Cañon del Diablo, but those looking for a technical climb on flawless granodiorite choose Pinnacle Ridge. Even in perfect conditions, the long route surprises almost everyone with its scale and complexity. On clear days summiters are rewarded with panoramas that extend to the seas on either side of the Baja peninsula.

Approach: Drive from the west up "Observatorio Road" and branch south to the road-end. In the past, vandals made it mandatory to arrange with people at the Meling Ranch or another safe spot to store your vehicle, or to have someone guard the vehicle during the climb. In recent years, however, climbers have been parking at the road-end without incident. The most common strategy is to hike with camping gear and water to a site below Blue Bottle, a 9,680-foot-high knob at the western end of the

ridge. Water might be found at the head of the ravine en route to Blue Bottle.

Route: From the Blue Bottle, the ridge is about 2.5 miles long, including sections of hiking. Expect difficulties up to 5.6 and at least a couple of 80-foot rappels. From the north summit scramble down 3,500 feet into the head of Cañon del Diablo to reach a bivouac site called Cedaroak or another known as *Campo Noche*; both have water. Then climb up Goring Gully to the Blue Bottle site and return to the road.

First Ascent: Walter Brem, Nathan Clark, Norman Clyde, Glen Dawson, Richard Jones and Bestor Robinson, June 1932

Difficulty: AD+, 5.6, with some rappels

Reference: *Parque Nacional San Pedro Màrtir; Topographic Map and Visitor's Guide to Baja's Highest Mountains*

Permit: A tourist permit and Mexican auto insurance are required to visit Mexico. A park permit is required to enter Parque Nacional San Pedro Màrtir.

The summit massif of Picacho del Diablo. Pinnacle Ridge is the right skyline. PHOTO BY STEVE ECKERT.

CHAPTER 7

Playing Immortal

As the best of North America's climbers grew more comfortable on steep terrain, they began to tackle routes of sustained and impressive verticality—some even compared to the extreme routes of Europe. Much of the progress in this pre-World War II period can be traced to the training that Americans started to do in earnest on small, accessible crags. The familiarity with steep ground grew to the point that North Americans began to aim for world-class objectives, most notably Mt. Waddington, new facets on the Grand Teton and ultimately K2.

Henry Hall aptly referred to Mt. Waddington as "surely one of the most remarkable culminating points of any mountain range in the world." Here was a fang as big and steep as the Grand Teton, yet usually pasted with rime and ice. By the mid-1930s, the challenge of its summit tower attracted many of North America's finest climbers.

The 1934 season held a lot of promise for climbing Waddington, as, in addition to the Munday-Hall-Fuhrer attempt (see Chapter 6), three other teams came to the mountain. A team from Winnipeg punched through an epic approach and became the first to make their way up the Tiedemann Glacier. They started up the snow-covered rock on the north face of Waddington's summit tower, but were turned back by bad weather and difficult climbing. A team from the British Columbia Mountain Club came, hoping that their extensive practice on steep crags and using pitons would make the difference. Neal Carter and Alec Dalgleish headed this team— Dalgleish, at 27, was the club's rock wizard.

They decided to follow the advice of the Mundays and Hall and probe the potentially drier rock abutments on Waddington's true south face, above the Corridor Glacier. A few hundred feet up, Dalgleish led out of a couloir, placed a piton, and came to an impasse. He decided to retreat but then fell. The piton held, but the fall swung him into a wall, and then the rope broke over an edge. He fell all the way down the couloir, and his mates found him dead at the base. The loss of their rising star stunned the Vancouver climbing community, and his mentor, Tom Fyles, virtually never climbed again.

The Rock Climbing Section of the Sierra Club had by now gained confidence that their climbing and belaying skills could get them up almost any piece of steep rock. Some of their best, including Jules Eichorn,

Ↄ Jack Durrance leading on the Grand Teton's *Exum Ridge.* PHOTO BY HANK COULTER, COURTESY MARGARET COULTER.

Elizabeth Woolsey, Bill House, Alan Willcox and Fritz Wiessner in New England before their trip to Mt. Waddington. PHOTO COURTESY ANDY WIESSNER.

Fritz Wiessner leading on the summit tower of Mt. Waddington. PHOTO BY BILL HOUSE, COURTESY ANDY WIESSNER.

David Brower and Bestor Robinson, tried the southwest face of Waddington in 1935, and a team including Robinson, Dick Leonard and Raffi Bedayan came in '36. Both parties focused on the face's rocky central buttresses, but these were too steep and tall to climb in a day, and the sustained difficulty made it impractical to carry bivouac equipment. Neither party succeeded. By its southern faces, Waddington was a problem as severe as any yet solved in the Alps, but raked by heavier and more frequent storms. Moreover, to get to Waddington required an expeditionary approach march with few or no porters, and of course the peak lay far beyond any rescue help.

Fritz Wiessner

Three climbers from the East Coast, Elizabeth Woolsey, Bill House and Alan Willcox, felt that if anyone could succeed on Waddington it would be their friend Fritz Wiessner. Wiessner had emigrated from Germany in 1929, and he climbed the New England crags with grace and power the likes of which America had never seen. His father had introduced him to climbing in Austria at a tender age, and Fritz grew up as a pioneer in one of the world's most severe climbing arenas, the sandstone and limestone towers of Saxony. There, climbers disdained pitons completely, and, to a degree unseen elsewhere, Wiessner helped advance the ethic that a climber must depend on free climbing

the features of the rock. In the early 1920s he and his peers climbed barefoot and pitonless on ground that now is rated 5.9 and harder, protecting 100-foot pitches with only a bolt or two and an occasional wedged knot of cord. In 1920, Wiessner proved himself one of the world's best rock mountaineers by putting up long, steep Dolomite routes on the Fleischbank and the Forchetta. When he showed up at the crags in New England, he led routes that the locals couldn't imagine, much less repeat.

Among Wiessner's early partners in America, only Yale Forestry graduate Bill House had the iron nerve and sharp determination that approached the German climber's. House had experience in Switzerland as well. As the 1936 season approached, Wiessner was in Europe preparing to try the first ascent of the vaunted Walker Spur of the Grandes Jorasses. When

THE CONQUERORS OF MOUNT MYSTERY: MR. FRITZ WIESSNER (RIGHT), THE LEADER, AND MR. WILLIAM P. HOUSE, WHO SUCCESSFULLY ASCENDED THE SOUTH PEAK, WHERE THE CLIMB WAS SO DIFFICULT THAT ONLY TWO COULD ATTACK IT AT A TIME.

Mr. Fritz Wiessner, who took the lead in this historic ascent, is a German-American chemist. of New York. He is thirty-six and has twenty years of climbing experience. He was a member of the German-American Nanga-Parbat Expedition in 1932. Mr. William P. House, of Pittsburgh, is also a well-known climber. He is a student at Yale University, and is twenty-three.

Bill House and Fritz Wiessner, down after their first ascent of Mt. Waddington. PHOTO APPEARED IN THE *LONDON DAILY NEWS*, COURTESY ANDY WIESSNER.

Willcox and Woolsey telegrammed and promised he would not regret a trip to Waddington, House's partnership won him over and Wiessner took a ship back to America.

When the foursome arrived below the southwest face of Waddington, Wiessner and House first tried to climb couloirs that the Sierrans had figured were too exposed to rockfall. They headed up the prominent couloir west of the summit, but steep rock glazed with ice forced them down—this was the 16th failed attempt on the peak.

On July 21, Wiessner and House tried a different route, leaving their high camp at 2:45 a.m. on a moonless night. This time they started up a couloir east of the summit. Near dawn, Wiessner dispatched a short pitch of steep ice by chopping steps and holds. Then the pair climbed a rising traverse leftward across hanging snowfields to reach steep rock within a few hundred feet of the top. Wiessner donned rope-soled rock shoes, and, as he always insisted, held on to the lead. As the difficulty was near his limits, he hammered in pitons regularly. House, burdened with the crampons, axes and extra boots, often needed help from the rope above. Their route led into a steep chimney,

HOW THE "UNCLIMBABLE" SOUTHERN PEAK OF MOUNT MYSTERY WAS CLIMBED:
THE ROUTE TAKEN BY MR. WIESSNER AND MR. HOUSE IN THEIR THIRTEEN - HOUR
ASCENT OF THE SOUTH FACE OF MOUNT WADDINGTON.

The visible parts of this route are marked by dots; the parts hidden by buttresses by dashes.
Rotten rock, rock glazed by ice, and falling stones presented great difficulties.   The couloir at
the left separates the North Peak (first climbed by the Don Mundays, of Vancouver) from the
higher South Peak.

The southwest face of Mt. Waddington, with the Wiessner-House route drawn. PHOTO APPEARED IN THE *LONDON DAILY NEWS*, COURTESY ANDY WIESSNER.

Fritz Wiessner on the summit of Mt. Waddington. PHOTO BY BILL HOUSE, COURTESY ANDY WIESSNER.

Bill House on the summit of Mt. Waddington. PHOTO BY FRITZ WIESSNER, COURTESY ANDY WIESSNER.

where Wiessner stemmed off House's shoulder and somehow avoided knocking loose stones onto his belayer. By late afternoon they had won the 13,177-foot pinnacle, the highest point for hundreds of miles, where only one at a time could stand. House wrote that, among his various sensations, "relief was the most dominant." But of course they had to descend, and their *Dülfersitz* rappels had to be carefully managed over the steep, loose rock. House described their final escape:

> *Progress became extremely slow in the dim light. At one point we found we had miscalculated our position in the gully. Tying our full 300 feet of line to a piton we rappelled to the end, to find ourselves still above a 15-foot drop.... No piton cracks presented themselves, so we tried a drastic remedy to our problem. I lowered Wiessner from my ice axe, driven in a crack, and once down he set himself firmly as I attempted to climb down, scratching with my crampons for footholds. When they disappeared I jumped, confident that Wiessner would stop me, which he did. From here we hastened onto the open glacier. The climb had taken 23 hours, most of it over difficult rock and ice. The next day the weather broke, and as we came down through the storm we felt grateful that the gods of weather had allowed us to play immortals.*

Wiessner and House had climbed with rare deftness on both rock and ice, and they had dug deeper into the well of commitment than any other climbers in North America. The Sierra Club group felt that a major factor in House and Wiessner's success was their willingness to take greater risks. This was partly true, but House and Wiessner also knew how to gauge alpine risks better than most North Americans. They succeeded where exploratory mountaineers could not climb, and where technical rock skills alone were not enough.

Back to the Tetons

The Tetons had gathered a reputation as the most exciting mountains south of Canada. A variety of climbers had found employment in the range, either as guides or national park rangers, and after Underhill's 1931 visit these locals led most of the new routes. Yet untried, though, was the *Nordwänd* of the range, the Grand Teton's north face, and keenest to claim this prize was Paul Petzoldt.

The Tetons shaped Petzoldt's adult life. At 16, he had been an impoverished youth with few prospects and little direction. In 1924, he and his buddy Ralph Herron got a route description from Grand Teton pioneer Billy Owen, then marched right up to the unclimbed east ridge of the Grand. Without a rope or any real climbing experience, they quickly got onto ground way over their heads and desperately scrambled back down. Then they looked more carefully at Owen's note, found their way to the Upper Saddle, and reached the top. Petzoldt later figured, "I don't think I ever underestimated a mountain again."

Paul Petzoldt in 1936. PHOTO BY KEN HENDERSON.

Back in town, locals and tourists cheered their ascent, and some asked the young Petzoldt to lead them up the peak. Thus began Petzoldt's long career as a charismatic guide. Petzoldt was not the first guide in the Tetons, but he was the first to make guiding a steady business. By the 1960s he would work his belief in wilderness mountaineering into a school for instructors, the National Outdoor Leadership School (NOLS).

Between his working ascents Petzoldt sought out harder climbing adventures. In December 1935, he, his brother Eldon and Fred Brown made the first winter ascent of the Grand Teton, discovering the upper peak to be blown free of snow and less frigid than the valley below.

Earlier, Petzoldt and Sterling Hendricks scouted the Grand Teton's north wall by rappelling the upper part of the north ridge. Their oblique view indicated that four ramps angling across the wall could be climbed readily, but the steep walls between these ramps looked very challenging. Late in August 1936, Wiessner, House and Woolsey came through the Tetons on their way back from Waddington. They met up with Petzoldt, who later said he discussed the north face's potential with them. On August 24 the three visitors climbed a new route on the northeast face of the Middle Teton, while Petzoldt guided a group up the Grand Teton. That evening, Petzoldt learned that the visitors had moved their camp to Amphitheater Lake and were planning to try the fabled north face.

Miffed, Petzoldt gathered his brother and a Dartmouth student he employed as a guide, Jack Durrance, and raced to beat the Easterners to the face. Durrance had first climbed in Germany as a youngster, when his parents were stationed there, and the Grand's north face would be the first in a string of new routes he would climb in this range. Well before dawn, the three men snuck past the visitors sleeping at Amphitheater Lake and got onto the face. Slabs, chimneys and moderate walls provided enough holds and cracks to connect the first three ramps. Above the third, however, they met a steep impasse. The

Jack Durrance on the summit of the Grand Teton after the first ascent of the *Complete Exum Ridge,* 1936.
PHOTO BY KEN HENDERSON.

sun was sinking low, so they rappelled back to the second ramp and escaped to the summit via the upper north ridge.

Wiessner, House and Woolsey saw the others on the face and decided not to follow. Instead, four days later, Wiessner, House, Percy Olton and Beckett Howorth climbed the north ridge, and Wiessner became the first to lead that route without direct aid, extending himself around the crux chockstone with some wild bridging moves.

The day after this, Jack Durrance and veteran Ken Henderson teamed up to make the first ascent of the complete Exum Ridge, which they later called their favorite climb anywhere. Below the Wall Street ledge where Glenn Exum had started his climb, they scouted some 800 feet of complex buttress. In just five hours, Durrance and Henderson danced their way up corners, ramps and steep faces, and then continued up Exum's upper ridge to the summit.

At the end of the season, Durrance went back to school at Dartmouth and founded the Dartmouth Mountaineering Club, which quickly became the Ivy League's second most active club.

Focus on K2

Wiessner, House, Petzoldt and Durrance were the cream of America's new generation of technical climbers, and their careers soon coalesced on the toughest peak climbers had yet considered: K2. The American Alpine Club got permission for an attempt in 1938, and in good weather the team nearly succeeded. In the finest piece of climbing yet seen in Asia, Bill House led a crux chimney. At their highest camp, Petzoldt felt capable of summiting but did not have adequate supplies to climb higher.

Meanwhile, back in the Tetons, Jack Durrance led a partner up yet another outstanding new route on the Grand Teton, the northwest ridge. This is the longest ridge in the American Rockies, and the upper part is renowned for some of the most exhilarating climbing in the region.

In 1939, the AAC returned to K2, with Wiessner leading the team. None of the '38 members could go back, and at the last minute the AAC dispatched Durrance to join the expedition. Durrance's boots didn't arrive in time, however, and he had to work in a supporting role. Wiessner and modestly experienced Pasang Lama Sherpa reached a camp near the top, but the loss of Lama's crampons helped foil what would have been one of the greatest mountaineering achievements of all time. Misfortune descended into horror as the expedition devolved into confusion, a storm, a rescue attempt and the deaths of three Sherpas and one American. Back home, Wiessner was upbraided amid rumblings of Teutonic selfishness. Wiessner resigned from the AAC, and thus essentially ended the alpine career of the most skilled climber America had seen.

Fritz Wiessner had impressed, intimidated and in some cases disturbed the American climbing community. American climbers embraced adventure, but, as historians

Fritz Wiessner in the 1930s. COURTESY ANDY WIESSNER.

from the northwest ridge, and in August he aimed for it with fellow Dartmouth man Henry "Hank" Coulter, who would later write the first Teton climbing guidebook.

They approached the west face up a spectacular and seldom-visited canyon, which they named Valhalla. When they woke clouds covered the sky, but Durrance insisted they head up. He would do most of the leading, while Coulter would follow with both packs—a 50-pound load of hardware and bivouac gear. A couple of pitches up, a plate of ice whizzed over Durrance's head, and then the clouds let loose a snowstorm. They hid in a nook until the weather changed again. As the sky cleared, Durrance led over mixed rock and ice, and then up a rotten chimney. Above, the face steepened past vertical, but Durrance rose to the challenge. A barrage of rocks rained down from climbers on the regular route above—never did they imagine anyone would be climbing in the abyss below—and Durrance and Coulter screamed upward until the rockfall stopped.

As Durrance started to lead out from the Great West Chimney, he had to yell again— this time at Coulter, who had fallen asleep at the belay. The hour grew late, and they decided to speed progress by leaving their packs behind (which were later retrieved by friends on rappel). As they struggled to find a way to return to the top of the Great West Chimney, Bob Bates happened to be looking over from the regular route and yelled down to suggest a blind traverse. Soon after this pitch, Durrance and Coulter emerged from the chimney and reached the top. They had completed the most challenging alpine rock route yet in the United States.

Andrew Kaufmann and Bill Putnam put it, "[Other] Americans played for fun, and Wiessner played for keeps." Ropemates acknowledged Wiessner as a considerate and technically safe climber, but he had come to trust only himself—and this was both his strength and his weakness. Although many would describe his attitude as competitive, Wiessner proclaimed that climbing was not a competitive sport but rather a private quest to work through the toughest terrain that nature could deliver. By trade a chemist and head of a pharmaceutical company, he was proud that financial interests never clouded his climbing. His intense and total commitment inspired later alpinists, and Reinhold Messner called him "the most pivotal climber of the 20th century." In 1966, the AAC restored Wiessner's stature within the club by bestowing an Honorary Membership upon him.

Durrance's Magnum Opus
Jack Durrance returned to the Tetons in 1940. He had heard Robert Underhill mention in a lecture that the most direct way to the top of the Grand Teton would be by the west face. Durrance had gotten a good view of this face

The Bugaboo of the Bugaboos
During the summer of 1938, Fritz Wiessner and Chappell Cranmer traveled to the Bugaboos to try the group's last unclimbed tower, Snowpatch Spire. Conrad Kain had felt "inclined to prophesy that this pinnacle will be the most difficult ascent in the Canadian Alps," and indeed eight attempts had yielded no real progress on any of the tower's smooth, steep walls.

Jack Durrance belaying in the Tetons, probably on Nez Percé, with Hank Coulter below. PHOTO COURTESY MARGARET COULTER.

Jack Durrance in the Tetons. PHOTO BY HANK COULTER.

Wiessner and Cranmer started up the southeast corner, under the namesake snow patch, where several fairly challenging pitches led to an overhang. To surmount it, Wiessner pulled out direct-aid slings. After leading this slow pitch he looked past the snow to a steep headwall that seemed to promise a lot more direct aid. Wiessner later wrote scornfully that such a mechanical effort "takes neither skill nor brains." (Also to the point, perhaps, was that "we had used up our pitons on the lower part of the climb.") He concluded that an ascent of Snowpatch "will only be possible with the use of a whole magazine of pitons and karabiners."

Two years later, in 1940, a group of Sierra Club rock technicians including Raffi Bedayan (later Bedayn) drove to the Bugaboos. The smooth cracks of this alpine granite were reminiscent of Bedayan's home walls in California, and he relished the chance to climb a route where Wiessner, his rival from Waddington, had backed off.

Bedayan and Jack Arnold took just a bit of bivouac gear and shared leads up the first pitches. Wearing crepe-soled tennis shoes, they neared Wiessner's high point, where Bedayan wryly noted that Wiessner had left "a magazine of hardware" in the cracks. They removed the pitons and replaced a couple for aid themselves, and then reached easier ground on the left flank of the snow patch. As evening approached, they rappelled to a ledge and spent the night shivering under a tarp. At dawn they found to their frustration that a technically proficient "snafflehound" (probably a pika) had raided their vitamin tablets.

As Bedayan neared the tiers of overhanging granite above the snow, he wrote later, "We had a 'rock-engineering' problem on our hands. This didn't mean we had to cut steps in the rock, hang by pitons or use other artificial aids. We would, however, want to place pitons, use adequate belays, anchors and double rope technique." Although most of the rock took pitons well, Bedayan ran into a few dead ends and overcame tenuous blank sections with only "moral support" pitons for protection. At one delicate stance, he "caught

Snowpatch Spire from the east. Bedayan and Arnold climbed near the left edge, over the top of the snow patch, and up to the top. PHOTO BY CHRIS ATKINSON.

sight of a...small brown animal, scampering on the friction pitch that I had given up.... It was undoubtedly the snafflehound, romping around full of our vitamins. I needed them now." Linking a couple of finger traverses and chimneys, Bedayan found a way to the summit without using direct aid.

The One-Man Tornado

In the Cascades, a new generation of Mountaineers was enjoying a renaissance on both technical and exploratory fronts. Lloyd Anderson started a buying cooperative (which he later named Recreational Equipment Inc.) that imported ice axes, ropes, pitons and carabiners directly from Europe. By the late 1930s, Seattle climbers were buzzing with enthusiasm for the North Cascades, and each new climb ended on a summit that looked out to more new objectives.

In 1939, a 16-year-old with almost disturbingly fearsome intensity joined the club. In his first full year of mountaineering, Fred Beckey climbed 35 peaks, including the first ascent of remote Mt. Despair with Lloyd

Anderson and Clint Kelley. Beckey's inspirational role model was the legendary Hermann Ulrichs—the original "outlaw" Mountaineer (see Chapter 5). Beckey seemed to know right away that one's guide to adventure should not be established routes but unclimbed terrain.

The next year, Beckey, his younger brother Helmy, Anderson and two others started the season early with a May ascent of a classic high pyramid that Ulrichs had attempted and named "Isosceles Peak." They succeeded on the granitic west ridge and renamed the mountain Forbidden Peak. For the rest of the summer the Beckey brothers climbed non-stop. With no car, they patiently hitchhiked along back roads, even to get to the remote northern Picket Range—the second time climbers had ever entered the range.

In 1942, most climbers were tied up in World War II, but Fred was able to delay his service. He plotted an incredible next step: the second ascent of Mt. Waddington. To the shock of every North American mountaineer,

RECREATIONAL EQUIPMENT COOPERATIVE
Price List No. 6
April 1, 1940

	Regular Price	Our Price		Regular Price	Our Price
*Air Mattress, 3/4 length	6.50	4.60	*Pants, mens all wool	9.95	8.00
Books, Bruning - Rook Climbing	1.00	.60	* " , womens " "	8.75	7.00
" Technique Alpine Mtng	1.25	.80	(Samples in store for size)		
" Wedderburn " "	2.00	1.25			
* " Young - Mountaincraft	7.50	6.00	*Parka, 8 oz canvas duck	5.95	4.50
Carabiner, pear or oval	.90	.50	* " womens gaberdine	6.75	5.40
" safety	2.00	1.40	* " mens "	6.75	5.40
Compasses, small scout	1.00	.85	(Samples in store for size)		
Crampons, 8 point swiss	8.50	5.45			
" 10 " Eckenstein	10.00	7.00	Pitons, lateral or vertical	.50	.25
Cups, tinned with wire handle	.15	.15	Piton hammers	2.00	1.50
Dehyd. Mixed vegetables ½#	.28	.17	Photographic hinges	.10	.08½
" Powdered eggs ⅓#	.55	.25	Primus stoves, small	4.15	3.11
" " milk ⅛#		.07	* " " medium	5.50	4.13
Almonds 1/5#		.10	" Radius type, large	6.35	4.76
Cashews 1/3#		.10			
Lemon drops ½#	.15	.10	Rope, climbing 7/16"x 100'	2.00	1.25
Nestles cocoa 1 1/8 oz		.03	" reepschnur ¼"x 100'	.75	.50
Duffle bags, heavy weight	3.25	1.67	Rucksacks, small	1.50	.95
First aid kits, scout	.75	.63	" "	1.75	1.00
Glasses, colored unbreakable		2.45	" , Medium 2 pocket	2.50	1.67
Film and camera orders			" large " "	2.75	1.67
on May 1, and July 1 (grouped)			" Steel frame, medium	8.95	8.95
Flashlights, 3 cell headlight	2.95	2.95	" dito with waist strap	9.30	9.30
Glasses, colored unbreakable		2.45			
Ice Axe, Swiss, no glide ring	8.50	5.75	Shoes, secure requsition		
" " with "	10.00	6.25	from salesman or store and		
" Austrian " " "	12.50	7.50	purchase from Currin-Greene		
" Leather guards	.95	.70	at 2715 Western Ave.		
" Glide rings and strap	1.00	.45	*Shoes, 6" suitable climbing		6.75
Maps, topographical	.15	.08	" " " "		7.25
			" 8" " "		9.00
Mittens, lined canvas	1.35	.75	" " hand made "		15.00
" " leather faced	1.95	1.00	Shoe laces, rawhide 54" for 8"		
" " all leather	1.65	.92	" " "	.20	.15
" all leather long	2.50	1.65	" " 72" for 10" boots	.25	.20
" " wool	.95	.69	" " 96" " 16" "	.30	.25
" " " Indian knit	1.25	1.00	Sno-seal, for shoes med.	.35	.35
" Womens all wool	.85	.69	" " " large	.50	.50
" " wool and leather	1.95	.98	Sole oil " " "	.35	.35
			Socks, white sweat	.29	.23
Nails, tricouni type no. 1	.05	.05	" , short about 7/8 wool	.65	.45
" " " " 2	.06	.06	" " " all " "	.75	.55
" #613, #615, #6H	.09	.09	" " 100% wool	.95	.69
(Amount per shoe listed at store)			" " wool cashmere	.50	.50
Buy you nails and take with you			" " " Indian knit	1.25	1.00
before purchasing shoes.			" " long white, all wool	.75	.45
			" " colored	.85	.69
Save on equipment - Spend it on trips.			* Sleeping bags 1¼# down, 2 pc	24.50	17.50
Store at 2121 Western.			" " 2# recom.	26.50	19.50
Hours 8 AM to 7PM, 6 days a week			" " 1½# one pc	22.50	15.50
Catalog and dividend information book in store.			" " 1 3/4# recom.	23.50	16.50
* Goods not in stock secured by store			* Tent, Tarp-N-Tent 4#	9.00	9.00
or Ken Norden, T.Davis Castor			* " Co-Op Tarp 4½#, 9'sq.		3.75
or Mary or Lloyd Anderson			Sunburn preparations, waterproofing in store		

The first price sheet (dated 1940) for Recreational Equipment Cooperative, the buying club organized by Lloyd Anderson that later became REI. IMAGE COURTESY MSCUA UNIVERSITY OF WASHINGTON LIBRARIES, ACCESSION # 2648, BOX 1.

Fred and Helmy Beckey succeeded. They climbed the southwest face using an upward-traversing route similar to that followed by Wiessner and House, except Fred donned felt slippers over tennis shoes to lead out of an icy chimney lower down and aim more directly toward the summit.

At ages 19 and 17, the Beckey brothers had found the skills and the cautious determination to succeed on the most demanding

alpine summit yet climbed on the continent. Helmy would continue to climb for many years on a recreational basis, but Fred had barely begun to astonish the mountaineering world. The challenge of mountain terrain became the driving force of his life, and already he had begun to accumulate a master list of first-ascent projects, from obscure to supreme, that would fill his time for longer than anyone could imagine.

SUGGESTED ROUTES
FROM THIS PERIOD

GRAND TETON (13,770 feet/4,197 meters)
Complete Exum Ridge

The Grand Teton has so many classic routes that it's hard to choose among them. The only complaint one might have with this Durrance-Henderson route is that it is too superb and therefore overpublicized. But no one will regret climbing it. The routefinding complexities, erratic weather and steep face and chimney climbing on firm, south-facing rock inspire and demand a competent effort. Detailed descriptions are readily available and need not be replicated here. Although very fit climbers can climb this route in a day from the road, most camp high in Garnet Canyon.

First Ascent: Jack Durrance and Ken Henderson, August 1936

The Grand Teton from the Lower Saddle (southwest). The *Exum Ridge* follows the sun-shade line. PHOTO BY ANDY SELTERS.

Difficulty: D, III, 5.7, 1,400 feet

Permits: A permit is required to enter Grand Teton National Park, and overnight camping requires a wilderness permit (reservations recommended).

Guidebooks: *A Climber's Guide to the Teton Range; Fifty Classic Climbs of North America*

GRAND TETON (13,770 feet/4,197 meters)
West Face

Climbers in the know regard this as the best and hardest of the classic Grand Teton routes. It is Jack Durrance's most brilliant achievement and the culmination of pre-World War II routes in the United States. In 1967, George and Mike Lowe made a classic direct start to this face by climbing a section of the *Black Ice Couloir* (see Chapter 10). However, at this writing climate change has made the *Black Ice Couloir* an uncertainty, and one must enquire locally each season as to whether it holds ice.

Approach: The original northern approach up Cascade and Valhalla canyons is a worthy experience for those with a bit of extra time. Most, however, approach this face from the south, via the Lower Saddle and the Valhalla Traverse ledges (discovered in 1959). In either case, one can access the original Durrance route by linking three wet and/or icy shelves. From the third shelf, traverse right to the meat of the route, the steep wall between the Northwest and Great West chimneys. The direct approach up four pitches of the *Black Ice Couloir* joins here.

Route: For about eight pitches you'll exercise a variety of alpine rock climbing skills, from mantels to jam cracks, face climbing to chimney moves, Class 4 sections to verglased slabs. Join the last segment of the *Owen-Spalding Route* to reach the top. Descend by the rappel variation to the *Owen-Spalding Route*.

First Ascent: Jack Durrance and Henry Coulter, August 1940; *Black Ice* pitches: Ray Jacquot and Herb Swedlund, July 1961; *Black Ice-West Face* linkup: George and Mike Lowe, July 1967

Difficulty: D+/TD-, IV, 5.8, 3,000 feet (AI 3 with *Black Ice Couloir*)

Permits: As above, a permit is required to camp on either of the approaches to this route.

Guidebook: *A Climber's Guide to the Teton Range; Fifty Favorite Climbs*

Route: Under the left edge of the spire's snow patch, start with six pitches of moderate fifth-class dihedrals that lead up and to the right of the Wiessner Overhang. Easy slabs, with bolts at the belays, run up left of the snow patch. A traverse above the snow takes one to the crux pitches, which weave through the overhangs above. The hardest two pitches require delicate thin-hold climbing. At this writing, four pitches are protected partly by fixed pitons. Follow the easy summit ridge to the highest point. Because of the traverses on this route, the best descent is to rappel the 1956 west face route.

First Ascent: Raffi Bedayan and Jack Arnold, August 1940

Difficulty: D, IV, 5.6, 2,200 feet

Guidebook: *Bugaboo Rock*; *The Bugaboos*

Permits: A fee is charged for staying at the Kain Hut or for camping within Bugaboo Glacier Provincial Park.

The west face of the Grand Teton. The original Durrance/Coulter route enters from the left, while the *Black Ice* variation is at the right. PHOTO BY LEIGH ORTENBURGER.

SNOWPATCH SPIRE (10,053 feet/3,063 meters)
Southeast Corner

Since the first ascent of Snowpatch Spire, granite climbers of every generation have found routes on this tower to match their aspirations, from aid walls to free climbs of every difficulty. This original route is still a popular outing, and at nearly 20 pitches it is long enough to require efficient climbing to avoid a night out.

Approach: The Bugaboos tower beyond the end of a long dirt road west of Spillamacheen, British Columbia. The steep approach hike takes half a day. One can camp either at the ACC's comfy Kain Hut or higher and cheaper at a bench known as Applebee. Take care here to sequester food from marmots.

Snowpatch Spire from the east. PHOTO BY CHRIS ATKINSON.

CHAPTER 8

Busting Through "Impossible"

When World War II ended, Americans erupted in total celebration. It seemed their determination, industry and technology had righted the world and put the future into their hands. Americans applied their technical and industrial momentum to all manner of challenges, and postwar climbers quickly took this pluck and enthusiasm to the mountains.

Many of America's best climbers had served in the Army's 10th Mountain Division, and their mountaineering skills proved decisive in battles in the Italian Alps. Early in the war, Japan had captured the Philippines—the world's primary source for manila rope fibers—and the American military urgently commissioned nylon ropes for its mountain troops. Nylon ropes proved to be superior in almost every way, from strength, stretch and water resistance to reduced friction. Nylon fabric also was made into lightweight tents and ponchos. Climbers Bill House, Dick Leonard and Arnold Wexler all worked with the military to develop this gear.

The Army ended the war with plenty of left-over nylon goods and hardware, including

pitons, carabiners, down sleeping bags, helmets, ice axes and protective clothing, and they made this surplus available for modest prices in stores around the country. As a result, many climbing camps of this period looked like military outposts. Using the new ropes, civilian climbers gained confidence in belaying and leading steep walls. Falling still entailed a serious risk, but no longer was there much fear of breaking a rope. With the new, lighter equipment on their backs and new roads pressing closer to the mountains, climbers were freed from the hassle and expense of approaches with pack animals or multiple carries.

Mountaineers after the war also began to climb in a new type of boot, featuring lugged soles of composite rubber. Italian Vito Bramani developed the new sole just before the war. Charlie Houston and Bob Bates had come across Bramani-soled boots in Europe in 1939, and they instantly saw the superiority of "Vibram" compared with nailed soles. The blocky rubber gripped much better on wet or dirty rock, and the nail-less soles were much lighter. Vibram soles did not serve so well on hard snow or ice, but climbers quickly started depending more on crampons, which eventually led to a revolution in ice climbing. After the war, Army-surplus boots

↻ Yvon Chouinard sorting hardware at Camp 4, Yosemite Valley, in the 1960s. COURTESY PATAGONIA HISTORICAL ARCHIVE COLLECTION.

with similar soles became available, but discriminating climbers imported European models. Lightweight *Kletterschue* with thin Vibram soles became *de rigueur* for pure rock climbing.

As Americans' new fascination with technology spilled into climbing, mountaineers found that the engineering approach worked particularly well on vertiginous rock and expeditionary sieges. Yet for the finest climbers the game remained more art than science, a matter of following passion and balancing it with technical logic and a gambler's instinct for the limits of acceptable risk.

Many experienced climbers did not like the trend toward what they saw as daredevil climbing. In 1947, 15 climbers died in climbing-related accidents in North America—a new high. The following year even more perished. The older generation was appalled. Walter Wood, president of the American Alpine Club, issued "An Appeal to Reason." He insisted that "the mountaineers of the country have a moral responsibility to exert every effort toward guiding the climbing cadets into the ranks of true mountaineers." Many no doubt inferred that Wood's "true mountaineers" would be climbers of his mold, with geographic exploration as their main calling—prudent people who avoid "unreasonable" terrain.

Another warning came from Hassler Whitney, one of the most talented rock climbers of Harvard's pre-war generation. He maintained through the 1950s that belaying the leader gave a false sense of security. As he had so ably demonstrated in his prime, when lead climbers used few or no pitons and did not trust a rope to hold a serious fall, the crucial matter was to succeed with certainty or to retreat. More than a few young climbers of this time headed up steep walls with more enthusiasm than security, and indeed some accidents were caused by failures in technique.

But skilled use of the new gear promised to help crack tougher climbs, and as the new equipment, techniques and terrain became more familiar through the 1950s, the older generation's calls to climb traditionally began

to gather dust in mountaineering's attic. The youthful drive to explore prevailed, and adventure was again redefined by those who would have it. Much of this post-war progress came through university clubs, especially those at Harvard and Dartmouth, as well as new clubs in California at Stanford and UCLA.

As Fred Beckey wrote of this period—and in fact helped to prove himself—the rate of progress into steep, technical uncertainty accelerated at such a pace that "'impossible' became a pedantic term."

Back to the Mountains, ASAP

A few people returned to climbing even before the war in the Pacific was over. In the summer of 1945, Shawangunks pioneer Hans Kraus and partners climbed a variety of new routes in the Wind River Range, including a long, interesting rock route on Mt. Helen. Andy and Elizabeth Kauffman, Maynard Miller and Norman Brewster initiated a Harvard renaissance in the Selkirks with an excellent new route up the north ridge of Mt. Swanzy, near Rogers Pass. At first Swanzy's summit block seemed insurmountable, but Miller succeeded by leading "a narrow, evil crack running perpendicularly up the east side of this obstacle."

A week after the Japanese surrender, Fred Beckey exploded out of the gate. With Jack Schwabland and Bill Granston, he went to climb the hanging Price Glacier on the steep and hidden northeast flank of Mt. Shuksan. The three had a tough time finding a way up steep slopes between crevasses and seracs, and they deployed many belays from chopped stances backed up with rammed axes. Beckey led a final headwall of glare ice. As the sun set they kept going over the summit, and in darkness they hoofed it to the trailhead on the opposite side. This was the toughest snow and ice route yet done in the United States, but for Beckey it was just a springboard into the next generation of big, wild routes.

The next summer, Beckey mounted essentially the first climbing trip since John Muir's in 1879 to the Stikine area of southeast

Approaching Devils Thumb. Beckey's first ascent route gained the east ridge (facing the camera) from the left.
PHOTO COURTESY ANDY WIESSNER.

Alaska, to try the almost mythical horn of Devils Thumb. He recruited two of the three climbers who had scouted the peak in 1937: Donald Brown and none other than Fritz Wiessner. Unfortunately, Wiessner wrenched his knee while ferrying loads out of the Stikine canyon, and he had to give up the trip. Back in Petersburg, Beckey sent telegrams that convinced Seattle climbers Bob Craig and Clifford Schmidtke to join him.

Before Beckey and his new partners tackled Devils Thumb, they made a snow and ice climb up Kate's Needle, the highest peak in the vicinity, at 10,002 feet. Their views of Devils Thumb showed only one reasonable route, especially for the limited windows of good weather that they might hope for: Avalanche-prone slopes led to the east ridge, where a rocky arête pasted with ice looked possible. Twice, the slow, difficult climbing met with storms that forced retreat. But just as their schedule and basecamp supplies dwindled to a couple of days, high pressure moved in. With previous knowledge of half

the route and a 3 a.m. start, the threesome reached the ridgecrest with August 25 still young. Beckey resorted to some aid around granite gendarmes with huge air below his feet, but after almost two months in the area, they finally reached the top in one long day. This was a breakthrough technical climb in the Alaskan environment, and soon afterward Beckey wrote, "It's the hardest climb I've ever done." Of course, harder climbs were still to come for Beckey, but no one else would brave Devils Thumb for another 24 years.

Beckey wasted no time heading for his next project. Right after he returned to Seattle, in September 1946, he and two others hiked for two days from the east side of the Cascades to make the first ascent of the comparatively modest but beautiful granitic tower of Liberty Bell.

In August 1948, Beckey climbed the north ridge of Mt. Baker, with cousins Ralph and Dick Widrig. The three stayed up late chatting below treeline at the old Kulshan Cabin, and before dawn Ralph had to drag a sleepy Fred into the day. As they crossed the Coleman Glacier and gained the ridge, the sun turned hot, but they quickly got after the business of hewing steps into ice hidden below a coat of snow. An epaulet of ice near the top presented the main challenge, and the climbers chopped carefully over 60-degree ground for two pitches. The belayer braced in an excavated seat while tied to a barbed, soft-iron ice piton. Ten hours after leaving the cabin, they stood on top.

Even though Beckey's resume of conquests was already the most impressive in North America, he wouldn't rest for a moment—what mattered to him was the essentially infinite number of unclimbed peaks and routes. He built an intensive mountaineering lifestyle, taking advantage of weather patterns as best he could. He started fitting in major trips to the far north, British Columbia and the Cascades in a single year, and usually began or ended each season with new routes in the Rockies and the Sierra.

A natural salesman, Beckey earned money during winters by working at department stores (a great place to meet women, he would confide), promoting ski films or wholesaling commodities such as paper and farm equipment. But during the high-sun months his life was a frenetic carom between climbing objectives. He plowed through countless long-distance drives, pausing only to make calls to check on the weather and to lock in partners for trips three and four down his calendar. Using hard-sell tactics, he became as tenacious on the phone as on the lead, plying partners with persistent descriptions of a superb objective, often without divulging its name or location. No one would know everywhere he'd been until the next year's *AAJ* came out—and that only included his successes.

Could even the most awed of Fred Beckey's post-war peers have predicted that his climbing would extend—with dedication and intensity—into the 21st century? His name is attached to pioneering climbs on almost every range on the continent, and at this writing he's still adding to the list. Yet Beckey's obsession has always been tempered with patience and an unquestioned willingness to retreat if something doesn't seem right. Dedicated as he is, Beckey also maintains a realistic perspective of how climbing fits into the broad scale of things, saying, "What does it matter whether it's a first ascent except to yourself or a few people?"

Evolution in the Rockies

Climbers in the Rockies also were exploring precipitous new possibilities. In Colorado's San Juan Mountains in 1947, Joe Stettner led John Speck and Jack Fralick up the 1,200-foot east face of Monitor Peak, a steep wall with few breaks. Stettner placed 19 pitons, including one for a pendulum. Three hundred feet from the summit, darkness forced them to spend a rainy night crowding under Stettner's jacket. In the still-cloudy morning, Stettner led one of the longest and most difficult pitches of his career. In fact, Speck had to

Bob Craig on the west ridge of Kate's Needle. PHOTO BY FRED BECKEY.

Fred Beckey. PHOTO BY JIM STUART. COURTESY STEVE ROPER, THE *ASCENT* COLLECTION.

move his belay to give Stettner an additional 20 feet of rope to reach a stance. Although Monitor's rock is not solid, this route is still considered one of the classics of the Colorado backcountry.

During this same August, two of the grandest of grand British climbers reluctantly employed hardware to climb an irresistibly geometric rock peak in the Canadian Rockies. Himalayan pioneers Frank Smythe and Noel Odell went with J. Ross to climb Mt. Colin, a sculpted fan of upturned strata near Jasper. They moved admirably up the northwest ridge, but near the summit an overhang blocked their way. A ledge allowed them to traverse onto the southwest face, but regaining the ridge required some steep, delicate climbing. Here Smythe resorted to hammering in a protection piton, the only one of his career. This indirect aid allowed them to continue to the first ascent of the peak. Smythe later referred to his delight at the peak and

his misgivings for the piton as "the success and failure of Mt. Colin."

Nearby, an even steeper rocky mount was proving resistant to all comers. Brussels Peak had seen attempts by A. J. Ostheimer, Sterling Hendricks, Bob Hind, Fred Beckey and others. Smythe tried it in 1946 but found that all the options "invariably end in overhanging rocks." Two prolific Sierra Club climbers, John and Ruth Mendenhall, came in 1948, but they also backed off, saying that bolts might be necessary and that, "It seemed wise to leave the climbing to braver, better-equipped men." While hiking out, they met a party of four other Americans hiking in: Jack Lewis, a young Teton guide; Ray Garner of Arizona's Kachina Mountaineering Club and his wife; and Ed George. In addition to an array of pitons, this team carried bolts. Garner had arranged for sponsorship from a New York foundation in return for making a 16mm film to be titled *First Ascent*.

Brussels Peak from the northeast. The controversial Garner-Lewis first ascent climbed along the sun-shade line. PHOTO BY LARRY STANIER.

Their climb became a flashpoint in Canada over the use of anchors in mountaineering. The facts and Garner's description of the climb hint that his team's confidence was based at least partly on the potential to sink a "tamp-in" (bolt) wherever they wanted. Before they even reached previous climbers' high point, they placed Canada's first bolt, and as they continued over the towers of the ridge they drove plenty of pitons and two more bolts. When the first day grew short, they retreated and left a rope hanging off a crux overhang.

The next day remained clear, but the group rested. The day after that, with the weather threatening, they returned with difficulty to their high point. Lewis led on, struggling up a chimney through an overhang. Garner described him using "what we like to call the 'flesh crawl' technique.... His legs stuck out into the air. When he finally grunted past it he drilled a hole and placed a tamp."

Soon heavy rain began to fall, and they cowered amid lightning strikes. To avoid attracting the current they hung their ironware off the edge, but when the storm passed and they tried to retrieve it a knot failed and the hardware all went clanging down the face. Luckily, George had some pitons left, but as they hauled these up they got stuck, and George had to climb unbelayed to free them. Though the weather threatened again, Garner and Lewis continued upward. In two more pitches they made the top. A blizzard pelted them as they returned to a shivering Ed George, and they struggled down to the notch where Garner's wife had the stove going.

Among the many traditional climbers who were offended by the style of this ascent, Frank Smythe wrote, "I still regard Mt. Brussels as unclimbed, and my feelings are no different from those I should have were I to hear that a helicopter was to deposit its passenger on the summit." The tactics inspired Bob Hind, a prominent, tradition-minded Canadian, to write a mocking satire in the 1951 *Canadian Alpine Journal.* "The Ascent of Dumbkopf Tower" not only described with alarm the evil frenzy of a mechanically minded climber, it also gave free air to the prejudice that associated technical climbing with Teutonic fanatics, even Nazism. Hind's protagonist was "Aldorf Hilter," and he went about the climb of Dumbkopf Tower with a mythical "spring anchor" device for cracks, a "Boltsetter" for instant bolts and a plethora of pitons. Through a mélange of technical tricks, Hilter and his partner conquered the virgin summit, where Hilter "pulled out a small red flag with a queer black crooked cross in the center.... 'I like to leave them around,' he said shame-facedly. 'It reminds me of old times.'"

Hindsight now gives us a broader perspective on this tempest. Lewis and Garner were admirably determined, but they were not the best ambassadors of technical climbing. To Canadians who had not yet seen how a practiced cragsman could flow up a cliff, their dependence on hardware seemed like an outrage that, if allowed to spread, would threat-en to divert climbers from "real" climbing skills. Vancouver climber Art Cooper said, "I have no use for this modern mechanical climbing—driving bolts and nails and pitons into rock. If you can't climb a thing with your two bare hands, forget it." Canadians also had plenty of easier routes on unexplored mountains to tackle. As Cooper put it, "I spent a lifetime climbing around [Vancouver] and I haven't touched half of it."

Climbers from more intensively developed areas, however, knew that pitons and even bolts weren't necessarily a crutch for the feeble but a tool for the skilled. In the years to follow, climbers who had honed their skills on steep crags would climb Brussels with relative ease and few pitons.

Virtuosos of the Steep

The Tetons and California were the continent's postwar hot spots for technical climbing. A year after climbing Mt. Brussels, Ray Garner convinced two Teton guides, Art Gilkey and Dick Pownall, that it was time to complete the north face of the Grand Teton by finishing the final headwall. The pitches Durrance and Petzoldt had led 13 years before were still difficult, and it was four in the afternoon before this 1949 team reached the old high point (the top of the third ramp). Pownall then led some of the most brilliant pitches of his fine career. First was a chimney to a ledge, at the end of which he lowered off a piton and swung into a crack where he could place another aid piton. A tension traverse got him to a shallow chimney that he climbed to the face's fourth ramp. With a rucksack hindering him, Garner could hardly believe what small holds he had to use as he struggled to follow. After a few more pitches of easier ground, the trio completed the Grand's north face at 10 p.m.

In California, one man was most responsible for restarting climbing's evolution after the war interlude: John Salathé. A Swiss iron-worker, Salathé immigrated to California during the Depression but didn't take up climbing until 1945, at age 45. He joined the Rock Climbing Section of the Sierra Club and started making stronger pitons, using carbon steel and a better heat treatment. Unlike the softer pitons of European tradition, Salathé's could be driven into narrow cracks in Yosemite's hard granite. Moreover, they could be whacked out and re-placed many times before they broke down. With such reliable and reusable hardware, Salathé began to plan longer and steeper routes.

In 1946, Salathé and his friend Anton "Ax" Nelson succeeded on a climb that a number of 1930s teams had found too severe, the southwest face of Half Dome. This was the first new route up Half Dome since George Anderson's, and its steep, smooth cracks required extensive direct aid on Salathé's pitons. They also made use of the prusik knot, a sliding/gripping hitch that allowed a climber to ascend the leader's rope. With this climb and its techniques as a model, "sixth class" climbing in Yosemite took off. A year later, Salathé and Nelson succeeded on the stunning Lost Arrow. Many climbers around the continent assumed that piton engineering was the primary skill involved in such ascents, but Yosemite regulars knew these climbs required a lot of toil and free climbing, especially in the strenuous chimneys.

In 1950, a group of RCS members climbed Castle Rock Spire, a Lost Arrow-like needle in Sequoia National Park. This was the first climb using Yosemite's high-angle methods in a remote location. Allen Steck, a member of this team, was fired up not only by the potential for new rock routes but also by alpine walls. He had been one of the first Americans to make a postwar climbing pilgrimage to Europe, where he learned the game swiftly enough to complete one of the Alps' major rock testpieces, the overhanging north face of the Cima Grande.

A couple of months after the Castle Rock Spire climb, Steck and Salathé teamed up for the oft-tried north face of Yosemite's Sentinel Rock. Despite sharing just a gallon of water between them over five sweltering days, they succeeded with strenuous chimney wrestling and aid on pitons and bolts. When some implied that such a climb was too technical, Steck, who knew there was much more than rote engineering involved, nevertheless responded, "Well, we are a technical society."

Barely a week after climbing Sentinel, Steck joined seven Sierra Club buddies for an expedition to try new routes up Mt. Waddington. The two who organized this trip, Richard Houston and Oscar Cook, had in 1947 found a lake where they could be landed by floatplane, just two days' walk from the Tiedemann Glacier. Following this plan, all eight Sierrans were perched at the 12,000-foot col below Waddington's summit tower only eight days after leaving Vancouver. A reconnaissance of the tower left them discouraged, but two vaguely possible routes suggested they split into two teams of four.

Bill Long, Ray De Saussure, Cook and Houston headed up to the notch below the southeast prow of the tower. An icy chimney loomed "unusually apparent and not very encouraging." However, banding in the gneiss disguised many holds, and Long cleared rime from enough edges and piton cracks to lead up the slot, passing three strenuous chockstones. A few more pitches of mixed climbing brought them to the top by 2:30 in the afternoon.

Around on the northeast face, where two 1934 parties had failed, Phil Bettler, Bill Dunmire, Jim Wilson and Steck were nearing the crest of the tower. They had been able to chop steps across steep snow and ice patches and connect sections of dry, sometimes loose rock. As the afternoon grew long, Dunmire and Wilson stayed behind on the summit ridge to allow Steck and Bettler to travel faster. As they approached the summit's final chimney, a gap 30 feet deep appeared at their feet. Steck was able to pendulum to the opposite wall and latch onto a knob, and from there they climbed up to see their friends' footsteps on the summit.

Thus after a couple of dozen attempts spanning almost three decades and yielding only two desperate successes, two teams in one day reached Waddington's summit by two new routes. For both teams, the ability to move over steep rock was so potent that they would declare their ascents were, by Yosemite standards, only moderately difficult. Within a couple of decades, the southeast chimney would become known as a "regular" route up Waddington, attainable by mortals with a well-rounded repertoire of skills.

Cragsmen Go High

In the 1950s, gymnastic, fair-weather climbing at accessible crags spread across America. In the east the centers were the quartzite balconies of the Shawangunks and the granitic ledges of New Hampshire. In Colorado it was the sandstone faces at Eldorado Canyon, the Flatirons and Garden of the Gods. In the Tetons it was a plethora of pinnacles and walls, especially in Cascade and Garnet canyons. Californians, of course, had Yosemite Valley and the crags and boulders near Los Angeles and Berkeley. Each

Climbing on the first ascent of the northeast face of Mt. Waddington's summit tower. PHOTO BY ALLEN STECK.

➲ Mark Landreville nearing the top of Mt. Waddington on the *Southeast Chimney Route*. PHOTO BY CARL DIEDRICH.

area allowed climbers to develop the joys of gymnastic ascent sheltered from alpine harshness.

The Sierra Club rating system soon expanded to accommodate the new climbs. At Tahquitz Rock in Southern California, the category "fifth class" now covered such a broad range of difficulties that Royal Robbins and Don Wilson decided in 1952 to add so-called "decimals" to indicate relative free-climbing challenge. Thus, a moderate pitch that required some piton protection might be 5.3, while a severe pitch might be rated 5.7 or even 5.9. This system soon was applied in Yosemite, and it spread to most other crag centers around the continent.

Crag climbers generally still thought of their game as practice for (or an offshoot of) mountain climbing. Their ultimate heroes remained the pioneers of fierce alpine north walls and Himalayan giants. But when these rock technicians took their new abilities to the mountains, they found scores of route opportunities their predecessors hadn't been able to consider.

Two dramatic technical achievements came in the Tetons in 1953. Guides Willi Unsoeld and Leigh Ortenburger and park ranger Richard Emerson went back to the north face of the Grand Teton, and where Pownall had needed a pendulum to cross blank rock high on the face, Emerson was able to use tiny holds to complete the traverse. A week later Emerson made a second breakthrough. Pioneering with Ortenburger and Don Decker, Emerson executed some crafty piton work and a wild pendulum to climb the huge and difficult south buttress of Mt. Moran.

Back in the Sierra, in the last wintry days of 1954, a pair of independent-minded Californians jokingly fancying themselves as Austrian alpinists made the first ascent of the northeast ridge of 14,375-foot Mt. Williamson, one of the longest ridges south of Alaska. Warren Harding and John Ohrenschall started from the ridge's toe at 6,000 feet, and their four-day odyssey to the summit—at least 9,000 feet of total gain over more than five miles of ridge—became a Sierra legend. On

their third day a fierce storm blew in, and as snow plastered the rock they resorted to frequent aid and rappels to pass towers that wouldn't even require a rope when dry. It was two more days before they could reach the main summit and bushwhack, soaking wet, back to their car.

In 1955, another team of Americans succeeded on one of Canada's longstanding challenges, Mt. Robson's *Wishbone Arête*. Since Walter Schauffelberger led to within a few hundred feet of the top in 1913, as many as 30 attempts had failed in the face of dozens of rock steps, icy rock and rime-feathered gargoyles. Don Claunch, a tiger from the Cascades, was touring the Canadian ranges that summer, and in early August he met a group of student climbers from Los Angeles. Among them were Mike Sherrick, a talented cragsman, and medical student Harvey Firestone. The three decided to try the *Wishbone*.

These climbers knew enough of alpine tactics to pare weight and prepare to suffer. At the base of the arête, 5,000 feet below the summit, they packed only their climbing gear and a small tent, some nuts and raisins, and candles. Sherrick's leads took them over most of the pure rock steps on the first day; he placed a dozen pitons and marveled at how Schauffelberger had led the same ground with no iron at all. By sunset they stopped at

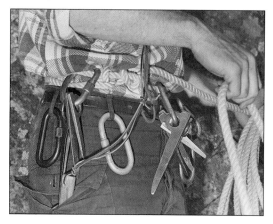

A Teton climber's rack ca. 1950, probably Richard Emerson's. PHOTO COURTESY JACKSON HOLE HISTORICAL SOCIETY AND MUSEUM.

Climbers starting up the northeast ridge of Mt. Williamson in winter. PHOTO BY ROBERT PARKER.

a small ledge at 11,500 feet, not far below the *Wishbone's* juncture. After a night of shivering, Claunch took over most of the leads on icier ground. Climbing with crampons on both rock and frozen snow, he arrived at the ridge's infamous gargoyles. Rime and ice in bizarre shapes and consistencies crusted big mushrooms of snow, making all movement insecure. Darkness came again when they were just a few hundred feet below the top, and they spent another, even colder night. The weather remained clear, though, and in the morning Claunch dug into his willpower to make one of the toughest leads of the climb, a 60-degree ice chute ending in a headwall of vertical rime. Of this pitch, he said, "It was a delightful feeling to drive in a long spiral piton and know it was secure." Not far beyond this they won the summit.

Enthusiasm for major climbs in Canada's outback also collected at the Stanford Alpine Club, and in 1957 John Harlin, Gary Hemming, Henry Kendall and Hobey DeStaebler shouldered big packs for a multi-day hike deep into the Selkirks. Chasing

Mike Sherrick leading on the first day of the first ascent of *Wishbone Arête*. PHOTO BY DON GORDON.

rumors of granitic peaks in the Battle Range, the foursome bushwhacked some 20 miles south from near Rogers Pass and then climbed over a high col to get to the Melville Group of peaks, where they'd arranged for an airdrop. They indeed found a superb alpine arête, the north ridge of Mt. Butters. This long knife-edge forced them to traverse mixed ground below its crest, and at the peak's headwall they had to take tension to reach a steep chimney that led to the top.

Unfortunately, their airdrop didn't arrive and they had to march back out after this first climb, hungry indeed. Harlin and Hemming would go on to make historic ascents in the Alps, and Kendall would later win the Nobel Prize in physics.

Canada Emerges

The technical climbing that Canadians had long scorned finally caught on in their mountains in the early 1950s, and ironically it was indeed Germanic climbers who sowed the seeds of progress. Leo Grillmair had gotten his first training in mountaineering as a soldier in the Third Reich. With postwar

opportunities slim in Austria, he convinced his friend Hans Gmoser to emigrate to Canada with him. In 1952 the pair visited a rock peak that Gmoser had seen at the foot of the Rockies while hitchhiking out of Calgary. On the broad southeast wall of Mt. John Laurie (now called Yamnuska) they found a steep, blocky chimney and climbed it without pitons. Gmoser wrote to other buddies in Austria that higher wages and unclimbed limestone walls in Canada made for an exciting new life.

Franz Dopf heeded Gmoser's call, and over the next decade these partners and other immigrants would bring the European standard of rock climbing to the Rockies. Mt. Edith, Mt. Louis, Sunburst Peak and other steep peaks attracted their expertise, but they developed their most famous routes on Yamnuska's 1,000- to 1,500-foot-high wall. In 1953, Gmoser and Dopf completed the *Calgary Route*, which required a few pitons for protection. Following a vision of climbing ideal descended from the 1930s master of alpine rock Emilio Comici, they next plotted a *direttissima*, the direct line that, as Comici

Leo Grillmair. COURTESY LEO GRILLMAIR.

Hans Gmoser. PHOTO COURTESY WHYTE MUSEUM OF THE CANADIAN ROCKIES.

put it, "a water-drop would take falling from the summit." In 1956, Gmoser and Dopf aimed for a prominent corner system dropping from near Yamnuska's highest point, but they couldn't find enough holds on the steep headwall and retreated.

In Austria such climbs would have been commonplace, but many Canadians once again rose to confront a perceived threat to their climbing values. They characterized the Austrian style as emotionless, mechanical and motivated by showboating. Gmoser answered in humanistic terms, writing that what was most important was that they were transcending the meanness of society:

> We wanted to inhale and breathe life again.... We were rebelling against an existence full of distorted values, against an existence where a man is judged by the size of his living room, by the amount of chromium on his car. But here we were ourselves again; simple and pure.... We were ready to trust each other, help each other and give to each other our everything.
>
> This mountain to us is not a sports arena. To us it is a symbol of truth and a symbol of life as it should be. This mountain teaches us that we should endure hardships and…not drift along the easy way, which always leads down.

Dopf, recalling Canadian climbers who threatened to remove all of his and his friends' pitons, retorted, "The places that we put a piton in they wouldn't even get to." His antagonists found that he was right, and it was this fact—that occasional protection anchors inspire skilled climbing up terrain otherwise unimaginable—that gradually brought the piton-haters to accept hardware as a tool not of decay but of advancement.

Don Morrison, a British climber who moved to the Calgary area briefly, also showed what a solid cragging background could achieve. He teamed with Calgary local Jim Tarrant in 1955, and Morrison led the whole way up the 3,300-foot northeast buttress of Odaray Mountain. Although Morrison did not place a single piton, he pulled through overhangs and sustained difficulties now rated up to 5.7. Gmoser called this "one of the most formidable climbs in the country."

In September 1957, Gmoser, Dopf and Heinz Kahl returned to Yamnuska to try their direct route for the third time. Kahl, who had immigrated to Canada in 1955, led the hardest overhangs, and they celebrated the finale with an ecstatic embrace. For younger climbers, the route *Direttissima* pointed the way to what was possible, and it remains one of the historic climbs of Canada.

Abilities were improving so quickly that Brussels Peak, the stumper of the 1940s, no longer seemed like a serious challenge. Californian Mark Powell handily led the second ascent of the Lewis-Garner route in 1955, and a few years later Gmoser and Kahl climbed this route, pointedly avoided the bolts, and used only four pitons for the whole ascent.

Brian Greenwood, wearing his "Alpine Guide" badge.
PHOTO BY GLEN BOLES.

It was another British immigrant who would finish ushering Canadian climbing into the modern era. Brian Greenwood learned to climb soon after he came to Calgary in 1955 at age 21, and just two years later he made his first new route on Yamnuska. He called the steep, 5.8 corner system *Belfry*, and for some of his protection he placed wedged machine nuts, probably the first time hammerless hardware was used in North America. Greenwood would dominate new-route development on Yamnuska through 1975, establishing a total of 13 new lines. In 1959, he came to the Bugaboos and met Fred Beckey and Hank Mather, who were working on the big, steep east face of Snowpatch Spire. Beckey decided to take a break from the daily toil of aid, prusiking and fixing rope on this relentless wall, and he joined Greenwood for a mostly free new route on Snowpatch's west face. The two dynamos needed just one day and a bit of aid.

By 1960, the camaraderie of the rope and the beer mug had bridged the ethical and ethnic divides among Calgary climbers, and various European immigrants around Calgary started the Calgary Mountain Club (another CMC). With experience and talent straight from the climbing centers in Britain and the Alps, this group got right down to the real business of climbing and fraternizing. Some would later describe their coalition as "a drinking club with a climbing problem," but with Greenwood's example the CMC laid the foundation for Canadians to take on some of the continent's most demanding alpine faces.

Beyond Yosemite

After Warren Harding drilled through the night to finish El Capitan's Nose route in late 1958, some Yosemite climbers—especially Harding—began to seek out High Sierra peaks to apply big-wall techniques. In northern Yosemite, one highly visible wall was the 1,000-foot-high south face of Mt. Conness. In 1959, Don Goodrich attempted this climb but fell off with a loose block and was killed. Harding, Glen Denny and Herb Swedlund

returned to the face later that summer. Goodrich's blood marked the route with a long stain, and as Swedlund led through this section his stomach turned and his ambition waned. He let Harding and Denny take the lead, and after three days they topped out.

The following July, two teams climbed major granite walls in the Mt. Whitney cirque. South African Denis Rutovitz and Pole Andrzej Ehrenfeucht climbed the full east face of Mt. Whitney, using occasional aid pitons and a bolt ladder to avoid an overhanging wide crack. Soon after this, Harding and Denny went to Keeler Needle, a 1,400-foot-high wall on a stunning *aiguille* next to Whitney. Harding's main goal in climbing was to have a good time, and he was famous for his lighthearted dedication to the enterprise he labeled "basically absurd." With this approach in mind, he invited two utter novices—Rob McKnight and Desert ("I never did get his last name") Frank because "they were good wine drinkers, and we all got along." Harding led all the pitches up Keeler Needle over another three-day ascent, and Denny coached the others as they followed, often with prusiks.

In 1959, Ray Northcutt and Layton Kor brought Yosemite-style climbing to the Colorado Rockies with an ascent of the lower half of the east face of Longs Peak, up to Broadway Ledge. Above this rises a plumb, 950-foot-high shield known as the Diamond—the steepest wall of alpine granite in the Lower 48. Boulder climber Dale Johnson first asked the National Park Service about climbing the Diamond in 1954, but park officials feared they would be unable to rescue an injured climber and announced that no one would be allowed to try it. It was six years before officials relented. In 1960, Californians Bob Kamps and Dave Rearick had just repeated the Northcutt-Kor route on the lower east face when the National Park Service suddenly announced that applications for climbing the Diamond would be accepted. Using substantial direct aid and a few fixed ropes, they were able to complete the first ascent of the wall via a route that came to be known as *D1*.

John Salathé and Yvon Chouinard in Camp 4, Yosemite Valley, 1961. PHOTO BY TOM FROST.

Roving Masters

During these years, a youth named Yvon Chouinard began to appear at many of North America's climbing centers. A French-Canadian born in Maine, Chouinard and his family moved to Southern California while he was still in grade school. He didn't fit in well, partly because he had yet to master English, and he took to hiking in the hills. At age 16 he joined a group trip to the Wind Rivers, the first real mountains he had seen. Chouinard broke away from this group to attempt a route on the west face of Gannett Peak, and somehow he succeeded even though he had only work boots and no ice axe. The high terrain got Chouinard's blood going, and from the Winds he went straight to the Tetons. Back in California, he decided that mountains and climbing would be his life.

Seeking to sustain a lifestyle with little distraction of employment, Chouinard made a summer basecamp below the Tetons in an old incinerator. He subsisted on "a mostly oatmeal diet...supplemented with the occasional poached (not a cooking term) fool's hen, marmot or porcupine. On special days there was spaghetti with a can of cat tuna." In 1957, at age 18, he borrowed about $800 from his parents to buy a portable forge to make pitons, and he began to earn money by traveling between the various climbing centers and selling hardware. Later he would procure a die from Alcoa to make carabiners. He became a keen observer of climbers' practices, but he never became attached to one area's methods or cliques.

In 1959, Chouinard went to Yosemite and saw that the firm rock and reliable weather made an outstanding laboratory for technical climbing. However, his instincts told him that the ultimate climbs would not be mere technical ascents but technical ascents in a high and demanding environment, like the big north walls of the Alps. The next year he went to Canada and saw such a challenge, the north face of Mt. Edith Cavell. The weather stayed bad, however, so he returned to the Tetons and met up with Yosemite climbers Royal Robbins and Joe Fitschen.

The big news in the Tetons was that Leigh and Irene Ortenburger and Dave Dornan had put up a steep, icy chimney route on the northwest side of the Grand Teton. A week afterward, Leigh Ortenburger, Pete Sinclair and Jake Breitenbach discovered a chain of sloping ledges that simplified the approach to the remote northwest face, a link soon labeled the Valhalla Traverse. Chouinard, Robbins and Fitschen followed this approach and repeated the Northwest Chimney all free, and then traversed right and finished their climb with the upper pitches of Durrance's west face route. Both Northwest Chimney ascents reached a new level of technical alpine difficulty for North America, taking on very steep terrain with a variety of challenges, including icy rock climbed with crampons, tenuous face climbing and complex routefinding.

An Amazing Season

The next year, Chouinard hooked up with Fred Beckey for what would be the era's landmark season. They started with the north face of Edith Cavell. For this climb, they teamed up with Dan Doody, a Teton climber who had collected sponsorship from the Canadian National Railway by promising a tourism-promoting film of Eigerwand-like climbing. The itinerant climbers waited out storms as honored guests at the CNR's deluxe Jasper Park Lodge. The hotel had a strict dress code, and since the trio owned only a single sport coat, they dined one at a time. Rain and storm persisted for days, and the three started to feel some pressure to produce a climb and a film. With a forecast for a brief window of good weather before another storm, they went for it.

They aimed for the face's steepest quartzite rib, which descends directly off the summit. Beckey led much of the way on the relatively easy first day. An approaching warm front loosened plenty of rockfall that whistled and crashed past them. They belayed at sheltered spots as much as possible and then sprinted through exposed areas. They continued into the night, finally reaching snow ledges for a bivouac at midnight, 1,000 feet below the top.

At dawn the storm broke. Chouinard took over the lead as rain, hail, flashes of lightning and crashes of thunder exploded around them. The icefield capping the summit had promised easier going, but loose graupel and hail lay over hard ice, and Chouinard had to tediously chop scores of steps. The final summit rocks turned out to be rotten, steep shale, and the trio's dire insecurity continued right to the top. But soon the region's first real *Nordwand* had been won, and the three descended the east ridge with great respect for the peak and for each other. They also looked askance at the temptations of sponsorship and how it and the film had pressured their judgment.

Beckey and Chouinard took the train south to the Selkirks, aiming for a north wall that had been on Beckey's list since his first year of climbing, the north face of Mt. Sir Donald. They found relatively firm quartzite layered with in-cut ledges, and Beckey wrote that it was "almost monotonous" as they repeatedly pulled up the ladder-like holds. Mindful of the safety inherent in moving fast, they climbed much of the face unroped, despite severe exposure and difficulty continuously at their limit for unroped travel, though they did belay at an overhang with loose blocks. The feared rockfall never came, and they reached the northwest ridge just below the summit only five hours after starting. Their bold approach, tempered by caution where it was really warranted, made a steep, 2,500-foot alpine face into a moderate day.

Next the pair went to the Bugaboos, where, two years before, Beckey, Herb Staley and John Rupley had glimpsed the awesome west side of the Howser Spires. Beckey later wrote, "The Howsers looked like Fitz Roy and Cerro Torre and their satellites all grouped together." This was the most sustained sweep of granite anyone had yet contemplated north of Yosemite, and a buttress reaching out from South Howser looked particularly stunning. They would need both Beckey's meticulous planning and Chouinard's technical wizardry. His new pitons—from wafer-thin knifeblades with an offset eye to big, aluminum "bong-bongs" for wide cracks—would be invaluable.

The Howser Towers from the west. Beckey and Chouinard climbed the sunlit prow on the right (south) tower. PHOTO BY CHRIS ATKINSON.

Beckey and Chouinard warmed up with three preliminary outings: a new route on Pigeon Spire's north face, then a circumnavigation of the entire Howser massif, and then the first ascent of their expected descent route from South Howser, the rocky and icy east face. This climb confirmed that they could descend in light *Kletterschue* and thus leave their heavy alpine gear at the base of the west buttress; afterward, they would borrow boots and ice axes to retrieve their equipment.

They gave themselves a jump on the big buttress by climbing a couple of pitches in the afternoon, leaving two ropes hanging to hasten their start the next day. In the morning, as Chouinard prusiked up, he found to his horror that a rodent had chewed into one of the ropes. After this scary start, however, the excellent rock and their practiced technique allowed them to climb 13 more pitches that day, about half of them with some direct aid. They used Yosemite wall methods the whole way, as the leader hauled

his pack on a spare rope and the follower came up using prusiks on steeper pitches. After a modestly uncomfortable bivouac, they finished the striking "white headwall" cracks with eight more fifth- and sixth-class pitches. A few hundred feet of easier ground put them on top. In Beckey's words, "Here was a climb of high Yosemite standards, almost 2,500 feet in height, and subject to all the dangers of mountaineering in an alpine range."

To finish off their summer, Beckey and Chouinard went south to meet Bill Buckingham and East Coast climbers Art Gran and John Hudson in America's perennially "secret" granite hideaway, the southern Wind Rivers. They focused on two very steep walls: the "impossible" northwest face of East Temple and the north face of Lost Temple .

The next summer, in July 1962, Beckey joined two other greats of this period, Brian Greenwood and Don Gordon (formerly Don Claunch—he changed his name around 1960), to hike into the Rampart Range, the spectacular quartzite chain south of Jasper. As they toured an area where no modern climbers had yet ventured, they unanimously agreed that the east prow of Oubliette was "perhaps the finest example of mountain architecture in an area full of classic lines." By starting unroped to gain as much height as possible before the warming day brought rockfall, they reached a snowy ledge that allowed them to traverse out to the east face proper. The steep rock proved to be excellent gneiss and quartzite, interspersed with dark strata of rotten shale. On one section, Beckey led an awful, decaying chimney, and on the very next pitch Greenwood led over very steep, superb quartzite. Fine rock continued to inspire them to move quickly, and they reached the summit just before dark. Luckily they found a fairly quick way to Oubliette's prominent descent chute and made it down without incident.

Coast Mountains Galore

In 1959, an unusual 19-year-old from Vancouver toured and climbed alone for a month in the Coast Mountains. So powerful was the experience that Dick Culbert decided to dedicate as much time as he could to climbing in this region, and to write a guidebook. In 1962, Glenn Woodsworth joined Culbert's scheme, and the two made dozens of first ascents of peaks. Both were gifted technical climbers, very familiar with the Squamish Chief. Culbert hatched a plan in 1964 to grubstake a climbing summer by making use of government incentives to prospect for minerals. They studied for and passed the geologic tests, and a summer's expense account was theirs. Their biggest goal was the last unclimbed major summit in the Waddington area, the intimidating tooth of Serra V.

Culbert and Woodsworth spent much of their stipend on chartering a ski plane to put them in position for Serra's north face. Woodsworth led as they swiftly climbed through an icefall and crevassed ice face littered with avalanche debris. At a more mature age Woodsworth would say, "It was not a good choice of route…. In hindsight it

was stupid." Nevertheless, by 3:30 p.m. they reached the Serra-Asperity Col. A storm was closing in, but with the top still visible they climbed excellent rock and then donned crampons to veer onto the spire's north face, where the granite was less steep but iced up. The storm came down in full fury as Culbert led to the top at 8 p.m. Rappels and traverses took hours in the blizzard, and it was midnight before they settled into a bivouac at the col. With new snow blanketing the terrain, their next day's descent was harrowing, but they got down safely. Many have since decided that Serra V is a summit even more inaccessible than Waddington. As for Woodsworth and Culbert, this was just the start of a five-week tour during which they climbed "dozens of first ascents" on their way back to the Bluff Lake outpost on the east side of the range.

Canadian Rocky Walls

As word of the Edith Cavell ascent spread, brave climbers began to aspire to other Eigerwand-like faces of the Canadian Rockies. The next major wall fell to a trio of "Vulgarians," a brazenly irreverent association of young East Coast rock climbers. Art Gran was a lead Vulgarian, and though he was most known as a Shawangunks cragsman, he considered summer trips to the Canadian Rockies a crucial part of his climbing career. In 1965, he convinced John Hudson and Pete Geiser to try the 5,000-foot-high east face of Mt. Chephren, a towering wall in plain view from the Icefields Parkway. They chose to go as a party of three, in part because they anticipated bad rock and would need more strength if they had to retreat in case of an injury.

Indeed, they dodged whistling stones and pulled off many holds on the route. At one point Gran felt his footholds give way and he tumbled for 60 feet, coming to a sliding stop by virtue of an ice-axe arrest in shale scree. After a night below the steep headwall crux, they used some aid as well as good routefinding luck to summit on their second day.

The obvious next great challenge of the Rockies was the 5,500-foot-high north face of

Mt. Temple. A few had made forays up chutes low on the right part of the face, and Brian Greenwood for years had eyed a direct line up the concave headwall right below the summit. At the summit icecap he thought he saw an ice ramp that would allow passage.

In 1966, Heinz Kahl convinced Greenwood and Charlie Locke that the time was ripe for this face. Greenwood was now tethered to a family and a job. But he quit the job to climb Temple, saying later, "I was brought up straight and believed that working was an essential part of life.... I got over that." This inspired Locke to quit his job too. Little did they know that Kahl was dying from leukemia, and that he hoped to make this his last major climb. Just a thousand feet up the lower snow chutes, however, Kahl fell behind and had to return. Although they wouldn't learn of his condition until later, Greenwood and Locke felt a little extra inspiration to finish the route for their partner.

The two men progressed toward the headwall, and as the face steepened they favored rock over the snow-covered ice (a preference that would be reversed a few years later, as ice climbing gear and techniques improved). Soon they saw that Greenwood's headwall appeared "devoid of cracks, the ramp through the ice was non-existent." They steered right to a prominent buttress instead and found steep and exhilarating climbing on generally firm quartzite. As they settled in to a bivouac ledge on the buttress, they watched in horrified relief as the summit icecap sent off an avalanche that swept the headwall they had intended to climb.

Overnight, a small storm moved in and they woke to see the crux rock prow now coated in snow. Undaunted, Greenwood led pitch after pitch of the steepest part of the route, only occasionally resorting to aid. Thus was completed the finest alpine route by the finest climber yet to tackle the Rockies.

Mt. Chephren's northeast face. The 1965 first ascent route gained the central (sun-shade) upper rib from the left, then worked up and left to the top. *The Wild Thing* (1987) climbed the face to the right. PHOTO BY BARRY BLANCHARD.

Heinz Kahl. PHOTO BY GLEN BOLES.

SUGGESTED ROUTES
FROM THIS PERIOD

MT. BAKER (10,781 feet/ 3,286 meters)
North Ridge

Mt. Baker is the Cascades' northernmost and snowiest volcano, and glaciers on every side of its graceful dome pour off to below treeline. Its north ridge is still a popular, moderate classic, and the epaulet of ice at over 9,500 feet provides an exciting challenge with ice up to 50 to 70 degrees.

    Approach: From Bellingham, Washington, drive to a forest trailhead off the Mt. Baker Highway. Most people hike to a camp either near treeline (about 5,000 feet) or on the Coleman Glacier.

    Route: Cross the Coleman Glacier (a maze of crevasses in late season) to either skirt the toe of the ridge and start up its flanks or gain a snow-ice ramp that climbs directly to the ridge. From there the route simply runs upward, although there may be a variety of options to surmount the ice cliff. Descend by Baker's standard route, down the northwest ridge and back to the Coleman Glacier.

    First Ascent: Fred Beckey and Ralph and Dick Widrig, August 1948

    Difficulty: AD, AI 2-3, 3,700 feet

    Guidebooks: *Cascade Alpine Guide; Selected Climbs in the Cascades (Volume 1); Alpine Select*

Mt. Baker from the Coleman Glacier. PHOTO BY ANDY SELTERS.

Mt. Waddington from just above the Tiedemann Glacier. PHOTO BY ANDY SELTERS.

MT. WADDINGTON (13,185 feet/4,019 meters)
Southeast Chimney

The "regular route" up Waddington is a classic. The climb demands a range of skills and the humility to know that the weather and myriad conditions found on this mountain have a big say in when it will be climbed.

Approach: Most parties charter a helicopter flight with White Saddle Air Services of Bluff Lake, a remote outpost east of Waddington. (It's a long day's drive to Bluff Lake from Vancouver.) Other parties find a great wilderness adventure by walking in. There are a variety of basecamp locations on or just above the Tiedemann Glacier, at about 6,200 feet. From the glacier, most teams plan three or four days roundtrip but carry extra supplies to wait out bad weather.

Route: From Rainy Knob, an outcrop just above the Tiedemann Glacier, the first challenge is to climb the Bravo Glacier's icefall. Open crevasses later in the season can make this a circuitous day, and midday heat can make it a trying, even hazardous climb over mushy snow bridges and under active seracs. Above the icefall's third tier, a bergschrund might pose difficulties en route to 9,850-foot Bravo Col. An easy but crevassed glacier leads up the southeast ridge to the most advantageous campsites for a summit bid. On summit day, take Class 3 and 4 ledges across the northern base of the Tooth and into the notch below Waddington's main tower. A traverse right gains the famous chimney. Two or three pitches past blocky chockstones lead to an exit left, where exposed but easier ground weaves to the top. Descend by the same route.

First Ascent: Oscar Cook, Dick Houston, Bill Long and Ray de Saussure, July 1950

Difficulty: D+, 5.7, often mixed, 6,900 feet

Guidebook: *The Waddington Guide*

OUBLIETTE (10,138 feet/3,090 meters)
East Ridge

This, the first technical route on the northeast front of the Rampart Range, is the most popular climb in the area—meaning it's one of the only routes to get any traffic at all. The climb is a one-day affair for qualified alpinists, after a long day's hike from the road.

Approach: Near Jasper, the well-maintained trail to Amethyst Lakes starts from the road to Edith Cavell. It's a good 20 kilometers to the lake, but the scenery alone is worth the walk. Unfortunately, mosquitoes are notoriously bad here, and grizzlies can present a serious threat. Check with Jasper National Park wardens on the status of the big omnivores.

Route: There are two ways to gain the ledge that leads to the main arête: an easier chute at the end of the descent gully, or the original route's Class 3 and 4 rock (one fifth-class pitch) under the north face. In this area of rockfall, it is best to climb very early in the day, and with some haste. From either direction, traverse the prominent ledge to the east arête. From there the general route is obvious, mostly just left of the prow, but complex rock makes for lots of small routefinding decisions and possible dead ends. Climbers who require perfect stone will be dismayed at some of Oubliette's strata, especially in Beckey's rotten chimney, but the climbing is easy where the rock is loose. Where the route steepens, the gneiss and quartzite provide firm, spectacular passages that will be memorable in anyone's career. Descend via the south couloir and ridge to the Paragon-Oubliette Col (one or two rappels), and then take the convenient broad couloir and one rappel down to the Tonquin Valley.

First Ascent: Fred Beckey, Don Gordon and Brian Greenwood, July 1962

Difficulty: D+, 5.7, 2,800 feet

Guidebook: *Selected Alpine Climbs in the Canadian Rockies*

Permits: A fee is charged for entering Jasper National Park, and a permit (additional fee) is required for backcountry camping. It's also recommended that climbers register and sign back in with park wardens.

Oubliette from the east. PHOTO BY GLEN BOLES.

MT. TEMPLE (11,624 feet/3,543 meters)
Greenwood-Locke Route

Some half-dozen routes have been made up this vast amphitheater of a wall, but the original *Greenwood-Locke* prow is the best, for it offers the safest and most spectacular positions, on the soundest and steepest rock. Nevertheless, this is a serious alpine wall, and aspirants should be well prepared to judge conditions for rockfall and to encounter everything from running water to rotten rock or verglas.

Approach: It's just a bit over an hour's hike on a good trail to Lake Annette, at the base of the face. It's smart to bivouac here to get the earliest possible start.

The north face of Mt. Temple. PHOTO BY GLEN BOLES.

Route: Start early on a cold morning up the right-hand "Dolphin" couloir (which unfortunately has completely melted dry in some recent years), and quickly gain a good 1,500 feet. Then branch right onto moderate rock climbing to gain a second icefield. The top of this icefield is where the business begins. A difficult chimney leads to easier climbing and an unsettling traverse for 200 feet left along a prominent but sloping ledge. This puts you in a position to start up the better limestone above. A variety of steep pulls, chimneys and occasional aid cracks interspersed with ledges make for exhilarating pitches. Halfway up this headwall one can find a protected bivouac site. The hardest and most spectacular climbing is a couple of hundred feet below the top. The summit is an hour's hike away, or you can head straight for the easy southwest ridge descent route.

First Ascent: Brian Greenwood and Charlie Locke, July 1966

Difficulty: TD+, 5.8, A2, 5,500 feet

Guidebook: *Selected Alpine Climbs in the Canadian Rockies*

Permits: A fee is charged for entering Banff National Park, and a permit (additional fee) is required for bivouacs. It is recommended that climbers sign out and sign back in with park wardens.

CHAPTER 9

The Giant Routes

For the core of America's exploratory mountaineers, World War II was a sobering but busy time. A number of leading climbers—notably the "Harvard Five" (see Chapter 6)—contributed directly to the military's development of mountain and cold-weather operations. As the *Harvard Mountaineering Journal* put it, their members endured the war with a "brave but pessimistic attitude." Afterward, they looked forward with renewed conviction "that mountaineering is bigger than war or any other catastrophe. Climbing is a thing of the soul, and as long as there are men who have souls, the quest and ascent of high places will continue."

This generation would take such ideals to the mountains for another 20 years or more. Besides the Harvard Mountaineering Club, other university clubs made significant postwar climbs in the continent's great ranges, especially the Dartmouth Mountaineering Club, the Stanford Alpine Club and the club at the University of Alaska.

At war's end, mountaineers looked north to the Alaska Range and the Icefield Ranges, which together hold 17 of the continent's 20 highest peaks, six of which were still unclimbed. The 11 that had been summited each had only one route, and only Denali had been climbed more than once. Giant routes were untouched, and vast areas of Alaska, the Yukon, British Columbia and the Northwest Territories had hundreds of peaks awaiting even the first perusal by climbers.

With so much exploratory climbing yet to be done, the adventure of mountaineering in the far north seemed to remain much as Allen Carpé had described it in 1931:

> *The ascent of each of these [Alaskan giants] may entail weeks of work and travel beyond the snow-line.... None so far accomplished affords the interest of serious 'technical' difficulties. Given a competent method of attack, success depends really on time, supplies and transportation.*

Soon after the war, however, as bush pilots and mountaineers became partners in adventure, approaches shrank from weeks of toil to a few hours of skilled and daring aviation. With the time and supply rules transformed, the subarctic peaks became more familiar and climbing teams started

➲ On the first ascent of the *Cassin Ridge*. PHOTO BY RICARDO CASSIN. COURTESY BRADFORD WASHBURN, HENRY S. HALL, JR. AMERICAN ALPINE CLUB LIBRARY.

taking on technical routes, generally following the ridges.

The Bunyanesque scale of these peaks still seemed nearly overwhelming, and Alaskan climbers developed siege tactics similar to those used on Himalayan peaks. Generally, this entailed making piecemeal advances up a route, extending long spools of "fixed" safety lines to each successive high point, and then ferrying provisions and climbing gear up those ropes to support the next advance. When a high camp was set within a reasonable striking distance of the top, some or all of the climbers would summit from there.

Late in this period, rock climbers also began to take planes into remote peaks that were spectacular beyond their dreams.

Among the leading climbers of the 1950s and '60s, the technical and exploratory branches of North American mountaineering were reuniting. Both groups of postwar climbers moved toward a grand and unified ideal of difficult and spectacular climbing over long routes, in remote and challenging environments.

Colossal Enterprises

During the war, Harvard men Bill Putnam, Andy Kauffman and Maynard Miller discussed a celebratory postwar expedition, and early in 1946 they decided to retrace the original 1888 approach to Mt. St. Elias. They collected five other expedition members, including Kauffman's wife, Elizabeth.

Mt. St. Elias from the southwest. The 1946 Harvard team climbed from the glacier prominent in the center up the ridge system facing the camera. PHOTO #2030 © BRADFORD WASHBURN. COURTESY PANOPTICON GALLERY, WALTHAM, MA.

Like the 19th century pioneers, this team had to start marching from Icy Bay. However, their efforts were greatly eased by the U.S. military. The Air Force enthusiastically agreed to practice making airdrops along their route, and the Army supplied them with new equipment such as crampons, radios, tents, clothing and rations. They labeled their logistical behemoth of an expedition the "Colossal Enterprise." The team proceeded to the north ridge of Haydon Peak and then traversed to the col below St. Elias. At a 13,500-foot-high bench, they received their final airdrop. Two boxes tumbled off the edge, so the climbers would go a bit hungry on the way down, but after fixing ropes past a 10th camp, all eight reached the summit five weeks after the start from Icy Bay.

Putnam then began a fine career of ferreting out information on alpine-scale peaks in expeditionary locations. He started in 1947 with a basecamp (supported by airdrop) east of Mt. Waddington, on the Tellot Glacier. He gathered a crew of Harvard undergraduates and invited Fred Beckey to add his expertise. Various members of this party succeeded on a number of prominent peaks, some of superb granite, others mostly of snow and ice. One significant, if risky, first ascent was Mt. Asperity. Beckey, Harry King, Francis Magoun and Graham Matthews worked out a complex route over ice walls and bergschrunds to access the prominent, avalanche-prone couloir between Asperity and Mt. Tiedemann. They made good time up the couloir and thereby completed the first route up the huge alpine front that sits across the Tiedemann Glacier from Mt. Waddington.

Beckey and three others then tried the spectacular Serra Peaks, but while traversing a snow slope they triggered an avalanche. All four were swept down until their ropes snagged over rock knobs. As Beckey and Harry King regained their footing, they discovered that Charles Shiverick had collided with rocks and was dead. They carried the news to basecamp, and Putnam and a partner hiked out to civilization. For another month the remaining climbers combined more first ascents with successful efforts to dissuade a massive and risky plan to recover Shiverick's body by airplane.

In 1948, Walter Wood renewed his Arctic Institute of North America (AINA) "Project Snow Cornice" trips deep into the Icefield Ranges, starting with an attempt to make the first ascent of Mt. Vancouver, a 15,787-foot-high massif 44 miles east of Mt. St. Elias. AINA used its own Norseman ski plane for access and airdrops at each camp, but the trip foundered when the Norseman's propeller nosed into soft snow. The next year, Noel Odell joined the team, and the airdrop supply chain helped ease the team up the long and scenic north ridge. Wood, however, became ill from stove fuel that contaminated his rucksack and had to bow out.

Robert Bates joined Wood in 1951 for a similarly well-supplied expedition to make the first ascents of Mt. Alverstone (14,565 feet) and Mt. Hubbard (15,015 feet), the twin white giants east of Mt. Vancouver. They worked the airdrop system to its maximum up the Cathedral Glacier, and the climbers didn't have to carry a thing between camps. Unfortunately, the flying proved to be more hazardous than the climbing, as Maury King's supply plane crashed while carrying Wood's wife, Foresta, and their daughter, and the three were never found.

During the war, as Bradford Washburn helped the military with cold-weather operations, he also began to work on a definitive map of Mt. McKinley and the surrounding mountains. In 1947, he led the fourth ascent of Denali, by the Muldrow Glacier. His team included Portland climbers Bill Hackett and Smoke Blanchard, along with Washburn's wife, Barbara. She became the first woman to climb the peak, even though she was saddled with a preponderance of the cooking and worry over the Washburns' new child in Boston. During this time, Washburn expanded his collection of large-format aerial negatives of the area, and with inspired scrutiny of those photographs he began to plot the next generation of climbing on Denali.

About this time the Office of Navy Research (ONR) began looking for a way to establish a research camp high on Denali to study particle physics. They asked Washburn to find the best route, and he proposed the west buttress, for he had seen by air that it would be reasonable to make a ski-plane landing on the Kahiltna Glacier. He correctly predicted that Kahiltna landings would make the west buttress the preferred way to climb Denali, and that it would bring new attention to the peak's southern aspects.

Word of this proposed route reached Henry Buchtel, a doctor in Denver. He contacted Barry Bishop, a climber from Cincinnati, and they wrote to Washburn for advice. Washburn asked if he might join them and arranged for Terris Moore to fly them in. Moore then designed the first aero-skis that retracted and extended, so he could take off from dry ground with wheels and then land on snow.

Bill Hackett on the first ascent of Denali's west buttress, packing a load using fixed rope on the headwall to gain the crest of the buttress. PHOTO #57-5893 © BRADFORD WASHBURN. COURTESY PANOPTICON GALLERY, WALTHAM, MA.

Washburn also arranged for ONR to deliver airdrops up to 10,000 feet.

As Washburn had predicted, the headwall below the 16,000-foot crest of the buttress proved to be the most difficult section of the route, and the climbers strung 600 feet of rope for use while ferrying loads. With their extensive experience, planning and support, the team could hardly fail, and on July 10, 1951, a second route to the top of McKinley finally was won. Washburn immediately pointed out how air support made a McKinley climb "possible for consideration by climbers of moderate means, or those without unusually extended vacation time." ONR soon afterward abandoned its idea for a high-altitude laboratory, focusing instead on particle accelerators.

Expanding the Expedition Game

The next year, 1952, two expeditions aimed for King Peak, the unclimbed 16,971-foot-high western bastion of Mt. Logan. First was a team led by Elton Thayer from the University of Alaska in Fairbanks. No ski planes operated in this area, so the Thayer expedition followed the 1925 team's approach up the Logan Glacier and then received airdrops for their basecamp. They proceeded up the west edge of King Peak's north face, and, placing two camps, eventually followed complex mixed terrain on the upper west ridge to the top.

The second King Peak team heard about Thayer's success just as they packed to leave Seattle, but they continued anyway, under the leadership of Pete Schoening. This party hired a pilot who agreed to try landing on the Seward Glacier with a Grumman boat-bellied floatplane. The Grumman landed fine but couldn't take off, and it remained beached like a whale. Half the team then had to walk up the Malaspina Glacier to basecamp. A cool, favorable wind eventually allowed the plane to take off.

Schoening and party started with the first ascent of Mt. Augusta, a beautiful 14,070-foot peak across the Seward Glacier from Mt. Logan. On the eastern of Augusta's two north ridges, they employed ice pitons to protect

Mt. Augusta from the north. The Schoening first ascent party climbed the broad, sunlit ridge curving toward the camera. PHOTO BY JOE JOSEPHSON.

ice angled over 50 degrees. After establishing just two camps, the entire party summited. Schoening, Bill Niendorff, Dick McGowan and Gibson Reynolds then crossed the Seward Glacier to try King Peak via its east ridge. The top of this ridge proved difficult, with steep ice, occasional rock, bitter cold and high winds turning back two attempts. On a third try, McGowan and Niendorff had to retreat with freezing feet, but Schoening and Reynolds succeeded. The weather improved the following day, and Schoening went up again, leading McGowan and Niendorff to the top.

This trip showed that climbers at high altitudes and latitudes needed a better boot design. Some members of the team had U.S. Army insulated rubber ("bunny") boots—these soft boots kept the feet warm but did not offer much support on steep ground, requiring more effort to be put into chopping steps. Others wore stiff-soled mountain boots of wool felt that climbed well and probably would have been warm enough during steady climbing, but were too cold during the climbers' frequent pauses. In subsequent years, manufacturers would design leather expedition boots with inner boots of felt.

The 1952 expedition also demonstrated the fortitude and commitment to partnership that would make Pete Schoening a legend the following summer. During the 1953 American expedition to K2, as the team was trying to evacuate gravely ill Art Gilkey, Schoening deployed the most famous belay in history, bracing his ice axe behind a rock to hold six tumbling climbers from certain death.

The Remarkable Season

Between 1952 and 1954, Bradford Washburn published recommendations for three huge new climbs in the Alaska Range: "the great west ridge" of McKinley's north peak, the western ridge of Mt. Hunter and McKinley's south buttress. All three would be climbed during the 1954 season.

Climbers at about 13,800 feet on the first ascent of the northwest buttress of Mt. McKinley. PHOTO COURTESY FRED BECKEY.

The Alaska Alpine Club had no accessible place to practice technical climbing, but their members knew how to travel and survive on Alaskan glaciers. They initiated the first two 1954 trips, and for the first time since the mountain's earliest ascents resident Alaskans would climb Denali.

The "west ridge of McKinley's north peak"—the same buttress that Frederick Cook had started up in 1903—came to be known as Denali's northwest buttress. Donald McLean and Charles "Bucky" Wilson from Fairbanks initiated the expedition to try it, and they invited along Henry Meybohm, a German ski instructor living in Anchorage, and Bill Hackett from Portland. A widely traveled veteran of World War II, Hackett was the only person to have climbed the highest peaks on five continents (all but Asia and Antarctica). The route looked technical, and so Hackett persuaded the team to invite Fred Beckey, who almost never joined trips that were not of his own design. Beckey coyly responded that, since

he had no serious romance going on, he would come.

The team landed at a lake north of Mt. Foraker and hiked to an appointed airdrop. Gusts tossed the plane carrying their supplies onto the Peters Glacier, near basecamp, and although the pilots were unhurt, the memory of this incident helped encourage the National Park Service to ban airdrops on Denali a decade later.

Up on the route, Beckey's expertise proved invaluable for the long sections of steep ice. At 15,000 feet he steered onto granite buttresses, placing the range's first pitons, to avoid tiresome step cutting. The team fixed rope over the steeper sections and established their sixth camp at 18,500 feet, an easy mile from the summit. On May 27, in marginal weather, all were able to reach the north peak.

Meanwhile, Elton Thayer and three other Alaskan buddies were at work on Denali's vast south buttress. This snaking spine incorporates a whole chain of mountains, and following its crest to Denali's summit promised to be a long wilderness odyssey. The four hiked from an Alaskan Railroad stop to the Ruth Glacier, where pilot Ginny Wood, the wife of teammate Mort Wood, airdropped a month of supplies, 400 feet of rope for fixing, a small supply of ice pitons and snow anchors, two canvas tents and a manuscript of Washburn's recommendations for the route.

Washburn's text said, "Those who attempt this side of McKinley [must] be equipped with ample reserves of food and fuel, as well as a reliable radio at least at their landing camp. Even a minor accident in this remote wilderness could easily develop into a terrible disaster, without good communications and a well-supplied route of retreat." But Thayer and friends had enough experience with wilderness that they planned a more daunting style—no stocked basecamp and no radio. Instead of returning down their route, they committed to a traverse

over the north side of Denali, to a cabin in Kantishna on the far side of the McKinley River. Thayer worked there as a ranger, and the previous summer he had stocked the cabin with supplies.

Aerial photographs had not prepared Thayer and his partners for the serious start to their climb. The narrow fork of the Ruth Glacier leading to their route proved to be frequently swept by avalanches off the huge faces above, and crevasses stretched all the way across the canyon. After managing these challenges, the group began chopping steps and ferrying loads upward. A few days from their airdrop, they reached the crest of the buttress and began to grasp what it meant that the top of Denali was still more than 10 miles away, beyond four summits above 15,000 feet. After climbing a second long slope to 14,000 feet, they came to a bizarre cornice of solid ice that, according to

High on the first ascent of Mt. McKinley's northwest ridge. PHOTO BY FRED BECKEY.

George Argus on the first ascent of Denali's south buttress. EXPEDITION PHOTO COURTESY BRADFORD WASHBURN, HENRY S. HALL, JR. AMERICAN ALPINE CLUB LIBRARY.

Three climbers on the first ascent of Denali's south buttress, leaving their highest camp (17,400 feet) to head for the summit. The north summit is in the background. EXPEDITION PHOTO COURTESY BRADFORD WASHBURN, HENRY S. HALL, JR. AMERICAN ALPINE CLUB LIBRARY.

Wood, extended 60 to 80 feet over the Kahiltna Glacier.

> *It formed a weird ice cave through which we walked and crawled a very long distance. In some places we had to remove our packs and push them ahead of us while wriggling on our stomachs to squeeze among the cold blue ice blocks and through the tiny passages.*

Sustained challenges put them behind schedule, but the weather remained excellent, and so, Wood wrote, "We decided not to relay any more. We would somehow carry both our loads together even though they would weigh about 90 pounds." When they reached the high basin that would later be named for Thayer, they decided to take a circuitous but less-steep route to the east side of the summit. Cresting the northeast ridge, they camped with a view over their route home and "realized that, not the summit, but this pass had been our objective." Two weeks after leaving the Ruth Glacier, they made an anticlimactic roundtrip to Denali's summit, and then reshouldered their loads for the descent to the Muldrow Glacier. Mort Wood's

and George Argus' ice axes were broken and repaired with tape. As they descended Karstens Ridge, Elton Thayer came last. Wood described what happened next:

> *Suddenly Elton slipped and began to slide. The best belays we could get were with the pick of the axe dug into the snow-covered ice.... In seconds Les [Viereck] was pulled loose and my belay was not strong enough to hold two men.... After that, I only remember tumbling end over end in the loose snow, now and then being pulled by the rope and always unable, because of the heavy pack, to roll over on my stomach and dig in my axe to check the fall.*

The team tumbled for some 800 feet, until Viereck fell into a crevasse. Thayer hung in free air off a serac wall, and the yank of the rope around his waist apparently broke his back. He was dead. George Argus lay incapacitated with a broken hip. After recuperating for six days, Wood and Viereck sledded Argus to a safe spot, then hurried out to Thayer's cache at the hut in Kantishna. A military helicopter rescue (the first in the range) was arranged for Argus, who had waited a week alone, confident his friends would find a way to return for him.

These companions had enjoyed a tremendous adventure far from the eye of civilization. But the loss of their friend Thayer eclipsed their gusto for the first traverse of Denali and one of the greatest expeditions of the decade, and the three survivors never did another major climb. Les Viereck later became a regional hero for helping to stop federal plans for using nuclear bombs to create a harbor on Alaska's northern coast.

Deborah and Hunter

Fred Beckey and Henry Meybohm didn't rest long after succeeding on Denali's northwest buttress. Back in Fairbanks, they happened to meet Heinrich Harrer, the Austrian who had participated in the first ascent of the Eiger's north face and who had spent the war years in adventurous exile in Tibet. From Fairbanks the three admired unclimbed Mt. Deborah.

Though this peak reaches a modest 12,540 feet, Beckey wrote, "Without doubt the summit of Deborah is one of the most impressive and spectacular sights in the Americas."

The three traveled by ski plane to the Yanert Glacier on June 17. To take advantage of firmer snow conditions, they climbed toward the west ridge at night, and by late in the morning of the 19th they started for the summit. They reached the south ridge at 12,000 feet, and from there, "The final south ridge seemed a nightmare of steep and exposed corniced knife-edged ridge," Beckey wrote. "The only route lay along the top of the ridge over the cornices, constantly exposed to the danger of a break." Climbing this final ridge added six hours to their long day, but the summit was theirs. Afterward, Beckey wrote, "It was our unanimous conclusion that Deborah was the most sensational ice climb any one of us had ever undertaken."

Just 12 days after summiting Deborah, all three men flew with the famous pilot Don

Heinrich Harrer and Henry Meybohm on the south ridge of Mt. Deborah, during the push to the summit on the first ascent. PHOTO BY FRED BECKEY.

Sheldon to the Kahiltna Glacier, at the base of the western ridge of Mt. Hunter. Washburn had written that this ridge was "the only feasible route" to Hunter's summit plateau. Beckey knew that summer storms soon would bring an end to the Alaskan season, so with a sense of urgency they decided not to ferry loads, even though the ridge was twice as long as Deborah's. They started up the route with eight days of supplies and one extra rope, which they fixed over a rock gendarme low on the ridge.

Although their route had plenty of hard ice (often under a layer of slushy snow), Beckey and Harrer led without cutting the usual number of steps, often kicking in their frontpoints instead. Harrer had first seen this calf-burning but speedy technique in use on the first ascent of the Eigerwand, when Anderl Heckmair and Ludwig Vörg caught up with him. At that time, Harrer commented, "I saw the New Era coming at Express speed; there were two men running—and I mean running."

On Hunter, at the end of an ice pitch, Harrer or Beckey would fashion the standard ice belays of the day, pounding in an ice piton and carving a substantial bucket seat to brace from. Ice was only one of the challenges, however, as big, wet cornices, unstable snow slopes and tenuous crevasse bridges made for insecure travel. To get the snow at its best, they climbed mostly in the cool glow of night. After a remarkable effort only five days long, they stood on top.

These four 1954 expeditions broke new ground in both strategy and terrain, setting standards that few would be able to match for some time. Beckey was enthusiastic about the possibilities in Alaska, but he also issued a "Word of Caution" that the big ridgelines were "unique alpine problems" that required a new level of savvy with cornices, avalanches and solar timing. Other climbers who began to look at big Alaskan ridges would continue to climb very conservatively.

More Northern Giants

Many other great peaks in the north still had only a single route to the summit. In 1955,

Gibson Reynolds and Keith Hart led a team from a variety of American universities, along with Canadian Leon Blumer, to try the north ridge of Mt. Blackburn, which had not been climbed since Dora Keen's first ascent. Along the ridge they met an overhanging ice wall flanked by loaded slopes, and this turned them back. Regrouping, they flew a short way southeast to 14,470-foot University Peak. Here the team had a week of harrowing travel through a basin swept by serac fall and avalanches. When one serac avalanche came straight for them, they dodged it by fleeing willy-nilly into separate crevasses and escaped with only minor injuries. After collecting an airdrop above the icefall, all six made a successful ascent up the steep and broken north ridge.

As of 1956, Mt. Logan had been climbed only twice, and by only one route, the King Trench. Among the gargantuan unclimbed buttresses that fly off its summit plateau, only the one leading to the east summit seemed reasonable. Seattle climbers had tried this ridge in 1953 and had been turned back by bad weather, but word of its potential made it to California. Don Monk and Gil Roberts (a Stanford Alpine Club graduate) set a trip for 1957. Their five-man expedition reached Logan's base by ski plane, but planned to return to the coast on foot.

The route began with a bergschrund and a steep 400-foot slope, and from the top of this the climbers hauled their supplies onto the ridge by using a counterbalance pulley rigged from a tripod. The ridge then confronted them with icy chimneys, narrow sections of ice and loose rock, and steep slopes, but thankfully only a modest amount of cornicing. They fixed ropes over the tough sections for load carrying. About halfway up, the ridge broadened and the challenges changed to steep snow with avalanche and crevasse hazards. As they looked far down to the tiny specks of their tents at basecamp, knowing that civilization was a two-week hike away, Roberts noted, "We had a feeling of extreme isolation tempered only by the knowledge that we had nearly ten days of food." Over three weeks they placed eight main camps on

Mt. Logan, with the east ridge facing the camera. PHOTO BY CHIC SCOTT.

the ridge, and on July 19 all five members reached the east summit.

In 1958 Leon Blumer and Hans Gmoser planned a return to Mt. Blackburn. They hoped to do a lightweight ascent up the east ridge, but the terrain above 13,500 feet was steeper and longer than they could manage without fixing ropes and ferrying loads, so they turned to the north ridge that Blumer had tried three years before. At the previous high point, safer conditions and Gmoser's expertise at cutting steps got them around the gendarme, and they reached the north-west summit. Surveyors later identified this as the highest point on Blackburn's extensive summit plateau.

New Boldness

Having tasted expeditionary climbing on Blackburn, Gmoser set out in 1959 to make the first fully Canadian ascent of Mt. Logan, by the east ridge. His team of six climbers had a slim budget, forcing some to hitchhike to Kluane Lake. There was no snow left for ski planes to take off, so they had to hike and ski about 100 miles to basecamp and receive an airdrop. The extended approach time cut into

their food and fuel stocks, and when they reached the base of the ridge they had only 12 days of supplies to tackle the giant peak.

Forced to hurry, they found they could run longer stretches between camps than the 1957 party had, although they also set up intermediate caches. They completed the ridge to the 16,000-foot summit plateau in only six days, but this pace gave them all the ripping headaches, lassitude and lack of appetite of mountain sickness. Nevertheless, on the seventh day, all six pushed themselves to the east summit, and the day after that they made it all the way back to the glacier. The team added some real exploration to their trip by returning to Kluane via the previously unvisited Donjek Glacier.

In the 1956 Swiss publication *The Mountain World*, Bradford Washburn had proposed two routes on the great south face of Denali. Few North Americans could imagine themselves in this league, and it was three years before a team of four Dartmouth-Teton tigers took up one of these futuristic challenges, which came to be called the *West Rib*.

Jake Breitenbach had been on Denali twice, once to try the southeast spur and once to summit via the west buttress, so he was the group's nominal leader. Barry Corbet and Pete Sinclair had dropped out of Dartmouth in search of a more adventurous and perhaps more powerful education in the mountains, notably the Tetons. Their fourth was Bill Buckingham, a native Jackson Hole guide, then enrolled at Princeton. All were proficient rock mountaineers, but they had much less ice climbing experience—Sinclair, in fact, had never done an ice climb. Imbued with the go-light legends of Himalayan hero Hermann Buhl, they considered themselves not an expedition but an alpine team taking on an expedition-size challenge. They had interested ABC in the project, and they carried a bulky tape recorder for post-ascent broadcasts.

When they unloaded from Don Sheldon's ski plane on the Kahiltna Glacier, their route looked so big and sustained that to Pete Sinclair it suddenly seemed as if "the world had not been constructed for a person my size, that a person was going to have to get bigger if he was going to get along around here."

They had hoped to climb rock, but even in their "bunny boots" and crampons without frontpoints the ice passages proved to be easier than the rock towers. They chopped thousands of steps, strung their 1,700 feet of 3/8-inch manila line to rock pitons and Marwa ("coat-hanger") ice screws, and ferried loads through the first fifth of the route.

Though the weather remained perfect, the spine of snow and ice soaring into the sky was intimidating, and when they ran out of rope to fix they went into a funk and considered retreat. Breitenbach had seen Denali storms, and he was worried sick as he imagined being pinned by a storm on such sustained, steep ground.

His buddies, however, soon regained their resolve, and Corbet and Sinclair probed higher. Since the going was no worse than before, Corbet and Buckingham pulled up half their fixed rope to use on the route above. With their ties to the ground cut, they set sail into serious commitment and gave the climb their all. Steady progress and teamwork generated exhilaration, and Sinclair wrote, "For the first time since childhood, I was where I wanted

Jake Breitenbach in the ice couloir gaining access to the ridge during the first ascent of Denali's *West Rib*. PHOTO BY BARRY CORBET.

to be, doing exactly what I wanted to do, with the people whom I wanted to do it."

They proceeded through six campsites, using what later would be called "capsule style," where members ferry loads to the next campsite but leave no tents or fixed rope behind them. Just 11 days after landing on the glacier, they staggered to the summit, suffering from altitude illness. After their return to the highest camp, a storm did materialize, though luckily without severe winds. In snowfall and whiteout, they traversed to the west buttress to descend. For Americans of this generation, the ascent became an inspiring reminder of how the biggest climbs call not only for technical skills but also calculated risk-taking and emotional commitment within a demanding environment.

A third great climb was made in 1959 in the far north. Leo Scheiblehner was a preeminent Austrian alpinist who had come to America that year. In March he had hooked up with Fred Beckey on Mt. Hood, where the two made a remarkable first ascent of the Yocum Ridge, a jagged spine plastered with rime.

When summer came, Scheiblehner and Richard Griesmann worked as guides to geologists in the Fairweather Range. They eyed the peaks and noted the conditions, and when they got some free time the two guides climbed the 7,000-foot southeast face of Mt. La Pérouse in a single day, as if it were a simple Alpine tour.

The two had noted how, during the daytime, avalanches and serac falls swept this face frequently, but at night the colder temperatures held the snow in place. They started up in the early evening, and, carrying little in their packs, cramponed upward in firm, stable conditions. Through the night they climbed snow and ice sustained at 40 to 60 degrees. Though they had to maneuver over some snowy rock slabs, they reached the safety of the summit ridge by 5 a.m. Their snow savvy, along with the fitness and confidence to climb steep ground quickly, allowed them to pull off a climb years ahead its time.

Remote Rock

During this decade, a Scottish-Canadian Arctic scientist named Col. Patrick Baird started bringing climbers to the incredible mountains of Baffin Island. An amateur climber himself, Baird had seen so many giant walls and amazing peaks that he knew modern technical climbers would love to visit the area.

The mountainous east coast of Baffin Island runs for over 1,500 miles, and every climber who experiences it, even today, comes to acknowledge that the potential for exploratory mountaineering here remains at least as profound as that for technical advance.

In 1950, Baird brought three Swiss and an American to the Sam Ford Fjord area, and the group climbed a number of peaks, most of which they labeled simply with elevation numbers. Three years later, Baird brought four Swiss to the Cumberland Peninsula, a concentration of peaks they noted to be more extensive than all of Switzerland's mountains. Three of this team, Jürg Marmet, Hans Röthlisberg and Weber F. Schwarzenbach, climbed a striking arête to Baffin Island's highest peak, 7,074-foot Tête Blanche.

Among the thousands of fantastic summits, Mt. Asgard, a joined pair of truncated towers, stood out as an astounding fortress of supreme impregnability. On Asgard's east side, however, the Swiss found relatively moderate slabs and ramps that led to the notch between the towers. From there, a rock prow demanded but a few steep pitches, including some aid with pitons, and to their surprise the climbers soon scrambled onto the tabletop of the north peak.

Across the continent, a Yale University Mountaineering Club team flew in 1952 to

Swiss climbers on the crux pitches of the first ascent of Mt. Asgard, 1953. PHOTO COURTESY ARCTIC INSTITUTE OF NORTH AMERICA.

On the summit after the first ascent of Mt. Asgard. PHOTO COURTESY ARCTIC INSTITUTE OF NORTH AMERICA.

the Logan Mountains (like distant Mt. Logan, also named after the founder of Canada's geographical survey) in the Northwest Territories. The Yale boys reached nine summits and reported some of the most jaw-dropping granite on the continent.

Three years later, Sterling Hendricks, Arnold Wexler, Donald Hubbard, Ray D'Arcy and Dave Bernays followed up on that claim, and as they hiked under huge, steep walls of fantastic shape and character, they coined the name Cirque of the Unclimbables. This team found a way to climb the highest peak in the area, Mt. Sir James MacBrien, and many of the spires of the Echelon and Pentadactyl groups. In all they made an impressive 18 first ascents, but they found the most awesome peaks distinctly unclimbable.

In 1960, four climbers based in the American Rockies took a six-week expedition to this legendary cirque. Bill Buckingham, Stuart Krebs, Pat Hoadley and Stanley Shepard worked out the least difficult routes to almost every important summit in the four arcs of the cirque and graced these fantastic peaks with colorful names: Mt. Meringue, Phenocryst Spire, Parrot Beak Peak, Tathagata Tower and Lotus Flower Tower. Most of the peaks required snow and ice climbing as well as rock climbing up to at least 5.6. Mt. Proboscis, however, seemed to lack any obvious possibility. After much scouting, they persisted with some aid up its south arête and continued over "sharp barn roofs" to the highest point. Buckingham said that this "certainly ranks among the most difficult rock peaks of North America" and that "this single cluster of peaks is at least the equal of any of the more famous areas."

North America's Ultimate Route?

In the same article that inspired the 1959 *West Rib* climb, Bradford Washburn proposed that a crack team could climb "the great central bulge on the fabulous 10,000-foot South Face" of Denali. He declared that the unmistakable spur that runs directly to the highest point on the continent was the "last and probably the most difficult and dramatic of all potential new routes on Mount McKinley…. This route may be classed as unequivocally excellent climbing from start to finish."

Washburn's proclamation eventually found fertile ground at the Italian Alpine Club (CAI). Mountains and climbing were part of the Italian national culture, and after major successes in the Karakoram the CAI was arguably the most advanced climbing organization in the world. The club assigned Carlo Mauri to lead a team to Alaska, and Mauri collected a team of five young "Lecco Spiders," an elite club from a small alpine valley. However, just before departure in the spring of 1961, Mauri broke his leg skiing and so Ricardo Cassin, the national hero and grandfather of the Spiders, took over as leader. Since Denali was substantially lower than peaks that club members had climbed in Asia, the Italians reasoned the challenges would be more technical than environmental. Partly out of

Bill Buckingham on the most difficult section of the first ascent of Proboscis. PHOTO BILL BUCKINGHAM COLLECTION.

Aerial view of the Cirque of the Unclimbables from the east. Prominent peaks include (from left to right): Mt. Harrison Smith (left forefront), Proboscis, Flattop Spire, Higher Polymer (center distance), Phenocryst Spire, Lotus Flower Tower, Parrot Beak Peak and Mt. Sir James MacBrien. PHOTO BY HARRISON SHULL.

naïveté, they were probably the first to prioritize a Denali challenge this way, and it led them to bring standard alpine mountaineering boots, a serious miscalculation that they would narrowly overcome.

Cassin organized the expedition in classic siege style, and under his leadership the Spiders were a united team. By extending the chain of camps and ropes up the route, climbers could exchange the tasks of leading and ferrying loads, and periodically return to basecamp to recoup. They were more comfortable climbing granite than ice, and with the much greater security of rock pitons versus ice anchors they avoided ice wherever possible. The steepest climbing on the route is in the first third, and it took 10 days to establish their first camp on a tiny bench. After another thousand feet of easier climbing, a better campsite was thoroughly stocked.

The team established just one more camp, at nearly 17,000 feet. From there, on a typically bitter and breezy day, all six made the summit after a very long 17 hours. When they struggled back to their high camp seven hours later, their bodies cried out for a long rest. But terrifying weather was approaching, their feet were freezing, and they were unprepared to weather a storm on that exposed perch. One member, Giancarlo Canali, had feet so swollen with frostbite that he could no longer pull on his boots. Gigi Alippi donated his larger boots, and they started the long retreat down the fixed lines with snow falling heavily and Alippi desperately trying to manage while wearing layered socks inside of overboots. As Cassin led them down, powder avalanches swept over them and their dependence on the fixed ropes was all too obvious. Over three days all made it to basecamp. Back in Anchorage, while some of the members received successful treatment for severe frostbite, a telegram offering congratulations arrived from President Kennedy. Cassin declared that this ridge, which now bears his name, was "one of the biggest satis-

On the first ascent of the *Cassin Ridge*. PHOTO TAKEN BY
RICARDO CASSIN. COURTESY BRADFORD WASHBURN, HENRY S. HALL,
JR. AMERICAN ALPINE CLUB LIBRARY.

Boyd Everett at basecamp during the expedition that
made the first ascent of Mt. Logan's west ridge, 1966.
PHOTO BY GRAY THOMPSON.

factions in my long life as a mountaineer
thanks to the effort and unmatched talent of
my five young teammates."

Alaska Range Triumphs

Although North Americans had already
mounted expeditions to big Alaskan routes,
the Italians' success seems to have inspired
even grander designs. At least a couple of
dozen other giant ridges waited on the highest peaks. In 1962, Harvard grad Boyd Everett
led the next big excursion, to Denali's southeast spur. Everett was a high-powered stock
analyst, 28 years old, with only a modest
sense of mountains and climbing but a penchant for attacking grand problems. Denali's
southeast spur would be the first in a series of
giant routes where he would apply his organizational talents and his bankroll, develop-
ing a consummate expedition methodology.

A team led by Bill Hackett, including Jake
Breitenbach, had attempted Denali's southeast spur in 1958, but they turned back from
rotten and unstable snow and ice. Everett
conscripted four New York friends and a
young Harvard climber named Hank Abrons
to try this ridge. Leapfrogging 2,400 feet of
fixed rope between camps, the team persisted through hollow cornices, over hard ice and
past all sorts of strange and unstable forma-

tions. As the prolonged effort stretched their
supplies, they decided that four of the team
should work in support to establish a final
camp at the end of the south buttress, from
which the two others would make a summit
attempt. This tactic worked, allowing Everett
and Sam Cochrane to climb directly up the
southeast prow of Denali's summit dome to
reach a bivouac camp and then continue to
the top. On the summit, Everett planted a jar
of soil carried from New York's Central Park.

For American mountaineers, the following
season will always be remembered as the
year when Americans first climbed Mt.
Everest. For years to come, American expeditions would keep in mind the success by Jim
Whittaker and Ngawang Gombu—and especially the amazing traverse of the peak that
Willi Unsoeld and Tom Hornbein pulled off.

While the cream of American mountaineers were in Nepal, three expeditions
headed for dangerous new routes on Denali.
First, a team of younger Teton and Rainier
guides went to the east buttress. Avalanches
were a big concern on the ramps leading up
to the buttress; one cavalcade almost took
out their basecamp, and another hit the
climbers, who luckily were held safe by fixed
ropes. Once on the buttress, the guides ferried loads to build a chain of supplies, string-

Three climbers on the first ascent of Denali's Wickersham Wall. PHOTO BY GUNTI PRINZ.

Hank Kaufmann in exhaustion during the first ascent of the Wickersham Wall. PHOTO BY GUNTI PRINZ.

ing ropes over the occasional steep sections. Warren Bleser and Rod Newcomb led through some particularly steep ice, and after joining the 1954 south buttress route, Newcomb, Peter Lev and Al Read reached the summit.

The other two 1963 expeditions went to the immense north face of Denali, the Wickersham Wall, one of the biggest sustained rises of real estate in the world. Although Bradford Washburn had detailed his proposals for this wall in the previous year's *AAJ*, he also warned that avalanches would be a risk.

Hans Gmoser, now a guide in the Canadian Rockies, led a group of fellow guides including his old partner Leo Grillmair as well as two Americans. Gmoser's swift successes on Blackburn and Logan had made him optimistic that big mountains could be climbed quickly and with little ferrying. They aimed for the western edge of the wall, the route thought to be the least dangerous. At 7,000 feet they received an airdrop, and in two days

of good weather they quickly proceeded to Camp III at 10,000 feet. Above rose the terrain that Washburn had noted to be particularly prone to avalanche loading, and in fact a 1961 team camped here had been swept down, luckily without injury.

A few inches of snow fell on Camp III, and with avalanche hazard on their mind Gmoser's team pushed in only three days to a high camp at 18,100 feet. They all began to suffer from the fast pace to such thin air. But since wispy clouds now warned of a storm, the Canadians pressed for the top. Just as Gmoser, Gunti Prinz and Hans Schwarz summited the north peak, the storm hit and a multiday nightmare of descent and self-rescue ensued. Half the team became almost incapacitated with altitude illness, and a dire retreat to the 16,600-foot camp barely saved their lives. When the weather cleared they had recovered enough to traverse to Denali Pass and escape via the west buttress.

As Gmoser's team celebrated back at McKinley Park Lodge, a team of seven mostly undergraduate members of the Harvard Mountaineering Club arrived. Hank Abrons was their leader, and they planned to do the eastern edge of the Wickersham Wall, a steeper route more exposed to serac avalanches. Sophomore David Roberts summarized the incredulity that will always come with seeing Denali, "It was impossible that a mountain that far away could take up so much of the sky, but there it was." Facing steeper terrain than Gmoser's route, the team progressed slowly, fixing ropes over schist cliffs and serac walls and occasionally using direct aid. Avalanches swept right along the subtle rib of their route, but the youngsters didn't know they were supposed to be scared. When they placed one camp below a disintegrating wall and watched substantial rocks rumbling past their tents, they whooped with excitement, figuring that this was part of the thrill on a big mountain.

After they had climbed past the worst terrain, a multiday storm delivered a massive dump of snow. When the skies cleared, pilot Don Sheldon flew over to check on them and saw their tracks disappearing into huge avalanche swaths. Sheldon readied the world for the worst. But good fortune and camaraderie prevailed, and the Harvard undergrads succeeded on Denali's ninth major route, one that no one has taken interest in since.

Washburn continued to send enticing letters and photographs of Alaskan peaks to the European centers of alpinism, and the 1964 season saw two crack teams follow his advice. A French group led by the great alpinist Lionel Terray had a variety of ambitions, starting with a "warm-up" on Mt. Huntington, a 12,240-foot peak just south of Denali. Mt. Huntington is so graceful and striking—especially in Washburn photos— that a variety of teams had been eyeing it. The cornice-toothed northwest ridge seemed to be the only potential route, and after three weeks of effort they succeeded. Like Cassin and many other visitors, Terray was impressed with Alaskan conditions, finding that the ancient subarctic ice is like brick-hard glass, the temperatures fluctuate fiercely, and the snowy crests are replete with unstable masses. Terray, in fact, injured

The *Hummingbird Ridge* team before their climb. From left to right: Frank Coale, Dick Long, Allen Steck, Jim Wilson, John Evans and Paul Bacon. PHOTO COURTESY ALLEN STECK.

Mt. Logan from the south, above the Seward Glacier. The *Hummingbird Ridge* is the prominent central spine. The first ascent party started from the opposite side, gaining the crest in the low section at left, and followed the ridge to the top. The upper part of the *Warbler Ridge* is visible at right, and the south-southwest buttress is to the left.
PHOTOGRAPH #7614 © BRADFORD WASHBURN, COURTESY ELMER E. RASMUSON LIBRARY/UNIVERSITY OF ALASKA FAIRBANKS.

his shoulder in a long fall. The Frenchmen had planned to try the south face of Denali as well, but Huntington was adventure enough and they returned home.

A German team flew to the Ruth Glacier to try the Moose's Tooth, a hulking molar southeast of Denali. The group worked upward to a campsite below the main west ridge, 2,500 feet and over one and a half miles from the summit. Pushing for the top, the team found corniced ridges, hard ice and loose snow requiring great care and effort. While traversing to the middle summit, Arnold Hasenkopf hit very hard ice and took a long fall over the south face. He climbed back up, though, and all four members of the expedition reached the highest point 22 hours after leaving their camp.

The *Hummingbird*

For the 1965 season, Boyd Everett gathered nine climbers, mostly from Harvard and Dartmouth, to climb St. Elias by its very long northwest ridge. This was Everett's second attempt on the route; his 1964 team had

reached the ridgecrest only 3,000 feet lower than the summit, but still three miles away. During that expedition, the area was rocked by two major earthquakes, a disturbingly common trigger for cataclysmic avalanches in this region. There were no earthquakes in 1965, but an avalanche still hit three of the climbers while they worked up their fixed ropes, injuring one. On the way to the summit this team strung 4,900 feet of fixed rope from an impressive total of 56 pitons. For climbing the fixed lines, they no longer used prusiks or other knots, but instead employed the swift new Swiss camming ascenders known as jümars.

As Everett and party neared the summit, a team of Californians was starting up the biggest, most spectacular flying buttress on the continent, the central south ridge of Mt. Logan. Starting from 6,000 feet on the Seward Glacier, this seven-mile spine rises through an almost overwhelming array of summits and towers, including a mile-long horizontal stretch of arabesque cornices. Anyone who made it through this gauntlet would still face a 7,000-foot headwall leading to Logan's main summit. Sacramento physician Dick Long originated the plan to attempt this ridge. Long had been awestruck at the prodigious spine during an expedition to Logan in 1953.

As the tactics for climbing big ridges became established during the intervening years, Long started talking about his dream with Allen Steck, physicist Jim Wilson and John Evans, who earned his money by wrestling crocodiles at a tourist trap in South Dakota. Figuring they would need to be comfortable on fixed ropes and steep terrain, they trained on wall climbs in Yosemite. During the fall of 1964, engineer Frank Coale and skier extraordinaire Paul Bacon joined the project. About this time they got a call from Boyd Everett, saying he wanted to join forces. In this exchange, Long obtained some valuable and intimidating aerial photographs of the ridge. But the Californians decided that familiarity and compatibility would be more important than Everett's experience, so they turned down his offer, and indeed teamwork would prove to be their most valuable asset.

In the second week of July they started climbing the ridge on its western flank, stringing fixed rope up a 2,800-foot rock buttress to avoid obvious avalanche chutes. It took a few days to haul over 700 pounds of gear, including 30 days of food and 4,200 feet of fixed line, up the buttress to the ridgecrest at 9,600 feet. During one of these trips, amid an icy wilderness nearly 100 miles from any flower, Steck was buzzed by a migrating rufous hummingbird that had come to investigate his red frame-pack. He later wrote:

> *My little friend, you and I are both intruders on this lifeless ridge; you have been blown off course by chance, while I, owing to forces I do not fully comprehend, have come voluntarily—like a moth to a flame—attracted by the elemental dynamism of the mountains. We are now both engaged in a struggle with our environment, though mine appears the more absurd.*

They decided to name the ridge for the little visitor—and to pull the fixed lines and

keep going. A long day of climbing across loose schist and wild cornices gained only a small lift in elevation. This first taste of ridge-line traversing was so frightening, with so much more yet to come, that the team quavered with the ambivalence that would be their partner for the whole climb. Each delicate step forward made the seemingly inevitable retreat more dispiriting, and they constantly asked each other, "How can we get off of here and when?" On the other hand, they agreed they wouldn't give up until they'd given it their best shot. At each challenge they dug deeper into a well of patience, assertiveness and ingenuity.

To get their loads atop one rotten rock tower, they transported their gear by rigging a "*téléferique*," a Tyrolean span some 600 feet

Camp 2 on the *Hummingbird Ridge*. This is the platform where the team spent a week in storm, and which fell away hours after they pressed forward. PHOTO BY ALLEN STECK.

Climbing along the heavily corniced "Shovel Traverse" section of the *Hummingbird Ridge*. PHOTO BY ALLEN STECK.

long. Looking beyond this gendarme to the mile-long chain of cornices, Steck marveled at their artistic grace and then recoiled at the prospect of climbing over them. As he probed the tottering structures, he found them "exciting beyond belief." He led along the billowy high wire to the only hope for a camp, a precarious site leveled from the top of one of the largest cornices. The group asked physicist Wilson how long their cornice perch would remain intact, and he gave it six days. They anchored to extra lines tied in way down the slope.

A storm then came and they had to wait out a week on that perch. By the time the weather cleared they had used up about half their supplies, and they had more than three-quarters of the route yet to go. They voted whether or not to press on, and with the count 2-2, Long and Wilson's votes would decide. Wilson had great trust in the younger, powerful Long. He asked, "Dick, can you get me off of this mountain safely?" Long replied that he could, and so on they went. That afternoon they happened to look back and watch the perch they had occupied for a week shear away. Bacon lightened the moment by suggesting that their tent lines had been holding it up.

In the lead now, Long found slow work cutting steps, as the crusty surface on south-facing aspects wouldn't release his adze. He tried clearing steps with their steel camp shovel and found it worked wonderfully. Looser snow on northern aspects also responded to the shovel, so this became their primary tool. Nevertheless, the scale and continuous tenuousness made it hard to be optimistic. They comforted themselves by agreeing that if they weren't finished with the cornices by August 2 they would retreat. As they led, fixed and ferried over the next five days, luck seemed to be with them. Evans dropped a boot (for the second time) and was able to recover it. Some of the ridge turned out to be more reasonable than expected. Two days before their deadline, a storm that probably would shut them down seemed to be brewing. But the next day was clear, and Evans quipped, "Looks like the beginning of the forward retreat." Buoyed by this notion—that going ahead was a better way to get back—they completed the *Hummingbird Ridge.* The headwall beyond the corniced ridge turned out to be moderate, and after fixing rope to the summit plateau they climbed to all three of Logan's highest summits. Then they descended to a cache that Coale had set at King Col, after a total of 30 days on the route.

This was the grandest ascent of the period and one of the greatest routes done anywhere in the world. Fred Beckey remarked, "When they got back we just couldn't believe that they had climbed that thing. We didn't think they had a chance." Subsequent attempts to repeat the entire route have failed, and the ridge now bears a nearly mythical mystique.

Advanced Organization
The following year, Boyd Everett compiled his advice for big trips into an unpublished manuscript, *The Organization of an Alaskan Expedition.* In this hand-typed tome one finds key insights into the expedition thinking of this era.

Everett recommended being aggressive in route choice because one could expect to climb almost any terrain that looked reasonable from afar; he maintained that weather and avalanche hazard would be greater factors than technical difficulty. While he noted that some younger climbers were beginning to challenge the use of fixed ropes, he held firm to the notion that it is inefficient and unsafe for a climber to carry a heavy pack without depending on a line anchored above.

Everett also offered an explanation for why climbing in Alaska and the Yukon usually went slowly. He noted that sleep and the chores of camping on ice left just 10 hours per day for climbing. Difficult ice and snow conditions made for slower going, colder temperatures required more insulation and stove fuel, and bad weather typically forced a team to be tent-bound about half the time. Gray Thompson and others later characterized Everett's methodology as the "Alaskan Wave Theory"—haul enough manpower and supplies to the base, and a wave of momentum will carry someone to the top.

Since these great routes were of such a different order from most alpine climbs, Everett also suggested special Alaskan ratings. He categorized routes relative to each other based on a subjective assessment of scale and overall difficulty. Examples of all six grades included:

Route	*Alaska Grade*
Mt. Steele, East Ridge	I
Mt. McKinley, West Buttress	II
Mt. Huntington, Northwest Ridge	III
Mt. St. Elias, Northwest Ridge	IV
Mt. McKinley, *Cassin Ridge*	V
Mt. Logan, *Hummingbird Ridge*	VI

In 1966, Everett mounted his most grandiose expedition yet, a climb of King Peak's west ridge that continued on to the summit of Mt. Logan. Nine climbers accompanied him, and Everett was seemingly proud to describe the use of a probable record of 10,300 feet of fixed rope and 83 pitons. Canadian authorities did not authorize American pilots to land within Canada at this time, so the team had to land on the Columbus Glacier across the border. To help with the load ferrying, Everett arranged for the first and probably only expedition use of a snowmobile. An Arctic Cat was brought to basecamp in the Cessna ski plane, and, at about 10 mph, the machine ferried supplies to the start of the climbing. They also used it to ferry supplies up the King Trench to place a mid-route cache near King Peak. Although Gray Thomspon was injured in a fall, the expedition persevered to success.

The following February, an eight-man expedition launched one of the more brutal adventures yet hatched: climbing Denali in winter. The party included Art Davidson (four months after climbing Kichatna Spire, see Chapter 12), Jacques Batkin, who had been on the first ascent of Huntington, and Ray Genet, an ambitious Franco-Swiss tyro who was cavalier about his complete lack of mountaineering experience. At first the team did not take the crevasse hazard seriously, and they traveled up the Kahiltna Glacier unroped. Not far from the landing site, Batkin plummeted through a snow bridge to his death.

After much soul-searching, the team pressed on. Enduring temperatures below –50ºF and wind chills estimated at –148ºF, Davidson, Dave Johnston and Genet reached the summit. During their exhausted retreat a storm hit, and they had to huddle in a cave at Denali Pass for some six days. After the weather cleared, they dragged themselves on frostbitten feet to the Kahiltna Glacier and a helicopter evacuation.

Expedition Extravaganzas

The subarctic's plethora of virgin summits, along with Canada's approaching 1967 centennial, inspired the moribund Alpine Club of Canada to launch what has been called the most extensive mountaineering expedition in history, the Yukon Alpine Centennial Expedition. Teams of mountaineers tackled 13 unclimbed, unnamed peaks in a chain north of Mt. Logan that was christened the Centennial Range. Each objective was named for one of Canada's provinces. A second phase of the extravaganza was a celebrity basecamp accessed by helicopter near the snout of the Steele Glacier, west of Kluane Lake. There, climbers could chum with the likes of Lord John Hunt, Fritz Wiessner and Walter Wood, and then venture out to make a first ascent. Twelve peaks were climbed here for the first time and named for the deceased presidents of the ACC.

That same year was also the centennial for the Alaska Purchase, and Boyd Everett made a sales pitch to the state to gain official status for another multiteam assault. Under the umbrella of "Alaska '67," 14 climbers would siege three different routes up the south face of Denali: one to repeat the 1954 route up the south buttress, another to the *Cassin Ridge* (where Everett himself participated) and a new route up the steepest part of the face, a mile to the east of the Cassin route. To boost morale, the south buttress team packed a five-pound portable record player and 15 LP albums up to 15,000 feet.

Four young Dartmouth climbers comprised the south face direct ("Centennial Wall") team: Dennis Eberl, Gray Thompson, Dave

Denny Eberl beginning the difficult second rock buttress on the first ascent of the *Direct South Face* of Denali. GRAY THOMPSON COLLECTION.

Gray Thompson on the icefield between the second and third rock buttresses, *Direct South Face* of Denali. GRAY THOMPSON COLLECTION.

Seidman and Roman Laba. Their proposed route worked through granite buttresses and slopes known to be prone to avalanches. As they strung their 7,500 feet of rope, they realized there was no genuinely safe way and, as Seidman said, "extreme chances had to be taken." As much as possible they belayed and set camps below rock features. All four were hit by avalanches, however, and for security they depended on their ropes, anchors and swift climbing, often on frontpoints.

As many Alaskan expeditions did at this time, they started in early July. Storms hammered the region for two weeks, forcing all four to stay in their two small tents on platforms chopped from steep ice. When the weather finally cleared, they were ecstatic to get moving again, even though they had yet to even start the 2,500 feet of steep granite and mixed climbing below the top. As the weather now held, they confronted the most technical (up to 5.7) high-altitude climbing yet done on the continent. Deploying fixed

↻ Gray Thompson on the *Direct South Face* of Denali; Kahiltna Peaks in the background.
GRAY THOMPSON COLLECTION.

ropes pulled up from below, they reached the summit on August 4. The south buttress team had cached supplies for them, so they descended that route.

Back in Talkeetna, they learned that the two weeks of storm had overwhelmed a team (the "Wilcox Expedition") climbing from the north, and seven climbers had perished. Two books and other commentators analyzed this disaster, but one undeniable factor was that repeated successes by technical routes on Denali had insidiously led climbers to lower their guard. The tragedy was a grim reminder of what Bradford Washburn had written: "I know of no spot where wind and temperature can be more powerfully combined than on McKinley's upper ridges—and I am referring to the summer months."

Two years later, Boyd Everett took his organizational expertise to the Himalaya to attempt Dhaulagiri. Gray Thompson and some other veterans were invited, but they decided not to go because of the serac-fall hazard on the chosen route. Their fears proved true: a gigantic avalanche killed Everett, Dave Seidman, Vin Hoeman and three others. In a single cataclysm, a major wing of America's expeditionary mountaineers was lost.

SUGGESTED ROUTES
FROM THIS PERIOD

MT. ST. ELIAS (18,008 feet/5,488 meters)
Southwest Ridge

This Himalayan-sized mountain, the fourth-highest summit in North America, is one of the most stupendous uplifts in the world. Although six or seven primary routes have been made to the summit, all of them have significant hazards, circuitous climbing or other uncertainties that defy the notion of a "regular" route. Ski-plane landings at nearly 10,000 feet on the Columbus Glacier have made the west face somewhat popular, but the classic route is the southwest ridge. Unlike on Denali, there is no easy access to high altitudes for acclimatization. However, Austrians Kurt Stüwe and Josef Hassler climbed this route alpine style in nine days of beau-

tiful weather in May 1984. Most parties plan to take two to three weeks.

Approach: At this writing the only pilot flying to St. Elias is Paul Claus of Chitina, Alaska. The landing spot is on the Tyndall Glacier at about 2,300 feet, depending on conditions. At least one party has recommended landing on the Libby Glacier and crossing the Chaix Hills to reach the foot of the ridge.

Route: The climbing starts with a good 7,000 feet of steady gain up the southwest ridge of Haydon Peak. The first half of this section is a slope of rotten shale, and then snow and ice allow better going to Haydon. Traverse around the north flank of Haydon Peak to the 10,000-foot col with St. Elias. From the col, the broad nose of St. Elias' upper southwest ridge is obvious. With snow, ice and mixed terrain up to 60 degrees, the first half of this 8,000-foot-high slope is the most difficult section of the route. Most parties break up the climb to the summit with camps or bivouacs at two or more decent sites. One can expect a variety of conditions, from ice to névé to deep snow. Descend by the same route.

Mt. St. Elias from the south-southwest. PHOTO BY WALT GOVE.

First Ascent: Benjamin Ferris, Andrew Kauffman, Elizabeth Kauffman, Bill Latady, Maynard Miller, Cornelius Molenaar, Dee Molenaar and Bill Putnam, July 1946; First winter ascent: Dave Briggs, Gardner Heaton and Joe Reichert, February 1996

Difficulty: TD, AI 3, 15,000 feet

Guidebook: *Alaska: A Climbing Guide*

MT. LOGAN (19,550 feet/5,959 meters)
East Ridge

Few expeditionary routes attract enough traffic to be called popular, but this route's balance of technical but manageable terrain and super-alpine grandeur brings a number of teams to it every season. As on St. Elias, an acclimatization program is hard to build here, especially if one plans to march beyond the east summit to Logan's highest point. If high altitude were not a problem, many parties would climb this route alpine style, but most place four to six camps and occasional stretches of fixed rope along the ridge.

Approach: From Kluane, Yukon Territory, or Chitina, Alaska, pilots can land at 7,000 feet on the west fork of the Hubbard Glacier, barely a mile from the start of the ridge.

Route: Parties have started up the ridge on both the south and north sides of its toe. Once on the ridgecrest, the first sections are narrow and exposed for some distance, but the snow, ice and rock are only moderately difficult. At about 11,500 feet a rock step gives passage to the first section of true knife-edge, which is generally uncorniced. The next challenging section is where crevasses force you to traverse fairly steep ground on the south face of the ridge. Then another knife-edge takes you nearly to the end of the technical difficulties at 13,600 feet. Above, the ridge broadens to more gradual terrain, where the concerns shift to hidden crevasses, storm exposure and avalanches. A final camp can be pitched between here and the base of the 19,357-foot east peak, which is a good 193 feet lower and almost two miles from Logan's highest point. Descend by the same route.

First Ascent: Dave Collins, Don Monk, Cecil Oulette, Gil Roberts, Kermith Ross, July 1957

Difficulty: TD, AI 3, 12,500 feet

Permit: Permission is required to climb in Kluane National Park.

The east ridge of Mt. Logan. PHOTO BY JOE JOSEPHSON.

DENALI (20,320 feet/6,194 meters)
South Buttress

Mort Wood, one of the first ascensionists of this route, wrote, "I would never encourage anyone to climb the mountain by this route, as it is not, in my opinion, either safe or practical." Since then, however, advances in snow and ice climbing, and especially the ski-plane option of beginning and ending this route at the Kahiltna Glacier, have made this arguably the finest moderate route to the top of the continent. It is an uncrowded, slightly more technical alternative to the west buttress—which is to say it is a serious undertaking.

A variety of routes reach the crest of the buttress. The 1954 team climbed moderately steep slopes out of the Ruth Glacier's west fork. In 1965, a Japanese team with Anchorage students Shiro Nishimae and Art Davidson gained the crest much higher, from the east fork of the Kahiltna Glacier, via

Denali from the south. The 1988 south buttress route line is drawn. The *Cassin Ridge* is prominent in the center of the main face. The 1967 *American Direct* ("*Centennial Wall*") is on the prow farther right. The 1984 *Slovak Direct* is on the *Cassin's* right flank. The sunlit face to its left holds the routes done in 1980, 1983 and 2001. The left skyline includes the upper west and northwest buttresses. PHOTO #5896 © BRADFORD WASHBURN. COURTESY ELMER E. RASMUSON LIBRARY/UNIVERSITY OF ALASKA FAIRBANKS.

a ramp somewhat threatened by seracs. In 1988, a team of Americans climbed a slightly steeper but safer spur to the right of this route. Not until 1994 did a team finally make the complete ascent of the buttress from the Kahiltna's southeast fork. The 1988 route is recommended here.

Approach: From the 7,100-foot-high landing site on the Kahiltna's southeast fork, travel around Mt. Frances Randall and up the east fork of the Kahiltna.

Route: Near the head of the glacier, gain a bench at 11,000 feet and then climb east up the broad rib that starts along the top of some huge rock cliffs. There are some small serac walls to work through before you reach the top of the buttress at about 15,400 feet. Now take the crest of the buttress on an unforgettable two-mile sky tour. Parties who want to follow Thayer's easier but much longer route will cross Thayer Basin and summit via the northeast ridge. Most climbers ready for moderately steep snow and ice will take the southeast ridge that Boyd Everett first climbed in 1962. Either descend the same route or go down the west buttress, which requires a carry over the top. As for any Denali climb, unless you are pre-acclimatized you should plan for a three-week excursion.

First Ascent: Mort Wood, Leslie Viereck, Elton Thayer and George Argus, May 1954; Via Kahiltna Rib: Bill Alexander, Andy Carson, John Chaklos, Chuck Crago and Zach Etheridge, May 1988

Difficulty: D, AI 2, 12,500 feet

Guidebooks: *High Alaska; Denali Climbing Guide*

Permit: Permission to climb Denali must be obtained 60 days in advance from Denali National Park. There is a $150 fee.

Period III

Better That We Raise Our Skill

The essence of alpinism has always been a commitment to the unknown—following time's arrow along its only path. And great routes follow the mountain's natural path. And good climbs are those following these one-way paths with an irreducible minimum of equipment. Economy, no extra gear, no wasted thought or motion. Every piece of equipment counts, no debilitating debates, no inefficiencies. And two climbers—the sine qua non of technical climbing. Two climbers—with more than the strength of two—the minimum of human society.

—Bill Sumner, 1974 *Ascent*

If mountaineers were simply interested in getting up routes, the post-World War II era might have been the peak of the game. For expedition climbers in North America, what could be greater than the giant ridges and faces that had been done in Alaska and the Yukon? For technical climbers, what could be more exciting than the great verticality of El Capitan? If route completion were the only guiding principle, mountaineers would simply deploy snowmobiles, airplanes, large teams, bolts and fixed ropes as much as possible.

But the nature of climbing is to optimize challenge, and climbers began to rebel against mechanization. During the 1960s and 1970s, a general mumble grew into a chorus to say that mechanized support and unbridled technology were no longer advancing climbing but inhibiting it. Progressive climbers understood that the future lay not in simply succeeding but in climbing better. They began to weigh anew the terrain and their potential, and to assert that, although the terrain would never get grander, the limits of personal effort were far from known. The term they adopted to point to the future was *style*.

As in any art, a definition of climbing style is subjective and constantly evolving, but perhaps the most important aspect is *engagement*. The idea was to engage more personal effort and to reset the level of uncertainty. Climbers sought not to tie their own hands or to make climbs more difficult; rather, their goal was to push themselves to climb tough terrain more effectively. Perhaps the best way to summarize style is that it is a search to find the simplest way to do more.

Of course, mountaineers long insisted that personal effort should take precedence over technological support—as shown by the decades-old debates over the use of pitons. Traditionally, a route's inherent difficulties dictated the style. But once technologies and tactics evolved to allow success on even the biggest and steepest routes, style became the front-burner definition of progress. Unclimbed terrain would continue to be a leading challenge, but climbers now became at least as likely to celebrate ascents of existing routes in better style.

Lito Tejada-Flores, an observant and superb skier and climber from California, developed a seminal definition of style in his essay "The Games Climbers Play." This article first appeared in the 1967 issue of the Sierra Club publication *Ascent*. By this time, climbing had branched into a range of specialties. From the shortest, most severe technical challenges—bouldering—to the hugest Himalayan faces, Tejada-Flores identified a spectrum of seven climbing "games." He showed how each game had its own "rules" of style. These unwritten rules, he argued, mandated "a handicap system...to equalize the inherent challenge and maintain the climber's feeling of achievement at a high level.... [The rules] are designed to conserve the climber's feeling of personal (moral) accomplishment against the meaninglessness of a success which represents merely technological victory."

On Himalayan-scale routes, for example, where the problems of scale and difficulty compounded so much that success and survival by any means were a great challenge, climbers could employ a range of siege tactics, including large teams with support personnel, fixed ropes, established camps and even ladders. But such means would be absurd on a crag climb or a more typical alpine face, and so the rules of style insisted that climbers adopt an appropriate level of handicap. New standards for style would be set when climbers completed a route with less than the usual amount of support. For instance, succeeding on a big wall or Himalayan route without fixed ropes would be one advance in style. Free climbing a steep crag route usually done with aid would be another. In the alpine climbing game, the dynamic and risky environment had long mandated efficiency and speed, but the new emphasis on style suggested taking on much bigger and more technical routes with the original tactics of alpine mountaineering.

During the 1960s, North Americans' insistence on climbing with style gathered momentum in Yosemite Valley. After El Capitan had been climbed a couple of times, Royal Robbins asserted that climbers should take on that great wall without using fixed ropes. He underscored the new imperative by saying, "Better that we raise our skill than lower the climb." The easy access and fairly benign environment in Yosemite made it a natural place to make long, technical routes in a single go. In the 1970s, Canadians and Americans took to frozen waterfalls with such aplomb that they opened a parallel realm on vertiginous ice. Soon leading climbers had begun to take their skill and alpine-style philosophy to technical routes in the high mountains.

When Tejada-Flores wrote his article, his "Super-Alpine Game" was just coming into play. This game "rejects expedition techniques on terrain which would traditionally have been suitable for it. Its only restrictive rule is that the party must be self-contained. Any umbilical-like connection in the form of a series of camps, fixed ropes, etc., to a secure base is no longer permitted. This rule provides a measure of commitment that automatically increases the uncertainty of success, making victory that much more meaningful."

In the 1960s super-alpine climbers were beginning to ascend expedition-scale routes with only a few fixed ropes and no fixed camps. As they climbed, they would retrieve and re-string their limited amount of rope, progressing without the lifeline of ropes and camps leading back to the base. The first teams on Denali's *West Rib* and Logan's *Hummingbird Ridge* climbed in this fashion, which became known as "capsule style." Meanwhile, the boldest European climbers were starting to take on big routes in the Andes with just a single lead rope, in pure alpine style. Before long this would become the game in Alaska and the Yukon.

The search for climbing renewal also gained momentum out of the general call for social renewal in the 1960s and 1970s. As corporations, urban sprawl and the war in Vietnam seemed to march against the interests of many, there was a growing realization in both North America and Europe that civilization's biggest problems were being created by civilization itself. As American cartoonist Walt Kelly wrote, "We has met the enemy, and it is us," Americans began calling for limits on population growth, pollution and the military. So, too, climbers began to grow more aware that there is only one world of mountains and that they had better make the most of it and treat it kindly. When leading climber and gear designer Tom Frost helped lead the call, in 1970, for restraint in the use of rock-damaging pitons, he quoted Goethe: "Whatever liberates our spirit without giving us self-control is disastrous."

American mountaineers took their concerns to Congress, where they pushed for legislation to establish officially designated wilderness areas, which would be permanently off limits to roads and motorized access. The Wilderness Society (Bob Marshall's organization), Sierran David Brower and a number of Cascade mountaineers were key members of the broad coalition that helped write and lobby for the Wilderness Act of 1964. This law adopted as U.S. policy the notion that wild lands are assets—places where we can know nature without the mixed blessings of civilization.

With even the poles, Everest and Denali becoming well trodden, some lamented what seemed to be obvious limits to the potential for discovery. In this regard, some climbers felt that even the dissemination of route information was damaging to the climbing experience, and they advocated an ethic of not describing or publicizing their first ascents. In 1972, leading Shawangunks climber John Stannard warned that the process of climbers competing to make their marks could usher in an endgame where "all the routes in all the climbing areas are fully cataloged, codified and prepared for the museum." As a remedy, he predicted that by 1984, "The reporting of first ascents will disappear because it serves no purpose, other than to hinder the process.... To one who climbs for intrinsic reasons it makes no difference whether it is the first ascent or not." Since guidebooks now codify most crag routes, Stannard's predictions look naïve, but in certain areas climbers still keep quiet about new routes, partly out of fear of the loss of adventure. In Montana, climbers talk about their routes but have agreed not to publish information, as a matter of honoring and continuing the ancient oral tradition of the region's Blackfeet Indians.

Across the United States and Canada, wilderness journeys and climbing became fashionable parts of youth culture. By the early 1970s, dropping out and tying in became a fad, and Yvon Chouinard wrote, "What was once a way of life that only attracted the oddball individual is now a healthy, upstanding, recreational pastime enjoyed by thousands of average Joes." New North American manufacturers sprouted to meet an emerging market for improved climbing gear, and commercial climbing magazines added new venues to disseminate information, heighten competition and develop climbing identities.

For those who kept their focus more on substance and progress than on fashion, climbing mountains in the best style possible became the beacon to an unlimited mountaineering future, a way to enhance both experience and accomplishment by engaging ever more closely with the character of the peaks.

CHAPTER 10

The Ice Revolution

Compared with rock climbing, the techniques for climbing ice did not evolve much into the 1950s. In 1953, the year that Richard Emerson made the brilliant first free ascent of the Grand Teton's rocky north face, a Harvard team finally repeated the ice face on Mt. Robson that Conrad Kain had pioneered in 1913. As it happened, the Harvard crew found firm but pliable snow and little hard ice. Their modern gear included crampons and rudimentary ice pitons, but their methods still depended on chopping steps, and in this skill they undoubtedly had nothing on Kain.

The insecure toil of hewing ladders of steps up steep ground made the attitude toward ice climbing something like paying taxes—a well-rounded climber had to participate, but the first choice was to avoid ice. However, as climbers developed the tools, techniques, the specific strengths and the audacity to lead steep ice without cutting steps, the bookkeeping changed. Eventually, frozen waterfalls became the ice climber's "practice" crags, and on big alpine routes ice climbers would move off the rock and onto ice as a

faster way to go. This opened up all manner of alpine and super-alpine routes. North Americans would be at the forefront of this revolution— arguably the most influential transformation in mountaineering history.

Beginnings in the Cascades

The Cascades are the primary snow and ice mountains in the Lower 48, and so it is natural that this is where American climbers actively started to trust their crampons' bite directly, without chopping steps. Fred Beckey and Bob Craig, for instance, made the second ascent of the north face of Mt. Shuksan (sustained 40- to 50-degree snow and ice) in firm conditions in the fall of 1947. Beckey looked down from above and took pride in seeing no steps, saying, "Nature's intimacy was inviolate that day." A year later, Craig joined with Dee Molenaar to put up an impressive new route through the Nisqually Icefall on the south flank of Mt. Rainier.

Crampons themselves had not improved since the hinged, 12-point design first came out in the 1930s, but on steeper ice a few climbers nevertheless began to experiment with the audacious technique of frontpointing while stabbing the ice with the pick of their axe in one hand and perhaps an ice dagger in the other. Beckey was a cautious

↺ Yvon Chouinard using a minimum of tools and a maximum of finesse on *Repentance*, a mixed climb near North Conway, New Hampshire, in 1976. PHOTO BY HENRY BARBER.

Mt. Mendel (right) and Mt. Darwin. The left and right Mendel Couloirs are visible on the north face. PHOTO BY ANDY SELTERS.

practitioner of occasional frontpointing in the 1950s, and climbers from the east side of the Cascades, unaffected by the "tried and true" tradition that still kept Seattle's Mountaineers chopping steps, also took to frontpointing. The east-side "Sherpa Climbing Club" guys innovated their own rigid crampon design, welding across the hinge to build a solid platform for secure frontpointing. In 1955, Sherpas Dave Mahre and Gene Prater made the second ascent of Rainier's Liberty Ridge with occasional flurries of frontpointing.

In June 1957, a team of premier ice climbers from both sides of the Cascades finally tackled Mt. Rainier's unclimbed west (Mowich) face. Fred Beckey, Tom Hornbein, Don Claunch, John Rupley and Herb Staley found that the face was not as steep as the intimidating frontal view implies. The 5,000-foot-high route was continuously 40 degrees and occasionally steeper. When the five saw from the top that a storm was brewing, they changed their descent plans and simply went back down the same face.

In September of that season, Mahre, Prater and Prater's brother Bill pushed a route through the northeast face of Mt. Stuart. Climbing up the Ice Cliff Glacier, they skirted an absurdly steep serac wall and finished up a steep chute to the northeast ridge. In subsequent seasons Mahre and Prater would return to climb the glacier two more times, adding to the challenge by moving onto the vertiginous granite of Stuart's northeast headwall.

Rink-Hard Couloirs and Relentless Faces

Sierra and Teton climbers generally had to negotiate snow and ice only during approaches and descents from rock routes. But in the late 1950s some began to go out of their way to look for hard snow and ice in steep couloirs. These chutes have sections of glassy, super-hard ice—the sort that no one yet was ready to climb without chopping steps. In September 1957, John Mathias and John Ohrenschall climbed the *V-Notch Couloir*, a 55-degree chute rising out of the Sierra's Palisade Glacier. The next spring, Stanford climbers Felix Knauth and John Whitmer climbed the striking 1,000-foot couloir that shoots up the north face of the Sierra's Mt. Mendel, with a bulge of ice over 60 degrees.

Teton climbers also began to consider steep ice chutes in the late 1950s. From ledges on the west side of the Grand Teton, they often looked down a bullet-hard, 1,000-foot-long gutter that earned the name *Black Ice Couloir*. In 1958, Ken Weeks, Yvon Chouinard and Frank Garneau started up it, but a volley of rockfall sent them back. Three years later, Fred Beckey and George Bell also retreated from the ice chute. A month after their attempt, in late July 1961, engineering student Ray Jacquot and guide Herb Swedlund skirted the rockfall challenge with a moonlit start from the Lower Saddle. They aimed to reach the route at 1 a.m., and to hedge their bets they donned helmets—something that, to traditional mountaineers, proved their plan was patently absurd. Jacquot and Swedlund gained the couloir's midsection by rock climbing the first few pitches of Durrance's west face route, and then moved onto the glassy ice. Chopping steps between occasional moves on frontpoints, they finished seven pitches of ice up to nearly 70 degrees. This was a remarkable burst of energy from the slender Swedlund, as it was only his second time wearing crampons and just four days earlier he had climbed a major new rock route on the right side of Mt. Moran's south buttress.

Jacquot and Swedlund protected their ascent with an impressive total of 30 ice piton placements. Ice pitons at this time included a variety of corkscrew and drive-in designs, and while these no doubt made the climbers feel more secure, their ability to actually hold a fall was dubious. In general, ice climbing was a game of boldness in the traditional sense—the leader must not fall.

A year later, Teton guides Al Read, Peter Lev and James Greig climbed the *Enclosure Couloir*, a chute less steep and dangerous than the *Black Ice Couloir*. It delivered them onto superb rock climbing along the Grand's northwest ridge.

Ron Perla, another Teton guide and also a leading snow scientist, went north in 1961 with talented Salt Lake City climber Tom Spencer to meet an impressive array of challenges on a long-tried route up Mt. Robson: the Emperor Ridge. From a camp at 8,000 feet, they worked their way up the ridge's vertical rock abutments, gradually coming to icy

rock at an overhang where they used some piton aid. Despite a cloud-cap wind that blasted the higher reaches, they made swift time through Robson's infamous comb of insecure rime-ice gargoyles. They wove in a margin of safety by running pitches around alternate sides of the ghostly towers, finding that the 150-foot rope was barely long enough to connect safe stances. Sometimes they had to chop into the big blobs to reach solid ice for aid pitons. A couple of times they had to traverse above the Emperor Face on steep ice and again use aid to regain the crest. They completed 30 pitches to reach easy ground at the summit area, where they shivered with light bivouac gear in a crevasse. Even with advances in gear and technique, few teams, if any, have climbed this big route so swiftly.

Bold Cascade climbers of the early 1960s had their focus on the most notorious face on Mt. Rainier, the Willis Wall. Park administrators deemed this face off limits, but a variety of the region's most ambitious climbers were willing to flaunt both the rules and the frequent devastating avalanches. Bad weather turned all away until late June 1961, when Charlie Bell climbed the left edge of the wall alone. He followed a spur that proved surprisingly moderate, weaving around rock cliffs and connecting to the upper *Curtis Ridge*. Because Bell had never done any major routes before, many dismissed his claims. A year later, though, he repeated the climb with a more central start and presented photographs as proof. Eventually he paid a fine for his violation of park regulations and noted, "I find it paradoxical that Bonatti got a medal for his Matterhorn solo and I paid a $50 fine for my Rainier solo; but if I were running Rainier Park, I would surely prohibit myself from doing it again."

Dan Davis and Pat Callis were students in Seattle studying mathematics and chemistry, respectively, and in January 1963 they made the much-discussed first winter ascent of the north face of Mt. Index, the impressive gateway peak to the Cascades northeast of Seattle. Davis and Callis climbed while a clear cold snap made the snow and ice firm and secure on the low-elevation peak (the summit is only 5,979 feet). They spent their second night on the summit in Callis' custom, two-person, nylon bivouac sack, and they engineered many rappels to get back down the 5,300-foot route.

Dave Mahre led the charge for a direct route up the center of the Willis Wall, and one night in early June of 1963 he and his east-side buddies Fred Dunham, Don Anderson and Jim Wickwire started up a rib to the right of Bell's route. In one long push they climbed over rotten rock cliffs, steep snow and glassy ice (where they chopped steps), all under an active serac wall. They traversed right to breach that wall at its central overlapping break, while the perched tonnage luckily held firm. As Anderson began to weaken from exhaustion and altitude illness, the team veered across the top to descend whatever way they could and made it down the Mowich Face.

Cascade ice climbers knew that one of the great challenges on the continent was the north face of Mt. Robson. Don Claunch had called this 2,600-foot shield in the sky "perhaps the most savage looking ice wall in the Rockies." Many parties tried it during the early 1960s, but bad weather and unstable snow on its lower third blocked suitors from the real challenge. Beckey and Ed Cooper retreated off it once, sensing that the snow was unstable, and the next day they saw their tracks carried off in an awesome avalanche.

It was loyal partners Callis and Davis who finally succeeded, in early August 1963, during their first trip to Canada. Starting in the middle of the night from a bivouac in the bergschrund, they kicked steps under an aurora display in soft, even "questionable" snow, without crampons. Soon, though, the powder thinned and they started to hit ice underneath. Dawn's light revealed profound exposure, and the view up the face showed an ice rink covered with powder and tilted to 65 degrees. They put on crampons and kept going "on all fours," frontpointing while poking into the ice with an axe in one hand and an improvised tool for balance in the other— Davis had an "ice hatchet" and Callis carried a snow picket. At the end of each rope length,

Jock Glidden showing classic form on the second ascent of Mt. Robson's north face, in 1968. PHOTO BY PETER LEV.

the leader chopped a stance into the ice and belayed from a couple of barbed ice pitons. After 10 hours the pair reached the top. They descended to the top of the Kain Face and found it laden with warm snow. They intentionally kicked off avalanches to clear the face before descending, which they did mostly by standing glissade.

Soon Cascade climbers took their growing expertise to the principle unclimbed facet of Rainier, the intimidating apex of the Mowich headwall, left of the 1957 route. In 1966, Dee Molenaar, Gene Prater, Jim Wickwire and Dick Pargeter first attacked the headwall, with Molenaar leading a crux chute of ice through rock bands. Key to their safety and success was long experience on Rainier that pointed them to a narrow time window between early-season avalanches and later-

The north face of Mt. Robson, shining in early light. The upper Emperor Face is to the right. PHOTO BY ANDY SELTERS.

season rockfall. Molenaar noted that, "Our steady upward progress on the 45-degree to 50-degree slope was expedited by use of front crampon points." A year later, Bill Sumner led an ice ramp that veered right from Molenaar's pitches, and the year after that Dan Davis, Mead Hargis, Mike Heath and Bill Cockerham pushed a route through the steepest part of this face. As this team worked through various cliff bands they had to pull on icicles, frontpoint ice up to 60 degrees, and use some aid on rock.

The Robson and Mowich routes represented the state of the art of North American ice climbing in the mid-'60s. These routes were comparable to classics of the Alps that had been extreme in the 1930s, but even the contemporary European masters would have climbed these American routes in a similar style.

The Tool User

After the landmark ascent of the North America Wall of El Capitan in the fall of 1964, Yvon Chouinard started to experiment with ice climbing. In December 1965, he and Dennis Hennek went to try the *Mendel Couloir*. This late in the year, the previous winter's snow was long gone and all that remained was old ice, black with grit and as hard as iron. No one had climbed the infamous route in

such a condition, but "too icy" was just what they were looking for—or so they thought. Chouinard wrote:

> I tried to chop a step, but even though I swung the axe with both hands it made only a nick. It was like trying to chop into an asphalt road.... I figured that since it was only about 45 degrees that it would be easier to frontpoint it instead of trying to chop steps.... I was standing on my frontpoints about 20 meters out [from protection] where the gully steepens to over 60 degrees. The pick of my axe was barely in because I couldn't get a good swing. It was so steep and I couldn't trust that wretched dagger [in his other hand] to hold me in balance.
>
> So there I was locked on, unable to move up or down and my legs were crapping out. It was snowing hard by now and spindrift avalanches were coming down in waves.... There was one point when you could have knocked me over with a straw.... Don't ask me how, but I got out of there and onto the rock, where I put in a chock and rappelled.... The thing that kept me going was thinking about how I was going to go back to the shop and forge a hammer with a long, thin pick with teeth on it for climbing ice. No more of this ice dagger bullshit for me.

The following summer Chouinard went to the Alps to see how the Europeans climbed ice. He found that, although many Europeans were very skilled, they were doctrinaire: Germans climbed on their toes and frontpoints, while French climbers were adamant that the only way to climb ice was with the feet flat. With his usual detachment, Chouinard came to see that both methods had their proper place and time; frontpointing was imperative on very steep ground and hard ice, yet on classic alpine terrain the efficiency of flat-footing was equally vital. He also decided that ice axes needed a better design.

Ice axes had become shorter since Conrad Kain's day, but they were still 80 or 90 centimeters long—the better for chopping steps and for use as snow anchors. For chiseling steps in hard ice, the pick was straight and pointed like an awl. Swinging the pick of one of these axes into ice for security was an ungainly effort that resulted, at best, in the pick resting tenuously in a nick. For decades, most climbers accepted this state of affairs. The ice axe was the very symbol of mountaineering, and climbers the world over had become attached to its historical design and use.

The idea of a curved or drooped pick had been floating around for decades, notably with Germans and Austrians even before World War II, but the idea was scattered among esoteric aficionados. Chouinard knew about Scottish winter climbers who had started using short hammers with drooped picks in the early 1960s. He decided that alpinists needed a pick on their ice axe that would embed itself securely when swung into ice. He went to the Charlet factory to request a short axe, only 55 centimeters long, with the pick curved to match the arc of the swinging head, a chisel-shaped tip and teeth to bite into the ice. He swung the new tool into some serac ice and liked it very much.

Late in that 1966 season, as the alpine faces turned icy and "out of shape," Chouinard happened to meet up with Layton Kor, the 6-foot, 5-inch "race horse of the mountains" from Colorado. Together they made the first American ascent of a major alpine ice route, the 3,000-foot north face of Les Courtes. Their ice tools provided much-needed portable security, but the stress of continuous frontpointing just about exploded their legs. From this climb, Chouinard realized he needed better footwork, and better crampons too.

Back in California, Chouinard described his ideas to his new partner in gear design, Tom Frost, an ace Yosemite climber and a graduate of Stanford's design school. In 1967, the two men introduced the "alpine hammer," a piton hammer with an extended, curved and toothed pick for biting into ice. A year later they issued the curved-pick *piolet* (ice axe) and rigid, unjointed crampons.

Chouinard's company also imported a new tubular ice screw from Austria. The need for

Yvon Chouinard on a Sierra ice gully, possibly on Mt. Mendel, in fall conditions in the mid-1960s. COURTESY PATAGONIA HISTORICAL ARCHIVE COLLECTION.

better ice pitons had become too clear after two fatal accidents in Pinnacle Gully on Mt. Washington, where Marwa "coat-hanger" screws—the best available ice pitons—failed to hold falls. One of the accidents, in 1965, killed Harvard man Craig Merrihue and Dan Doody, Chouinard's partner on Mt. Edith Cavell. While the tube screws would require much improvement in the years to come, they immediately put some genuine security into the ice climber's belay system. With the new tools backed up by ice screw protection, the ice revolution began.

Revolution at Hand

Californians Roy Bishop and Michael Cohen used the new implements in July 1967 to make the first ascent of the most technical summer ice chute in the Lower 48, the *Left Mendel Couloir*. They took a long day's leave from a Sierra Club group they were guiding to march over a high pass and climb the very narrow and steep couloir just left of Mt. Mendel's original ice line. The chimney reared up at an average angle well over 60 degrees, with sections over 75 degrees, and one chockstone dribbled overhanging ice. Pushing himself beyond his experiences in the Canadian Rockies, Bishop led every pitch of the glassy ice, chopping small steps on occasion but also kicking in his crampons deftly and using bridging technique to span the crux.

In September 1969, Chouinard met Doug Robinson and the two laid plans to climb "late-season, out-of-shape" ice chutes in the Sierra. They climbed the Palisades' notorious *V-Notch Couloir* without chopping steps, and soon afterward they repeated that route with Tom Frost and Doug Tompkins. Then Chouinard, Frost and Tompkins went to the *Right Mendel Couloir* and climbed that without chopping steps too. Back at company headquarters, Chouinard, Frost and Robinson developed a campaign to inspire North American climbers with the belief that climbing ice in style—precise, strong footwork, solid ice-tool placements and only an occasional chopped rest or belay stance—was the mark of a complete alpinist.

Andy Selters in Mt. Mendel's left couloir. PHOTO BY DOUG ROBINSON.

In February of 1970, Chouinard traveled to New England to sample the region's waterfall ice and to disseminate the new techniques and tools in workshops. One novice who bought the new tools was Rick Wilcox, who then went to Huntington Ravine and bumped into Jim McCarthy and Bill Putnam, two of the region's veteran hard men. McCarthy asked the impressionable young Wilcox if he might test the new gear and then led the whole group up Pinnacle Gully without cutting steps. They reached Mt. Washington's summit plateau in the unheard-of time of less than five hours. That summer, Chouinard demonstrated the new ice game to classes in the Tetons, and among the students was Greg Lowe. Soon the ice revolution was in full swing, as almost overnight the new tools and methods opened up route possibilities that just a couple of years before had been unthinkable.

In his 1972 catalog, Chouinard ran a favorite quote, from the French aviator and author Antoine de Saint-Exupéry, to express how he felt about tools and style:

"Have you ever thought...about whatever man builds, that all of man's industrial efforts, all his calculations and computations, all the nights spent over working draughts and blueprints, invariably culminate in the production of a thing whose sole and guiding principle is the ultimate principle of simplicity? It is as if there were a natural law which ordained that to achieve this end, to refine the curve of a piece of furniture, or a ship's keel, or the fuselage of an airplane, until gradually it partakes of the elementary purity of the curve of the human breast or shoulder, there must be experimentations of several generations of craftsmen. In anything at all, perfection is finally attained not when there is no longer anything to add, but when there is no longer anything to take away, when a body has been stripped down to its nakedness.

With effective tools and protection, even free-hanging frozen waterfalls became climbable routes—the ice climber's equivalent of crag climbing. The sustained, fairly steep ice of alpine faces and Alaskan buttresses soon would be easier to climb than the neighboring rock. Even though technology was making all this possible, this technology did not simply increase security but also speed and effectiveness. New gear or not, it took a bold and tenacious climber to start up a pitch of steep ice without the aid of chopping steps. Chouinard reflected on the paradoxes of technology and style in his 1978 book *Climbing Ice*:

> *The technological imperative of industrial man has always been that if it can be done it should be done. There is no choosing; if it's possible it must be right. Modern man, enslaved by his technical imagination, is shoveling coal to a runaway locomotive. But technology should set him free, opening choices instead of dictating them. Declining a possible technology is the first step toward freedom from this bondage—and returning human values to control. The whole direction of climbing moves against the technological gradient. Here personal qualities like initiative, boldness and technique are supported rather than suppressed by the tools of the trade.*
>
> *In the last few years, as I became more sure of myself and more poised in balance on the ice, I found myself stretching technique. For instance, I used only the ice axe for clawing in steeper and more brittle situations. My Alpine hammer stayed holstered for whole pitches and climbs. This is the technological inversion: fewer tools applied with increasing delicacy. I was rewarded for walking this edge by seeing more sharply what was around me, and I felt more deeply what comes boiling up from within.*

The Lowes

In the American Rockies, a single family generated a parallel revolution. In the late 1950s, brothers Mike, Greg and Jeff Lowe all were taken up the Grand Teton at very young ages by their father, Ralph, who had climbed in

Yvon Chouinard on an ice climb in New Hampshire, 1976. PHOTO BY HENRY BARBER.

Chouinard teaching ice climbing on Mt. Hood, 1975. PHOTO BY HENRY BARBER.

Mixed climbing on the first winter ascent of the Grand Teton's north face. PHOTO BY GEORGE LOWE.

that range since the 1920s. Mike in turn initiated their cousin George, and climbing became a family focus for brotherly provocations and collaborations. From the early 1960s on, the Lowes compared notes and designed new challenges—from 5.10 and 5.11 pitches on short crags to climbing the Tetons in winter.

In the summer of 1967, George and Mike tested the full range of their alpine skills as they climbed the lower half of the *Black Ice Couloir* on the Grand Teton and then veered left onto Durrance's west face route. These two also started probing light and fast style in the Tetons, making the first winter ascent of Mt. Owen in a day from the car.

In February 1968, George, Greg and Mike Lowe, along with Rick Horn, made the most advanced alpine ascent of the time in the Lower 48: the first winter ascent of the north face of the Grand Teton. Starting from a snow cave in the bergschrund, they found the first "easy" pitches to be choked with mushroom-like ice. Fixing some ropes, it took them two days just to nick and stem their way to a bivouac on the First Ledge. There they took shelter from the bitter cold by worming into the shallow snow, parallel to the wall. Above, they found patches of dry rock for a pitch where they could edge upward in their leather double boots. But the face beyond was pasted with white rime and verglas. In crampons again, they chipped placements with their ice axes and daggers and excavated cracks for piton protection. They reached dry rock near the top of the route with daylight to spare, and Greg and Rick were able to lead through the infamous pendulum section without aid. George then took them almost past the Fourth Ledge and to the top, but darkness came too soon. They survived another worm-hole night and climbed over the top and down the next day.

At a time when most North American mountaineers still used crampons to balance up hard snow and chopped steps, wearing them to climb steep, icy rock like that on the Grand Teton on winter seemed only somewhat more reasonable than flapping your arms to fly. The Lowe-Horn ascent was not publicized and few recognized how advanced it was. Soon, though, the Lowes would be applying their mettle to even greater alpine faces and redefining North American alpinism.

Canadian North Faces

Ever since Europeans began to tackle the great alpine north walls in the 1930s, the *Nordwänd* had become a symbol of ultimate mountaineering challenge, the realm where steep terrain and harsh conditions unite. Leading American climbers knew that the Canadian Rockies had *Nordwände* as big as any in the Alps, and steeper. Such major ice and rock faces are more than just extended technical challenges—they are fraught with potentially serious hazards from falling rocks, ice and snow avalanches, and frequent foul weather. In 1970, cousins George and Jeff Lowe decided it was time to tour the Banff-Jasper highway and start picking off new north faces.

They first attempted one of the most severe but accessible possibilities, the north wall of Mt. Kitchener. Just three years before, Chouinard, Joe Faint and Chris Jones had dismissed this face as too steep. But newly won ice climbing confidence led Jeff to consider the face's awesome central couloir, admiring how it "falls from the summit like the tail of a white comet." He and George started up it as sunlight angled onto the wall and melt-loosened rocks started screaming past them "like trains at Grand Central Station." They unroped and ran back down as fast as they could, referring to the chute as the *Grand Central Couloir*.

The cousins moved to the north face of Mt. Temple and started up a central rib that ascends directly to the summit serac wall. Above the initial 3,000-foot prow of broken, surprisingly moderate terrain, they climbed three pitches over the bulging wall of hanging ice, using aid on ice screws to surmount overhanging sections.

At about the same time, Chris Jones teamed up with Gray Thompson, by then a geology professor at the University of Montana. Jones, a British immigrant to North America, was building one of the most brilliant alpine careers of this period. Along with Denny Eberl, Jones and Thompson hiked for two long days up the Athabasca River to try the northwest edge of Mt. Alberta. Steep and poorly protected rock turned them back, and then Eberl became ill and had to hike out.

Jones and Thompson then hiked in farther, to Mt. Columbia, where they hoped to climb the north face. From Columbia's base, Jones and Thompson guessed they might be able to climb the 5,000-foot face in eight hours, and perhaps get back across the Columbia Icefield that night. They made reasonably swift progress on an ice apron at the edge of the face's hanging glacier, but as they neared its top they came to steeper ice at some seracs. Then an ice-choked "Scottish gully" that promised passage to another icefield proved to be nearly vertical. On such ground they had hoped to employ the new techniques they'd seen in the journals, but in such a remote setting, with weighty wilderness packs, they stuck with the tried and true method of nicking steps and holds, and were

Looking down at Chris Jones from the top of the "Scottish Gully" pitch of Mt. Columbia, during the first ascent of the north face and north ridge. GRAY THOMPSON COLLECTION.

Chris Jones below the north face and north ridge of Mt. Columbia from the Athabasca River during the approach.
GRAY THOMPSON COLLECTION.

forced to bivouac. On the second day, ice chutes and rock bands kept rearing up steeper than they'd anticipated, and with the top still out of view and storm clouds darkening their second sunset, they huddled on a sloping ledge as a near-blizzard swarmed over. The next morning they struggled over the last steep ice rib to the windswept summit, then dragged themselves across the Columbia Icefield and down to the highway.

During this same July of 1970, Denny Eberl and his Dartmouth buddy Peter Carman joined Yvon Chouinard to climb the easternmost ice tongue on the 1,000-foot-high north face of Mt. Fay. Carman marveled how, "The ice changed continuously in texture ranging from Nirvana Névé to black ice overlaid by a loosely attached layer of brittle ice and was consistently steep with bulges of 70 degrees." The trio climbed most of the face using the mixed footwork technique that Chouinard now advocated for alpine faces, with one foot on frontpoints and the other foot turned flat against the ice.

The next year, 1971, the Lowe clan cranked up the intensity. Greg had started building his own drooped-pick tools and exploring their limits. On a bitter January day, he and his brother Jeff made the first winter ascent of the *Black Ice Couloir*. These two started venturing up frozen waterfalls in the Wasatch Range, where Greg led through chandeliers so steep they required sustained climbing with his body weight completely hanging off his arms. Then, in July, Greg repeated the *Black Ice Couloir* alone and unbelayed.

That summer, Jeff mostly lived out of his little truck and climbed as much as possible. In August he based at the Icefields Parkway and met up with Gray Thompson and Chris Jones. These two had already made an attempt on the *Grand Central Couloir*, and Jeff was keen to go back. Jones and Thompson's experience indicated that the central couloir ran out of ice at steep, sheer rock, so they aimed for the right-hand ramp-couloir. Their first day ended at a miserable bivouac without the security of either a ledge or a trustworthy

Gray Thompson and Jeff Lowe brewing tea on the summit of Mt. Kitchener, after making the first ascent of the *Ramp Route*, August 1971. PHOTO BY CHRIS JONES, COURTESY GRAY THOMPSON.

anchor. In the morning they followed the ramp, which proved to be barely a weakness. Traversing up and right on sustained thin ice and friable rock, they wrestled through the summit cornices to the top at 6 p.m.

A New Era, By George

The next year, George Lowe began to show the depth that would make him North America's premier pioneer of modern alpine routes. His "day job" was systems analysis, the highly sophisticated field that solves super-complex problems by analyzing their components and varied levels of interactions; most of his work has been for the government and too secret to discuss with anyone. This career would keep Lowe from ever becoming a full-time climber, but his penchant for solving multifaceted problems helped turn his vacation breaks into a progression of extreme new routes. He knew better than anyone else how to digest the intensity of one ascent and use that as a basis to push his abilities on a higher challenge. "If

you're going to survive in big mountains, you don't do wild things immediately," Lowe said. "You do them after you've learned…. If you're careful and keep it together, you just keep plugging and get there."

In February 1972, George and cousin Jeff kicked off the year with a stormy, three-day, first winter ascent of the *Black Ice*-West Face link-up on the Grand Teton. In August, George and Teton climber Jock Glidden began hiking to an awesome Rockies face that George had seen in a photograph, the north face of Mt. Alberta.

A long day's approach hike left Lowe and Glidden still a couple of hours away from the 3,300-foot face, and the next morning they didn't start up Alberta until 10:30 a.m. The weather was chilly enough that no rocks came down, and after a few easy pitches they reached the face's big ice apron. This 55- to 60-degree sheet took a few hours, and just before dark they climbed one pitch of rotten yellow rock at the base of the headwall. This rock proved so crumbly that they could readily unearth a bivouac ledge from it under an overhang. Above here the real challenge would begin, as they looked past three pitches of rock resembling graham crackers to a plumb-vertical wall of dark, hard limestone.

Lowe followed a discontinuous crack system up the gray shield of the headwall (where many others since have gotten lost). He took all the leading and discovered that—as is generally the case in the Canadian Rockies—the steeper rock proved the soundest. The headwall provided just enough edges and cracks to allow progress, albeit sometimes on aid. At the end of this day they reached easier rock a couple of pitches below the summit ice sheet and enjoyed a pleasant perch for the night. It took them all the next day to gain the top, traverse the summit ridge and descend to a third bivouac, halfway down the original 1925 route.

George Lowe's big objective for the next year, 1973, was the southwest face of Devils Thumb. He partnered with Chris Jones, but during the drive to Alaska Jones' car broke down in Calgary. With the repair expected to

Jock Glidden enjoying sunset at the first bivouac on the first ascent of the north face of Mt. Alberta. PHOTO BY GEORGE LOWE.

Jock Glidden following the hardest pitch on the first ascent of the north face of Mt. Alberta. PHOTO BY GEORGE LOWE.

take a couple of days, the two caught a bus up the highway toward Lake Louise to try another line on George's list, a striking couloir on the north face of Mt. Deltaform. The chute (now called the *Supercouloir*) went smoothly until its very top, where it butted into a headwall and Lowe led one of the hardest pitches of his life, a steep chimney of shattered shale coated with ice.

Back on the road, they joined Lito Tejada-Flores at Devils Thumb. Pushing through a storm that pasted them and all their gear with icy snow, they persevered up the 2,400-foot Yosemite-like wall on the southwest face.

Drama on North Twin

With a stream of major ascents now pooled into a deep well of experience, George Lowe and Chris Jones hiked to the base of arguably the most awesome *Nordwänd* of

the Canadian Rockies, the north face of North Twin, in midsummer of 1974. As they descended toward the wall from Woolley Shoulder, they watched it drop from the west edge of the Columbia Icefields deeper and deeper, in profound Gothic pillars, for a full 4,500 feet, ending in a basin often called the Black Hole. Lowe reasoned that the giant, grim pillars would present fairly reliable rock, similar to that on nearby Mt. Alberta—just a lot more of it. For his part, Jones wrote, "I was intrigued to know my limits, wanted to push myself as never before. I had a feeling that North Twin might provide the answer."

They started out with a substantial bandolier of pitons, three ice screws, just one rope for leading and one for hauling, and supplies for six days. They wisely included a bouquet of thin pitons, including Chouinard-

Chris Jones midway up the first ascent of Mt. Deltaform's *Supercouloir*. PHOTO BY GEORGE LOWE.

Frost's stamp-sized Rurps, although neither had used these before.

The vertical and overhanging rock on North Twin proved to be fairly seamless, and the two men were forced into frequent aid and repeated pendulums. Though the main buttresses presented challenges as steep and technical as those on El Capitan, loose and lower-angled sections precluded pack-hauling, and falling rocks forced them to veer onto some of the steepest prows. After two days they were barely halfway up the wall and the most imposing tiers loomed above. At the end of two more days of difficult work they came to the only ledge within sight, a perch barely big enough to sit on. By now the realization gnawed at them that pendulum points and the usual amount of stuck and dropped gear had left them with too few anchors to retreat.

On day five they kept improvising aid and free climbing while a storm began to gather. As the evening darkened, Lowe worked left toward the edge of the face and an ice chimney, which promised to take them to the likely easier 60-degree ground beyond the upper edge of the wall. He aided on a sequence of tied-off knifeblades and then their last Lost Arrow piton. Some holds allowed him to climb free, but as the next crack appeared he realized he didn't have any pitons that would fit. He asked Jones to send up a couple of pins that were part of the belay anchor. As Lowe held on with one hand and pulled up the haul line with his teeth and other hand, he shifted and then fell off, plummeting for 60 feet before a good piton held. He swung back to the belay with a bad bruise, but fretted only over the loss of that crucial Lost Arrow. Jones decided it was time to circle the wagons and bivouac, even though they had no niche to set their cartridge stove upon, much less a ledge for sleeping.

Neither Lowe nor Jones could compete as technical climbers with the new virtuosos in Yosemite or Eldorado, and even on ice pitches there were better technicians. Yet on alpine walls they may have formed the strongest partnership in the world at this time. They had met in the Alps in 1965 and promptly made the first American ascent of the *Bonatti Pillar* on the Dru. They were solid at a level much deeper than technical skill; profoundly endowed with determination and character, both could peer upward from a stressful situation, see through curtains of even greater

Chris Jones leading on the first ascent of the north face of North Twin. PHOTO BY GEORGE LOWE.

Chris Jones arriving at a belay high on the first ascent of the north face of North Twin. PHOTO BY GEORGE LOWE.

George Lowe at a high, sloping bivouac on North Twin.
PHOTO BY CHRIS JONES, COURTESY GEORGE LOWE.

stress, and figure how to do what had to be done. Each had an utterly honest, untainted sense of his own abilities and limitations, and consequently a deep trust in each other. As Lowe put it, "With Chris, the chance of us not making a critical mistake was pretty high." At this point on North Twin they had few cards left to play.

After a wretched night, Lowe tried to escape left along a slab that headed toward the icy chimney. The slab steepened and ice hung over it, but he realized he could grab the edge of ice and lieback along it, pressing his knee into some plastered snow. Beyond this he found a thin crack for a tiny piton, and by traversing past this with rope tension he reached the chute. Then, as he started up this lower-angled ground, the clouds let loose and waves of hail streamed over them. The imperative to reach the top only increased. They endured another thousand

A thoroughly exhausted George Lowe on the hike out from the first ascent of the north face of North Twin. PHOTO BY CHRIS JONES, COURTESY GEORGE LOWE.

Chris Jones, shown here at a tiny bivouac cave on Mt. Kitchener, 1971. PHOTO BY GRAY THOMPSON.

feet or so of mixed climbing in severe conditions before they could bivouac on the summit. The next day they made the long march across the Columbia Icefield to the Banff-Jasper highway.

Although this climb was so steep and hardware-dependent that it can be considered a wall route, it was mountaineering savvy that allowed Lowe and Jones to succeed. Their route has turned back all subsequent attempts. For Chris Jones, this was the last great Rockies first ascent he would do, although he still made substantial climbs during breaks from his computer work. He also would compile the first definitive book of climbing history for the continent, *Climbing in North America*. Lowe kept his progression going—five years later he would do the huge north face of Mt. Geikie in the Rockies, and from Alaska to the Karakoram and Mt. Everest he would be the key climber on some of the most advanced climbs in the world. Only later would many realize that Lowe was at the front of a revolution in technical alpine climbing that ran parallel with Reinhold Messner's well-publicized revolution in Himalayan mountaineering.

The *Nordwänd* Trend

In 1975, Jeff Lowe returned for another try at Mt. Kitchener's *Grand Central Couloir*, partnered with another talented American, Mike Weis. Knowing too well the artillery-like rockfall that roared down their objective during daytime thaws, Lowe wrote that they "geared up psychologically for a different sort of rhythm and a more classical, longer-lasting twirl through an immense mountain dance hall." The two carried minimal food, water and bivouac gear and started climbing at 6 p.m., planning to climb through the night with headlamps.

The evening chill indeed held back most rockfall, and in darkness they gained the initial 2,000 feet. An aurora swirled above them, and Lowe took this as an auspicious omen. As they reached the steeper neck of the couloir, dawn lit the sky. At 6 a.m., they faced not a simple ice chute but a vertical chimney. Above that, very thin ice over rock slabs butted up to a mushroom-plug of snow. Protection cracks were infrequent, thin and flaky, but they delicately balanced crampon points on rock and managed a couple of pendulums. Above the mushroom they found solid ice for another few pitches, but this ended at a second head-wall of steep rock dusted with snow. To its right they found a narrow ice chute, and this delivered the two tired climbers below the summit icecap. A pitch of vertical rotten snow took some time, but 26 hours after starting they stood on top. They had danced perfectly between the interacting risks of rockfall, exhaustion and technical difficulty.

One more great Rockies *Nordwänd* fell under scrutiny in this era—perhaps the most enormous and terrifying of all. Along the west edge of Mt. Robson's north face soars a stupendous stack of shale and ice, 6,500 feet of strata layered so steep and dark that it makes the Eigerwand look moderate. It's hard to know how many attempts were made on this Emperor Face during the 1970s, but Americans Pat Callis, Jim Kanzler, Jim Logan, and Jeff and George Lowe were among the suitors.

Coloradan Jim Logan returned to the face in 1978 with a partner fairly new to big climbs but with remarkable strength and enthusiasm: Terry "Mugs" Stump. Earlier in this season they had attempted Mt. Logan's *Hummingbird Ridge* alpine style, starting from the toe of the ridge. Perhaps in comparison with this colossal vision, the Emperor Face seemed more attainable. Logan had seen a unique aerial photograph from John Barstow that showed a ribbon of ice running through the steepest upper bands, and both men knew that modern ice techniques made even vertical ice much more climbable than steep, loose rock.

They waited out a week of rain, and when clear, chilly skies came they found thin ice pasted all over the rock—just what they wanted. Nicking their way up with crampons and ice tools, they made steady progress, but with ice clogging the cracks they had very little protection. In the first half of the face, the steep tiers were only 15 to 20 feet high, interspersed with bands of snowy scree and easy but very loose rock. By the third day, however, they reached tiers that stood 50 or 60 feet tall and very steep. Frequently they had to resort to aid. Finally they reached the ribbon of ice they'd seen in the photograph. Though it was plumb vertical, Logan started up it in glee, and Stump had to remind him to place some protection. The ribbon lasted for four pitches. Above this, they chopped seats and spent a third night on the wall.

The next day Logan started up one of the most notorious leads in North American climbing history. He contrived every aid trick he could imagine, from thin pitons and hooks to a tapped-in ice hammer, and even tied-off icicles. With his rack diminishing, he moved to free climbing. In all, Logan spent eight hours on the lead before he made a desperate, clawing mantle onto the next ledge. The tiers eased above this, and Stump led to a fourth bivouac atop the Emperor Ridge. In the morning they descended the bowl that George Kinney and Curly Phillips had climbed 69 years before. In light of having solved the problem of the face, few challenged their decision to forego the summit, and thus began a trend among some climbers to put less emphasis on the summit as a definition of success. It was Logan's last major new route and Stump's first.

At the end of the decade, in the early fall of 1979, Montanans Jim Kanzler and Terry

Jim Logan waiting out bad weather. PHOTO BY MUGS STUMP.

Kennedy made a little-known ascent of an American *Nordwänd* as grim as most any in Canada, the 3,500-foot-high, sedimentary north face of Mt. Siyeh in Glacier National Park. These same partners had succeeded on the nearby north face of Mt. Cleveland—at 4,000 feet high and 6,000 feet across, this was the biggest expanse of vertiginous wall in the Lower 48. But Siyeh had defeated them three times previously. Kanzler and most Montana climbers felt the oral traditions of the state's Blackfeet Indians should be respected, and that information about Montana mountaineering should not be published but only passed on through private conversations. However, Kennedy later published an article on their Siyeh story.

Kanzler and Kennedy figured that September offered the best chance of finding the face held together by cold before snow covered the rock. Storms kept beating them back, though. During their 1978 attempt, the skies darkened, wind shrieked and rocks peeled off the top. Kanzler, who had roped up with some of America's best, said to his partner, "I don't know what to tell you, Kennedy; Fred [Beckey] would go down, George [Lowe] would go up." When a cinder-block-sized stone exploded onto their previous belay ledge, they bailed.

In '79 the weather held. The climbing, however, was sustained and serious enough to make them doubt their chances. Free climbing ideas fell away with every loose hold, and the leader pulled or stood on pitons, Friends, shifting blocks of "petrified mud" and verglas over primordial algae beds and crumbly limestone—whatever would hold. The second had to climb with the bulk of their gear, because hauling would dislodge too many rocks and they didn't trust anchors enough to jümar. Kennedy led most of the first half of the wall, to the point where it was safer to keep going than to retreat. On the second day, Kanzler came to a long, 1.5-inch crack and leapfrogged on aid using the only two Friends that would fit for some 75 feet. Halfway through their third day, he wrestled unprotected up a 50-foot offwidth and then up a "gutter drain" he aided on nuts; when

one of his nuts popped he stopped his fall by pressing against the walls of the gutter. That proved to be the last of the worst of it, and late in the afternoon they pulled onto the sunny summit.

Winter's Icy Grip

The great 1930s and '40s alpinist Giusto Gervasutti wrote, "A climber who is strong and sure of himself should prefer winter ascents because these more than any other give him a chance of measuring his strength against mountains in severe conditions." In 1973, as European alpinists began to fear that the future might be empty of new challenges, the legendary Briton Doug Scott called winter "the great white hope for Alpine climbing." In the Canadian Rockies, winter comes harsher than in the Alps. Temperatures below 0°F are the norm, and the thin snowpack makes rotten and avalanche-prone snow all too common. Nevertheless, Rockies climbers began to take on winter routes in the 1960s.

Leif-Norman Patterson was a Norwegian who emigrated to the States and later to Canada, and he loved snow and ice the way fish love water. In 1963 and '64, he and Californian Les Wilson made three attempts

Leif-Norman Patterson on the first winter ascent of Mt. Robson. PHOTO BY ALEX BERTULIS.

to climb Mt. Robson in winter, but the wicked cold made even mildly stormy weather too fierce, and rotten snow conditions made for awful travel. In March 1965, Patterson returned with Seattle climbers Alex Bertulis and Eric Bjørnstad. Bertulis had left messages for Fred Beckey to join them, and Beckey drove from Colorado to Seattle, collected Tom Stewart, and raced up to Canada to join the climb. Bjørnstad stayed behind, and with somewhat better conditions Bertulis and Patterson succeeded up the Kain Face in two beautiful days. Just as they began their descent, Bjørnstad, Beckey and Stewart arrived in their footsteps.

This was the first winter that the new highway over Rogers Pass was plowed for travel, and Beckey and Bertulis immediately drove down there to try for the first winter ascent of Mt. Sir Donald. Meeting with Don Liska and Dave Beckstead, they found the original route deep in snow but free of its notorious summer rockfall. They snuck in this summit on March 20, 1965, one day before the deadline that didactic observers call the end of true winter.

Calgary climbers also took to serious winter climbing during this same month, as Brian Greenwood and Lloyd MacKay climbed Mt. Louis by a new route on the south face on sun-dried but frigid limestone. In December 1966, Greenwood, Charlie Locke and Chic Scott made a multiday trip to climb steep and loose Mt. Hungabee. A year later, the same three, plus Eckhard Grassman, Don Gardner and Archie Simpson, went to Mt. Assiniboine. Gardner, Grassman and Scott hurried up the north ridge and made the summit, but the short day ended on their way down and they had to endure a windy, bitter night up high in their sleeping bags.

In February 1969, a joint Sierra Club and BCMC team made the first winter trip into the core of the Coast Mountains, taking advantage of ski-plane access to the Tiedemann Glacier. To their surprise, they got a spell of good weather. Even more surprising, there were no avalanches, and, except for cold, long nights, the conditions seemed nearly as favorable as in summer. Dick Culbert, Allen Steck, Bob Cuthbert, Les Wilson, Barry Hagen and Bill St. Lawrence were able to make the only winter ascent of Mt. Waddington to date, via the southeast chimney.

Colorado ski pioneer Fritz Stamberger teamed with Gordon Whitmer in 1972 to make one of the more legendary winter ascents in their state. They climbed the notoriously loose direct north buttress of Capitol Peak in one long day, and settled into a memorable bivouac on the summit.

A few of the most hardcore big-wall climbers began attempting their routes in winter. Back in 1967, Wayne Goss and Layton Kor had sieged the first winter ascent of Longs Peak's Diamond, by a new route. Now, in 1972, Greg Lowe talked his ski-racing friend Rob Kiesel into trying the first winter-conditions ascent of a Grade VI, the northwest face of Half Dome. Lowe had

Alex Bertulis on the summit of Mt. Robson, after making the peak's first winter ascent. PHOTO BY LEIF-NORMAN PATTERSON, COURTESY ALEX BERTULIS.

Bill St. Lawrence traversing into the crux chimney on the first winter ascent of Mt. Waddington. PHOTO BY BOB CUTHBERT, COURTESY LES WILSON.

designed the world's first portaledge or hanging tent (a "LURP"), and this would be its big test. On their sixth day, as their food supply ran out, darkness and a storm forced them to hide in their tent a heartbreaking single pitch from the top. The storm tossed their capsule around all night, and when the morning dawned with a raging blizzard Lowe wrestled out of the tent and into the cauldron. Lowe spent six hours on this last pitch and "began the final section depending entirely on the adhesion of thin snow clumps to barren rock."

Icy Pillars and Faces

In New England by 1973, hardcore enthusiasts were exploring their technical and muscular limits on dozens of frozen waterfalls. In February of that year, a band of long-haired men and women from North Conway skied up to Chimney Pond, below the northern cirque of Katahdin, the great peak in the cen-

ter of Maine. Among them was Henry Barber, the period's touring superstar of rock climbing. Barber had tried some easy ice climbing in 1970, but had temporarily given it up as "too mechanical." He got back into it during this winter of 1972-'73, realizing he could approach ice as he did rock—not just as verticality to muscle over but as a complex structure with subtle angles and features to make use of. On either medium he was a severe proponent of style. Most modern ice climbers used wrist loops on their tools, to allow them to pull or hang from a relaxed grip, but to Barber this seemed an ethically dubious form of aid. When he and Dave Cilley started up the most prominent stairway of ice pouring off Katahdin's north face, they had only the grip of their leather gloves to hold onto their *piolets* and alpine hammers.

Though the temperature was about -20°F, most of the climb went well. About two-thirds of the way up, Barber led through the crux pitch, a curtain of wind-twisted icicles that required finesse, care and power. When he finished the pitch and stepped onto an easier slope, he found no ice for anchors, just wind-hardened snow. To belay, Barber swung his tools into the snow and tied into them, sat down, braced his feet, and deployed a hip belay. Then Cilley fell from the steep ice and pulled Barber off his perch. As Barber's axe levered out he clawed at the snow and felt both their weight come onto the buried pick of his alpine hammer. Barber screamed while Cilley pulled back onto the ice, and they finished the route unscathed.

During the mid-'70s the ice climbing revolution exploded in the Canadian Rockies, and climbers fought their way up many of the awesome frozen waterfalls along the Banff-Jasper highway. Calgary climbers—many of them immigrants from Britain—led this charge and broke new ground on pure ice routes steeper and longer than anything yet imagined outside of North America. Much of the steepest ice they climbed by attaching aid ladders to their ice tools.

American Carlos Buhler put in a couple of Rockies waterfall seasons, and then decided to take winter climbing to the area's big north

Henry Barber pauses below the crux section on the first ascent of the *Cilley-Barber Route*. PHOTO BY DAVE CILLEY, COURTESY HENRY BARBER.

Dave Cilley following one of the first hard pitches on the first ascent of the *Cilley-Barber Route*. PHOTO BY HENRY BARBER.

faces. In January 1977, Buhler and young Canadian Phil Hein climbed the north face of Mt. Temple, starting with the Greenwood-Locke chutes and traversing to the upper Lowe spur. The climb took them six frigid days. Soon after this, Buhler and Canadian Mark Whalen climbed the more technical *Supercouloir* of Mt. Deltaform. Calgary climbers were already chagrined that Americans had claimed so many first ascents of their north faces, and this pair of winter ascents fired them into action.

John Lauchlan and Jim Elzinga had started climbing together as teenagers, and although they were barely into their 20s in March 1977 they catapulted into the big time with a brutally cold ascent of the *Ramp Route* on the north face of Mt. Kitchener. Their second bivouac on the face was a grim, shivering affair where they had to "half sit, half hang from tied-off screws." On the ramp, poorly protected, snow-covered rock made for slow going and a third awful night. Spent, Lauchlan led over "snow-covered slabs. Nailing. Roofs. Steep ice, bad belays, black fingertips…fucked. The world, time is frozen and only Jim and I remain…. I mantle over

the cornice and roll into the frozen gale…. We stagger off down the ridge…two men, alive." Lauchlan later summed up the rush of being forced to push beyond what seemed possible: "When there is no choice there can be no hesitation."

The following January, two Californians grabbed the first winter ascent of Kitchener's *Grand Central Couloir*. Jack Roberts and Tobin Sorenson were on their way to very big projects around the world, and this was one of their harshest tests yet. They had planned to climb it as Lowe and Weis had done in summer, straight through without a bivouac. But amid the toughest climbing their newfangled headlamps gave out, and they were forced to halt and dance through the night to survive. Though Roberts especially suffered some bad frostbite, they climbed for their lives to reach the top.

In 1978, Lauchlan and Elzinga helped to push the style of climbing frozen waterfalls "free," with no aiders—their only connection to the tools was through their hands and wrist loops. At the end of 1979, they succeeded on an ice route in a very alpine setting, on the east face of Snow Dome.

Tobin Sorenson starting one of the crux pitches on the first winter ascent of Mt. Kitchener's *Grand Central Couloir*.
PHOTO BY JACK ROBERTS.

Many had noticed how winter seizes this face into a great sweep of glistening blue that rears up between 50 and 90 degrees for 2,200 feet. It took the pair three days to make the ascent, and they called it *Slipstream* for all the loose snow washing down it. Spectacular position and sustained steep ice made the route an instant classic, but since then the Damocles' Sword of seracs that hang over the line has become even more dangerous, and today the route is no longer recommended.

John Lauchlan simmered with merciless intensity, and this helped project him into the role of Canada's first high-profile climber. He started to appear across the nation on television shows and in newspaper articles. In 1982, he went to solo *Polar Circus*, a big waterfall spilling off of Cirrus Mountain, but avalanche danger was high and his hubris in confronting this hazard

Jim Elzinga. PHOTO BY BARRY BLANCHARD.

John Lauchlan. PHOTO BY BARRY BLANCHARD.

Dave Cheesmond on Denali. PHOTO BY MICHAEL KENNEDY.

meant his death. Vancouver climber Bruce Fairley wrote a tribute poem:

…He faced all the knives I couldn't face,

entered the tunnels that I avoided…

drank the wine you didn't have time for;

swallowed the fire you couldn't put out.

Don't give me this bullshit we don't need heroes,

only a dishrag doesn't have heroes.

Historian Chic Scott wrote that, "Lauchlan was the first [Canadian climber] to toss his life willingly into the pot and play the game for keeps."

5.9, A2

Just a few months before Lauchlan's death, Calgary was energized by another lightning bolt in the form of two South Africans: Dave Cheesmond and Tony Dick. They were fresh from an epic of survival on Alaska's Mt. Deborah, when a mix-up in airdrops left them with a starvation march out. As they drove down to the Rockies, they ate non-stop the whole way. Then they hiked into the first big peak they came to—Mt. Robson—and

swiftly climbed the *Wishbone Arête*. Back at the base of that route, they woke from their bivouac to blue skies, which called them onto another climb. The two traversed around the mountain on the "Yellow Ledges" at 8,000 feet to the Emperor Face. There they promptly climbed a new route. Although this was not the direct challenge of the Logan-Stump line, they pushed through some very serious terrain. They summarized what must have been a ferocious couple of days with this sentence: "There was much hard ice climbing, much rockfall and rock climbing up to 5.9, A3."

As Cheesmond looked around the Rockies and saw all the big routes yet to be done, he promptly set up an engineering practice and made Calgary his new home. With Cheesmond leading the way, 5.9, A2 (or A3) became a standard "sandbag" rating applied to the series of big faces Canadians would pioneer in the ensuing years. Anyone aspiring to repeat these routes needed to know that this misleading application from the purely technical, California-centered rating system really meant "at or near the modern limits of hard and scary."

In 1982, Cheesmond and Dick warmed up on some established *Nordwände* and then made another extreme route without

Barry Blanchard heading for the first crux on the first ascent of *Andromeda Strain*. PHOTO BY DAVE CHEESMOND, COURTESY BARRY BLANCHARD.

publishing an account, the awesome east face of Mt. Assiniboine. The following year Cheesmond began to team up with some of the local climbers, and this invigorated crew took on the moniker the "Wildboys." One primary focus was an obvious 1,800-foot gash in the east face of Mt. Andromeda, where six years of attempts had resulted in retreats from the line's steep rock, thin ice and "chockstones" of snow. On April 16, Cheesmond, guide Barry Blanchard and attorney Tim Friesen swung leads for two days through all the difficulties and completed one of the classic hard routes of the range, *Andromeda Strain*.

Just a week later, Cheesmond and Kevin Doyle survived a stormy new route up ice walls, snow and loose rock on the north face of South Mt.Goodsir. In low visibility, they mistakenly ended up descending another flank of the same face. This descent alone proved to be a two-day ordeal with avalanches of loose snow pouring over them for up to half an hour at a time. Even Cheesmond called it "unimaginably scary."

Accelerating the formula established by such predecessors as Gmoser and Greenwood, the Wildboys trained on Yamnuska and then went to the big faces. Cheesmond commonly got in a hard route on Yamnuska after a workday in Calgary. His motto was, "It's all good training, man," and every time he got into a tight situation he thought of it as training for something even

bigger. He trained right into the Himalaya, contributing to a new route on Mt. Everest, an ascent of K2 and the first alpine-style ascent of a route on Rakaposhi with Blanchard and Doyle. His compatriot Tony Dick wrote of him, "There's nothing more committed than a guy who never stops training. You just can't keep up; that's all."

In peak fitness, Cheesmond and Blanchard went in 1985 to try a new route on the north face of North Twin. After a couple of thousand feet of climbing often exposed to whistling rockfall, they aimed for a headwall more sustained than the Lowe-Jones route. This proved to have almost Yosemite-like corners and cracks, with "some of the best [rock] either of us had seen on limestone." Lady Luck also led them to end one day of sheer verticality at a small cave with a flat floor, a perfect campsite. Although the rock at times proved to be more friable than it appeared, the two men completed the second route on one of the most legendary faces on the continent after a seven-day excursion.

Colder is Better

A new generation of Seattle-area climbers also began to look to winter for extra-alpine challenges in their home mountains, and the snowy months delivered experiences that would serve many of them well on major climbs in Alaska and around the world. Each year after Thanksgiving they watched for the couple of clear cold spells that usually break Washington's winter parade of maritime storms. Callis and Davis had already shown in 1963 that Mt. Index, with its flinty rock and many bushes, was a much better climb under good wintry conditions than in summer. In 1978, Doug Klewin and Dan McNerthney climbed an icy route up Index's middle peak, and Todd Bibler, Steve Swenson, Reese Martin and Don Fredrickson climbed the '63 north face route and then traversed all three of Index's rimed summits.

Bill Pilling and Steve Mascioli decided, in 1985, to take a winter trip deep into the North Cascades from the east, to climb the big northeast buttress of Mt. Goode. They found that gullies leading up the right side of the

buttress were filled with water ice, providing better climbing than the fourth-class rock of the summer route. Exhilarating mixed climbing carried them along the top of the buttress, and then another gully of ice led right to the summit.

The chief advocate for Cascade winter ascents was Kit Lewis, a wild, hard-drinking carpenter who had decided to make the first winter ascents of the hardest routes in the Cascades. He found a solid partner in Jim Nelson, and their determination took them to the top of Nooksack Tower on Mt. Shuksan in 1983, Burgundy Spire (near Liberty Bell) in '84, and the Yosemite-esque *Girth Pillar* on the north face of Mt. Stuart in '85. Nelson has said that Lewis' rules for climbing style are two: "Make it safe and have fun." In the classic Warren Harding tradition, "fun" included a lot of hard work during the day and drinking at night, and the two men eagerly tackled the Cascades' winter bushwhacking with heavy packs.

Kit Lewis at a camp en route to the first winter ascent of *Girth Pillar* on the north face of Mt. Stuart. PHOTO BY JIM NELSON.

Dave Cheesmond leading on the 1985 first ascent of the north pillar of North Twin. PHOTO BY BARRY BLANCHARD.

The big Cascade prize was the first winter ascent of the northeast buttress of Slesse, but half a dozen Lewis-Nelson attempts were thwarted by storm and the scale of the approach. In early March 1986, they solved the approach problem by flying to the base by helicopter. Climbing snowy, glazed rock in plastic double boots, working in étriers about 10 percent of the time, and hauling the leader's pack on many pitches, it took them five days to climb most of the route. When they were just a couple of hundred feet from the summit, a storm hit hard and they had to hide in their bivy tent for two days. When it cleared somewhat, they swam down snowy rappels and slopes, and then made a march

out in the rain that extended the epic to washed-out bridges, treacherous cliff traverses and stream crossings.

Two years later, Lewis and Bill Liddell pushed their way up the notorious jungle of Marble Creek to make what Lewis thinks of as his best winter ascent, the beautiful, jagged spine of Eldorado Peak's west arête. This under-appreciated, 22-pitch, 5.7 backbone was first climbed by Richard Emerson and Walter Gove in 1969, and Lewis led the whole way during the winter ascent. About the same time, Nelson and Mark Bebie found superb conditions on a new route on the west side of that bastion of Cascade winter climbing, Mt. Index. Their ascent began with

Kit Lewis leads out of the third bivouac on the first winter ascent of Slesse Mountain's northeast buttress. PHOTO BY JIM NELSON.

Jim Nelson high on the first winter ascent of the northeast buttress of Slesse Mountain. PHOTO BY KIT LEWIS.

Jim Nelson at the high, stormy bivouac on the first winter ascent of the northeast buttress of Slesse Mountain. PHOTO BY KIT LEWIS.

accessible cliffs, but once in a while teams would add commitment by heading for ice streaks they noticed high on a mountain face. The 1987 and 1988 seasons brought three particularly severe ascents.

In early 1987, logger Ward Robinson warmed up with Ian Bolt by making the first deep-winter ascent of *Andromeda Strain*. Then, in March, Robinson joined guides Blanchard and Peter Arbic to attempt a face that Blanchard had tried four times before, a chute-and-head-wall route on the high ramparts of the east face of Mt. Chephren. While leading a crux icy overhang with crampons, Robinson took a fall into space. He regained the rock and finished the pitch, but after just two rope lengths their day of work ran into darkness. The third day presented more reasonable terrain, but Blanchard still had a fierce time leading steep mixed ground with dubious protection, and it was past dusk before they topped out. They called the route *The Wild Thing*.

Success on Chephren after so many tries was like a passage for Blanchard, and the climb had a lot to do with making him a top-drawer alpinist. He described the mix of magnetic allure and extreme stress he'd experienced as "the beautiful white lady with the red dagger…. The lady is calling me again, and I know I'll go. But I'm going to follow her hands with a sober eye. I'll watch for the dagger."

a couple of pitches of monkeying up forested cliffs, which put them in the throat of a 3,000-foot-long ice chute that Bebie likened to the famous north face of Les Droites.

By the late 1980s, Calgary's Wildboys had started to think winter was the best time to climb the big Rockies faces. Ice tools had evolved into steep-drooped instruments offering very reliable purchase, and climbers began to understand that winter's cold and avalanche hazards were—with care—more manageable than summer's loose-rock problems. As Barry Blanchard put it, "In the Rockies, winter provides a better climbing experience."

Come November, Canadians started keeping track of bluish streaks dripping over some of the hundreds of limestone walls in this region. They searched mostly for ice on lower,

Ward Robinson, one of the strongest pioneers of north walls in the Canadian Rockies, shown here on the first ascent of Howse Peak's north face. PHOTO BY BARRY BLANCHARD.

Ward Robinson in an overhanging chimney on the first ascent of Howse Peak's north face. PHOTO BY BARRY BLANCHARD.

The major route of 1988 came when Blanchard and Robinson chased their armed siren to another chute-and-headwall route on the north face of Howse Peak. As their second day on this face turned to darkness, Robinson took a swinging fall while aiding over a roof. Nevertheless, he went back up to finish the pitch. On the upper headwall the next day, 70-degree thin ice steepened to almost vertical, even thinner ice. Without the option of falling or retreat, Robinson pulled through, and on their fourth day they made the top.

In just a few short seasons, ice climbing had changed from an exercise in step construction to efficient elegance, and in less than a decade climbers used the new style on ice as an avenue to the fiercest alpine walls. As we'll see in Chapter 11, rock climbing also was on a rocket-like evolution into extreme difficulty. Gradually, climbers were pulling together a unified model of total alpinism—climbing technical ice, rock and snow on the biggest scale and in the best style imaginable.

SUGGESTED ROUTES
FROM THIS PERIOD

MT. MENDEL (13,710 feet/4,179 meters)
North Face Couloirs

The north face of Mt. Mendel is visible from few places in the Sierra, and when California climbers in the 1970s first looked straight at it from Lamarck Col, more than a few turned tail. The right couloir is the obvious "comet tail" streaking down the face; the core of the left couloir remains hidden in a chimney until you're nearly under it. For most climbers this is a two- or three-day trip.

Approach: The hike in from North Lake (9,200 feet) follows a steep, never-finished trail up to alpine plateau country. One may bivouac at springs or snowmelt gullies in this area, or else continue over 13,000-foot Lamarck Col to camp at beautiful lakes in Darwin Canyon. The climbing for either couloir

The north face of Mt. Mendel, showing the two ice couloirs. PHOTO BY ANDY SELTERS.

begins above the 30- to 50-degree glacier nestled above the lakes.

Right Couloir: A drought during the early 1990s melted out the legendary "asphalt road" black ice in the right couloir, and at this writing the route features less-ancient and more-forgiving blue alpine ice. In early summer most of the couloir is hard snow, and in late spring it even has been descended on skis. Climb the couloir in six or seven rope lengths, followed by some Class 4 rock to the summit ridge. From there it's a couple of Class 4 and 5 rope lengths to the summit terraces. Descend via the southeast side, where a short rappel delivers you to Class 3 terrain.

Left Couloir: The ice in this couloir comes from spring and summer meltwater that drips out of a summit snowdrift. The lowest part of this couloir is a slot chimney that holds ice only into midsummer. This three-pitch section was first climbed by Doug Robinson and Dale Bard in July 1976, and they continued to the top mistakenly thinking they had climbed a completely separate couloir, which they called *Ice Nine*. If the bottom chimney has no ice, keep right and gain the main chute via a difficult mixed pitch. Once in the upper narrows, the climbing is on steep ice with bulging cruxes, which may become dry rock later in the season. The protection options are mostly adequate on either ice or rock, but in thin conditions the crux chockstone can require some tricky nut work.

First Ascents: Right Couloir: Felix Knauth and John Whitmer, June 1958; Left Couloir: Roy Bishop and Michael Cohen, July 1967

Difficulty: Right Couloir: D-, AI 3, 5.4, 1,400 feet; Left Couloir: TD-, AI 5, 5.9, 1,400 feet

Guidebooks: *The High Sierra; Sierra Classics*

Permits: To spend the night in the John Muir Wilderness, it's necessary to obtain a wilderness permit from the Inyo National Forest office in Bishop.

KATAHDIN (5,267 feet/1,605 meters)
Cilley-Barber Route

In winter the northern cirque of Katahdin is draped with ice, and, except for the fact that the rock is granitic and solid, the tiered headwalls resemble a scene from the Canadian Rockies. A number of exciting ice and mixed routes venture through the cliff bands, and the most striking ice stairway is the

Looking up the *Cilley-Barber Route* on Katahdin. PHOTO BY MARTY MOLITORIS/ALPINE ENDEAVORS GUIDE SERVICE.

Cilley-Barber. Don't let Katahdin's modest elevation fool you, for this peak in winter is a serious undertaking. Aspirants must be ready for fierce weather and must be able to judge avalanche conditions. With this region's wild temperature fluctuations, there's also a history of water building up inside the ice and bursting forth when a climber's tool breaks the dam.

Approach: It's a 17-mile trip into the Chimney Pond basecamp, and climbers' plans are dictated by Baxter State Park. Some parties in the past didn't make the long trip before nightfall, and the park now requires all parties to take two days for the approach. Most stay at a shelter at Roaring Brook, at the start of the woodsy climb into the cirque. At Chimney Pond there is a hut with a woodstove that eases nights of arctic conditions, although the park charges $25 per person per night to stay there and reservations must be made well in advance. There are also some lean-tos available for sheltered tent sites. Most people plan a trip of five days or more.

Park rangers have the authority to ban climbing because of weather or snow conditions, and to check climbers for proper equipment.

Route: The *Cilley-Barber Route* is the most prominent cascade of ice pouring from the snowy basin below the summit. Ice screws offer the only reliable anchors for the hard climbing. Two tiers of steep ice lead to snow and then a 200-foot section of rolling ice. Another snow segment takes you to an intimidating crux of sustained steep ice that butts into an overhanging tier of icicles, which are usually twisted by wind into Medusa-esque wickedness. Usually one can find a steep but reasonable passage to the right of the main tangle. Above the crux, moderate snow and rock lead to the top. Go west along the summit ridge to descend via Cathedral Saddle.

First Ascent: Henry Barber and Dave Cilley, February 1973

Difficulty: TD-, WI 4+, 2,100 feet

Guidebook: *An Ice Climber's Guide to Northern New England*

Permits: A permit to enter, camp and climb is required from Baxter State Park; apply months in advance if you plan to use the cabins.

MT. ALBERTA (11,873 feet/3,619 meters)
North Face

This face is big but not huge and much of it holds fairly moderate climbing. First ascensionist George Lowe believes that it should be reasonable for a fit party to climb this route without a bivouac. Why then, almost 30 years after the first ascent, have fewer than a dozen parties climbed it? The answer is simply that this face's combination of difficulties makes for a very serious undertaking. Routefinding, rockfall, weather, ice and steep rock, a complex descent—it all adds up to a classic and complete mountaineering challenge. Recent dry years have diminished the ice on the face, and there is some concern that the small hanging glacier atop the wall has become unstable and potentially threatening.

Approach: It's a tough, long day in to Alberta. The hike from the Icefields Parkway starts with an icy wade across the Sunwapta River, then a march up Woolley Creek and over Woolley Shoulder. A mile beyond the shoulder there's an ACC hut, and you may want to break up your approach with a night here, especially in marginal weather. From

The north face of Mt. Alberta. PHOTO BY GLEN BOLES.

the hut, traverse a small glacier to make an end run around Alberta's northeast ridge. Most people rappel (160 feet) from the end of a spur off the northeast ridge, and then bivouac in the moraines below.

Route: The climb begins with a few easy rock pitches (possibly snow) that give access to the big ice apron. Run pitches up the ice to the rock headwall. Most parties bivouac here, but faster parties have kept going and reached a bivouac ledge two-thirds of the way up the headwall. The headwall is complex, dark and steep, and whatever scouting you've been able to do will be a big help. It's a solid 10 or 11 pitches through these cliffs, starting with two or three rope lengths through moderate but rotten yellow rock. On the dark and firmer rock above, corners and a quartz-rich wide crack lead to an overhang and a pendulum right. Aid climbing (a hook is said to be useful) through more overhangs reaches a nice crack heading farther right. The climbing eases and you pass a bivouac ledge, but the last pitches are often icy with melt from above. The summit icefield should go smoothly, but then you'll be faced with the descent: a long traverse along the blocky and sometimes corniced summit ridge, followed by various rappels, downclimbing and traverses on the original 1925 route.

First Ascent: George Lowe and Jocelyn Glidden, August 1972

Difficulty: ED2, 5.9, A3, AI 3-4, 3,300 feet

Guidebook: *Selected Alpine Climbs in the Canadian Rockies; Fifty Favorite Climbs*

Permits: A backcountry camping permit is necessary for overnight stays in Jasper National Park, and it's recommended that you register your climb with park wardens as well. A permit from the ACC is necessary to stay at the hut.

MT. KITCHENER (11,417 feet/3,480 meters)
North Face

Roadside scouting and a short approach have helped make this great wall one of the continent's more popular severe alpine challenges. The *Grand Central Couloir* is the striking line, but the original *Ramp Route* is scarcely less serious, just less technical at its cruxes. The face's reputation for rockfall hopefully has been emphasized enough to deter aspirants from being caught here during thawing temperatures, especially on the face's lower two-thirds. It's now assumed that anyone heading up these routes will climb in the style of Lowe and Weis, with minimal or no plan to bivouac.

Approach: From the Icefields Parkway, it's a couple of hours' walk over talus to bivouac sites that are well positioned for an early start.

Route: A team should make quick time up the 50- to 60-degree apron and lower couloir. On the *Ramp Route*, an S-shaped weakness allows access to the "ramp," which presents surprisingly challenging climbing with very thin protection for some eight pitches. The *Grand Central Couloir* route is obvious until the chute narrows, whereupon you have the option of either going straight up mixed ground (rarely done 5.8, A2), or working right and then up a steep ice hose. A few hundred feet higher you come to the second crux rock wall. Icy conditions there might allow a direct finish, but more typical condi-

tions will encourage you to veer right up an ice chute that gets you higher up the wall. There's usually enough dry rock to require a poorly protected 5.9 pitch, with possible aid, to access the summit cornices. Descend via the east ridge, which requires one short rappel and a bit of downclimbing.

First Ascents: *Ramp Route*: Chris Jones, Jeff Lowe and Gray Thompson, August 1971; First winter ascent: Jim Elzinga and John Lauchlan, March 1977; *Grand Central Couloir*: Jeff Lowe and Mike Weis, August 1975; First winter ascent: Jack Roberts and Tobin Sorenson, January 1978

Difficulty: *Grand Central Couloir:* ED+, 5.9, A2, AI 5, 4,300 feet; *Ramp Route*: ED, 5.8, A1, AI 4, 4,300 feet

Guidebook: *Selected Alpine Climbs in the Canadian Rockies*

Permits: A backcountry camping permit is necessary for overnight stays in Jasper National Park, and it's recommend that you register your climb with park wardens as well.

Jeff Lowe and Chris Jones just after completing the first ascent of Mt. Kitchener's north face. PHOTO BY GRAY THOMPSON.

CHAPTER 11

Style on Rock

Through the 20th century, American climbing steadily moved away from the tradition of mountaineering as developed in the European Alps, and toward a homegrown identity. Most American mountains are drier and rockier than much of the Alps, so the American focus naturally shifted to rock mountaineering and crag climbing. This technical focus intensified during the late 1950s and '60s, to the point that Americans became—at least on granite—the premier rock climbers in the world. Colorado, the Tetons, the Northeast and British Columbia all had clusters of brilliant rock climbers, but it was the walls of Yosemite that inspired the highest standards on sustained vertical ground, and the climbers who trained there would change the mountaineering world.

Many or even most rock climbing specialists never ventured to high mountain routes, but through the 1960s they still climbed even short routes as if they were mountaineering problems. The paramount guide to style was efficiency—it was best to climb free wherever possible, but when the terrain reared up one should get on with efficient direct aid rather than waste time trying to figure out how to climb free. As Yosemite pioneers began to move smoothly up the big walls, they added an ethic that all routes should be done alpine style—even major El Capitan ascents should be made with minimal or no fixed ropes.

The traditional mountaineering community did not fully apprehend what rock climbers were doing. Elders of the American Alpine Club only began to admit minor mention of major Yosemite ascents in their journal in the early 1960s. By the 1970s, however, every leading mountaineer in North America arrived at high-standard mountain routes only after training on accessible crags and walls, and most would put in many seasons of low-elevation rock climbing.

Rock climbing was so popular by the early 1970s that overuse became a widespread concern. Most obvious were the holes being chewed in the rock by repeated placement and removal of pitons, even in Yosemite's steely granite. The popularity also fostered a sense of aesthetic decay among some of America's best climbers—a dismay that the joys of discovery were being replaced by demanding but familiar technical exercises. When El Capitan—the defining challenge of the era—started collecting a number of ascents each year, climbers sought a new

↻ Doug Robinson leading on hammerless gear in the Sierra. PHOTO BY GALEN ROWELL/MOUNTAIN LIGHT.

infusion of imagination. The result was a three-pronged evolution in style.

First, gear companies attacked the crack-damage problem by designing and promoting nuts (chocks), the alloy wedges that are slotted into cracks rather than hammered in. After using them skeptically for a few years, climbers found that, with practice, nuts were not only benign but also reliable and efficient, and hammerless ascents soon became the norm.

Second, the search for technical adventure led to a more intense focus on free climbing. This brought improved rock shoes, hand chalk and, by the mid-1970s, the development of spring-loaded camming anchors. Free climbers started to claim the stylistic and athletic high ground. Eventually, the "rules" for free climbing began to liberalize. Free climbers spent extra time figuring out moves, taking short falls and resting on hardware. With these developments, free climbing advanced to previously unimagined terrain.

Third, rock climbers began to head for high ground. In the 1970s, broad-minded rock athletes gradually rediscovered the notion that an ascent in high mountains can be more complex, uncertain, aesthetic and profound than simple cragging.

In the 1963 *AAJ*, Yvon Chouinard had written this manifesto: "The future of Yosemite climbing lies not in Yosemite, but in using the new techniques in the great granite ranges of the world." Chouinard foresaw that technical proficiency soon would be exported to alpine and super-alpine routes:

> These extraordinary climbs will be done by dedicated climbers who are in superb mental and physical condition from climbing all year round; who are used to climbing on granite…and who have the desire and perseverance needed to withstand the intense suffering, which is a prerequisite for the creation of any great work of art. Yosemite Valley will, in the near future, be the training ground for a new generation of super-alpinists who will venture forth to the high mountains of the world to do the most esthetic and difficult walls on the face of the earth.

Even as Chouinard wrote this, a renaissance of high-country climbing had begun on granite walls of the Sierra, the Cascades, the American Rockies and southwestern Canada.

Beckey Rocks

In the North Cascades the Yosemite manifestos took seed in 1963, with a partnership between Fred Beckey and a younger Seattle cohort, Steve Marts. Like most of his generation, Beckey generally hadn't questioned siege techniques. In fact, he had developed a habit of hanging ropes partway up peaks and then moving on to other routes; some said he did this to stake claims and keep competitors away. Marts, on the other hand, had spent a season in Yosemite and fully embraced the daunting challenge of going big without fixed ropes. Beckey, as usual, had plenty of ideas for big new routes up his sleeve, and he was game.

In mid-July they got going with a two-day first ascent of the complete north ridge of Mt. Stuart. In 1956, Don Claunch and John Rupley had found an easy ramp that led to the midpoint on this dramatic buttress, and from there climbed to the summit. The obvious goal, however, was the whole buttress. Starting from just right of the toe, Beckey and Marts climbed many pitches of steep, classic alpine granite to a bivouac just below the junction with the 1956 ramp. In the morning they completed the 2,800-foot-high route, an impressive breakthrough for the region and still a favorite. However, this was only a warm-up for what would become the greatest alpine rock route in the Cascades, the awesome northeast buttress of Slesse Mountain in southernmost British Columbia.

Beckey had climbed on Slesse twice and had developed "a proprietary interest in the great east face." Miles of densely forested wilds hindered his attempts to get to the hidden cirque until 1958. When he finally was able to reach ledges descending across it, "The upward look was overwhelming; so

Slesse Mountain: The northeast buttress is the prominent sunlit feature on the right. PHOTO BY DON SERL.

enormous was the wall we could scarcely concentrate on checking potential routes." In the following years, however, growing familiarity with big granite, as well as logging roads that shortened the approach, combined to give Beckey and Marts secret hope. Soon after climbing Stuart they hiked in to Slesse.

With just two ropes and a little survival gear, they climbed halfway up the 3,000-foot buttress to reach a nice bivouac ledge. Overnight, however, a thick cloud bank came in, and in the morning they retreated into the ghostly mist, rappelling toward cairns they had built just for this contingency. They left their ropes hanging from the lowest steep sections to ease their next attempt.

Beckey and Marts decided that the challenge called for added horsepower. They approached Eric Bjørnstad, an eclectic climber who ran Seattle's favorite climbers' hangout, Coffeehouse Eigerwand. They plied him with mythic tales but refused to disclose the name of the peak or even what direction it lay in. Bjørnstad only learned the goal as they arrived at the start of the approach. As a team of three, the climbers moved more surely but slowly, and they spent their first night below

Fred Beckey leading in a dihedral on the first ascent of the southeast buttress of Pigeon Spire in the Bugaboos, another climb that he and Steve Marts did during July of 1963. PHOTO BY STEVE MARTS, COURTESY FRED BECKEY.

Fred Beckey in the 1960s. PHOTO BY GALEN ROWELL/MOUNTAIN LIGHT.

the earlier high point. The next day, the ridge steepened and they had to resort to some aid. As darkness came Beckey and Bjørnstad reached a ledge, but Marts had to spend the night below, standing in aid slings in the middle of the last hard pitch. Clear weather held, however, and in the morning they reached the summit after climbing a total of 34 pitches and placing 63 pitons and one bolt. Beckey wrote that they were "very, very happy…. We had separated myth from reality."

For Beckey, this was no reason to rest and he raced east for his nearly annual late-summer visit to the Wind River Range, to try the El Capitan-steep north face of Mt. Hooker. For this he enlisted Layton Kor, who was dominating the advance of technical climbing in Colorado. Just before meeting with Beckey he had made the first two one-day ascents of the Diamond, with Royal Robbins, one of them a new route. When Kor and Beckey started up Hooker, though, September cold made the shaded face unreasonable. They retreated and moved to a sunnier prow, the west face of Musembeah Peak.

With Kor along, Beckey knew they would move fast, so they took just a light pack with some water, a snack and a little spare clothing. Wearing *Kletterschue*, they tiptoed up fine edges and finger-sized cracks, jiggling and

hustling to keep warm until the afternoon sun arrived. A wind came up, and soon it began to rain and sleet. As they began to shiver, it became imperative to get up and over the top. Kor veered off the main prow onto easier ground on the north face, but, as Beckey recalled, "Every crack was full of water, and the major couloirs dropping toward the flanks were horrible waterfalls." Kor pulled furiously through long, wet cracks, rarely pausing to put in a protection piton. Then Beckey led "an overhanging wall…partly on aid to avoid a terribly loose chockstone. When we finally got up, we felt as if we had been in an icy water tank half a day. We literally ran down to camp," where they built a much-needed fire.

A National Rating System

By the early 1960s, American climbing was popular enough that climbers from a variety of areas were compiling guidebooks. As climbers traveled between different regions, the desire for a unified rating system grew. Californians Royal Robbins, Steve Roper and Leigh Ortenburger started a lively discussion of how climbs might be compared and categorized, and it was Ortenburger, a statistician and Teton guide, who compiled the results. The National Climbing Classification System, or NCCS, was introduced in *Summit* magazine in 1963. This system was designed to replace the unwieldy 5.X "decimal" grades with a simple digit indicating the difficulty of a free climbing pitch. It also incorporated a five-level category, A1–A5, for direct-aid pitches, as well as the Roman numerals I–VI that Yosemite climbers had started using to grade the overall length and difficulty of climbs. The system was logical and climbers quickly came to understand, for instance, that VI, 7, A3 described a major technical climb, probably on El Capitan.

In the long run, however, the NCCS free climbing digits never supplanted the similar and already well-established 5.X ratings. The A1-A5 ratings were useful for some time, but because aid climbers took A5 as the gospel limit of difficulty and refused to allow expansion into A6 or beyond, drastic discrepancies between similarly graded climbs eventually made this system nearly meaningless. The

The Cathedral Traverse (left to right): Teewinot Mountain, the Grand Teton and Mt. Owen from the northeast. PHOTO BY ANDY SELTERS.

most enduring part of the NCCS has been the overall grade, which came to be based on technical climbing time. Teton rangers had recorded scores of ascent times over the years, and Ortenburger used these figures to calculate the standard times for many Teton routes, accurate to within minutes. Using this data, he categorized Teton routes from I to IV. In Yosemite, Mark Powell articulated the generally accepted times for I to VI routes. A Grade III would take about half a day; Grade IV a full day; Grade V a single overnight; and Grade VI at least two days and usually more.

Grand Traverses

Another style path climbers periodically have taken has been to link multiple summits. The Tetons and the Sierra present some especially logical peak-clusters. In 1938, Jack Riegelhuth and W. K. Davis traversed the northern Pali-sades, from Mt. Winchell over Thunderbolt Peak to North Palisade. Twenty years later, John Ohrenschall and John Mathias traversed in two days the ripsaw between Thunderbolt Peak and Mt. Sill. In the same season, in the North Cascades, Ed Cooper and Walt Sellers covered a similar skyline challenge, the mile-long spine that links Mt. Torment and Forbidden Peak.

In the Tetons, a new level of linkup challenge sprang, so legend has it, from the fertile mind of Willi Unsoeld. A guide for Glenn Exum, Unsoeld first proposed in the early 1950s that a traverse over all seven of the core Teton summits might be done in under 24 hours. He convinced Pete Schoening and Dick Pownall to try the big traverse, but after bogging down in routefinding on Teewinot, they had to call it a day after continuing to Mt. Owen and the Grand Teton—a long, brilliant day nonetheless. Their highline soon became known as the Cathedral Traverse, and their experience suggested that to do all seven peaks it would be easier to start from the south and thereby rappel down the north ridge of the Grand Teton rather than climb up it.

During the summer of 1963, Californians Dick Long and Allen Steck, along with alligator wrestler John Evans, came to the Tetons during an extended tour of western mountain areas. Long persuaded the other two to try Unsoeld's south-to-north challenge. On their first attempt they made it over five of the peaks, but at 5:15 p.m., as they neared the top of Mt. Owen, lightning and drenching rain forced a retreat. They finally straggled back to their car at 2:45 a.m. Three days later they tried again, leaving at 11:30 p.m. Now familiar with the route, they made it over Nez Perce, Cloudveil and the Middle Teton and on to the summit of the Grand Teton by 10:30 a.m. Though lightning approached again, they snuck to the top of Mt. Owen and then over to the summit of Teewinot by 6 p.m. Two hours later they were back at the car, three and a half hours ahead of Unsoeld's 24-hour target. Traditionalist Leigh Ortenburger labeled their exertions "a high school trick," but as the elegance and effort of this link-up became well recognized, the tour became known as the Grand Traverse.

That summer, Seattle climbers Alex Bertulis and Half Zantop made, in 10 days, the first tour along the remote Picket Range. They traversed below the spires of the Terror Creek cirque, then climbed the west ridge of Mt. Terror. They left the southern Picket group with 2,000 feet of *Dülfersitz* rappels down Terror's north face—this alone took one and a half days. Carrying only ponchos for shelter and no stove, they descended to treeline for a campfire, and then continued to the northern Pickets to climb Mt. Fury and hopefully finish over the top of Mt. Challenger. As their food ran low a whiteout enveloped them, blocking their way out via the heavily crevassed Challenger Glacier. By pure luck, the only two other climbers to visit the Pickets that year appeared in the mist, having crossed the glacier when it was clear. After summiting Mt. Challenger, Bertulis and

Zantof followed these two and their footprints to Perfect Pass and out.

In the Canadian Rockies in 1965, Calgary youngsters Charlie Locke and Don Gardner completed one of the grandest traverses yet done on the continent: all of the peaks along the Continental Divide that ring the Valley of the Ten Peaks and the Lake Louise cirque. On their first day they climbed Babel, Fay and two more peaks before reaching a shelter. The next day started with three lesser peaks before taking on the first ascent of the east ridge of Deltaform. On the third day they worked over Mt. Neptuak and struggled down loose, steep rock to Wenkchemna Pass, where relatives met them with a small resupply. The southeast ridge of Mt. Hungabee then proved to be their greatest technical challenge, for the notoriously loose rock was wet. Onward they pushed over lesser peaks to the hut at Abbot Pass, from which they tagged Mt. Lefroy before continuing north over Mt. Victoria. Overall, the grand tour took them six and a half days and included 22 summits.

Granite Classics

In 1964, Royal Robbins, Dick McCracken and Charlie Raymond brought their Yosemite talents to the Wind Rivers, to the 1,800-foot-high north face of Mt. Hooker, the wall that Beckey and Kor had passed up when it was too cold. Their route required much direct aid over three and a half days of climbing, and their line was hailed as the first wilderness wall big and technical enough to rate a Grade VI.

Back in the Valley, in 1965, Eric Beck looked across the crackless expanse on the west face of Half Dome and noticed an upward-wiggling line of crystalline feldspar—a dike that might provide holds. He recruited two other Valley residents, Chris Fredericks and 21-year-old Jim Bridwell, to try to climb it.

Through the 1960s, most routes up Yosemite's fine-grained granite followed cracks, and there was only an occasional tenuous and usually unprotected foray onto friction and face holds, mostly on the Apron below Glacier Point. Beck hoped his route on Half Dome would go free, but the only anchor

Half Zantop on the 1963 traverse of the Picket Range. PHOTO BY ALEX BERTULIS.

possible for most of the way seemed likely to be bolts. Beck is often remembered as a wry proponent of the live-cheap-and-climb-more lifestyle, and for his observation that, "At either end of the social spectrum there lies a leisure class." These three climbers had leisure time, but at their end of the social spectrum they could scrape together only 10 bolts for their Half Dome attempt.

Beck led the first pitch, placing their first bolt to protect a gap before the dike. They found the two-foot-wide stripe to be rich with surprisingly angular, crystalline holds. As they alternated leads, each leader tried to preserve their precious few bolts. Although the holds thinned dramatically in places and the three were climbing in lug-soled *Kletterschue*, they edged upward with little hesitation and on most pitches without any intermediate protection, unless a piton seam appeared. In this way, 90 years after George Anderson completed his siege ascent, this trio made the first free ascent of one of the world's unique summits in a single day. At the

top they still had four bolts left. They called the route *Snake Dike,* and when their friend Steve Roper went to repeat the route the next year, Beck convinced him to add some bolts.

In 1968, three of America's finest cragsmen went to the Cirque of the Unclimbables and found a route so stunning and suited to their style as to lift them beyond their wildest dreams. Where climbers of the previous decade had found these walls embodied their definition of unclimbable, stone masters Jim McCarthy, Tom Frost and Sandy Bill saw routes they could hardly wait to get on. None was more astounding than the southeast buttress of Lotus Flower Tower. This spear rises in a continuous, 2,200-foot-high thrust with what Bill described as "a long, long crack hanging straight, like a thread, from the very peak of the tower—The Great Line." Moreover, the rock bristled with phenocrysts—crystal-knobs that made superb holds. A third of the way up the tower, in need of a bivouac site, Frost came to a ledge he described as "all right, if you happen to

like flat grass." For two more days they followed this supreme crack system, sure and
straight, virtually floating in high spirits to
the cairn left by Bill Buckingham eight years
before. The whole climb had been too good
to be true, and its aesthetics instantly became
famous the world over.

In 1969, veterans George Lowe, Leigh
Ortenburger and Jack Turner set their sights
on the most impressive unclimbed area of the
Grand Teton, the steep and shaded north face
of the Enclosure. After working up remote
Valhalla Canyon, they climbed a pitch across
the tongue of the *Black Ice Couloir* and continued on mixed ground to attack some of the
most sustained verticality on the peak.
Wearing a down jacket and full mountaineering boots, Lowe led a long, unprotected and
icy offwidth crack. Turner continued up this
fissure for another short pitch before a fierce
storm forced them to bivouac and then

retreat. A few weeks later, Lowe came back
with his cousin Mike and re-led the offwidth,
which remains one of the most intimidating
pitches in the Tetons. They continued for
seven or eight more pitches to the top of the
Enclosure.

Palisade Renaissance

Before he joined the Harvard Wickersham
Wall expedition of 1963 (see Chapter 9), Don
Jensen had dropped out of college and
returned to the Sierra. Though it was midwin-
ter, he went to the Palisades, a Teton-like
arena of granodiorite splinters that soar up to
14,000 feet, all fairly untouched by modern
technical climbers. He spent half the winter
and spring of '63 camped at 11,000 feet in the
southern Palisade cirque, climbing and skiing. Jensen made regular trips from this her-
mitage down into the hamlet of Big Pine to
get supplies and to busy himself taking

Lotus Flower Tower. PHOTO BY GALEN ROWELL/MOUNTAIN
LIGHT.

Don Jensen on the east face of Mt. Sill in the Palisades,
Sierra. PHOTO BY KEITH BRUECKNER.

The Palisades section of the Sierra crest. The Thumb is barely visible on the left, and to its right is Middle Palisade and Norman Clyde Peak, with *Twilight Pillar* prominent. Right of center is Mt. Sill, then North Palisade and its neighbors. Mt. Agassiz is the last peak on the right. PHOTO BY ANDY SELTERS.

anthropologist-style notes on small-town life. Later that year he found work with Larry Williams, who had started Mountaineering Guide Service in the late '50s; Jensen became his most accomplished guide.

Whether with clients, partners or alone, Jensen started pioneering routes up the boldest walls in the chain, including the east face of Mt. Sill and the *Eagle Face* of Norman Clyde Peak, along with many first winter ascents. In 1966, he and fellow guide Frank Sarnquist set a new Sierra standard for sustained free climbing on the *Twilight Pillar* of Norman Clyde Peak. Jensen also grew keen on ridgeline traverses, and as he guided clients along various segments of the Palisade spine he mused that an ultimate tour would follow the entire nine-mile backbone between The Thumb and Mt. Agassiz.

Wilderness mountaineering came to boom in subsequent years, and other fresh-faced dropouts found their way to the Palisades. Climbers like Doug Robinson, John Fischer and Carl Dreisbach came to the mountains to get away from cities, political turmoil and even the intensive scene in Yosemite. Although these long-haired climbers' psychedelic habits contrasted with the steadiness of Jensen and Williams, they all developed a brotherhood in climbing, and some of the youngsters worked their way into guiding jobs.

In 1969, a heavy winter forced the Palisade guides to set up a lower basecamp, below Temple Crag. This convoluted monument stands east of the main crest and doesn't

quite reach 13,000 feet, but its complex structure ripples with some of the grandest buttresses in the Sierra. For six years Jensen had accepted the common lore that Temple Crag had worse rock than the crest peaks, but then John Fischer pointed out that the morning light gleamed with the promise of firm stone when it skipped across these fins. In July 1969, Jensen climbed a third of the way up one spectacular fin with student Mike Graber. This foray made him realize that Temple Crag held some of the best climbing in the Sierra, and he called the arête that begged to be finished *Sun Ribbon*—the first of four big spines that would collectively be known as the *Celestial Arêtes*.

On September 2, Jensen and Fischer teamed up to complete the *Sun Ribbon*, while their buddies Carl Dreisbach and Pat Armstrong climbed the adjacent *Moon Goddess Arête*. When Jensen got to the gap that had slowed his first attempt, he made quick work of it by lassoing a horn; the two howled to their *compadres* across the way as they slid across the gap on a Tyrolean traverse. Then Fischer led around the gendarme that had blocked Jensen before, wearing a secret weapon on his feet: EBs, the tight-fitting, smooth-soled rock shoes that were helping to revolutionize free climbing in Yosemite. The two parties continued whooping it up on their adjacent arêtes, completing a day they would never forget.

Near the close of the following season, in 1970, Robinson, Chuck Kroger, Jensen and

Looking across the northeast face of Temple Crag. The
Celestial Arêtes are in profile (left to right): *Venusian,
Moon Goddess, Sun Ribbon* and *Dark Star*. PHOTO BY ANDY
SELTERS.

Fischer went to Temple Crag's biggest prow.
Robinson and Tim Harrison had climbed a
few pitches up this spine (one of hard 5.10)
and labeled the potential route *Dark Star*,
after the "space sections" at Grateful Dead
concerts. Jensen and Fischer started up that
way, while Robinson and Kroger began a
variation to the right, which Robinson
named *Barefoot Bynum*, after their favorite
cheap wine. Worn out from a long summer
of guiding, they all expected to climb slowly,
and so they hauled bivouac gear. For Fischer
and Jensen, this led to a night hanging in
slings. The next day they reached the top of
the prow's main tower, but then escaped off
to the northwest. A year later, Jensen and
physicist Keith Brueckner climbed up that
retreat route and then ascended the upper
towers of *Dark Star*. Not until 1975 did

Fischer, Robinson and local youngsters Jay
Jensen (no relation to Don) and Gordon
Wiltsie climb all 30-plus pitches of *Dark
Star*.

Tragically, the two leaders of this Palisade
renaissance did not live to mentor into middle age. In 1967 Larry Williams went down
with his light plane, and in 1973 Don Jensen,
then studying in Scotland, was hit by a car
while riding a bicycle.

Climbing Clean

In 1967, Royal Robbins climbed in Britain and
came back with a bouquet of anchor nuts—
some were regular machine nuts threaded
with cord, and some were custom nuts specially designed for wedging into cracks. He
wrote an article advocating nuts because they
left the rock unscarred and were simple to
use. One reader who became particularly
enchanted with these elegant tools was Doug
Robinson, then a novice Palisade guide. He
found that the Palisades' angular cracks
accepted nuts readily, and soon other guides
started supplementing their racks with
"chocks."

A couple of years later, Robbins and Allen
Steck (who had assumed part ownership in
Williams' business, now called Palisade
School of Mountaineering or PSOM) sent
the guides the latest British designs. Soon
PSOM guides were taking nuts to the
smoother cracks of Tuolumne and Yosemite,
and crowing to the technical hard core
about the ethical, aesthetic and efficiency
benefits of climbing "clean." Robinson
joined the team at Chouinard Equipment
just as Frost and Chouinard were committing the company to reducing piton scarring
and to designing a new generation of nuts.
Breakthroughs came in 1971 and 1972, as
the company developed prototype chocks
and as Robinson and Jay Jensen pioneered
the first hammerless ascents of Yosemite
Grade IV and V routes.

Chouinard Inc. unveiled Stoppers and
Hexentrics in its 1972 catalog, along with an
influential manifesto for their use by
Robinson. Drawing connections to living
light on the land in general, "The Whole

The Great Pacific Iron Works, the manufacturing arm of Yvon Chouinard's equipment company, ca. 1960s. Chouinard is second from left, Tom Frost third from right. COURTESY PATAGONIA HISTORICAL ARCHIVE COLLECTION.

Yvon Chouinard wearing his company's new selection of hammerless anchors, in 1971. PHOTO BY TOM FROST.

Natural Art of Protection" read, in part, "There is a word for it, and the word is clean. Climbing with only nuts and runners for protection is clean climbing.... Clean is climbing the rock without changing it; a step closer to organic climbing for the natural man."

A year after this essay came out, Bruce Carson convinced Yvon Chouinard—who had felt that nuts would have important but limited value—to join him for the first hammerless ascent of El Capitan's *Nose*. Inspired both by nut use and the developments in ice climbing, Robinson later encapsulated the ways technique promotes better style:

> *Technology is imposed on the land, but technique means conforming to the landscape. They work in opposite directions, one forcing a passage while the other discovers it. The goal of developing technique is to conform to the most improbable landscape by means of the greatest degree of skill and boldness by the least equipment.*

Wild and Free

By the early '70s, the gap between rock specialists and adventure-focused rock mountaineers had widened. In crag centers like Yosemite, free climbers developed astounding, ever-higher levels of tenuous and strenuous challenge. In the mid-'70s, at Jim Bridwell's suggestion, the "decimal" rating system for free climbing expanded to 5.10a, b, c and d and to 5.11. Partly due to grade inflation and partly to greater abilities and better gear, the numbers would keep rising. A majority of American climbers focused on expanding the potential of short, hard rock climbs.

By contrast, a smaller number of climbers felt a strong pull to develop advanced technical skills specifically so they could take them to wilderness peaks. Bay Area-based climbers Galen Rowell and Chris Jones were committed to this idea, and in 1971 they climbed the striking and generally hidden west face of Mt. Russell, near Mt. Whitney. Pulling through clean 5.9 cracks at 14,000 feet, they found that the joys of discovery heightened the pleasure of technical challenge. Then they climbed a new wall route on the big face in Sequoia National Park known as Angel Wings. This was all in preparation for a trip north to

Galen Rowell on the summit of Mt. Williamson in the Sierra, after making the first ascent of the northwest ridge, solo, in 1970. PHOTO BY GALEN ROWELL/MOUNTAIN LIGHT.

the biggest prow in the Bugaboos, the west pillar of the North Howser Tower. In July, while Jones was between his two forays on Mt. Kitchener (see Chapter 10), he and Rowell hooked up with Berkeley climber Tony Qamar. The three climbers used two racks of anchors to move quickly up North Howser by having the second person jümar a spare rope while the first hauled the gear; as the second took the next lead, the third man extracted gear from the previous pitch. Despite needing a fair bit of aid, they completed this El Capitan-sized wall in just two days.

Rowell then drove back to Yosemite and found that within the climbing scene there,

> *The simple joys of exploration were on the wane; in their place was a trend to count and compare experiences with those of others who had climbed the same routes. I had no doubt that many Yosemite climbs demanded greater skill than the hardest routes of the highest ranges, but a big red flag went up when I saw climbers far more talented than myself unwilling to test in the nearby wilderness those skills acquired in this fair-weather womb. There was little I could do personally to reverse what I considered an unfortunate trend, except to bow out of it. I decided to go to Bear Creek Spire, alone.*

Rowell left his bicycle at the usual trailhead for the High Sierra's Bear Creek Spire, and then drove 40 miles to the trailhead that leads to the peak's more remote south face. This 1,000-foot face proved steeper than he expected, so he belayed himself for much of the climb. After much 5.8 and a couple moves of aid, he was able to reach the summit at sunset and then get down to a chilly bivouac. The next day he hiked to his bicycle and rode back to his car.

The Wildest Walls

By 1971, David Roberts (see Chapter 12) had joined the staff at Hampshire College, and that summer he collected a team of nine from the school to explore unclimbed towers in the ultra-remote Arrigetch Peaks of Alaska's Brooks Range. They arranged for an airdrop of supplies and then landed by float-plane at Takahula Lake. After a couple of days of hiking, they found what Roberts called "a glimpse of the Perfect Place," utterly apart from civilization, a tundra carpet rolling over the hills, wildlife roaming everywhere and sweeps of smooth granite lifting into big, fantastic forms. Among the various sheer tusks, Shot Tower was the most remarkable.

Shot Tower's only forgiving route seemed to be its west ridge, and Roberts and Ed Ward started up the smooth, moderately steep stone in their stiff Yosemite "RR" boots (designed for wall climbing by Royal Robbins). Even though they were miles north of the Arctic Circle, the day was so warm that they were nearly too hot in the afternoon sun. For pitch after pitch, just enough beautiful cracks appeared in the granite to, in Roberts' words, "lure me into commitment." After a dozen pitches they came to a 60-foot overhanging headwall, with only an incipient crack wiggling up it. With étriers and a series of nested pins, Ward led up the seam. The top waited just a couple of easy pitches beyond, capping what Roberts called "the happiest climb of my life."

On the other side of the continent, the wild walls of Baffin Island soon lured Yosemite-trained climbers. In 1970, Briton Doug Scott had made (with Tyrolean Peter Habeler) an early European ascent of an El Capitan Grade VI. A schoolteacher by trade, Scott was on his way to becoming one of the most accomplished and versatile professional mountaineers in history. At this time he was refining his own sense of style. On rock, he insisted on what he and others called "natural lines," routes where one could climb free or mostly free, and, most importantly, where there were enough cracks to proceed without a drill. Scott had made the acquaintance of Patrick Baird, the Canadian Arctic expert who facilitated the 1953 Swiss expedition that first climbed Mt. Asgard. It didn't take Baird long to convince Scott that Baffin was the place to go.

Scott's 1971 team comprised nine scruffy vagabonds, including Mick Burke as cinematographer and Californian Dennis

Hennek, one of Yosemite's most experienced wall rats. Around the Weasel Valley the team climbed a variety of peaks and found that many of the area's walls were composed of "the best rock that a climber could wish for." They looked in awe at the huge east face of Mt. Thor, but the stone was too steep and blank for climbing without drills. Near the head of the valley, however, the giant twin stumps of Mt. Asgard magnetized the climbers. Striking corner systems lay on either side of the north tower, but the late-August weather never cleared enough to allow a serious attempt.

Hennek and Scott came back the next July, without the burden of a film crew and with just two partners, Paul Braithwaite and Paul Nunn. They got a snowmobile ride up Pangnirtung Fjord and then packed 130-pound loads 25 miles up the thawing Weasel Valley to a basecamp at Summit Lake. Their first foray up Asgard's vertical west face came to crackless stone, so they retreated to try a more "natural," crack-rich line on the north tower's east face. As they laid plans for this 4,000-foot-high wall, their biggest fear was that a long, drawn-out ascent would butt into an arctic storm that would paste them to the wall with cold and ice. With continuous daylight, they decided to go without bivouac gear and just keep climbing until they reached the top. To their delight, most of the climbing went free, but the strain of such a long push in a threatening environment made Scott say, "We were within a stone's throw of a supreme test of our abilities." On the penultimate pitch, Hennek shed much of his clothing so he could squeeze deeper into a narrow chimney. This proved to be the hardest pitch of the climb, and 30 hours after they started they arrived at the summit plateau.

In 1974, Galen Rowell joined Dave Roberts and Ed Ward, the Shot Tower pair, to climb one of North America's biggest granite walls, the 5,100-foot east face of Mt. Dickey. This stands as the hugest of the monumental walls lining the Great Gorge of the Ruth Glacier. After fixing a few ropes, the trio led some 20 mostly free pitches in a single blue-sky day. But their fun turned serious when they came

Ed Ward belays David Roberts on the first day of climbing on the first ascent of the east face of Mt. Dickey.
PHOTO BY GALEN ROWELL/MOUNTAIN LIGHT.

into bands of rotten granite that Rowell described as "granola." After just four hours of sleep they charged into another long day, while clouds enveloped their position. Working up misted cliffs with a mix of free and aid, they managed another 10 difficult pitches—the last couple in a driving rain—to reach the top of the granite. In the morning, as rain turned to snow, they faced banks of ice, snow and schist. To trim weight, they had carried only one pair of crampons and one axe. Using this gear Roberts led onward, chopping steps for the others to follow, driving rock pitons into ice for desperate protection, and routefinding with a Bradford Washburn photo in his pocket. In all, they climbed 41 pitches to complete one of the most demanding climbs of the decade.

Extreme Free

During the 1970s, some of America's finest free climbers ventured beyond Yosemite and Eldorado to high mountain walls, although in friendlier settings than Alaska or Baffin Island. In the Tetons, for instance, Colorado stone masters Steve Wunsch and Art Higbee climbed one of Mt. Moran's south buttress routes at a 5.11 standard.

In Colorado, the big prize at this time was to climb the Diamond free. The *D7* route seemed the most likely possibility, but its sheer final headwall forced a number of aspirants into aid. In 1975, locals Jim Logan and Wayne Goss free climbed some hard 5.10 pitches of *D7*, and then linked to other routes that took them to Table Ledge, which allowed them to escape from the top of the face. Within a couple of weeks, the young California phenomenon Tobin Sorenson free climbed the *Pervertical Sanctuary* route on the Diamond's left edge, including one pitch at 5.11a. Sorenson and fellow Californian Rick Accomazzo then went up to the Bugaboos and nabbed the ultra-classic first free ascent of Chouinard and Beckey's buttress on South Howser Tower.

Colorado free climbers David Breashears and Art Higbee also went to the Bugaboos in '75 and climbed a new traversing route up the north end of the great east face of Snowpatch Spire. The 1,800-foot *Sunshine Wall* included some 5.10, but surprisingly no aid, and the two climbers reached the north shoulder of the peak in a single day. In 1977, Americans Steve Levin, Mark Robinson and Sandy Stewart free climbed the Lotus Flower Tower, using the full range of crack techniques and pulling 5.10 moves through a roof.

Californian John Bachar, the best and boldest free climber in the world, had begun to spend his summers guiding and climbing in Colorado. In 1977, John Long, Bachar's friend from California, suggested they try to free climb the Diamond. When they reached the peak, Long decided to stay in the meadows below with his girlfriend, while Bachar and Richard Harrison made their way to the base of the wall. Bachar and Harrison had never even scouted the Diamond, and as they wandered along Broadway Ledge they shouted down to Long for directions on where to start a possible free ascent. Long's yells put them on *D7*, and Bachar started leading up the almost flawless granite. Several pitches up, above the

The east face of Longs Peak. The Broadway ledge runs across the face at about 1/3 height, and the Diamond waits above. PHOTO BY ED WEBSTER.

Chris Vandiver on the first free ascent of the east face of Keeler Needle. PHOTO BY GALEN ROWELL/MOUNTAIN LIGHT.

section Goss and Logan had free climbed, he powered through a series of desperately thin cracks and liebacks. On the next lead, a crack gradually widened from finger-width to offwidth and wider. These intimidating 5.11 leads were the key to *D7*—the most dramatic alpine free climb yet on the continent. Near the top, they exited the face on Table Ledge.

In 1978, Bachar's fellow guide Billy Westbay suggested they try to free climb *D1*, the original aid line up the center of the Diamond. Bachar led the cruxy middle section up thin, gritty cracks and a small roof, with moves that are now rated up to 5.11. As they reached the final headwall, a lightning storm started crashing around them. With no time to lose, Westbay started up the logical but untried conclusion to the line, a ferocious offwidth seeping with water. Though his only protection was a fist-sized chock wedged a quarter of the way up the pitch, Westbay wrestled his way up the awful crack and onto the summit slopes. Purists consider this to be the Diamond's first real free ascent, since there was no escape

below the top. Two years later, Boulder local Roger Briggs repeated the free ascent of *D1* but followed the original aid corner on the last pitch, thus avoiding Westbay's offwidth and creating the first 5.12 lead on the Diamond.

During these years, a whole wave of climbers escaped Yosemite to seek high challenge on the Sierra's granite peaks. In 1975, Yosemite maestro Dale Bard led a beautiful 5.10 route up an 11,000-foot peak north of Yosemite, locally named the Incredible Hulk. The following year, Galen Rowell brought granite wizard Chris Vandiver to lead free ascents of Warren Harding's two great Sierra routes, the east face of Keeler Needle and the south face of Mt. Conness. Both required sustained technical climbing up to 5.10+ and 5.11. Rowell noted that, where the previous generation had approached climbs like Keeler as multiday big-wall climbs requiring direct aid, "[We] approached the route as an ordinary rock climb." He characterized these efforts as "part of a larger trend to merge the two disciplines of wall climbing and free climbing."

Advanced Protection

Intense free climbing begged for secure protection that was easy to place, and Greg Lowe, one of the most fertile minds in climbing, developed a variety of nuts with a continuous-angle camming action. These included both "passive" cams, which eventually developed into the Tri-cam, and a spring-loaded, cam-lever device called the "crack jümar," which expanded at a continuous angle to fit a range of placements.

Ray Jardine, a muscular man obsessed with extreme crack climbing, clandestinely took Lowe's camming concept and brought it into full flower (and eventually paid Lowe a patent settlement). With a British manufacturer, Jardine developed a four-cam unit called the Friend, with a spring-loaded injection trigger. In favorable cracks, one of these Friends could be placed or removed in an instant. When Friends hit the market in 1977, many

First light on the southeast buttress of Mt. Queen Bess.
PHOTO BY DON SERL.

climbers at first were skeptical of their reliability and some traditionalists maligned them for making protection too easy. But by 1980 no serious rock climber was without a set or three, and rock climbing speed, capability and security all rose another notch.

B.C. Granite

As always, the potential for brilliant new climbing in the Coast Mountains of British Columbia lagged years behind the developments in other ranges. Few had looked to these peaks with an eye for modern routes until Vancouver climber Don Serl began to poke around. In August 1976, Serl, John Wittmayer and Doug Herchmer used the 1950 Sierrans' approach (fly to Ghost Lake and receive an airdrop on the Tiedemann Glacier) to reach one of the biggest mountain walls south of Mt. Fairweather, the 5,000-foot south face of Mt. Tiedemann. Snow couloirs enabled relatively moderate climbing much of the way, but a band of loose granite and a heavy storm gave the trio a real education in alpine survival. To Serl, this climb revealed the area's promise as a premier arena for modern alpine climbing.

By the late 1970s, Vancouver-area climbers were well rehearsed on Squamish and Yosemite granite, and helicopter service helped inspire them to explore British Columbia's hinterlands for new challenges. In 1979, Serl, Dave Jones and John Wittmayer took a helicopter to the col north of Mt. Waddington and then dropped north to climb the 5,000-foot north face of Mt. Hickson. During their second day of climbing, the granitic upper part of this face presented them with "hour upon hour of unrelenting difficulty," much of it on steep rock with runnels and arêtes of ice and snow.

The following summer, Serl teamed with Michael Down for a premier Coast Mountain season. They started with a steep ice route on the 3,900-foot-high north face of Razorback Mountain, a striking peak on the east side of the main range. Then they took a chopper to Mt. Queen Bess, where they found sustained wonder-climbing on the beautiful granitic edge of the southeast buttress.

Don Serl, one of the great pioneers of Coast Mountain climbing. DON SERL COLLECTION.

Michael Down leading on the first ascent of the *Tuning Fork*, Mt. Bardean. PHOTO BY DON SERL.

Next, Serl took Down to another hideaway, the Chehalis Range. This collection of fine-grained granite peaks, reaching no higher than 7,100 feet, bristles just 50 miles east of Vancouver, yet none of the peak's stunning walls had been touched. Serl had been pointed to the area by Paul Binkert, a Coast Range veteran who pioneered some of these summits in the early 1970s. Rockies hardman Jim Elzinga joined Serl and Down to climb a 2,000-foot prow on the north face of Mt. Bardean. As on Queen Bess, they were able to climb to the summit in one long day, and they had to stand on aid pieces only for one short section. They called their line the *Tuning Fork*.

In March 1981, Vancouver climbers Scott Flavelle and Phil Hein started a series of outstanding granite climbs with a winter ascent of the west buttress of South Howser Tower. The two worked as ski guides in the area, and they used this connection to hitch a helicopter ride to the base of the climb. Over five days they persisted through a variety of weather, resorting to aid on a number of steep pitches in the fierce cold.

The following August, Flavelle, Down, Tom Gibson and Rob Rohn gathered to make high-standard routes in another granite

stronghold, the Adamant Group of the Selkirks. Among the highlights of this trip, Gibson and Rohn free climbed a route on Ironman, the northernmost summit in the group, at a 5.10+ standard.

The following year, 1982, Flavelle and Dave Lane made the first foray onto the extensive granite buttresses above the Tiedemann Glacier, across from Mt. Waddington. From the Waddington-Combatant Col, they climbed the nearest south-facing upper pillar on Combatant, working upward on almost flawless granite for 22 pitches up to 5.9, in one of the most spectacular settings imaginable. They called it *Skywalk*, and it has become one of the most legendary routes in British Columbia.

Beyond the Hyper-Technical

Progress at cragging centers became so dramatic, so fascinating and so accessible for so many that the definition of climbing itself was being transformed. Those focused on free climbing asked themselves not so much the traditional question, "Can I get up there?" but the hyper-technical, "Can I make the moves?"

The search for technical challenge leapt into pure expression when some Americans adopted the new European crag ethic of pre-placing protection bolts on rappel, most notably at Smith Rock, Oregon, and Eldorado Canyon in Colorado. Thus they dismissed the mountaineering-based need to plan and place protection as they climbed. With safety concerns pre-rigged, the standard of delicate and powerful moves reached even higher extremes. In this new context, many climbers wondered why anyone would go through all the hassle and risk to climb pitches with lesser technical challenge in the mountains.

As a result, although climbing generally was more popular than ever, all but a handful of highly publicized mountain routes were less traveled than they had been a decade before. However, committed adventure climbers continued to find satisfying unclimbed walls.

Washington-based Alan Kearney was a staunch veteran of wilderness mountaineering. He would write, "To understand the true spirit of Northwest mountaineering, it is necessary to carve away the outer tissue of accessible peaks and dig deep into the wild and rugged interior." Late in the 1980 season he convinced his friend Bobby Knight to hike way in to the little-known, 2,300-foot north face of Bear Mountain. Fred Beckey and Mark Fielding had climbed this face in 1967 by working up a snow and ice tongue as high as possible and then traversing onto a prominent rock buttress. Kearney saw the potential to climb this buttress in its entirety.

With weather and route uncertain, he and Knight started the buttress with a few days of supplies and bivouac gear. Right from the start the buttress delivered wonderful climbing up wildly exposed, steep cracks. They bivouacked on a terrace halfway up and then continued with more steep climbing and just a few points of aid to another bivouac. On the third morning they finished the final headwall with two more pitches of clean cracks splitting the narrow edge of the buttress.

In the Sierra, in July 1981, Galen Rowell and Dave Wilson made the first route up any of the big west-flank buttresses of the Palisades. Their route tackled the most prominent headwall on North Palisade with four pitches of thin 5.9 and 5.10 climbing, then continued

over a long arête to the summit. In a similar spirit, Jeff Lowe and a variety of partners established various difficult routes in the Wind Rivers. Chapter 13 will take up the further progress on high-country rock in the 1980s.

Traversing Revival
During the late 1970s in the Sierra, guides were starting to talk seriously about following Don Jensen's dream of traversing the whole crest of the Palisades. A PSOM client named Jerry Adams heard the guides muse about it, and in 1978 he proposed to John Fischer that they try it. Adams volunteered to set three caches at the base of peaks along the route. Partway along the comb, however, thunderstorms forced them to exit.

A year later, Adams set caches for another attempt with Fischer. Starting from Southfork Pass, with Fischer leading or "short-

John Fischer readying a rappel on the Palisade Crest section of the first traverse of the Palisades. PHOTO BY JERRY ADAMS.

The Minarets, from the east. PHOTO BY ANDY SELTERS.

roping" the entire way, they made their way along eight miles of toothy stone. For the most part they stayed along or near the main crest, nabbing every significant summit and making over 20 rappels. They spent their sixth bivouac near the summit of Thunderbolt Peak and the next morning descended to the Thunderbolt Glacier, where Adams had set their final cache. Fischer was somewhat revitalized by the cigarettes in that stash, but their anchors and energy were so depleted that they decided to compromise and climb their penultimate peak, Mt. Winchell, by its easier north face instead of its long and technical crestline ridge. Then they labored over to the top of Mt. Agassiz and descended north through Superior Col to treeline, essentially completing Jensen's dream—a feat of technical endurance that few appreciated.

During the early 1980s, Tuolumne/Yosemite partners Vern Clevenger and Claude Fiddler started to get fascinated with ridgeline traverses like this. It dawned on Clevenger and Fiddler that traversing many peaks in one long push was like creating a new ultra-route. As the two pored over Sierra maps looking for continuous skylines, they locked onto the Ritter Range—a fortress of metamorphic rock broken into a cluster of spires called the Minarets, along with the dominating twin summits of Mt. Ritter and Mt. Banner.

In August 1982, Clevenger and Fiddler started from a lake at the southern base of the Minarets, carrying a couple of days of supplies and bivouac gear, and climbed north over a dozen of these pinnacles. Their need for speed and the crags' complexity prompted them to disregard routefinding hassles and just force their way up and over the towers, climbing unroped until the terrain got harder than 5.8 or 5.9. At nightfall they settled into a bivouac near a trickle of water. In the morning they finished the last four connected Minarets and continued across a pass to Waller Minaret. As they headed over to Ritter, a subtropical storm unleashed lightning, hail and basketball-sized rockfall that chased them down. As with the Palisades traverse, only a few esoteric climbers understood the accomplishment of traversing the Minarets, or even considered it a route.

In British Columbia, Peter Croft was free climbing granite at the world's highest standard, and he too looked to the potential of traversing mega-routes. Croft had started rock climbing at Squamish, and he was so enthused that when his partners packed up with daylight to spare, he often just kept climbing, alone and unroped. He always chose easy routes, climbing down as well as up, just for the love of added mileage. As a result of so much disciplined joy, he developed a mastery that can only be called extraordinary. His roped climbing standard eventually rose to 5.13, but more remarkable was how he developed the naked confidence to climb unroped on 5.11 and even some 5.12—up and down. He began to notice that, without the hassle of belaying or anchoring, he could amaze even himself with how much ground he could cover quickly. He later said, "It was as if I'd learned to fly."

In July 1983, Croft was in top form. He traveled to the Bugaboos with Hamish Fraser, and together they headed for the Chouinard-Beckey route on South Howser Tower, each carrying a rope to pair up for rappelling the east face. With steady and careful unbelayed climbing, both stood on top with the morning still young. After the rappels, Croft went alone to Snowpatch Spire and climbed it via the 5.8

Kraus-McCarthy route on its west face. He rappelled and downclimbed the same route, then stashed the rope and went over to the 5.10 *McTech Arête* on the south face of Crescent Spire, the only route in this link-up that he'd done previously. After that, he hiked over and climbed Bugaboo Spire's northeast ridge. As he descended Kain's original ridge, Croft got off-route and had to downclimb some insecure 5.10. Fourteen hours after leaving, he was back at the hut, exhilarated and fulfilled—although he was kicking himself for not climbing easy Pigeon Spire, the only tower in the main group he hadn't tagged.

A year later, in 1984, Clevenger and Fiddler teamed up for another epic traverse, along a spine of summits that they called, for lack of a map name, the southwest ridge of Mt. Ritter. A traverse of this long chain of metamorphic summits, they argued, had the logic, challenge and length to be given a rating of Grade VI. Croft, Clevenger and Fiddler were making parallel assertions that mountaineering progressed not only by climbing harder but also by climbing longer.

Claude Fiddler on the first traverse of the Minarets.
PHOTO BY VERN CLEVENGER.

Vern Clevenger on the first traverse of the Minarets.
PHOTO BY CLAUDE FIDDLER, COURTESY VERN CLEVENGER.

SUGGESTED ROUTES
FROM THIS PERIOD

With so many of North America's peaks offering such superb rock mountaineering, this period has given the world perhaps the richest route legacy of any in our history. Only a few fine routes can be suggested here.

MUSEMBEAH PEAK (12,593 feet/3,838 meters)
West Buttress

This excellent buttress route provides a superb, memorable climb on a variety of sound rock. It presents some exposed and reasonably technical climbing, as well as routefinding puzzles and the commitment of climbing deep in a range famous for fickle weather.

Approach: Start with an 18.4-mile hike west from Dickinson Park Work Center, rambling over passes to a headwater of the Wind River at Baptiste Lake. Most hikers with a full pack will take one and a half to two days for this scenic sojourn.

Route: Musembeah's west buttress is the left of the two prominent ones seen from the lake. The climbing begins in the chute between the two but-

Musembeah Peak from the west. PHOTO BY JOE KELSEY.

tresses. Work left up corners and face moves for six pitches to the middle section of the west buttress. Follow this easier crest to the upper headwall. On the first ascent, Beckey and Kor veered onto the north face, where complex terrain gives ample opportunity to find dead ends—scout your route carefully. With dry conditions, climbers have been able to climb the route free and complete a direct finish. The summit area is a complex of converging arêtes, so take care with routefinding. Head east until it's possible to drop into the easy terrain of the peak's "south cwm."

First Ascent: Fred Beckey and Layton Kor, September 1963; First free ascent: Joe Kelsey and Richard Goldstone, 1976; Direct finish: Keith Cattabriga and partner, ca. 1990

Difficulty: D, IV, 5.8 or 5.10a, 1,500 feet

Guidebook: *Wind River Mountains*

Permit: Musembeah is within the Wind River Indian Reservation, and visiting this area requires a "fishing permit," available in stores and offices in towns near the Wind Rivers. A self-issuing wilderness permit for camping in the surrounding National Forest is available at the trailhead.

MT. BARDEAN (6,332 feet/1,930 meters)
The *Tuning Fork*

The *Tuning Fork* has all the elements of a classic alpine rock route: an elegant line, high-quality rock, sustained and moderately difficult climbing, and a wild alpine setting. The one- or two-day approach is reasonable by B.C. wilderness standards, but climbers expecting, say, Sierra- or Teton-like trails will find extra challenge.

Approach: The Chehalis Range is about two and a half hours' drive east of Vancouver, much of which is spent on 21 miles of dirt logging road. Climbers with a high-clearance 4WD can reach the old trailhead, but others have to walk an additional three miles up "decommissioned" road. From the old trailhead, the hike takes a solid day, starting with a rough trail that gets more overgrown past Statlu Lake, then some talus scrambling and cliffy cedar climbing. Bivouac on a bench below Bardean, being careful to choose a site that's not threatened by chunks of pocket glacier sliding off.

Route: The climbing starts on the right side of the lowest reach of Bardean's prominent north buttress, with some fifth-class climbing among small cedars.

Mt. Bardean on the left and Mt. Ratney on the right, in unusually snow-free conditions. PHOTO BY KEVIN MCLANE.

Easy ground then lets you work left to the rib that forms the left tine of the Tuning Fork, where you aim upward toward a prominent left-facing dihedral. The difficulties steadily increase as you approach this corner, and you might find a hammer and a few thin pitons helpful. Work left around some roofs to the superb upper pitches, staying generally on the left edge of Bardean's north face. From the summit, descend by scrambling along the skyline west to the top of Mt. Ratney. Downclimb and rappel Ratney's bushy north ridge to a pass, and then rappel and climb down to benches that lead back to the base of Bardean.

First Ascent: Michael Down, Jim Elzinga and Don Serl, July 1980

Difficulty: TD, IV/V, 5.9, 1,800 feet

Guidebook: *Alpine Select*

BEAR MOUNTAIN (7,931 feet/2,418 meters)
Direct North Buttress

Rave reports from alpine rock enthusiasts have made this a route that gets done almost every year—downright popular by regional standards.

The north face of Bear Mountain. PHOTO BY JOHN DITTLI.

Approach: From Vancouver, an hour of highway driving and 30 miles of dirt road heading south up the valley of the Chilliwack River reach a gate on the road. From here, it's a steady seven-hour hike on a rough trail through magnificent forest and along a panoramic ridgeline to a bivouac site (waterless after midsummer) on the west ridge of Bear Mountain. Make a straightforward descent to the western base of the north face. An icy traverse to the toe of the buttress usually makes alpine gear mandatory.

Route: Ten pitches of alpine crack climbing, mostly 5.8 to 5.10a, lead to a large terrace, which can provide an excellent bivouac. More 5.9 cracks and blocky climbing continue right on the crest of the buttress to a long offwidth crack, which can be mostly avoided to the right. Three more pitches up to 5.10 maintain the challenge and spectacular position virtually to the summit ridge. The summit is a short distance to the east, and the descent is a straightforward cruise back to the bivouac site.

First Ascent: Alan Kearney and Bobby Knight, September 1980; First free ascent: Brian Burdo and Yann Merrand, August 1985

Difficulty: TD, IV/V, 5.10a, 2,500 feet

Guidebooks: *Alpine Select, Selected Climbs in the Cascades; Cascade Alpine Guide (Rainy Pass to the Fraser River)*

Permits: The approach to this climb crosses from Canada into the United States and North Cascades National Park. Climbers must notify both U.S. Customs and the national park offices in Sedro Woolley, Washington.

SHOT TOWER (6,069 feet/1,850 meters)
West Ridge

The granitic Arrigetch ("fingers of the hand outstretched") Peaks are a beacon for climbing deep in one of the most fantastic wilderness areas on the continent. Position, quality of rock, history and sustained moderate climbing make Shot Tower's west ridge the classic of the area.

Approach: From Bettles, hire a floatplane to either Takahula or Circle lake. Airdrops are now prohibited within Gates of the Arctic National Park, and climbers usually figure on ferrying loads to basecamp. The hike from Circle Lake is steeper but shorter and less brushy, but either way, it's a one- or two-day hike to basecamp at Aiyagomahala Creek.

Shot Tower. The west ridge faces the camera.
AERIAL PHOTO BY DAVID ROBERTS

Route: About 12 pitches lead up the ridge, with superb crack climbing sustained at 5.6 to 5.8. This ends at the vertical final headwall, where 60 feet of aid on pitons and nuts up a bottoming thin crack get you to moderate terrain below the top. Rappel the route using two ropes; the slightly traversing headwall pitch may require a directional anchor.

First Ascent: David Roberts and Ed Ward, June 1971

Difficulty: D, IV, 5.8, A2, 1,500 feet

Guidebook: *Alaska: A Climbing Guide*

MT. ASGARD (6,600 feet/2,012 meters)
North Tower, East Pillar

Every visit to Baffin Island is an unforgettable journey into a landscape so powerful and fantastic that no one comes back unchanged. And within this surreal realm, the twin towers of Mt. Asgard stand out with such character and scale that this peak is universally acknowledged as one of the most distinctive in the world. From a distance, the walls seem unapproachable without big-wall tactics, but the 1972 route on the southeast face of the north tower offers a reasonably quick route to the top. There are a couple of bivouac sites on the route and the summit has plenty of sleeping space, but climbers capable of moving swiftly on 5.8 to 5.9 ground should plan to do the route in the single-push style of the first-ascent party, with the freedom of minimal gear.

Approach: Start with a flight from Ottawa to the main town on Baffin Island, Pangnirtung. From there, hire a boat (or snowmobile in early season) to go up Pangnirtung Fjord to the mouth of the Weasel Valley. There you start a 30-mile hike on a good trail to Summit Lake. The trip includes some brutally cold stream crossings. In some cases, it's wise to wait for the midnight sun to drop as low as possible, so runoff is at a minimum. From Summit Lake, the obvious choice for a basecamp, it's still a long four miles to the climb. Either follow climbers' paths directly up moraines to a rappel onto the icy glacier below the peak or continue on the trail to circle onto the glacier.

Route: The 24- to 30-pitch climb is characterized by three roughly equal segments: the lower apron, the middle buttress and the upper headwall. The apron has a line of cracks that offer delightful 5.8-ish climbing. The middle section is mostly fourth class with loose rock, and a bivouac could be made here. The headwall's 5.8 and 5.9 climbing is steep and sustained, with some 5.10. At the start of the final chimney there's a nice ledge. Unfortunately someone has defaced the route with a ladder of poorly placed bolts right of this chimney.

To descend from the summit plain, rappel into the notch between the two towers using fixed piton anchors. Be prepared for snow and possibly ice on the hanging glacier while descending to a pass above Summit Lake. Some parties have rappelled the line of ascent.

First Ascent: Paul Braithwaite, Dennis Hennek, Paul Nunn and Doug Scott, July 1972. Note: In 1998, Canadians Jia Condon, Rich Prohaska and Sean Easton climbed a route to the right of this line, which, at 5.10, A1, appears to offer more sustained and possibly even more aesthetic climbing.

Difficulty: ED, V/VI, 5.10+, 3,700 feet

Permit: A permit to enter Auyuittuq National Park is available in Pangnirtung. The national park offices also hold a detailed record of climbing in the area.

⟳ The north tower of Mt. Asgard. The east pillar that the British and American team climbed is approximately the left skyline. PHOTO BY DOUG SCOTT.

CHAPTER 12

Style in the Super-Alpine

In the giant ranges of Alaska and the western Yukon, the huge and distant mountains remained exotic to most climbers, and few would give up siege tactics before feeling more at home in this great white realm. During the 1950s, occasional lightweight or even alpine-style forays punctuated the parade of siege expeditions, but they started no trends. As noted in Chapter 9, three brilliant 1954 ascents in Alaska adopted alpine-style tactics, and the 1959 ascents of Denali's *West Rib*, La Pérouse's south face and Logan's east ridge certainly were landmarks for their style. This chapter picks up the go-lighter story in the 1960s, when a disillusionment with expedition-style efforts and a fascination with smaller teams gained momentum.

The push for style grew partly out of familiarity with the terrain, partly out of the aspiration to climb steeper routes, but mostly out of a desire to escape the repetitious toil inherent to stringing fixed ropes and supplying camps. When the 1970s ice revolution sent climbers swiftly up icy ground, the doors to alpine-style climbing in Alaska really opened.

↻ Looking back along some of the more wildly corniced sections of the southeast spur of Mt. Hunter. PHOTO BY GLENN RANDALL.

Even with advanced ice techniques, however, those who aspired to Alaskan routes alpine style still looked across big crevasses of grave uncertainty. Proponents invoked the tried-and-true alpine formula—that go-lighter tactics should deliver a net gain in safety. By moving only once up a route, a team would spend less time exposed to such hazards as storms and avalanches. And by climbing with just a few, familiar partners, a team would unify more naturally. But small teams also faced greater risks if a storm or other unforeseen problem hit them while exposed up high. More than one traditional expedition had been thankful they had extra supplies and manpower, as well as a line of fixed ropes to escape down.

The gradual shift from expedition style to alpine style can be characterized as a shift from military campaigns to guerrilla strikes. Guerilla climbers count on their capacity to climb very efficiently, their commitment to keep moving, and the accuracy of their expectations. But the question of whether super-alpine peaks might be done this way couldn't be answered in war games, only with live-ammo sorties. Climbers could only make educated guesses that their technical skills, fitness and luck would be just enough to keep the cry of uncertainty at a pitch something less than a wicked scream.

Dissidents to the North

If, as many believe, modern mountaineering is a game of civilization looking for its antidote, we can look to a classic case of frustration and its cure at Harvard College. David Roberts, a Colorado youth who was a freshman at Harvard in 1962, had come to hate most of what the grand school stood for. He blamed the agony of trying to come of age there on an ossified system of arrogant professors, hyper-competitive peers and an obligation to hold oneself in a posture that was "glib, cruel and invulnerable." In those stringent hallways, young men with a proclivity for wild endeavors found an island of vitality at the Harvard Mountaineering Club.

To the administration, the HMC was like an annoying nephew. Officials relegated the club's headquarters to a basement closet. Only after much petitioning did the school allow that one whole weekend of climbing was worth the same phys-ed credit as an hour's swim. To Roberts, however, the club was a major-league conduit for eye-popping adventure, and the institution would change his life. Not only were undergraduates climbing all over the buildings, crags and ice gullies of New England, they also were succeeding—on their own—on expeditions to Mt. Logan and the Waddington area. Patriarchs Bradford Washburn, Adams Carter, Robert Bates and Ken Henderson gave presentations and kept the semi-underground club blazing with the

Don Jensen in the Sierra. PHOTO BY KEITH BRUECKNER.

torch of high ambition. Still tying it all together was Henry Hall, the club's founder, who attended every meeting until his death in 1987. One can't help but wonder how Hall and his peers—the venerable core of America's mountaineering gentry—felt about the '60s dissidents and discontents they now shepherded.

Besides Roberts, the class of 1965's keenest climber was Don Jensen, a math and philosophy student from California. With climbing and rebellion their bond, these two became best friends. At the end of their sophomore year, both Jensen and Roberts joined the HMC trip that climbed Denali's Wickersham Wall. The following year's annual expedition was an expensive trip to the Andes, so Jensen and Roberts looked for a more affordable adventure in Alaska. As they searched the club archives for an objective, they heeded an instinct—the same call that second-generation pioneers have heard in most ranges around the world—that the finest routes would be found not on the biggest mountains, but on the steeper flanks of elegant secondary peaks. They settled on the crazy-looking east ridge of Mt. Deborah, a

David Roberts. PHOTO BY GALEN ROWELL/MOUNTAIN LIGHT.

peak that had not seen a single party since its 1954 first ascent. As no one else they knew was interested and qualified, Roberts and Jensen mounted the first two-man expedition to attempt a major peak in Alaska.

HMC patriarch Adams Carter counseled that Alaska and its heavily crevassed glaciers was no place for a lone pair, and that the arête they proposed would probably be the hairiest route yet tried in the state. Its crest rose in billows of steep, corniced spurs and thin ice that linked to prows of steeper, rotten-looking rock.

Nevertheless, the youths laid their plans. Jensen crafted special harpoon-style ice pitons, extra-long for rotten ice. For bivouacking on exposed perches, Jensen made a tiny, lightweight, single-wall tent with a ridgepole that would hold tight under heavy snow or fierce wind. It was still inconceivable to risk complete alpine-style commitment on such a difficult route, so they packed 3,000 feet of rope, supplies for two months and a radio.

What the pair found was difficult climbing on a mountain spectacular beyond their imagination. Atop a horizontal stretch of the ridge, Roberts and Jensen festered under days and days of snowstorms, and their tent was repeatedly buried. During clear spells they climbed and strung their fixed ropes as best they could, but the weight of storms and difficult climbing grew oppressive. It seemed likely that their basecamp cache of supplies for the trip home might be lost under the new snow. Then their radio broke down. Most disturbing, in the isolation of a two-person vacuum, their personality differences became exaggerated. They stuck together, however, because both wanted to define their lives by mountaineering, and because each admired in the other what he himself lacked.

In early July the weather finally cleared, and they progressed up overhangs of crumbly rock and around filigreed cornices. Where they had hoped to set a bivouac, however, they found an airy ribbon of double-corniced meringue, and beyond loomed a nearly vertical, ice-pasted, rotten cliff. They could not

find an anchor, they could not climb the cliff, and there was no place to sleep, so home they went. During the 10-day trip out, Jensen plummeted twice into big crevasses, just as Adams Carter had warned. Only luck kept him from serious injury.

This experiment in extreme wilderness mountaineering taught lessons that all Alaskan climbers will recognize. First, the summer snowfall and long Alaskan days made for conditions that are seldom as favorable as those on temperate-latitude mountains. Second, waiting out long storms in tents is not just a chance occurrence but a mandatory skill. Most important, failure and accepting failure are as much a part of the Alaskan experience as snow is to the glaciers. Finally, the two young men soon displayed the final ingredient for a successful Alaskan career: a selective memory that mutes the suffering and heightens the brilliant moments and incredible positions. The next season they would be back to try a new route on another spectacular peak, Mt. Huntington.

Roberts graphically described Huntington as a mountain made with "a sense of arrested grace...a sculptured frailty too savage for any sculptor's hand." The previous year, one of the world's most powerful climbing teams, led by Frenchman Lionel Terray, had sieged the peak's first ascent (see Chapter 9). Terray called Huntington "as big and majestic as the finest Himalayan peaks."

At Bradford Washburn's office, Roberts looked through the master's new stereoscopic photos of Huntington's striking west face, a wall banded with arching granite and trimmed with fluted snow and ice. Roberts had learned that the first criterion for choosing a route in Alaska is to find ridges or spurs that keep climbers at least reasonably safe from avalanches; in the 3-D views he identified a long arête that led to a central spur that would probably be safe. The prow looked even more technical than what they had tried on Deborah, and obviously it would be steeper than the Frenchmen's ridge. Although he figured the chance of success was less than 50-50, Roberts mailed the idea to Jensen out

Mt. Huntington from the west. The Harvard team climbed the central sun-shade line and angled up the summit snowfield to the top. The French first ascent route follows the left skyline. The west face couloir (p. 267) runs up the shaded area to the left, and the *Phantom Wall*, climbed in 1991, is at the right. PHOTO #8187 © BRADFORD WASHBURN. COURTESY PANOPTICON GALLERY, WALTHAM, MA.

in the Sierra. The two agreed that failure on a brilliant possibility would be better than success on a mediocre objective.

They were able to recruit two other Harvard cohorts, Matt Hale and Ed Bernd. This was still a small, young team for such a serious route, and again there was no doubt they would string fixed rope and establish camps along the route. Some rock sections were steeper than anything on Deborah, including a 50-foot overhang, but the rock proved to be very firm granite. Over 31 days they made their way up and down, up and down the face. In one near disaster, a falling Hale pulled his belayer Roberts and their pitons into a 30-foot tumble that miraculously ended when the rope hooked over a small knob. Still, the fixed ropes kept inching higher, and after a month of effort all four summited. The toil and fatigue took their price, however, and on the descent Bernd made a mistake arranging his body-wrap rappel and fell to his death.

In his book about this expedition, *The Mountain of My Fear*, Roberts explored the paradox of a profound experience coming out of a materially pointless endeavor:

> *After all, it would be nice to believe that climbing could somehow be a search for truth as well as for a summit. Yet I have come down from mountains comprehending no better who I am or why I climbed than when I set out, and still been happy. Climbers take risks, and to climb is so all-involving that it temporarily approximates life…. We had found no answers to life; perhaps only the room in which to look for them.*

An Absurd Joke

Later this same 1965 season, another New England team went in search of new routes in the Alaska Range, after having solved the slyest hoax in U.S. climbing history. The

The "Riesenstein" hoax pages from the June 1962 issue of *Summit*.

prank started in 1961, when geologist Austin Post showed aerial images of Alaskan peaks to a private Seattle gathering of mountaineers. Edward LaChapelle, America's dean of avalanche science, recognized most of the peaks Post displayed, but a cluster of incredible Patagonia-like towers was unfamiliar to everyone in the room. The spectacular and unknown forms gave LaChapelle and Harvey Manning the idea for a great ploy. They bet that even Fred Beckey wouldn't know of these peaks and plotted to get the goat of the man who had already run away with 10 times as many first ascents as anyone had a right to.

Manning clandestinely sent one of the photographs to the California offices of *Summit* magazine, with a bogus description of their location and phony route lines drawn in and credited to a mythical German team. *Summit* took the bait, hook, line and sinker. In the "Know Your Mountains" section of the magazine's June 1962 issue, *Summit* ran a stunning picture of the "Riesenstein Peaks of northern British Columbia." Climbers promptly solicited Canadian map offices for information that didn't exist. But not Fred Beckey. He knew right away that northern B.C. held no peaks like these. By carefully studying the clouds, snow and lichen streaks in the photo, he deduced that the towers must be somewhere in Alaska, below 10,000 feet. He was furious that he couldn't figure out exactly where, but, as he tells it now, he had plenty of other things to climb anyway.

For three years no aspirant climbers could find the exact location of "The Riesenstein." Finally, Al DeMaria and Brownell Bergen, working in the New York library of the American Alpine Club, discovered that the peaks lay at the western tip of the Alaska Range—they were the Cathedral Spires of the Kichatna Mountains. DeMaria immediately gathered John Hudson, the new prodigy of the Dartmouth Mountaineering Club, and four other New England climbers for the coming June. As the first pair stepped out of Don Sheldon's Cessna onto the Cul-de-Sac Glacier, De Maria wrote later, "The immensity of the walls around them suddenly took on the proportion of an absurd joke…. One could place the entire Bugaboo group…in a single cirque of this Kichatna range."

The Kichatnas are positioned to get the worst weather of the Alaska Range, and the six endured tent-sitting on an Alaskan scale. When weather windows did come, they summited three subsidiary peaks, including "Whiteout Spire," climbed by Hudson and Pete Geiser. Overall, however, the trip left them more humbled and impressed than triumphant. They declared Peak 8985, the highest in the area, "to be one of the outstanding peaks of North America."

After Ed Bernd's death, David Roberts was despondent about climbing, but Alaskan Art Davidson reignited his interest by persuading him to try the mysterious Peak 8985 the following year. In 1966, Roberts and Davidson collected two other teammates, and though they couldn't get free time until September—

Kichatna Spire from the northeast. The first ascent team started up a couloir hidden against the main mass of the peak, and then climbed the headwall just left of the right skyline to reach the summit. PHOTO BY DAVID ROBERTS.

a chilly season without the 24-hour daylight of midsummer—the excitement of the objective bid them to go anyway. They decided to christen the tower "Kichatna Spire." To their delight, they found a hidden, 1,600-foot couloir slicing up the north edge of the east face. As they kicked steps up this chute, they were glad for the late date, "for the snow conditions…were superb, whereas in the middle of summer such a couloir might have held only rotten snow, or worse, blue ice."

Near the top of the couloir, the climbers found vertical granite and steep ice. They hung fixed ropes on this headwall and retreated to basecamp, where bad weather pinned them down. Soon the need for efficiency mandated that only two, Davidson and Pete Millikan, could go for the top. They extended their fixed lines across snow-covered rock slabs and then retreated to a tiny ledge. Having dropped part of their stove, they were without water. That night the weather cleared, and in the morning, with Davidson leading most of the way, the pair emerged on the summit ridge. Easy walking led to a double cornice guarding the summit area, where Davidson finally swam his way up airy snow plastered to the highest block.

After their descent, the team climbed back up and removed their fixed ropes. They were perhaps the first expedition to take such care, and it would be another decade or more before climbers made route cleanup the standard Alaskan ethic.

In 1968, Royal Robbins, America's priest of technical-climbing ethics, came to the Kichatna Spires. Robbins, Charlie Raymond and Joe Fitschen flew in to the Tatina Glacier and made the first ascents of "Mt. Nevermore," Mt. Jeffers and "Sasquatch" (the latter has come to be known by Roberts' name, South Triple Peak). For these Yosemite hard men, these climbs were long one-day affairs, achieved alpine style without the risk of a night out in the notorious climate. Although none of these climbs were quite the scale of the biggest walls in the area, the masters had set the standard and afterward routes in the Kichatnas would be done with few or no fixed ropes.

Climbers below the summit of Barbeau Peak, Ellesmere Island. PHOTO BY JANE KOSKI.

Also in 1968, a year after they played lead roles in Boyd Everett's Denali south face campaign, Dartmouth climbers Dave Seidman and Todd Thompson took the small-team torch to Mt. Kennedy's north buttress, an amazing prow that Bradford Washburn had discovered in 1935. Seidman and Thompson invited Phil Koch and Joe Faint along, but took on most of the leading themselves. Ice on the buttress was very hard, and so they climbed rock as much as possible, with some aid. En route to the summit they established three camps linked by fixed ropes.

These 1960s "light" climbs were not alpine-style ventures, but they were deliberately smaller than the expeditions that traditional wisdom called for, on routes that were steep and technical rather than simply huge. Young climbers were increasingly convinced that their way led to the future. In fact, Boyd Everett repeatedly tried to persuade Roberts and Jensen to join his campaigns, but neither accepted those invitations.

Distant Discoveries

The marvel of exploring unvisited areas was still very much alive for this generation, and in the summer of 1968 Art Davidson, David Roberts and four other Harvard grads were the first climbers—almost the first humans— to visit a remote range of 8,000- to 9,000-foot towers and peaks west of the Alaska Range. As they scouted this hidden wonderland, their conversations trended toward themes of cosmic awe, and they named their surroundings the Revelation Mountains. Although rainy weather halted attempts on their main objective, "The Angel," just short of the top, the trip left them profoundly moved.

A few climbers of this era specialized in climbing obscure and remote peaks. Among them, Alaskan Vin Hoeman collected the most, from the Tordrillo Range to the Kenai, and from the Chugach to the St. Elias area. Hoeman also became the first person to climb the high points of all 50 states. He began accumulating information for a comprehensive guidebook to mountaineering in Alaska, which, unfortunately, was never published.

Far, far to the northeast, at 77 degrees north latitude, basic mapping and exploration was just getting started on the ice-blanketed realm of Ellesmere Island. In 1967, Geoffrey Hatersley-Smith led a party of British Air Force pilots to make the first ascent of 8,769-foot Barbeau Peak, the highest point of the island and all of eastern North America. It looks over thousands of square miles of icecap and toward countless peaks that offer interesting objectives well into the future.

Southeast Alaska

The Fairweather Range remained a rarely visited wilderness with plenty of room for exploration. In Glacier Bay National Park, ski planes and airdrops were not allowed onto the glaciers until 1987, and clouds are so ubiquitous that depending on air support is a dubious prospect anyway. Thus the area attracted those who relished a sea-to-summit wilderness experience, carrying all their own gear. Loren Adkins was a Juneau-based artist who started taking trips into these mountains, often teamed with Tennessee sociology professor Walter Gove. In 1968 they and Paul Myhre, John Neal and Kent Stokes finally climbed the west ridge of Mt. Fairweather, the route that parties had eyed since the 1920s. From an airdrop at 3,000 feet, they worked through threatening icefalls to the easier upper reaches of the ridge.

In 1972, Adkins, his wife, Marsha, and three others made the second ascent of Mt. Crillon, via the unclimbed west ridge. They started from Lituya Bay and steadily worked north to gain the ridge at 6,500 feet. From there they climbed the exposed ridgeline through cornices, bergschrunds and rotten rock, making an impressive two-day push to the 12,726-foot summit.

A year later, Fred Beckey and Jim Wickwire initiated a wave of Seattle-based expeditions to this region with a plan for the southwest ridge of Mt. Fairweather. To their surprise, they found that four East Coast teenagers, who had qualified for AAC youth grants, were gunning for the same route. Both veterans phoned the youngsters and tried to persuade them that

On the first ascent of Mt. Fairweather's west ridge. Above Camp 1, the route climbed out of the photo on the right and over the top of Fairweather's west summit, the high, sunlit peak. PHOTO BY WALT GOVE.

Approaching the site for Camp 3 on the first ascent of the west ridge of Mt. Fairweather. Beyond this dome the climbers found an unexpected cliff of rotten rock. They persisted over the west summit, above, and to the main summit (in cloud cap). PHOTO BY WALT GOVE.

Mt. Fairweather was no place for kids. But Henry Florschutz, Lincoln Stoller, Toby O'Brien and Peter Metcalf were so impressed by the reputation of the callers, they decided that, even if their heroes climbed the route first, it must be a worthy objective. At ages 16 to 19, they needed parental notes to travel unaccompanied through Canada, and Metcalf had to obtain his first driver's license to help with the driving. Both teams gathered in Yakutat at the same time, but Beckey was stuck in British Columbia in bad weather, trying to squeeze in another climb. Thus the kids flew to Cape Fairweather with two days' head start and got onto the ridge first.

As it turned out, both teams had successful expeditions. The teenagers built their enthusiasm and awe into a fine balance of drive and caution. Their ridge—the major divide between the 1931 Carpé-Moore route and the 1968 west ridge climb—started with bands of rotten rock where they hung their only significant length of fixed rope. Atop this buttress they set their only major camp on the route, and beyond this, in stormy weather, they stretched a couple of lengths of rope over steep ice sections. When the weather cleared, they made a two-day push to the summit.

Meanwhile, Beckey's group went farther up the Fairweather Glacier and decided to try unclimbed Mt. Salisbury. However, dangerous conditions there prompted them to switch to the east ridge of Mt. Fairweather, and it became clear that the best way to get there would be over the top of Mt. Quincy Adams. Beckey stayed in camp, not feeling well, and Wickwire, Greg Markov and Dusan Jagersky started the traverse as a threesome. This was early in the ice revolution, and Jagersky, one of Seattle's finest frontpointing aficionados, led much of the way. As they crossed Quincy Adams and headed toward Fairweather, they realized they could complete a horseshoe circuit by descending Fairweather's original south ridge route. In poor visibility, they accidentally veered down an unclimbed spur to the east but made it down fine. Their alpine-style tour had taken eight days. During this month a 5.9 earthquake shook huge avalanches off every face

in the region—luckily both expeditions were in safe, ridgetop locations at the time.

A couple of weeks later in the 1973 season, another Seattle trio—Jim Nelson and Dave and Diana Daley—also hiked up the Fairweather Glacier. The go-light mandate had become the new buzz in Seattle, and they approached in a single five-day march and promptly started up their objective, the north ridge of Lituya Mountain. They expected little ice and hoped to do the route in a day, so they took only one ice screw, a stove, minimal food and no tent. After a number of unprotected ice pitches and three hungry days, they climbed the peak and circled back to the base.

Big-League Alpine Style

"The drawback of climbing most major high-altitude mountains is that they require siege tactics," wrote Seattle climber Alex Bertulis. "More time is spent ferrying loads between camps and less time is spent climbing." In 1972, Bertulis and five others resolved that it was time to try lightweight style to make the fifth ascent of the *Cassin Ridge*. Bertulis, Tom Stewart, Jim Wickwire, Leif-Norman Patterson, Charlie Raymond and Robert Schaller decided to head up without tents, counting on digging snow caves. After fixing some rope on the Japanese Couloir at the start, they gained the ridgecrest but promptly found too little snow for a cave and lots of difficult ice to climb. They retreated and moved a mile west to try alpine-style strategy on an easier, snowier climb.

Their variation to the 1959 *West Rib* route proved to be much more suitable, and even though they shouldered packs weighing over 50 pounds with two weeks of supplies, they climbed in just six hours from 10,000 feet to 14,000 feet. A storm was gathering, but Patterson displayed his remarkable instinct for snow shelters and unearthed a covered crevasse that held a chockstone of ice big enough to sleep all six. In this blue-toned ice-box they comfortably waited out a two-day tempest. Then they split up. Bertulis and Patterson climbed a steep and direct new line to the east, while the others continued on the rib's crest. They rejoined that night at 16,800 feet to dig into a ledge for half-shelter. As they huddled barely warm enough, pilot Cliff Hudson happened to fly past, and on their radio they hailed him for a weather forecast: "24 hours of good weather, then a storm moving in with winds in excess of 50 mph!"

After arguing about the risks and strategy, they finally decided that if they went for the top with virtually no weight, carrying neither food nor water, they could get back to their bivouac in about nine hours. However, plowing through new snow at this altitude drained them, and the roundtrip took a full 24 hours. Luckily the forecasted storm hesitated, and they were able to recuperate in the sun before traversing to descend the west buttress.

As the Americans descended, the storm moved in and trapped a team of five Japanese women near the top. They also had climbed the *West Rib*, but in more traditional ferrying style, and when they were caught in the storm all five perished. Bertulis assessed what had happened: "Had they had a shovel along, they would have been able to dig in and might have survived.... Both [expeditions] underestimated the unpredictable Mount McKinley."

At Hampshire College, a youth named Jon Krakauer came under the wing of David Roberts. Krakauer followed his mentor's path to Alaska in 1975, with buddies Tom Davies and Nate Zinsser, to try a new route on Kichatna Spire. As they flew in, persistent clouds blocked the landing and forced them to quickly choose a new destination. They opted for the Ruth Glacier, even though they had only a rough idea of the Ruth's topography. On the south face of the Moose's Tooth they saw an ice chute rocketing straight toward a notch below the summit and decided to try it.

The three men's first attempt on this gutter ended in a washout in July rain. When the weather seemed to clear, they decided to try the 2,800-foot route in one push, without bivouac gear. They pressed on despite snow squalls that threatened to flush them out again, and after 21 pitches of ice and mixed climbing they reached the summit ridge, where they could see nothing but white cloud. They sat down and pondered how to find the summit. Krakauer fumed, "I just wanted to do the damn climb, without having to think another thing about it, and then get the hell out to friends, music and beer." They joked that this was like saying, "If we had some ham, we could have ham and eggs, if we had eggs." In due time the clouds cleared, and three hours later they became the second team to sit atop the Moose's Tooth. Krakauer then became more poetic: "The sense of singular, unwavering purpose, as clear and definite as the straight line of our couloir, was a rare, incredibly good feeling." They rappelled in a sleep-deprived but satisfied stupor, and their route became known as the *Ham and Eggs Couloir*.

This 1975 season was pivotal for alpine-style climbing worldwide. British and American teams focused siege campaigns on Everest and K2, respectively, and when the dust had settled from those trips many of the participants longed for simpler, more committing climbs. Then two Tyroleans pulled off the most stunning ascent of the decade. Peter Habeler and Reinhold Messner climbed a new route on Hidden Peak (8,068m) in four days roundtrip, as if it were just a big alpine route.

That same season, Messner's book *The Seventh Grade* hit North American readers, and in this summary of his meteoric alpine climbs to date, Messner laid out a vision for the potential of severe mountaineering. European climbers had long rated mountain routes in the I-VI rating system advanced by Willo Welzenbach in the 1930s, a system based on the grading of terrain difficulties. The sixth grade represented very steep routes, "the absolute limit of the physically possible." Messner began to climb Grade VI climbs solo, in winter and without aid. He implied that, by virtue of better style, he was embarking on a new level of severity, a seventh grade. Although no one articulated a clear definition of the seventh grade, big, fast ascents by Messner and other masters in the Alps and Himalaya made it clear that some new standard had arrived. In fact, Messner argued that Walter Bonatti had ushered in the seventh grade during the late '50s and early '60s.

Doug Scott and Dougal Haston were certainly pleased to have summited Everest during the British siege of the southwest face, but they also heard the call for big ascents by simpler means. A year after climbing Everest, they came as a lone pair to the south face of Denali.

At the end of April 1976, Scott and Haston started up the 1967 "American Direct" route with 10 days of food and a double bivouac sack in lieu of a tent. After three days of steep snow and ice climbing, they veered left onto the face's big, hanging icefield. Toting their heavy packs took so much effort that they abandoned some of their food, some pitons and a spare rope, and continued upward through frequent snowfall. As they climbed higher, they found themselves pushed to their limit. In Haston's words, "Frostbite was waiting to jump at the slightest weakness…. We were drawing heavily on all our Himalayan experience just to survive, and it was a respectful pair that finally stood on the summit ridge." They dug a bivouac cave at over 20,000 feet.

As they descended the next day, they came across two west buttress climbers who had collapsed from exhaustion and altitude sickness, their hands bare to the elements and already severely frozen. Desperate to get down themselves, Haston and Scott helped the feckless pair into their sleeping bags, went down to rest, and then returned with the injured pair's partners to rescue them. The evacuation saved the youths' lives but not their hands. This well-publicized saga had a poignant impact on the American mountaineering community. Climbers were graphically shown, on the one hand, how easy it was for the ill-prepared to fall into disaster. On the other hand, in Scott's words, "a long and painful apprenticeship" had made a major new route possible in the same style with which mortals would climb lesser mountains.

Just a few weeks later, one of the most remarkable climbers in American history showed just how far these ideals could be taken. Charlie Porter had quietly led the latest revolution in aid climbing on El Capitan, and in early June of 1976 he switched venues and made one of the boldest super-alpine ascents ever in North America—he climbed

Charlie Porter in 1976 in Alaska. PHOTO BY RUSS MCLEAN.

the *Cassin Ridge* alone. After one foiled attempt, he climbed back up the Japanese Couloir to Cassin's Camp I ledge, and from there he reached the summit in just one and a half days. Part of Porter's make-up was to shun publicity, so we know little of his methods or his trials, except that his rapid ascent made him suffer from the altitude. A year later, Ruprecht Kammerlander repeated the *West Rib* in similar style, although, again, few details of the ascent are available.

Unfinished Business
Though alpine style was becoming the rage, the scale and complexity of many big, unclimbed ridges that begged to be done encouraged at least some expedition-style tactics through the 1970s. In April 1975, for instance, an Alaskan team made the second ascent of Mt. Deborah, by a new route. From the west they ferried loads up to the long south ridge and then continued over classic corniced terrain to the top. In June, another team climbed a beautiful, direct ridge on the remote north side of Mt. Foraker, calling it *Archangel*. Around this time, the same youngsters who climbed Fairweather in '73, with Angus Thuermer taking the place of Toby O'Brien, climbed a new spur on Denali. Going "capsule style," in 42 days they worked their way from the Ruth Glacier up to the

southeast spur and over to the south buttress to finish via that long route to the top. Rotten snow conditions and sustained challenge kept forcing them to adjust to new reality, and so they called their route *Reality Ridge*.

In 1976, a Canadian scientific/survey team climbed a new ridge on the north side of the Mt. Logan massif. East of Logan, meanwhile, a Swiss team made a variety of climbs, including an alpine-style ascent of the big northwest ridge of Mt. Hubbard. The same year, a team of six French (including one woman) and one American climbed Mt. Foraker's most strikingly fluted and corniced spine, which cascades due south from the summit on a scale almost comparable to Logan's *Hummingbird Ridge*. They extended 10,000 feet of fixed rope along the crest twice, and the whole effort took 45 days.

Over a period of 34 days in 1978, four Americans climbed one of the longest ridge complexes on Mt. Logan, the northernmost west ridge. Just to reach the lower crest of this complex they had to climb 27 ice pitches. Then they went capsule style with about as much fixed rope as they could tote, and covered some three miles of ridge on their way to an arm of the summit plateau. From there they sledged for 13 miles of high, rolling terrain to the west summit.

Packaged Efficiency

During the 1970s, high mountaineering in North America grew into what could almost be called popularity, and this helped spur creative climbers and manufacturers to develop new gear that would help climbers do more with less. Cartridge gas stoves and other light stoves became available, and synthetic insulation that remained fairly effective when wet replaced down for jackets and sleeping bags used in wet climates. A couple of years later, waterproof/breathable Gore-Tex fabric came out and also helped to keep climbers dry.

Frame packs had been the ungainly standard for carrying loads, but about 1977 Lowe Alpine Systems started selling Greg's design for an internal-frame sack that carried expedition-size loads closer to the body, offering more freedom of movement and cleaner hauling. For high and light shelter, Seattle climber Todd Bibler used Gore-Tex fabric to make tiny, single-skin, two-person bivouac tents that weighed about four pounds. He brought one of the first of these to Mt. Salisbury in 1977. Bibler became ill, but his buddies Steve Swenson, Jim Nelson, Jerome Eberharter and Greg Thompson made the peak's first ascent.

Steve Swenson and Todd Bibler on the 1977 expedition to Mt. Salisbury. PHOTO BY JIM NELSON.

George Lowe at the end of the mushroomed ridge on the first ascent of the north face of Mt. Hunter. On the previous attempt, Jeff Lowe fell in the vicinity of the sunlit patch to the right. PHOTO BY MICHAEL KENNEDY.

The Future in High Gear

If the two big Denali ascents of 1976 showed what was possible alpine style in Alaska, Jeff Lowe, George Lowe and Michael Kennedy sent the concept into full speed a year later. Their primary goal was a steep, continuous spur on the Himalayan-size south face of Mt. Foraker. For a "warm-up," they would climb a new route on the north face of Mt. Hunter. This first route went well for 4,000 feet. But when Kennedy led to the top of a triangular ice face, he discovered a 300-foot-long phantasmagoria of bulbous cornice-dollops drooping from an incredibly narrow fin. As Jeff led across this convoluted tight wire, a cornice gave way and he took a 60-foot swing, coming to a stop with a broken ankle. An alpine-style nightmare was now their reality.

Though they had but two ropes and a couple of handfuls of snow and ice anchors, in two days Kennedy and George Lowe were able to get Jeff down to safety. The two healthy men then went back up and climbed the 7,500-foot route on Hunter in four days.

After some rest and much deliberation, Lowe and Kennedy skied over to Foraker's 8,800-foot south face. Between the two long, catenary ridges that had already been climbed, a spur that Jeff had scouted soared direct and to the point. The first third of this spur was a blocky granite buttress, and then a very long stretch of moderately steep snow and ice narrowed to a headwall of ice, granite and schist. Above this, a slender spine connected to the summit slopes.

The two men started up with heavy packs but just two ropes. The lower buttress proved challenging but workable, with a couple of short sections of hard rock climbing. Then they took on the bulk of the route: moderately difficult climbing on a seemingly infinite scale. As pitch after pitch led only to more climbing, Lowe, the most competent alpine climber in North America, began to mutter, "We're so far out there," yet the focus of movement put his concerns aside. As major features on the glacier below diminished into indiscernible blips, they left it unsaid that going over the top had become not just their objective but their only way back. At some

George Lowe and Jeff Lowe (left), with a broken leg, during their retreat from the north face of Mt. Hunter.
PHOTO BY MICHAEL KENNEDY.

point the snow thinned to ice and Kennedy took a 20-foot leader fall onto an ice screw.

So much climbing wore them down, and as their third day continued past midnight, they butted into the headwall of steep, rotten schist, with no bivouac site in view. Lowe admitted he was exhausted, and so Kennedy came into his own with effort like he'd never known before. He led a steep traverse across the snowy schist, and then up an even steeper mixed chute. At dawn another hard pitch finally brought them to easy ground, where they spent the day recovering in the sun. There they decided to name the route the *Infinite Spur*.

The following day they made it through a long, rising traverse under the spur's final crest, and then bivouacked again after their 80th pitch. A storm came in, and in their tiny Bibler tent they nibbled at their remaining supplies, hoping they would not be stranded for long. Luckily, the next day the weather was unsettled but good enough to summit. On the way down the insidious southeast ridge, though, Lowe walked too far onto a cornice. Down he went "in the midst of tons of ice," dragging his partner upward until Kennedy could dig in just 20 feet from the ragged edge. Lowe was only banged up, and they made it down safely. They had met a profoundly complex challenge of hazards, tough climbing and odds-on risk taking, all on a huge scale—and all alpine style.

George Lowe on the lower rock section of the *Infinite Spur*. PHOTO BY MICHAEL KENNEDY.

Earlier in this 1977 season, Jon Krakauer bolted from his construction job in Boulder to confront a wall that had enticed him ever since childhood, when he'd seen a rare photograph of it—the north face of Devils Thumb. In a fury to do something he could be proud of, he went alone. En route to the base, in poor visibility, he threw his fate into the crapshoot of an active icefall with tenuously bridged crevasses. Then he made two unbelayed forays up the icy, hoar-coated northeast flanks, both ending in quaking retreat. Sobered, Krakauer circled to the southeast face, where he persevered up snow ramps that butted into technical mixed ground near the top. With neither rope nor anchors, Krakauer hooked his way to the summit, and, regretting that he had no rappel rope, edged his way safely back down.

Canadians also entered the modern game of big, technical routes in the north during 1977. The Calgary climbing community, which was thick with hard-climbing and hard-drinking British immigrants, organized several expeditions. In a single, 12-day effort, four Calgary guys climbed a ridge on the 10,000-foot-high west face of Mt. Vancouver. John Lauchlan, John Calvert, Trevor Jones and Mike Sawyer succeeded on this route in an abbreviated capsule style, repeatedly extending, fixing and retrieving their 370 meters of rope each day.

David Jones, an engineer whose trade in applied logic (not unlike George Lowe's)

George Lowe following the last technical pitch on the first ascent of the *Infinite Spur*. PHOTO BY MICHAEL KENNEDY.

helped him analyze his way up dozens of excellent climbs, organized a Vancouver team (plus one Swiss) for the big spur on Mt. Logan east of the *Hummingbird Ridge*. Going capsule style, this team found the ridge "continuously interesting but predictable and safe," although big cornices

Late-evening sunlight shining upward across Mt. Logan's *Warbler Ridge*. PHOTO BY DAVID P. JONES.

David P. Jones in 1971. JONES COLLECTION.

cracked away under their feet more than once. Wherever they camped on the ridge, they arranged safety lines from anchors well downslope and slept tied-in. Like the Californians 12 years earlier, they also had avian visitors, and they named the route the *Warbler Ridge*.

In August of this year, when everyone assumed the Alaska season was over, Montana climbers Dave Stutzman and Bob Plumb hiked in from near Petersburg to try Devils Thumb by the tremendous pillar that divides the northeast and northwest faces. They aimed toward a striking couloir that shoots right up to the pillar, but found horribly loose rock running with waterfalls. They exited left to climb the fringe of an icefall, and then ramped upward to meet their prow. There, on featured granite broken with bands of snow, they found the going much more reasonable. After a total of 57 pitches over four remarkably clear days, they completed probably the most obscure big technical route on the continent.

Jack Roberts arises after an open bivouac on the north face of Mt. Huntington. PHOTO BY SIMON MCCARTNEY, COURTESY JACK ROBERTS.

Jack Roberts on lead on the north face of Mt. Huntington. PHOTO BY SIMON MCCARTNEY, COURTESY JACK ROBERTS.

Embracing Extreme

As Europe's master alpinists in the late 1970s took to climbing huge Himalayan routes alpine style, a few North Americans began to embrace a parallel vision for Alaska and the Yukon. Alpine-style guerillas on big, technical routes would need not only a very high level of fitness and ability on sustained, steep ground, they also had to ration a minimum of food, bivouac gear and anchors, and be ready for extreme stress.

In the Alaska Range in 1978, Californian Jack Roberts and British climber Simon McCartney paired up to try the intimidating north face of Mt. Huntington. Much of this 5,500-foot-high face is riddled with active serac walls and avalanche slopes, but the two plotted a linkup of spurs and chutes that they decided would be safe enough. They hoped to complete the face in three days and descend the French Ridge in just one more, so they took only a small rack and rations of just two energy bars per day.

Their super-light plan worked great for moving fast up the lower 1,500 feet of steep rock and ice climbing, but when they emerged onto the main face it seemed unlikely they had enough gear to rappel. Thus, from this early

point, survival meant reaching the top.

As they kept aiming to climb wherever it seemed avalanches and calving seracs would miss them, Roberts pondered how each of us defines what is crazy and what is sane. He was certain that life in his home metropolis of Los Angeles was certifiably insane. Yet, "climbers who choose to pioneer first ascents up difficult and dangerous faces on high mountains have chosen to be crazy.... For my part I have chosen to be crazy in order to cope with a crazy world and have adopted craziness as a lifestyle." Indeed, "A climber entering the sub-culture of a climbing community accepts his alienation from larger society and proclaims he is a full-fledged 'normal' person—that it is others who are abnormal." Taking note of McCartney, he felt "some comfort to know that I am tied onto somebody who is also crazy."

As they pushed into their third day, light storms kept sending snow down the face, and Roberts noted that, "Whereas in the past we had kept up our pace out of sheer exhilaration at being free and unique, we now continued because we were afraid to stop."

On their fourth day they neared the summit and reached a fine if hungry bivouac. In the morning they topped out and started

Mt. Hunter from the south. Johnny Waterman's southeast spur is the prominent buttress in the center.
PHOTO #5934 © BRADFORD WASHBURN. COURTESY PANOPTICON GALLERY, WALTHAM, MA.

down the billowy curls of the northwest ridge. As Roberts lowered him across a cornice, McCartney broke through, falling 50 feet and wrenching his ankle. This prompted them to change their descent plan to the steeper but easier-to-rappel west face, which would take them into a different basin from the one where their basecamp waited. They came across anchors from a variety of ascents, but then lost most of their rope when it wouldn't pull. Gradually they were able to salvage enough old fixed rope for more rappels, and in a 48-hour haze of dire fatigue and starvation they struggled to the Ruth Glacier, 10 days after they'd left.

During this same season on Mt. Huntington, two teams tackled the west face, bringing the ice revolution to an obvious couloir that connects up high with the 1965 spur. John Evans, Denny Hogan and Vic Walsh were the first to climb this couloir, but bad conditions forced them to retreat from the spur. Californians

Dave Nettle and Jim Quirk completed the couloir route to the summit in 1980. This has since become the most popular route on Mt. Huntington, and perhaps the most popular technical climb in Alaska.

Even as Roberts and McCartney were making their way back to basecamp, the most fanatic climber in Alaskan history had already been climbing on Mt. Hunter for over three months—and he still had another month to go on his route. If any person could epitomize both the strengths and agonies of obsession, it would be John Mallon Waterman. During his childhood in New England, mentors including his father, Guy, and Dartmouth climber Dave Seidman pointed him toward climbing, and he promptly carried that torch whenever and wherever he could. After an intense apprenticeship in the Canadian Alps and U.S. Rockies, he joined Dartmouth teams that made siege ascents of the east ridge of Mt. Huntington and the south ridge of Mt.

Hunter. To the right of this latter route, Hunter's southeast spur rose in a proud, continuous and unclimbed Gothic prow of sound granite capped by a long ribbon of snow and ice. Waterman's dream was to climb this great spur alone and then continue north for a complete traverse of Mt. Hunter.

He started the epic with 74 days of supplies, 3,600 feet of rope and about 100 pounds of anchor hardware. Confronting rock overhangs, vertical ice walls and perched, delicate cornices, he took on Sisyphean cycles of self-belayed leading, cleaning and hauling. On the solstice, after 88 days, he finally reached the summit plateau, where pilot Cliff Hudson airdropped 36 more days of food. Waterman stretched this for another 44 days as he ferried all his gear across to the northeast ridge and then descended that route. The total trip took almost five months.

Though Johnny Waterman had persevered through more than anyone had thought humanly possible, some demonic judge within him denied the pleasure of success. A number of his mentors had died climbing, and perhaps this encouraged his mind to reason, during his internment on the peak, that "living through it would mean that Mt. Hunter wasn't the mountain that I thought it was." Although his accomplishment made him an iconic legend to many who would have their lives defined by wilderness mountains, in general society his feat was, like most Alaskan climbs, more obscure than a minor-league batting record. He came back to a dishwashing job, an occasional slide show, and, eventually, eccentric campaigns for political offices.

Three years later, Johnny Waterman disappeared in a crevasse on the northwest fork of the Ruth Glacier. His tracks and his mood suggested that this was the culmination of his obsessions, that he went there to die.

The 1978 season on Mt. Logan also was marked by tragedy and drama. A team of four Americans tried to repeat the *Warbler Ridge*, but a cornice broke under a camp and Matthew Maytag and David Sturtz fell to their deaths. A Calgary team made a second attempt on the south-southwest buttress of Logan, but rockfall wiped out one camp, and

then John Lauchlan pulled off a block that knocked out Jim Elzinga, his belayer. With a radio they were able to call for a daring but successful helicopter rescue.

This epic rescue on Logan's south-southwest ridge made the national news in Canada, and many began to label this route the greatest unmet challenge in the country. Lauchlan and Elzinga returned in 1979, with Raymond Jotterand and British immigrant Alan Burgess.

Cautiously using ropes still hanging from the previous year, they were emboldened to go without ferrying, and they left the 9,000-foot-high basin below the ridge with supplies for 12 days. It took them nine days of effort to reach the site of the previous year's accident, and they passed the high point with some very steep climbing. Tenuous traverses along the spur then put them beyond the Styx, where the best and probably only way home was up. They pushed on to the base of the big final headwall, where they had to dig a bivouac shelter to wait out a big storm. As they lay battered by winds and snow, an avalanche blasted over Burgess and Jotterand, but the team was unscathed. Lauchlan then led tough ground through the high rock bands. At the top of the face, with their food about gone, they were pinned again by high winds. The two pairs had not been amicable during the whole climb, and they decided to split up on the easier ground near the top. When the winds diminished to a manageable gale, Burgess and Jotterand went to the nearby west summit, while Lauchlan and Elzinga went east to the main summit.

Big Steps
Peter Metcalf was acquainted with Johnny Waterman, and in fact had made an attempt on Waterman's big spur in 1977. He realized that this route would be a fantastic challenge alpine style. A student at the University of Colorado, Metcalf organized fellow students Glenn Randall and Pete Athans. They started early in the 1980 season, at the end of April, in the hope of finding cold and stable snow conditions. Figuring that light packs would allow them to climb 2,000 feet per day, they

Pete Athans and Peter Metcalf on the first alpine-style ascent of the southeast spur of Mt. Hunter. PHOTO BY GLENN RANDALL.

started with just six days of supplies. However, conditions were colder than normal and it took them a week just to join the south ridge. From there they spent two days carefully working across what Waterman had called the "Happy Cowboy Pinnacles," a knife-sharp arête with surrealistic, wind-whipped snow towers, which climbers are wont to straddle like a buckaroo and inch their way along. The ordeal continued with cold, stormy travel across the summit plateau and down Hunter's west ridge. Two weeks after starting, they reached the Kahiltna with Randall and Metcalf suffering from fairly serious frostbite.

Jack Roberts and Simon McCartney also returned to Alaska in 1980, aiming for the south face of Denali, west of the *Cassin Ridge*. Granite ramparts 3,000 feet high guard the lower third of this face, but the two worked through this challenge in three days of sustained climbing up to 5.9. Easier ground above this prompted them to off-load some food, and they progressed more rapidly. But then McCartney came down with altitude illness, so they rested a couple of days at about 16,000 feet. Even so, when they joined the *Cassin Ridge* at 19,000 feet, McCartney's condition worsened into high-altitude cerebral edema. He was almost comatose, and Roberts suffered from frost-bitten toes (sensitive from his winter ascent of Mt. Kitchener). In dire straits they pushed to get over the top.

On the upper *Cassin* they happened into Bob Kandiko and Mike Helms, who didn't have any food left either. They agreed that Kandiko would stay with McCartney, and that Roberts and Helms would go over to the west buttress to collect rescuers. En route, however, these two had to lend a hand in another rescue, and after waiting three days with no sign of help Kandiko began taking the barely mobile McCartney down the *Cassin Ridge*. With nothing to eat but a few amphetamines, the effort dragged into more than a week of desperation, including a tumble into a crevasse where McCartney broke his wrist. Eventually all four made it to safety. One of the most extreme climbs ever in Alaska had succeeded, more or less, but the margin had been cut so thin that both McCartney and Kandiko felt very lucky to have survived, and McCartney never climbed mountains again. Roberts proved himself as one of the toughest climbers ever in Alaska.

People began to see that it was easy to underestimate the time and effort required for an Alaskan climb. Going alpine style in Alaska did not mean going at alpine speeds. There still seemed to be some "Alaska Factor," some extra 20 percent to 40 percent of time and effort tacked on to every Alaskan climb. The Alaska Factor is a compounding of such factors as storms that require extra supplies, cold that necessitates extra clothing and slows every move of technical climbing, deep snow and extra-hard ice, and, above 14,000 feet, altitude that is more debilitating than most expect. However, if you were almost superhuman in endurance, wary of hazards

270

Simon McCartney heading into the big granite walls on the first ascent of the southwest face of Denali. PHOTO BY JACK ROBERTS.

Simon McCartney following the difficult "Roberts Traverse" section on the first ascent of the southwest face of Denali. PHOTO BY JACK ROBERTS.

and skilled in technical climbing, going light in Alaska offered plenty of exciting new challenges. In 1981, a man of such stature came into his own.

Terry "Mugs" Stump was a dreamer and college football star who'd come to a personal crossroads in the early 1970s. While on his way to Texas to try out for a professional football career, he felt his dreams recrystallize toward the mountains and he returned to the Wasatch Range. Soon his combination of Conan-like strength, his penchant for envisioning incredible potential, and his almost non-stop climbing trips would sweep him to the forefront of Alaskan mountaineering. In March of '81, he and Yosemite master Jim Bridwell flew into the Ruth Gorge, hoping to find late-winter ice. When they saw only powder snow draped on the walls, they made a snap decision and asked pilot Doug Geeting to drop them instead on the Buckskin Glacier, under the legendary east face of the Moose's Tooth.

This awesome wall had drawn attempts during the 1970s from such greats as Tom Frost, Chris Bonington, Galen Rowell, Yvon Chouinard, Warren Harding and Jim

McCarthy. To the right of the Yosemite-like wall of bad granite that these climbers had tried, Stump and Bridwell perused the possibility of linking snowy rock on an upward traverse into the steepest upper ramparts. The loose snow over rock looked absurd, but then a huge cornice fall swept the face and packed the snow into a more climbable medium. Bridwell looked at the face while sharing a bottle of whiskey, and when the liquor's effects were at their peak they decided it was time to go, "before we realized what we were getting into." Of their preperation in bitter cold for their gamble, Bridwell wrote:

The minimum would be the rule: four days of food and fuel to be stretched to six or seven if need be. Food was an austere assortment of gorp and coffee with sugar plus two packets of soup. The hardware rack was skeletal. We trimmed away the fleshy bolt kit...[leaving] 10 ice screws, 15 rock pitons, six wired nuts, one set of Friends and the essential Chouinard hook.

They started up icy chimneys and turned left across snowy rock slabs. Stump led most of this first part, although anchors often were so poor that neither man could afford to fall. Their bivouacs were fiercely cold, and they had to wait for morning sun lest frostbite start to unravel their gamble. On their second day,

> Mugs pressed the attack up the 80-to 85-degree gouge. In places he encountered overhanging bulges which the dry, cold winter had turned into airy, unconsolidated granola. Ice axes and hammers became useless weapons. Crampon points barely held, scraping on tiny edges, and we used shaky pitons for handholds.

They emerged from their second bivouac to climb some vertical ice, and then Bridwell linked tenuous aid and mixed climbing. As the day grew late a storm gathered, and there was no bivouac in sight. Stump led another desperate aid pitch up vertical and gravelly granite to an ice tongue, and in the dark they climbed two more pitches to a fortunate snowpatch where they could dig a cave. Easier climbing the next day led to the summit. Now the diciest part of the ordeal began. They rappelled to the south down an unknown vertical wall, and a few rope lengths from the bottom the wall smoothed into a crackless curtain. Swinging back and forth, Bridwell could find only a single flake for a small nut (a #3 Stopper). With their prayers hanging from this subtle wedge, they reached safety. Although they had pulled off a climb at the technical and environmental limit, Stump admitted that the route was probably "not worth repeating."

Steep and Solid

A couple of months later, Stump came back for the most coveted unclimbed buttress in Alaska. In plain view of the usual landing site for Denali, the north buttress of Mt. Hunter erupts out of the southeast fork of the Kahiltna Glacier with a 4,000-foot prow of granite crisscrossed with ice. A who's who of 1970s and '80s virtuosos had made forays up this buttress,

Mugs Stump leading the "Tamara's Traverse" pitch on the first ascent of the Moonflower Buttress of Mt. Hunter. PHOTO BY PAUL AUBREY, COURTESY MUGS STUMP COLLECTION.

starting with Wayne Arrington and Tom Bauman, then Dale Bard, Charlie Fowler, Pat McNerthney and Doug Klewin. To many, this wall embodied the logical step beyond Yosemite, an El Capitan of super-alpine terrain. Sustained climbing near and beyond the vertical and harsh spindrift avalanches during storms had thus far turned back all attempts. Stump felt ready to solo something big, and he thought this would be the place.

When he landed, however, the buttress looked pretty serious, and Paul Aubrey, an experienced New Zealand guide, offered his partnership. Planning together, they packed little besides a stove, Stump's hammock and a food sack that Aubrey found disturbingly light. They approached while a Seattle party was already a few pitches up. This team was taking on the buttress siege style, with portaledges, plenty of supplies and a stereo. Stump and Aubrey started farther right and worked upward at a pace that launched them ahead of these competitors. Aubrey quickly

Mugs Stump leading through "The Shaft" section on the first ascent of the Moonflower Buttress of Mt. Hunter.
PHOTO BY PAUL AUBREY, COURTESY MUGS STUMP COLLECTION.

saw that Stump could lead steep ice "like no one I'd ever seen"—while still wearing his pack. They ended their first day at a semi-hanging bivouac at the start of the prominent "Ship's Keel" corner.

After climbing past the corner the next day, a tenuous traverse right set them up for the key to the route, "The Shaft," a passage of super-steep—even overhanging—ice that somehow poured through the granite. Even Stump had to use aiders. He wrote later:

> The last 15 feet were a frothy, brit-tle curtain.... I pulled myself up. Never had concentration made such a deaf-ening roar in my head. I was a shell of forces and movement.... My excite-ment was explosive as I screamed in order to release the fullness: I felt that I belonged there.

Over two more days they continued up brilliant, difficult climbing, marveling at how ramps and runnels of ice linked very steep walls. At the end of their fourth day, they accidentally dropped the remains of that

food sack. The next day Stump led thin ice into the last rock band, and at a fist crack he fell out. He got back on, reached his tools high into a pocket of ice, and pulled to the end of the rock band. The summit of Hunter still lay some 2,000 feet of snow and ice climbing above, but they decided that, since the most technical climbing was over, they would rappel from there. The route was unfinished but the technical challenge had been solved, and Stump christened the line the *Moonflower Buttress*.

In one season, Mugs Stump had become a beacon of amazing potential. As many scratched their heads over his wild intensity, he wrote to his mother about his drive: "Climbing is the ultimate spiritual connec-tion with our center—God!"

Persistence Alaskan Style

Montana climber and Teton guide Jack Tackle had begun to look carefully at the huge faces draped along Denali's vast east, southeast and south buttresses—huge mountains in their own right. In 1979, he chose the 7,000-foot-high east face of the south buttress, and he and Ken Currens started up the face alpine style. Currens was in the lead a few pitches up when a snow ledge gave way under him. He plummeted for 240 feet, breaking his femur. Tackle stabilized him and hustled to the Ruth Glacier landing site to get a flight to Talkeetna. There he found Mugs Stump and Jim Logan. The three flew back in and res-cued Currens just ahead of a big storm. Stump's fortitude in a tough situation was an inspiration that Tackle would conjure on many future climbs.

This was Tackle's second trip into the big northern mountains. His first, in the St. Elias region, had shown him that difficult condi-tions and bitter nights made it naïve to go super-light with the expectation of alpine-like climbing. On the trip with Currens, how-ever, he felt they had overcompensated and carried too much. He came back to the south buttress' east face in 1980 with Jim Kanzler, but storms and horrible snow conditions kept them off. Then he returned a third time in 1982 with Dave Stutzman. Even though illness slowed Stutzman, they climbed 78 pitches over eight days and reached the top of the south buttress. Tackle wanted to continue to Denali's summit, but Stutzman's condition forced them to go down. Tackle named the face *Isis*, after an Egyptian goddess that bestowed fertility and resurrection, as well as the muse of a Bob Dylan song.

During that same May of 1982, the seasoned partnership of Peter Metcalf and Glenn Randall tried to climb the next spur to the south of *Isis*, calling its fluted cornices *The Ridge of No Return*. Cautious from their Hunter trip, they carried more food and fuel, but the route demanded many steep and narrow traverses—too much to climb with big packs. They descended and went back to *Reality Ridge*, the route that Metcalf had climbed with fixed-rope ferries in 1975. In 10 days of steady alpine-style climbing, they made the second ascent of this long, long route to Denali's summit. Almost simultaneously, another team made an alpine-style ascent of Denali's 1963 east ridge route.

Risk and Reward

In the 1983 season, six teams came to Alaska with plans to climb new, technical routes alpine style, and half succeeded unscathed while the other half found the risks of such climbs were very real indeed. Todd Bibler and Doug Klewin hoped to finish the *Moonflower Buttress* all the way to Mt. Hunter's summit. Unsettled weather sent snow down the route part of almost every day they climbed, but despite these conditions they reached a bivouac not far below the 1981 high point in four days. There, in one of Bibler's tiny tents, they waited out four days of bad storm. When it cleared they continued up the buttress and pushed through another storm to Hunter's summit. They descended the complex west ridge having made the first complete ascent of a coveted route through fierce conditions.

Glenn Randall and Peter Metcalf traveled to Mt. Foraker this year, adding a long wilderness approach and traverse to a big new route. Carrying everything on their backs for the approach, ascent and traverse, they made the 75-mile hike into Foraker's 11,400-foot

north face. They were only the third team to confront the northern flanks of Foraker, and the first to come without the assistance of horses. When they arrived at the peak's base, they already had consumed half of their 15 days of rations.

Luckily, the northwest ridge turned out to be uncorniced and they made steady progress. Their limited supplies pressed them to gain altitude a bit too fast; however, Metcalf got headaches, and just below the summit Randall came down with pulmonary edema. He barely had energy to walk, and their only way to safety was over the top and down the southeast ridge. While Metcalf double-ferried both their packs, Randall crawled over the top. Then, in poor visibility, Randall stumbled off the southeast ridge, and as far as Metcalf could tell he'd tumbled some 10,000 feet to his death. Metcalf resumed the descent, lonely indeed. However, he happened to glance back, and there was Randall

Peter Metcalf high on the *Highway of Diamonds* on Mt. Foraker. PHOTO BY GLENN RANDALL.

crawling back up. A small ledge a couple of hundred feet down had stopped his fall. He had a broken leg, cracked ribs and other injuries, and since he couldn't continue down and his altitude illness was not improving, his fate was still very much in doubt. Metcalf set up camp and they waited for a rescue—four days later they were evacuated by helicopter.

Bryan Becker, a talented and powerful climber and guide from Colorado, had a young client named Rolf Graage who wanted to be trained into a world-class alpinist. Becker took Graage's hopes to a new route on the southwest face of Denali, right of Roberts and McCartney's. Unfortunately they forgot their main rope and their ice screws. Becker led most of the route with only one rope, usually with his pack on. The difficulties included aid over a 25-foot roof and severe mixed climbing. Graage led some, too, but then suffered a long fall. Later his feet began to freeze from cold and neglect, and after two weeks their 10 days of supplies were gone. Becker managed to get to the summit and then led Graage over to the upper west buttress. Other parties helped lower him to the doctors who now spent each season at the 14,000-foot bench on the west buttress route. In Becker's words, "Denali gave us a thrashing I shall never forget." Recalling the granite in Colorado, Becker called the route the *Denali Diamond.*

On the east face of Mt. Huntington, Coloradans Robb Kimbrough and John Tuckey found wonderful if sustained and exhausting climbing on the first ascent of a beautiful granite prow. During the descent, however, as Tuckey approached their last rappel stance, a snow ramp gave way and both climbers tumbled off. Tuckey landed unhurt, but Kimbrough suffered a broken ankle and would not be able to climb out of their isolated basin. Tuckey tried to climb out to get help, but rotten snow again gave way and he fell back 1,000 feet, receiving a concussion. Three days later he recovered enough to gain the ridge and attract the attention of other climbers. A helicopter rescue pulled them out. They declared that it would be their last big trip.

Bryan Becker, pioneer of one of the hardest climbs on Denali, shown here on an ice climb in New England. PHOTO BY ED WEBSTER.

In the Hayes Range, two parties met by coincidence on the east ridge of Mt. Deborah, attempting to complete the arête that had been the dream of Don Jensen and David Roberts 19 years before. British climbers Roger Mear, Rob Collister and John Barry had slogged up to a camp on the col near the start of the route when a plane flew over and unloaded packages that thudded nearby. The next day, Dave Cheesmond and Carl Tobin arrived to claim those supplies, and also started up the ridge. After climbing what Mear called the ridge's initial "china shop of sails and webs all which way," both teams shared leads, and with great skill they worked a way across and over the wall of shale and ice that had turned back the 1964 pioneers. Above this, they had to swim up masses of unconsolidated snow over ice, and it was a new Alaskan dawn before the five settled into a tent site. As the day warmed, they got up and Tobin led over one last overhang of ice and then across easier "cauliflowers of rime, all helter-skelter to the top"—one more success in a wild season.

SUGGESTED ROUTES
FROM THIS PERIOD

MT. FORAKER (17,400 feet/5,304 meters)
Infinite Spur
This route has become one of the most legendary challenges in North America, and it is one of the very few technical giants to receive many attempts. Many accomplished climbers have gone to climb it, but only six or seven teams have succeeded. When conditions are favorable, it is a great experience for the elite climber.

Approach: From the popular landing site on the southeast fork of the Kahiltna Glacier, plan a couple of days to ski and climb to near the base of the wall.

The *Infinite Spur* of Mt. Foraker. PHOTO BY MICHAEL KENNEDY.

En route you cross over two low passes, where avalanche conditions can be a concern. The second pass is steep, requiring about five pitches of mixed climbing. Once inside the isolated subcirque below the spur, it's wise to spend time scouting the route and trying to assess snow conditions. Many capable teams have retreated when they found rotten snow conditions on this south-facing wall.

Route: Move quickly to the start to spend as little time as possible below the seracs and avalanche slopes on the west flank of the spur. Once at the base you're sheltered. Start with a dozen pitches of blocky rock and mixed climbing, up to 5.7 or 5.9 depending on routefinding luck. Then begin the long arête of snow and ice, involving more than 30 pitches. Typically, parties have climbed this section with belays in a long day, and then met the toughest climbing of the route late and tired. Faced with the choice of pushing through the pitches above or spending some hours to excavate a bivouac ledge, most have chosen to keep going, by one of three ways. The first-ascent party veered right and then found difficult mixed climbing for three pitches through the shale bands, followed by more steep climbing through seracs. Other parties have veered left onto slow-going snow slopes. The most recent teams have found an ice gully to climb directly. Above all these options, at about 15,000 feet, there's a flat spot. After that there's a traverse to the spur's knife-edge finale. At least one party, however, has found a few more pitches of mixed climbing to connect directly to the summit mass. Above here, there's still over 2,000 feet of easier terrain to the top.

Few peaks engender as much worry over a descent route. The obvious way, the southeast ridge, is notoriously prone to avalanches and deceptive cornices. Some have advocated rappelling the west face of the southeast ridge, but there are no details available. Most parties now recommend descending the circuitous but scenic *Sultana Ridge*, where the principal danger is storms, though the usual Alaskan crevasses also have caught some climbers. First climbed in 1979, this ridge tours east up and over the summit of Mt. Crosson, and it takes a couple of days to descend in good conditions.

First Ascent: Michael Kennedy and George Lowe, July 1977

Difficulty: ED 2, AI 5, 5.9, 9,400 feet
Guidebooks: *Alaska: A Climbing Guide; High Alaska*
Permit: A permit application must be submitted to Denali National Park 60 days in advance. There is a $150 fee.

MT. HUNTER (14,570 feet/4,441 meters)
North Buttress

A convenient approach, perfect granite, sustained steep climbing and rave reviews have made this the most sought-after technical route in Alaska. In fact, this shield of Mt. Hunter has come under such intensive scrutiny and traffic that it has become a goal almost apart from the rest of Alaskan mountaineering.

Approach: The buttress waits just a couple of flat miles away from the popular landing site on the Kahiltna Glacier's southeast fork.

Routes: A number of routes and variations have been done. From a traditional alpine perspective, the unrepeated 1984 French route makes the most sense, for a team that climbs on a storm-free day up the slashing couloir quickly gains half the height of the buttress, and above this the climbing looks as stimulating as anywhere else on the wall. *Deprivation*, on the right flank of the buttress, is also a logical testpiece that has seen repeat ascents. The *Wall of Shadows* sees repeat attempts, and in the superbly iced season of 2002 Jimmy Haden and Russ Mitrovich climbed the crux pitches of this route without aid. The most popular classic, however, is the *Moonflower*.

All routes on this buttress depend on ice from seasonal melt-freeze cycles; in stormy years there may be barely enough ice to climb. In ideal years it may be possible to free climb on ice where aid is normally required. During colder storms, spindrift pours down this wall by the bucket load. Rockfall and slab avalanches are almost nonexistent on the steep and solid buttress, but warm storms can paste blobs of mushy snow into the corners, and one of these fell and killed veteran Steve Mascioli; at least one other climber has been injured this way.

Climbers have used every sort of bivouac strategy, from sacks to hammocks and portaledges, but a tent is now most popular as long as one is willing to work with the limited number of places it can be set up. The usual time to reach the summit is nearly a

Mt. Hunter, showing the upper half of the north buttres and the route to the summit. About 2,000 feet of the lower buttress is blocked from view. PHOTO BY ANDY SELTERS.

week, although teams have done it in four or five days. Some parties retreat from the Cornice Bivouac at the top of steepest climbing; there is an established line of rappel anchors.

The usual start is left of the lowest extension of wall (which is a few hundred feet lower than it used to be since the ice apron fell away in 2002). Aim toward the "Ship's Keel," a striking granite prow. The first hard pitches run up the right side of the keel. Then climb or pendulum right to a chute that leads to "Tamara's Traverse," an 800-foot ramp of thin ice that is key to reaching mixed ground that breaks through the first major rock band. Head to the second rock band at "The Shaft," a 500-foot chute choked with ice that repeatedly bends beyond the vertical. A short ice band then leads to "The Vision," a section of sustained, steep wandering up mixed ground—this is the technical crux of the route. The difficulties ease for a few pitches as you trend right to the best break in the final rock band, which presents Bibler's "Come-Again" exit pitch, a short, overhanging offwidth that should have ice to climb. This empties you onto the upper pyramid of ice and snow. A few pitches of 50- to 60-degree ice and snow lead to the top of the buttress. The route then continues to the summit slopes. The obvious descent via the west ridge is a serious undertaking fraught with cornices, crevasses, avalanche slopes, and icefall and routefinding hazards. Therefore, some summiting parties have chosen to descend the north buttress.

First Ascent: Todd Bibler and Doug Klewin, June 1983

Grade: ED 2, 5.9, A3, AI 6, 6,300 feet

Guidebook: *High Alaska*; *Alaska: A Climbing Guide*

Permit: Climbers must register in Talkeetna to climb within Denali National Park.

MT. KENNEDY (13,970 feet/4,258 meters)
North Buttress

Few pieces of mountain architecture soar so grandly and prominently as this continuous sweep of ice, rock and snow. Jack Tackle has called it "the most beautiful route in the world." It is a line sustained for most of its length at 55 to 70 degrees, with a crux steeper section, and in a remote and stormy setting. During the 1990s, many leading climbers attempted to make the first alpine-style ascent. Crack British climbers Andy Cave and Mick Fowler finally succeeded in May 2000, and Bill Pilling and Andy Selters repeated the line in this style in July 2001.

Approach: Ski planes from Chitina, Alaska, or Kluane Lake, Yukon, can land a party within a short distance of the buttress.

Route: Head for a straightforward break in the first rock band. Sustained ice and/or snow climbing leads for many pitches toward the next rock band, which you flank to the right. Continued ice and snow climbing leads to the snowier midsection of the route. A spur branching left from the buttress here offers the only good bivouac site during a storm. Continue up and right on steep snow slopes, aiming for a mixed chute that breaks right to the base of the upper rock headwall. The route's most difficult climbing works through the beautiful granite-and-ice headwall via a variety of difficult lines. The first two parties used aid up a groove system

near the prow, and the two alpine-style parties found difficult mixed climbing farther right. Above this band, break onto snowier ground again on the crest of the main buttress. Climb until you can cut right again at another hidden chute across the prow, and gain the steep upper snowfield that leads to the top.

Descending the south side of the peak is easy, but the two alpine-style ascents of this route did not work out a completely satisfactory way of returning to basecamp. Descending the north buttress is an option, but the steep snow sections would be slow going and dangerous in stormy weather. The 2000 team radioed their pilot from the summit and descended east onto the Cathedral Glacier to a pickup spot below 9,000 feet. The second alpine-style team planned to tour west over nearby Mt. Alverstone and descend the fairly easy 1966 Beckey/Lowe route. This would be a particularly

Mt. Kennedy, with the north buttress in profile on the right. PHOTO BY ANDY SELTERS.

good option if a cache could be placed between Kennedy and Alverstone. Unfortunately, a storm pinned Selters and Pilling on the Cathedral Glacier until their pickup date, and on takeoff from that location the plane crashed into a crevasse, killing pilot Kurt Gloyer.

First Ascent: Dave Seidman, Todd Thompson and Phil Koch, July 1968; First alpine-style ascent: Andy Cave and Mick Fowler, May 2000

Difficulty: ED, AI 4, 5.8, 6,700 feet

Permit: Climbers must register in advance with Kluane National Park.

MOOSE'S TOOTH (10,335 feet/3,150 meters)
Ham & Eggs Couloir

Here's a *line*, a classic, straight split in the broad south-facing wall of a great peak. Modern ice techniques make this the most reasonable route to the summit of the Moose's Tooth, as long as fair weather holds.

Approach: Traditionally, parties approached from the landing site on the Ruth Glacier, skiing four miles

of heavily crevassed glacier and then climbing an icefall to the south face of the Moose's Tooth. In 2000, Talkeetna pilot Paul Roderick began landing climbers on the glacial bench at 7,400 feet, below the start of the route.

Route: From the bench, the general route is obvious: 2,000 feet of steep chute, hopefully choked with ice. Three to four pitches of rock or mixed climbing might be needed to access ice deeper in the chute. In the couloir, chockstones and thin or rotten ice provide technical cruxes. Over halfway up, a subtle split allows two options. Most go right, up mixed ground. From the top of the couloir, the summit is reached by an 800-foot climb up steep snow. Descend the route.

First Ascent: Tom Davies, Jon Krakauer and Nate Zinsser, July 1972

Difficulty: TD, AI 4+, 5.9, 2,800 feet

Guidebook: *Alaska: A Climbing Guide*

Permit: Climbers must register in Talkeetna to climb within Denali National Park.

Looking across the south face of the Moose's Tooth. The German first ascent team climbed the ice face at lower left to gain the skyline ridge and follow that to the summit. The *Ham & Eggs Couloir* is the chute leading to the notch just below and left of the highest point. PHOTO BY GALEN ROWELL/MOUNTAIN LIGHT.

Period IV

When "Why" Disappeared

The modern era has brought an explosion of climbing in all its forms. While previous generations spoke of their climbing community with special familiarity, today we refer to many large and separate climbing communities. From bouldering to mixed climbing, from sport climbing to wall climbing, each game is distinguished by different goals, styles and favored terrains, and by specialized participants. Even within each discipline, so many trends have emerged that the dominant one is simply expansion.

During the late 20th century, North American culture became increasingly consumerist, and as broader segments of the population have started climbing it has been no surprise to see increasing commercial influence. Refined technical ratings, timed speed ascents, training, sponsorship and corporate teams, media coverage and celebrity personalities—all these add up to the unmistakable buzz of performance athletics. But the mountaineering game is much more difficult to package than any form of purely technical climbing. Those who might hope to beam images of genuine cutting-edge alpinism into mainstream living rooms face nearly overwhelming technical and cultural challenges. Nevertheless, as international climbing organizations work toward including some well-tooled version of "mountaineering" in the Olympics, one could be excused for expecting that the logical progression for our life-game will be toward an industry catering to audience ratings.

Underneath the commercialism, however, mountaineering as a journey apart has flourished to ever-higher levels. Our most dedicated alpinists continue to expand the envelope of what's possible by taking the old recipe for progress to higher peaks of fitness and deeper wells of commitment than most of us can imagine. We can mark the progress in athletic parameters—harder routes done faster and climbing days of incredible endurance—but the most vital climbers still measure their success in the soul, by the depth of engagement and the force of commitment. In North America, this spiritual and athletic evolution still mixes with the wild card of unexplored terrain, right into the 21st century, as climbers continue to find worthy summits and major faces that have never been climbed.

What do we make of the apparently divergent modern trends? Is mountaineering a sport for consumption or is it a personal quest? The answer is both, for what we're seeing is the modern act of the old interplay between accomplishment and experience, the give-and-take going on since the days of John Muir and Clarence King.

As the modern era brings climbers and society into closer weave, the social context of mountaineering has changed. North American climbers were long used to being asked, in an incredulous tone, "Why do you climb?" By the late 1990s, however, mountaineering had become a fairly accepted curiosity, partly because of hyper-publicized tragedies and discoveries on Mt. Everest. As the social value of mountaineering has risen, the "basic absurdity" and carefree intensity that Warren Harding embodied so well has washed away. Modern climbers often take it for granted that at least some part of the world is very interested in what they do. The outdoor equipment industry aids this process with ever-finer gear. From plastic-shell expedition boots to hanging stoves, extra-sure ice tools, efficient clothing and sticky-rubber rock shoes, the modern climber can choose from an amazing array of equipage. Cell phones and pocket-sized radios have been a particularly interesting addition—by keeping climbers in touch where they once were very isolated, these devices have saved lives but also have been used as a convenient crutch.

Meanwhile, the threshold for entering and leading the modern climbing game keeps rising. The price of advanced gear, for instance, soars over the entire living budget of the previous generation of climbers. As climbers now number in the thousands and the gentry buys second homes in the mountains, our major climbing areas have been transformed from backwaters into desirable real estate. From North Conway to Jackson Hole, from Yosemite to Canmore, the cost and hassle of living near—or even visiting—the mountains keeps rising dramatically. These forces have transformed the climber-vagabond, and today a leading climber needs at least a modest revenue stream. As Christian Beckwith, editor of the *AAJ*, wrote in 1997, "Today, when most high-caliber climbers have ties to the climbing industry, the realization is that climbing in its upper echelons is a professional, not amateur, occupation." In North America, at least, sponsorship for climbers rarely amounts to more than subsistence help, but the gear, grants and rare, modest salaries definitely contribute to higher standards. This support can also pump up egos and add pressure to complete routes or exaggerate accomplishments.

In climbing—as in society in general—the accelerations of the modern era have parceled time into perhaps the most precious resource. As we compress more activity into the same span of life, hurry has become the hallmark of the age. It's probably no coincidence that climbing excursions now are more likely than ever to be measured for speed and timed in hours or even minutes instead of weeks and days. In Yosemite, the longtime harbinger of mountaineering trends, some measure their ascent times to the second. This is partly a matter of finding new challenge and partly a sign of climbing moving more into the forum of competition.

Another modern concern is that environmental care has to be embedded into the style of every trip. Actual and potential impacts on the mountain environment have put mountaineering on the agendas of public land managers in the United States, Canada and Mexico.

In many areas, the modern era has seen a maturing of route development, and this has increased the focus on route quality. People are now more likely to travel not to climb new routes but to repeat routes that are well known for strong architecture, sustained challenges at a given standard, outstanding position and other aesthetic pleasures. Also, while few women were active mountaineers in the post-World War II era, modern times have finally brought women back into the climbing game. In rock climbing, some women perform as well or better than almost any man. Women are still rare at the leading edge of mountaineering, but modern mountain climbing is very much a game for both genders.

The growth of climbing has not been painless. In the 1980s the encompassing vision that had been straining to hold together all types of climbing fell apart, as technically focused rock climbers decided that the advance of free climbing demanded pre-placed protection. Traditional climbers fought to hold a line on style, while sport climbers saw no reason not to remove protection worries from the challenge. The two camps came to blows over the best way to define and achieve higher technical standards. Mountaineering fell into temporary obscurity, as many Americans dismissed it as the obsolete grandfather of the climbing game, where a lot of hassle was necessary to access moves of modest difficulty.

By the mid-1990s, however, the two streams of rock climbing had split into different channels, as sport climbing's distilled focus gradually limited its practice mostly to suitable crags, indoor gyms and judged competitions. As the distinctions between sport climbing and traditional climbing became clearer, traditional climbers and mountaineers were freed from arguing over definitions of higher standards, and they began to reexamine and seek out the intangibles of engagement, commitment and position found on big natural terrain.

Now mountaineering in North American is enjoying a post-technical resurgence. Many North Americans have reembraced mountaineering as climbing's most demanding and complex discipline, where any level of technical difficulty might be found but the technical challenge is compounded by scale, environment, uncertainty and risk. Classic hard routes in the Tetons, Bugaboos and even the Selkirks and Coast Mountains that were rarely climbed in the early 1990s can now be said to have "traffic." Even the Moose's Tooth has received multiple ascents in one season. The "grandfather" of the climbing game—where "making the moves" is little more than the basic threshold for success—is more alive than ever.

CHAPTER 13

High Country Freedom

As difficult free climbing came to domi-nate the ascent game in North America, most climbers focused on short, accessible crags. During the 1980s, talents rose (and ratings inflated) into the 5.13 and 5.14 range, while mountain rock walls seemed like for-gotten relics. However, a few upward-looking cragsmen enthusiastically sought new standards on the high peaks.

The Diamond on Longs Peak waited in sur-prising neglect during the early 1980s, and Boulder climber Roger Briggs practically had the wall's free climbing potential to himself. Briggs was a student of high-level yoga and a staunch disciplinarian of free climbing style. In 1980, he initiated a new level on Longs Peak by linking the *Diagonal* route on the lower east face (first done as an aid route by Layton Kor and Ray Northcutt in 1959) and the Diamond in a single day, with Australian Kim Carrigan. Then he free climbed the *D1* route with Jeff Achey (see Chapter 11). During many trips up the Diamond, Briggs gradually became attuned to the weather, thin air and the nature of stone on the wall. He continued to pioneer the most difficult

➲ Peter Croft traversing in the southern group of the Palisades. PHOTO BY ANDY SELTERS.

mountain free climbs on the continent, including outstanding routes like *Ariana* (5.12a) and *The King of Swords* (5.12a) in 1985, and *Eroica* (5.12b) in 1987.

Charlie Fowler was another Coloradan who thirsted after high-mountain free climbs. In 1980, on Chiefs Head, also in Rocky Mountain National Park, Fowler and John Harlin III climbed sheer, almost crackless slabs, committing themselves to linking minuscule 5.10 holds with only sparse, tiny nuts for protection and belays. They named the route *Seven Arrows*. In the Wind Rivers, in 1981, Fowler paired with Jeff Lowe to jam up a brilliant crack route on the southeast face of Warbonnet, a spectacular peak at the south edge of the Cirque of the Towers. The steep line became severe when a splitter crack widened past fist size, requiring a 5.11 effort on the 1,000-foot face.

The Sierra Nevada's friendly weather and extensive granite also attracted a new gener-ation of high-country climbers. In 1981, John Bald freed the 1959 route up the com-plete east face of Mt. Whitney, wrestling with strenuous 5.10 offwidth cracks at 14,000 feet. Dale Bard went back to the Incredible Hulk in 1986 with Tom Lyde, and they free climbed the most sustained crack system (previously done with aid) on this 1,200-

foot-high tower, a 5.11 line known as *Positive Vibrations.*

Ropemates Stephen Porcella and Cameron Burns stormed into the Sierra in 1989, energized by map research suggesting a surprising choice of major features yet unclimbed and a plan to compile a guidebook to California's 14,000-foot peaks. They began by climbing one of Mt. Williamson's south arêtes, followed by a west buttress of Middle Palisade, two west-facing routes on North Palisade, a rib on Mt. Tyndall and (in two stages) the long southwestern arête of Split Mountain. A year later, the pair came back to the remote west side of the Palisades and put up two more 5.10 and 5.11 routes at high altitude.

Sport Tactics on High
In 1990 some climbers started to take preanchoring tactics for free climbing to high mountain walls. During August, Mark Rolofson, Stuart Ritchie and Annie Whitehouse went to the Wind Rivers to free climb the 1964 aid route on the north face of Mt. Hooker. With a week of effort, some route variations and 16 new bolts, they freed most of the route at 5.12. They had to aid just one wet, 50-foot section.

Two weeks later, Todd Skinner, Paul Piana and Tim Toula came to the same route. As the weather chilled, the 50-foot aid section dried out and Toula led it at a more difficult 5.12 standard; the team thus freed the whole route. Galen Rowell climbed with this group, and, although he had ethical concerns about bringing sport climbing tactics to a mountain wall, his photographs and articles gave this ascent a high profile.

Controversy had collected around Skinner and Piana during the 1980s, especially in Yosemite, when they shirked traditional free climbing ethics by pre-placing protection and resting on those anchors while figuring out the severe moves. Skinner began a high-publicity campaign to climb major walls using sport tactics, saying, "Aid climbing is not a valid form of ascent...and is little different from a helicopter ascent of a peak. One move of aid means total failure on a wall."

Todd Skinner at work on *The Great Canadian Knife,* on the southeast face of Proboscis. PHOTO BY GALEN ROWELL/MOUNTAIN LIGHT.

Paul Piana drilling a bolt hole on *The Great Canadian Knife,* the route he climbed with Todd Skinner and Galen Rowell on the southeast face of Proboscis. PHOTO BY GALEN ROWELL/MOUNTAIN LIGHT.

Others retorted that Skinner and Piana's tactics were contrived free climbing, as they used substantial aid for preparing the protection, set belays in the middle of crux sections, and seconded pitches on jümars. Rowell summarized the issue by saying that Skinner and Piana dreamed to make, "depending on one's point of view, either the world's most continuously difficult alpine free climb or the world's biggest sport climb."

Two years after climbing Hooker, Rowell brought Skinner and Piana to the Cirque of the Unclimbables. They were magnetized by a striking 1,000-foot-high outside corner on the southeast face of Proboscis. The edge showed almost no cracks, and essentially all the protection would be bolts. Over nine working days they prepared the corner by aiding up, cleaning the holds, placing bolts with a power drill (recharged with a gas-powered generator in camp), and then working the moves. After seven pitches they had placed almost all of their 100-plus bolts, and so they veered away from the edge to difficult cracks. All three climbers then packed for a continuous ascent. They led those first seven pitches at a standard up to 5.13b. Then, in the wide cracks above, they let 51-year-old Rowell take the lead, except at one particularly severe section that also needed "preparation" before being climbed free.

After watching Skinner and Piana at work, Rowell concluded that this was "a giant sport climb.... Regardless of how hard the pitches are when done free, with known ground that you've worked the hell out of, the connection with mountaineering is lost.... I don't think that this is the wave of the future."

Extreme free climbing using degrees of sport tactics came to a few other mountain walls in the 1990s. In 1991, Californians Mike Carville, Kevin Steele and Kevin Browne spent a number of days on a direct route up the prow of Keeler Needle. Following a prominent dihedral that arches left to the original Harding route, they progressed on aid, placed protection bolts, and then practiced the free climbing moves before climbing the route at a 5.12 standard. Carville and Browne later came back and pushed the route directly up the rest of the prow, freeing most of the upper section with more moves up to 5.12.

In the Cascades, Peter Doorish and others pioneered a number of difficult routes on Mt.

Baring and its satellite Dolomite Tower, some of which included rappel bolting. Back in the Northwest Territories, Kurt Smith, Jeff Jackson and Scott Cosgrove went to Proboscis in 1994, and over 19 days completed a 5.12 route. A year later, European master climbers Kurt Albert and Stefan Glowacz developed a long, well-bolted 5.12 route in this area on Mt. Harrison Smith. In the Bugaboos, in 1996, two Germans sieged a very difficult free route on the north side of Snowpatch Spire's great east face, using a power drill only to protect a slab pitch and for belays.

In 2000, Albert, Glowacz and two other Germans applied "redpoint" tactics (the German-originated term for free climbing after rehearsal) to an unclimbed tower on Baffin Island. They planned an ambitious overall adventure, starting with a memorable kayak approach from Clyde River. Rough sea forced them to turn into Eglinton Fjord, where they focused on a spire they named for the bears they frequently saw. Polar Bear Spire proved to be about 2,000 feet high, and on the harder pitches they drilled and prepared protection before lowering down to free climb the pitch.

In the late 1990s on the Diamond of Longs Peak, Eric Doub placed more than 20 protection bolts on a five-pitch line that branched off from *Eroica*. Unable to free the route, Doub recruited Tommy Caldwell, who in 2001 free climbed *The Honeymoon is Over* after just one day of reconnaissance. With two pitches of 5.13 and two pitches of hard 5.12 at nearly 14,000 feet, this was the first high-country 5.13 in the Lower 48.

With this scattered but growing collection of high-standard routes, where climbers could push their gymnastic efforts on a high mountain unburdened by worries about anchor safety, one might have predicted that sport climbing held the future of rock mountaineering. However, pre-anchoring tactics have been on the wane in the mountains since the late 1990s. It would seem that, in general, those who climb in the high country prefer to take on a mountain's whole challenge, including the uncertainty inherent in finding protection.

Increased bolting also attracted the disdain of wilderness purists, and in 1998 the U.S. Forest Service issued a ban on all fixed anchors within designated wilderness areas. Purists had said that all anchors left *in situ*—whether bolts or rappel slings—were "installations" that violated the 1964 Wilderness Act. Later, the agency was pressed to rescind this general ban in favor of "negotiated management plans" specific to each area. But the precedent was set; no longer could mountaineering be taken for granted as an activity of pure wilderness enjoyment—rather, it could be targeted as an intrusion on wilderness.

Old Ways to New Levels

Though they gathered fewer headlines, free climbers who stuck with traditional climbing methods had little problem finding new mountain routes at a high standard. Examples include Galen Rowell and David Wilson, who in 1991 completed another new route on Mt. Whitney's east wall. Their line included a 5.11 corner and a 5.10 wide crack that had stumped Rowell a year before; this time he brought extra-wide camming protection. The next year, the hyper-athletic couple Andy deKlerk and Julie Bruegger climbed a superb pillar on Mt. Chamberlain, a remote peak west of Whitney. They pulled through 13 pitches of almost continuous 5.10 and 5.11 climbing.

In the Canadian Rockies, Yamnuska-trained climbers also took higher standards to bigger peaks. Pull-up champ Jeff Marshall made a 1992 free ascent of the very steep Greenwood route on the east face of Mt.

The north face of Mt. Moloch. PHOTO BY NEAL BEIDLEMAN.

☾ Looking across the southeast face of Proboscis.
PHOTO BY GALEN ROWELL/MOUNTAIN LIGHT.

Babel, climbing wide cracks through the summit roofs with a 5.11 effort.

The year after that, Swiss-Canadian guide Ruedi Beglinger and Coloradan Neal Beidleman completed one of the most intimidating alpine rock climbs ever done in North America. This was the north face of Mt. Moloch, a 3,600-foot wall of rotten limestone in the western Selkirks. After a spell of foul weather they started up the face without bivouac gear. Soon they found that the rock made it, "for the most part, impossible to place protection...secure climbing was imperative." Beglinger's account continues, "The top 1,500 feet was nearly a winter ascent, with over a foot of new snow, iced-up rock and cold temperatures. The climbing was 5.9, but it was only every now and again we could place a piton, sometimes no more

Reudi Beglinger high on the north face of Mt. Moloch.
PHOTO BY NEAL BEIDLEMAN.

than a couple in a 60-meter pitch." Perhaps the lack of protection options kept them moving, for they reached the summit less than 11 hours after they left the glacier.

In the Bugaboos, during the same 1996 season when the Germans were working their route on Snowpatch, two very strong pairs of American traditionalists went in to the Howser Towers. Both wanted to free climb the prominent west buttress of North Howser, where the obvious plum was a 1,000-foot-long corner, previously aided as *All Along the Watchtower*. Coloradans Kennan Harvey and Topher Donahue got there first. Taking a minimum of bivouac gear, they climbed 10 pitches to ledges at the base of the great dihedral. After shivering through the night, they started up what Harvey called "the quintessential free climbing feature." Where the corner crack pinched off they had to dig into 5.11 moves. Then the corner jogged across a wet section. Harvey had to aid on nuts and wipe the holds dry with his shirt before he could lower down and re-lead the pitch free at 5.12. They summited after a second bivouac. Not far behind them were their friends Mike Pennings and Cameron Tague, who reached the summit via the same route in a single super-fast day from the Bugaboo basecamp.

Bugaboo crack systems yielded to other bold free climbers. In 2000, Canadian Guy Edwards and Bostonian Micah Jessup pulled off the first mostly free ascent of the east face of Snowpatch Spire, more or less following the original Beckey-Mather aid route. (Canadians Tom Gibson and Rob Rohn had freed the upper pitches of this route back in 1980.) Edwards and Jessup had a challenging day linking thin and somewhat dirty cracks, and then pulling over the face's big roof to reach a bivouac ledge. In the morning they found, in Edwards' voice, "the essence of free climbing: hard moves near our free climbing limits on steep, clean rock, with 'make you think' protection. And if you don't know whether it'll go free, or if it doesn't even look as if it'll go free, the challenge is much more than gymnastic—it's completely mental." Despite difficulties up to 5.12-, they led all 14 pitches without bolts, though on one pitch

Jonathan Copp leading on the first free ascent of the original route on the southeast face of Proboscis. AERIAL PHOTO BY HARRISON SHULL.

Peter Croft starting up the crux of the southeast chimney of Mt. Waddington, during the traverse of the Waddington/Tiedemann peaks. PHOTO BY DON SERL.

the leader apparently took a couple of rests on their hammerless gear.

In the Cirque of the Unclimbables in 2001, a team of super-advanced American granite hounds proved that powerful blasts of ultra-efficient climbing can get things done even when stormy weather offers only brief windows. On Bustle Tower, Jonny Copp and Brooke Andrews found thin cracks and 5.12 holds over a roof to make the first free ascent of the peak. Then Copp and Tim O'Neill climbed a more logical and direct route up this wall. Whenever the climbing was "moderate"—i.e., no harder than 5.9 or easy 5.10— these teammates used the efficient strategy of "simul-climbing," or moving together with the rope clipped only to occasional anchors between them. Josh Wharton joined Copp for

another impressive wall-in-a-day on Parrot Beak Peak. For the season's *coup de grace*, Copp and Wharton free climbed the original wall route on the southeast face of Proboscis. A stretch of continuous and runout 5.12 climbing had stumped previous attempts, but Wharton led through it, even though he found only two slits for protection on the whole pitch. Just nine and a half hours after leaving the ground they gained the summit.

Technical Endurance

After his 1983 Bugaboo linkup (see Chapter 11), Peter Croft had become one of the world's most accomplished crag climbers and rock soloists, confidently going up and down 5.11 without a rope. He aspired to combine these advanced technical skills with comparable levels of endurance. Probing into the regime of long-distance runners, Croft experimented with climbing hard for five days at a stretch on no more than 600 calories per day. He found that, after passing a tough threshold, his metabolism responded. He looked for a place where he could test his climbing endurance and decided on the entire Stuart Range—a continuous east-west stegosaur of Cascade granite some seven miles long.

Croft started from a Stuart Range trailhead in the wee hours carrying only a peeled banana inside a one-liter bottle of water. At first light, he scurried up the long north ridge of Mt. Stuart, a 20-pitch, 5.9 climb that forces many climbers to bivouac. From Stuart's summit, he turned east along the blocky, serrated, knife-edge crest of the range, along steep and sometimes untraveled ground. He scrambled, rambled, pulled and hustled over Sherpa, Argonaut and Colchuk peaks, and on this last summit he found a fig bar left for him earlier in the day by his friend Greg Foweraker. Croft then kept going over Dragontail and Little Annapurna to finish the whole ridge system. With daylight to spare, he detoured north to another massif and climbed the handcracks of the south face of Prusik Peak. By now he was as high as a kite but dry as a raisin, and as he hiked back to the road he struggled with the temptation to drink from creeks whose potability he couldn't trust.

A couple of weeks later, Croft teamed up with Foweraker and Coast Range veteran Don Serl for a much-discussed fantasy: traversing the entire horseshoe of the Coast Mountains' supreme peaks, from Mt. Waddington over Combatant, Tiedemann and Asperity to the Serra peaks. Stepping out from a helicopter below Fury Gap on a July evening, the three started for Mt. Waddington. At dark they settled into an abbreviated bivouac, and at dawn they went over Waddington's northwest

Peter Croft heading toward Mt. Asperity on the Waddington/Tiedemann traverse. PHOTO BY DON SERL.

Peter Croft and Greg Foweraker descending the north face of Mt. Asperity on the Waddington/Tiedemann traverse. PHOTO BY DON SERL.

Looking up the Tiedemann Glacier at Mt. Waddington and the Tiedemann group. PHOTO BY DAVE KNUDSEN.

summit and on to the main tower. A sunny spell had left the rock on the 1950 *Southeast Chimney Route* mostly ice-free, and they found the climbing so moderate they never broke out the rope. Then they reversed course and started for the main part of the tour, to the north ridge of Combatant, where they rested to let the evening chill firm the snow. At dusk they worked over Combatant and up the icy and rocky west ridge of Tiedemann, reaching a bivouac at midnight on the other side of that summit.

The next morning their luck soured, as Foweraker woke with a stomach flu. They pressed on but then, while descending from Asperity, Serl was hit in the arm by falling ice. Clouds gathered as they tended to Serl at the Asperity-Serra Col, with the steepest climbing just ahead. Croft ran the rope up four new, direct pitches to lead them to the second ascent of Serra V. Then, as they rappeled the overhanging east side of this thumb, a big, loose block crashed just past the cowering Croft. They regrouped again, and, Serl wrote, "We jabbered, jittered, and ate convulsively, the ancient animal in each of us unquenchable in hunger for life." Luckily the weather held, and after five days of climbing they descended to the hut by the Tiedemann Glacier, having completed one of the most brilliant excursions of modern North American mountaineering.

Peter Croft leading on the second ascent of Serra V, during the traverse of the Waddington/Tiedemann peaks. PHOTO BY DON SERL.

In the late '80s, Croft moved to California. He and John Bachar astounded the rock world by linking both El Capitan's *Nose* and Half Dome's northwest face in one day; Croft and Dave Schultz then climbed both the Nose and El Cap's *Salathé Wall* in a day. The media took more notice when he and Hans Florine did the Nose in only four and a half hours, yet to Croft the emerging Yosemite speed game started to feel like sport, and, "The closer I moved to sport, the closer I felt to science—and the closer I moved to adventure, the closer I felt to magic." He decided that, "In a realm defined by diversity, the stopwatch becomes ridiculous." Instinct told him there was a crucial distinction between speed for rivalry's sake and climbing better and longer as a matter of deepening engagement. To deepen his engagement, Croft went to the High Sierra.

The Enchainment Principle

Late in the summer of 1992, Croft made the second link-up of the Minarets, but he did it in a day from his car. During the 12 hours of daylight he climbed 15 summits, using a short rope only for rappels. While hiking back by headlamp, he was so wasted that he fell asleep on his feet and woke up in the woods some distance off the trail.

Croft realized that the concept of climbing mountains as singular, isolated challenges was an artificial limitation. With an ever-fresh instinct to push limits, he articulated what he calls "the enchainment principle":

> *If size matters—and I say it does—in a world where the biggest mountains and biggest faces have been climbed, where do we go and what do we do? When we travel to the mountain regions of the world, the thing that leaves us awestruck is, more often than not, the whole picture; the collection of high faces that wall a deep valley or poke out of a glacier, the continuous knife-edge ridges that go from peak to peak and are so clearly etched at sunset and sunrise. The idea then, is to take in as much of them as possible in a single adventure, either in the form of a linkup (or enchainment) or a traverse.... The potential is essentially unlimited.*

As Croft looked over the maps of Muir's Range of Light, he saw high, spiny ridges that were "routes bigger than any face in the Himalaya." The 1979 Fischer-Adams traverse

Peter Croft on the 5.8+ summit block of Thunderbolt Peak in the Palisades. PHOTO BY GALEN ROWELL, MOUNTAIN LIGHT.

of the Palisades was, he figured, "an achievement comparable to Warren Harding's first ascent of El Capitan." Of course, these 20,000- to 50,000-foot-long serrations do not demand the same commitment and environmental challenges of a face in the Himalaya, but the stress of covering exposed, steep and variable rock for hours and hours is very real. Best of all, Croft thought, traversing skylines "is like being on a summit all day."

In 1996, Croft traversed the northern cirque of the Palisades, starting with a scamper up the long *Moon Goddess Arête* on Temple Crag. He kept going over Gayley, Sill, North Palisade and Thunderbolt Peak and over to Mt. Winchell. Like Fischer and Adams, he tagged Winchell by its north face. Unacclimatized to 14,000 feet, he could barely keep trudging up the final summit, Mt. Agassiz. One of the greatest rock mountaineers in history, Croft saw this non-technical peak as the greatest challenge of the day.

The next summer Croft traversed most of the Evolution group, partly accompanied by Galen Rowell. They started with Mt. Mendel and climbed over Darwin and Haeckel, where Rowell headed down, his hands worn raw. Croft kept going over Wallace, Fiske, Warlow and Huxley, plus a number of other unnamed high points. He realized, however, that the complete skyline included a 13,000-

Peter Croft on the *Evolution Traverse*. PHOTO BY GALEN ROWELL/MOUNTAIN LIGHT.

easy routes than short, hard ones."

In the Tetons, swift climbers took to repeating the 1963 Grand Traverse, except by going north to south. This way you can enjoy the climb up the Grand Teton's north ridge and the easier peaks come at the end of the day. With routefinding always a challenge in the Tetons, even experienced and fit climbers still take a long day to tour the seven major peaks. However, when Alex Lowe (no relation to the other famous Lowes), completed the route in 1995 in 8 hours and 40 minutes, taking not even a water bottle, the temptation to measure the traverse with the stopwatch became irresistible. In the dry summer of 2000, a number of climbers completed this traverse, and Rolando Garibotti did it three times, once in 6 hours and 49 minutes.

The popular Cirque of the Towers in the Wind Rivers presented another obvious high-traverse challenge, and during 2001 NOLS instructor David Anderson took it on. In one day from his car he toured over the 10 main peaks in this arc, climbing at least 30 fifth-class pitches connected by many thousands of feet of easier but exposed climbing.

Untamed Alps

The almost countless subranges of the Coast Mountains still presented one of the biggest fields for exploratory mountaineering anywhere on the continent—in fact anywhere in the world. Esoteric groups of climbers continued to find delight in unclimbed routes, peaks and even whole ranges into the new century. Klattasine, Toba, Pantheon, Niut, Tchaikazan—the names roll off the maps and journals like exotic myths.

Fred Beckey entered the 1980s still at it. From Galen Rowell to Layton Kor, from Gray Thompson to Dan Davis, many of North America's most wide-ranging mountaineers traced at least some of their new-route inspiration to trips with Beckey, and in 1983 the still-determined old hand introduced a new generation of Seattle partners to the Coast Range. Greg Collum, Chuck Gerson, Bill Pilling and Jim Nelson flew in with Beckey, and among the group's various ascents, Pilling and Nelson climbed the huge south face of

foot peak connected to Mendel, and two years later he returned to do them all. Croft took in eight miles of climbing on mostly excellent granite up to 5.9 in a single day. "My friends in Yosemite don't understand," he said, "but this has been my best summer ever, and I haven't made a move over 5.9."

Croft and other leading climbers were redefining the old notion that mountaineering challenge is more than just technical—that, for instance, covering thousands of feet of difficult terrain can write a bigger chapter in your soul than any hundred feet of super-difficult crag climbing. Many talented climbers quickly became proficient at short, extremely technical routes, but the number of climbers—Americans in particular—who could move swiftly over thousands of feet of fairly technical terrain were few. Rolando Garibotti, the Argentine-American who honed his endurance and efficiency to a world-class standard in Patagonia—and who climbed the *Infinite Spur* on Mt. Foraker in one long day—put it this way: "It's harder to get good at big,

Fred Beckey on an unclimbed route in the Sierra, in 1998. PHOTO BY ANDY SELTERS.

Mt. Tiedemann. They took snow couloirs and whatever rock passages would help them veer around and between the peak's tiered towers. On their third day, they were able to trend west into a couloir system that led to the summit ridge. After waiting out a storm they made the summit in two hours and descended the dangerous Tiedemann-Asperity Couloir.

Soon after this, Collum and Gerson linked couloirs and buttresses on the west side of Tiedemann's south face, completing another new route. Pilling and Nelson also climbed the first tower on Tiedemann's south buttress ("Tiedemann Tower"), getting a 2,000-foot taste of the spectacular rock mountaineering on this massif.

This trip was the seed for a friendly but energetic Coast Mountain rivalry between Seattle and Vancouver alpinists. In 1986, paths collided at the 2,600-foot west wall of Bute Mountain, a granitic tower southeast of Waddington. Canadians Don Serl and Greg Foweraker topped out after 26 pitches and one unplanned bivouac, and as they returned

The west face of Bute Mountain. PHOTO BY DON SERL.

to the base Jim Nelson, Kit Lewis and the 63-year old Beckey were exiting their helicopter. Beckey was disappointed to have been scooped on this one, but Lewis and Nelson wanted to do the climb anyway. After a five-pitch direct start, they repeated the Canadian ascent, raving over the quality of the cracks.

Two years later, Nelson came back with Carl Diedrich and Jim Ruch to climb the obvious great challenge on Tiedemann—a line directly up the rock towers of the south buttress. They packed supplies for a few days and started by repeating the pitches up Tiedemann Tower that Nelson and Pilling had done before. Wearing rock shoes, they were able to lead with packs on, except for the occasional 5.9 or 5.10 sections. Clouds started to gather, so they took cramped shelter in a chimney, but the next day the weather cleared up and they continued to the top of the tower, rappelled a few rope lengths into a notch, and kept going along a rising crest of very clean granite to a second bivouac. At the top of the second tower, they covered their rock shoes with clever, lightweight overboots

and then veered left across a big snowfield to the cleanest-looking prow of Tiedemann's upper tier. Halfway up this, it looked like they'd made a mistake, for few cracks appeared. But knobs and crystals continued to pepper the superb rock, and they kept going for another dozen or more 5.9 and 5.10 pitches, needing just a few moves of aid. They made a third bivouac on the summit ridge, and then climbed to the top and struggled with flimsy footwear down the Tiedemann-Asperity Couloir.

Greg Collum was the first to lay plans for climbing the complete south face of Tiedemann's sister peak, Mt. Combatant. Late in the summer of 1994, Greg Child and Steve Mascioli joined him to climb the easternmost and biggest of Combatant's buttresses. They needed four days just to climb the seams leading up the first tower. Another four days took them along a complex knife-edge and onto the final buttress. There they found an exquisite blend of clean 5.10 cracks with amazingly airy position, and they finished their route, *Belligerence*, to the top. They'd

Jim Nelson leading on the first ascent of the south buttress of Mt. Tiedemann. PHOTO BY CARL DIEDRICH.

Jim Ruch leading on the first ascent of the south buttress of Mt. Tiedemann. PHOTO BY CARL DIEDRICH.

Jim Ruch and Jim Nelson rise for their third day on the first ascent of the south buttress of Mt. Tiedemann. PHOTO BY CARL DIEDRICH.

Jim Ruch on the first ascent of the south buttress of Mt. Tiedemann. PHOTO BY CARL DIEDRICH.

off-loaded extra food along the route, though, and with their scheduled pickup days away they faced a very hungry wait. On the summit, they stood shivering until they were able to make a radio connection to pilot Mike King, and the next day King picked them up at the Combatant-Waddington Col.

Scotsman Simon Richardson heard what was going on in the Coast Mountains, and in 1997 he brought compatriot Dave Hesleden for a look. They decided on the southeast buttress of Mt. Asperity, a long spine of towers. Richardson figured it looked like the north spur of Les Droites in Chamonix, only much bigger. They committed to it alpine style and made excellent time on complex but reasonable ground. Late on their second day, the spine narrowed and Hesleden rigged a Tyrolean traverse that got them to the main mass of Asperity. An easy day led to the top. The two men balked at descending the adjacent rockfall- and avalanche-prone chute, so they kept going east over the Serra Peaks, mostly following the 1985 traverse team's route.

For decades many have tried to compare various ranges in North America to the alpine homeland of Chamonix. These routes woke a few climbers to the fact that the Waddington area most closely resembles the birthplace of

The south faces of Combatant, Tiedemann, Asperity and Serra V and IV. The vertical scale in the photograph is about 1,500 meters (4,900 feet). PHOTO BY ANDY SELTERS.

mountaineering—except the setting is vastly more remote and the scale is even grander.

In 2000, two teams came to finish the last of the unclimbed major rock buttresses of the Tiedemann group. Veteran Alan Kearney brought youthful Brendan Cusick to the central rib of Combatant, and in 17 pitches of generally excellent rock, up slabs and over roofs (with some difficult aid), they reached Combatant's "shelf." They hiked over to the closest upper pillar and climbed another 12 pitches, first done by Canadians in 1982.

As Kearney and Cusick were finishing their climb on their fifth day, Simon Richardson returned to the range with another partner, Doré Green, to climb the westernmost south pillar on Mt. Tiedemann. Sustained and complex free climbing up to 5.10+ characterized their first day. Just as the prow seemed to be blanking out, Green turned a corner to find another crack system, and after a number of additional 5.10 sections they reached the perfectly flat crest of a tower to set up their tent.

They continued up easier mixed ground to the top. Once again, Richardson was wary of a gully descent in warm weather, so they toured over the top of Combatant and then worked a difficult descent off the Combatant-Waddington Col to the glacier, completing a four-day circuit.

As Far As the Ridges Run

The Coast Mountains have been the modern-day venue for one of the most extensive careers in the history of mountain exploration. Starting in 1967, Vancouver-born John Clarke spent three to six months of almost every year—over 30 years—touring and climbing in these mountains, and every one of his more than 100 expeditions visited a place no one else had ever been. His career is a surprising reminder in a technical age that engagement with mountains comes not only with difficulty but also with exploration and discovery. Clarke never counted the number of peaks he was first to summit, but that number reached into the many hundreds. More to the point, he felt, was his estimate that, over the years, he covered on foot and skis between 15,000 and 20,000 miles.

Clarke was a student at the University of British Columbia when he realized that the Coast Mountain path of the Mundays, Dick Culbert and others was beautiful and far from completed. He made his first three-week solo explorations with a pack heavy with idealism and only a pillowcase of granola to eat from. Gradually he perfected his methods for traveling these mountains, including a tasty and cheap menu system, airdrops and a whole order of strategies for climbing alone and staying dry. The brush of Coast Mountain canyons is so heartbreaking that Clarke would attempt to stay above treeline for an entire trip, cruising as far as the alpine ridge systems run. He took snowy crevasses very seriously, and when alone he would simply

John Clarke builds a cairn on another unnamed peak, above the Tahumming River. PHOTO BY JOHN BALDWIN.

detour around dangerous glacial terrain, no matter how many hours or days it might take.

Freedom from work commitments was crucial to his goals, so he set himself up with winter work in his parents' stained-glass business, squirreling away funds and drying food. Clarke refused to allow bad weather to shut down a trip, and he arranged plenty of extra supplies to wait out storms. Only occasionally would a partner join him—not because Clarke didn't welcome them but because of his one steadfast rule: "There will be no set return date, we will hang in there until the trip is done." As he put it, "There's a lot of things that keep people out of this country." Apparently so, for on dozens of excursions Clarke never encountered another mountaineering party.

One partner Clarke often could count on was John Baldwin, and in 1986 he and Baldwin pioneered the only Clarke tour that anyone has repeated, a 16-day traverse of all the peaks circling the Tahumming River, near Toba Inlet. Clarke called himself a roamer, but we have solid evidence of his climbing prowess. In 1986, eying the Klattasine Group of granitic peaks southeast of Mt. Waddington, he wanted a partner competent at rock climbing, and so he contacted Peter Croft, who eagerly joined him. At the first technical ground, Clarke switched to basketball sneakers—his usual rock footwear—but didn't ask for the rope. Wearing full packs, they made their way over exposed, wet slabs and up lieback corners. Clarke asked Croft what the terrain would be graded, for he had never done a rated climb. Croft told him it was about 5.6, and Clarke was taken aback—he had assumed such a number would describe much harder terrain. Croft realized that Clarke had a history of wild climbing, and he came back saying, "At what he does, he's the best in the world."

Starting in 1995, Clarke took a three-year hiatus from his journeys, partly because he had just about filled in his wall of maps with trips, but mostly because he had decided to help fight the systematic logging that is tearing down the Coast Mountain rainforests. Not unlike John Muir 100 years before, John

Clarke came back to civilization with a message and a mission. He felt his excursions gave him a broad perspective on civilization:

> *Early man had a really precarious existence and we are so comfortable these days. The more precarious, the more of a connection you get. You are getting a sense of what it felt for man living on earth for most of the time he has been on earth.*

In 1998, Clarke returned to climbing with a trip to northern British Columbia, west of Kitimat, with partners and kayaks. After many days out he wrote:

> *We are in such a wonderfully stunned state that we wonder what we'll be good for when we get back to the city. The word urgency is gone from our vocabulary unless it means paddling fast to get around a point while the water is calm.... Scanning the horizon, 60km to the southeast, we saw a continuous line of peaks so extensive it seemed to make a joke of peak bagging. 'Wow, where the hell is that?' Trevor asked. 'That's where we're going next year,' I said.*

Old Games Still Strong

The Coast Mountains aren't the only North American region with plenty of unclimbed terrain. From Canada's interior ranges even to the Tetons, modern climbers have found that the continent's array of "classic" routes is far from completed. "British Columbia," says Fred Beckey, "is my favorite part of the world," and he continued to bring younger climbers to ranges all over this province. In 1988, Beckey, Jim Ruch and Dave Pollari helicoptered to the Melville Group of the southern Selkirks. On Ahab, the threesome climbed a steep glacier route. The following day, Ruch and Pollari went up a beautiful, curving corner system on the north face of the same peak, moving delicately and delightedly up ice and rock to put up a route called *Boomerang* that bears repeating.

Until 1991, stunning Downie Peak in the northern Selkirks had not been repeated

John Clarke above Toba Inlet, on the *Tahumming Traverse*. PHOTO BY JOHN BALDWIN.

since Bill Putnam led the first ascent in 1959. Downie's north arête had long been considered a possible classic, and as logging roads made the peak more accessible, Adamant Lodge employees Franz Fux and Erich Unterberger finally made the effort. In a two-day adventure from the road, they climbed the 4,000-foot arête, finding the limestone reasonably firm, with a number of sections up to 5.7.

Vancouver scientist Dave Jones, who grew up on the west side of the Selkirks, has put up new routes in the area's many subranges since the early 1970s. By the 1990s he decided to get systematic about it, plotting numerous trips to this original range of North American alpinism. As late as 1998, Jones' records showed, 132 of the 545 peaks of the Selkirks were still unclimbed, and only 879 routes had been done.

Jones, his wife, Joie Seagram, and a variety of Canadian partners made two or more trips each summer to tick off beautiful ridgelines and steep walls. In 1999 they based in the Melville Group, and Jones, Guy Edwards, Greg Foweraker and Torben Johannson climbed a variety of fine granite routes on the south face of Mt. Ahab. In 2000 they went to the most "popular" block in the range, the granitic Adamant Group. Even here, Jones and teammates found plenty of new routes to be done, including the south face of Mt. Adamant (climbed by Peter Oxtoby and Todd Craig) and the southwest face of Montezuma's Finger, an amazing splinter climbed by Foweraker and Tim McAllister.

The Tetons, that most famous and compact range in America, also continues to yield new and worthy routes. Among the most active climbers has been worldwide big-wall veteran and misfit Jim Beyer. He focused much of his attention on the big, complex south flanks of Mt. Moran. In 1982 he and Dave Koch completed the spine of an obvious and very long gable above the popular south buttress, calling it *Revolutionary Crest*. Sixteen years later, Beyer was on probation from the law, feeling his "hectic hell called life totally melt[ing] down," and looking for a new adventure to clear his head. He worried that sport climbing ethics might have "corrupted" the Tetons, but found that, "While sport climbers everywhere else have been waging war on the rock with their power drills and grid bolting, the Tetons have been ignored." Belaying himself, he found free climbing up to 5.10c between two decades-old routes on Moran's south buttress.

In 2000, Beyer came back with talented free climber John Kelley. They pushed directly through many of the steepest facets of Moran's south buttress, resorting to aid on hand-drilled bolts and hooks on one section, but mostly linking stretches of dicey free climbing. Some 13 pitches up, Kelley led a very thin, 5.11 slab with widely spaced, hand-drilled bolts. They made a tactical retreat when they ran out of bolts, but a few days later they climbed back to their high point and completed the face to a bivouac ledge. The next day they met the south buttress crest and followed it another 2,000 feet to Moran's summit.

Climbing relatively small and technical alpine routes in winter can, of course, resemble the demands of the Greater Ranges, but relatively few North Americans take advantage of the low-sun months. A few months after Beyer and Kelley's climb, Teton ranger Renny Jackson collected locals Hans Johnstone and Mark Newcomb to try Moran's original south buttress route in winter. Many had attempted this project, and Jack Tackle and Alex Lowe had reached the top of the steepest climbing a few years earlier but did not summit. Jackson received a forecast of clear weather in early March 2001, and in one day out of Leigh Canyon they climbed the 10 or so pitches of the steep foot of the buttress and settled into their sleeping bags. In the morning they climbed many pitches of easier but still fifth-class terrain, burdened by sleeping gear and winter boots. By noon they met the east-trending gully where they planned to descend, and so they stashed their packs. However, as the relatively few parties who have done the complete south buttress have found, the terrain continued to be complicated, and at 5 p.m. Newcomb confronted a steep tower, still 1,000 feet from the top. The scary thought of a Teton winter night unprotected had them discussing retreat, but a "'Traverse of the Gods'-type of ledge" delivered them to snowy chutes, and at 7 p.m. they were on top. As they rappelled and climbed back down, a full moon rose and lit their way back to the packs.

Fairbanks resident Jeff Apple Benowitz has for years been exploring his adopted state for new peaks, and in the mid '90s he locked onto the 3,000-foot east face of The Thorn, at the eastern edge of the Alaska Range. Benowitz wanted ice on this face, and so he chose to try it in winter, but approach challenges including temperatures of -50°F and a half-frozen river turned him back twice. He finally got to the face in 1997, alone, but had to retreat when he came to blank rock with no ice. March of 1998 proved to be the right time, and over two days Benowitz and Rick Studley linked ice smears and "scary snow tunneling" to a rocky and snowy arête that got them to the top of the face. Benowitz said, "It will probably be 100 years before this hidden gem gets climbed again."

Rockies Rule

In the Canadian Rockies in 1996, Salt Lake City-based Seth Shaw avoided the problem of loose rock by going to one of the steepest—and therefore, presumably, most solid—big faces in the range. With extensive aid and difficult free climbing, Shaw led client Scott Simper up a gigantic shield on the 5,000-foot north face of Mt. Geikie. Much of the wall is vertical and overhanging, but the quartzite indeed proved quite strong, and so Shaw was inspired to complete the most sustained technical route in the Rockies.

Steve House helped revitalize the lineage of demanding winter routes in the Canadian Rockies, joining Barry Blanchard, Joe Josephson and others for some very steep and committing ascents. On a new winter route on the oft-attempted east face of Howse Peak, House led a vertical pitch of pasted thin ice so steep, tenuous and poorly protected that partners Blanchard and Scott Backes figured they didn't know anyone else who could have done it. They bivouacked in a worm-hole snow cave, but in the morning a storm came in. Against their better judgment, they decided to keep going even as snow accumulated, so that House's lead would not be forgotten on an unclimbed route. They gained the northeast ridge and then rappelled down their route from there. During one of these rappels, Blanchard was hit by an avalanche that almost swept him away. They named the route *M-16*, only half jesting that the collected challenges on a high alpine route in winter made it twice as hard as any roadside M8 mixed climb.

The following winter, House, Blanchard and Rolando Garibotti climbed an even steeper route on the east face of Mt. Fay. Sustained, very steep and occasionally thin ice tried even House. Avalanche conditions forced them to escape after the steepest climbing, but their climb helped establish an even higher standard in Rockies alpinism.

Steve House leading the third pitch of *M-16* on the east face of Howse Peak. PHOTO BY BARRY BLANCHARD.

Barry Blanchard leads on into a storm on the final section of climbing on *M16*. PHOTO BY STEVE HOUSE.

Barry Blanchard on *M16*. PHOTO BY STEVE HOUSE.

SUGGESTED ROUTES
FROM THIS PERIOD

WARBONNET PEAK (12,369 feet/3,770 meters)
Southeast Face *(Black Elk)*
Climbers making the usual approach to the Wind
Rivers' famous Cirque of the Towers know the end of
the hike is near when they pass beneath this
impressive wall. This sight has enhanced the reputa-
tion of *Black Elk* as a somewhat popular testpiece.
Very fit climbers have done it in a day from the Big
Sandy trailhead, but most will camp near the base,
at North Lake.

    Approach: It's a six-mile hike with 1,000 feet of
gain to North Lake, and from there the southeast
face of Warbonnet is obvious.

    Route: The climb goes up the left third of the face,
reaching easy terrain on the southeast ridge a few
hundred feet below the summit. The key to locating
the route is to spot the big chockstone-roof that caps

twin dihedrals facing each other at the top of the
route. The last difficult pitch goes up the left of these
corners and exits behind the chockstone. Third-class
ramps gain a steep crack system that will take you to
that corner. The most demanding and infamous pitch
is a sustained and steep wide-fist crack. Those with
less meaty hands are likely to give this section a 5.11a
rating. Descend easily by the south slopes.

    First Ascent: Charlie Fowler and Jeff Lowe, 1981
    Grade: TD, IV, 5.10d or 5.11a, 1,000 feet
    Guidebook: *Wind River Mountains*
    Permit: Overnight trips into the Bridger
Wilderness require a permit, available at the trailhead.

MT. TIEDEMANN (12,625 feet/3,848 meters)
South Buttress Direct
Scotsman Simon Richardson called this "one of the
world's great alpine routes." It has scale, sustained but
reasonable challenges, solid granite and superb position, making it indeed a brilliant modern challenge.

    Approach: Most parties helicopter in from Bluff
Lake.

    Route: The route starts with a climb of a 2,000-
foot tower, which a few teams have enjoyed as a 5.9

The southeast face of Warbonnet. PHOTO BY JOE KELSEY.

The south faces of Mts. Combatant and Tiedemann.
PHOTO BY ANDY SELTERS.

route in its own right. Easier climbing along a granite crest leads to a hanging snowfield on the left. Above here, the first-ascent party climbed the middle pillar of three that lead to the summit ridge. They found a dozen superb 5.9 and 5.10 pitches, with just a few moves of aid. Subsequent parties have also climbed an easier chute system to the right of this pillar.

Descent is by the avalanche-prone Tiedemann-Asperity Couloir, a gamble perhaps better taken at night.

First Ascent: Carl Diedrich, Jim Nelson and Jim Ruch, August 1988

Difficulty: ED 2, 5.10, A1, AI 2, 5,100 feet

Guidebook: *The Waddington Guide*

CENTRAL SIERRA NEVADA
Evolution Traverse

Here is the culminating vision of one of North America's most visionary climbers; the traverse's position, difficulty, quality and especially length all combine to make this line in the sky one of the most intensive high-rock engagements on the continent. General routefinding is easy; just follow a distinct ripsaw running for about eight miles, where the most logical climbing usually is right atop the crest-line. However, there are hundreds of small routefinding decisions, and the only reasonable way to complete the route is to move swiftly—with little or no use of a rope—on moderately technical, exposed terrain. Since the first complete ascent, two or three parties have repeated it, including at least one that used ultra-light bivouac gear for one night and accessed natural water sources along the route.

Approach: As per the approach to Mt. Mendel (see Chapter 10), cross Lamarck Col and then cruise down Darwin Canyon to camp at the southern edge of Darwin Bench, at 11,200 feet. The start of the route is the ridge rising directly east from there.

Route: The initial 3/4-mile of ridge gains a couple of thousand feet on firm Class 4 and some Class 5 rock up to Peak 13,385. Descending into the notch toward Mt. Mendel brings some real exposure, and this continues on the ridge toward Mendel, including a short, steep hand crack. From the top of Mendel, take the picket-fence line, with some 5.8, running to the route's highest point, Mt. Darwin

Dave Melkonian on the *Evolution Traverse*. PHOTO BY DAN PATITUCCI.

If you like our books, you'll love our membership benefits!

- Worldwide rescue insurance
- Unrivaled mountaineering research library
- Internationally renowned publications
- Domestic and international conservation projects
- Advocacy on policy issues

Photo: The Magic Line

For more information, return this postcard, visit www.americanalpineclub.org, or call (303) 384-0110.

Name _____

Address _____

City _____ State _____ Zip _____

Phone (___) _____ Email_____

If you like our books, you'll love our membership benefits!

- Worldwide rescue insurance
- Unrivaled mountaineering research library
- Internationally renowned publications
- Domestic and international conservation projects
- Advocacy on policy issues

Photo: The Magic Line

For more information, return this postcard, visit www.americanalpineclub.org, or call (303) 384-0110.

Name _____

Address _____

City _____ State _____ Zip _____

Phone (___) _____ Email_____

BUSINESS REPLY MAIL
FIRST-CLASS MAIL   PERMIT NO. 192   GOLDEN, CO

POSTAGE WILL BE PAID BY ADDRESSEE

AMERICAN ALPINE CLUB
710 10TH ST STE 100
GOLDEN CO 80401-8953

NO POSTAGE
NECESSARY
IF MAILED
IN THE
UNITED STATES

BUSINESS REPLY MAIL
FIRST-CLASS MAIL   PERMIT NO. 192   GOLDEN, CO

POSTAGE WILL BE PAID BY ADDRESSEE

AMERICAN ALPINE CLUB
710 10TH ST STE 100
GOLDEN CO 80401-8953

(13,381 feet). Descend chimneys (5.9 or rappel, some loose rock) down the south ridge of Darwin and return to knife-edge climbing for some of the most technical and memorable parts of the route, with climbing possibly up to 5.9 on superb rock. After these difficulties, a logical and easy escape heads west from Peak 12,996 over Mt. Spencer. On the main crest, moderate , sometimes sidewalk cruising leads south (look below to the east for water) to the fine, easy cracks up Mt. Haeckel. The line continues over Mt. Wallace and curves southwest with more easy fifth class to Mt. Fiske. If you're getting tired and think that the final climbing may not be worth it, trust the exhilaration of previous parties and keep going with fourth- and easy fifth-class climbing over Mt. Warlow and Mt. Huxley. Descend the west flank of Huxley to reach the John Muir Trail, which leads back to slopes below Darwin Bench.

First Complete Ascent: Peter Croft, June 1999

Difficulty: ED, 5.9, 40,000 feet of traversing

Guidebook: *The Good, The Great and The Awesome; Fifty Favorite Climbs*

Permit: A wilderness permit, available in Bishop, is required for camping in the John Muir Wilderness and Kings Canyon National Park.

TAHUMMING TRAVERSE

This horseshoe-shaped mountain tour about 120 miles north of Vancouver has become known as a classic introduction to the vast Coast Range wilderness. Technical climbing challenges are modest, but the demands of logistics, extensive alpine travel, the stormy climate and essentially no opportunity for

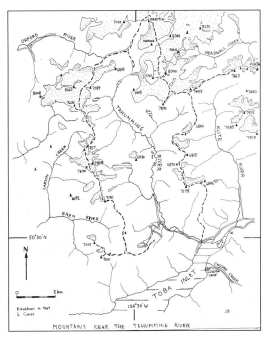

John Baldwin's map for the Tahumming Traverse.

escape make this a scenic, high-value engagement. Half a dozen parties have completed this route, covering the 60 miles and 24,000 feet of elevation change in two to three weeks.

Approach: Make helicopter or fixed-wing arrangements with air services in Campbell River (on Vancouver Island) for drop-off, pickup and air-drops along the route.

Route: From your drop-off at tidewater, get under way with the toughest part of the trip: a 5,000-foot climb through forest to snowline. Snow will be your companion for the rest of the tour, as the route arcs from ridgeline to summit to ridgeline to glacier crossing, again and again. A few summits require scrambling or pack hauling, but the main reason to bring a rope is for crossing crevassed glaciers. Make time while the sun shines, for even the most compass-savvy will be unlikely to cover much ground during low-visibility storm days. From late July well into August, stretches of fair weather almost always arrive.

First Ascent: John Baldwin and John Clarke, July/August 1986

Grade: D, Class 3, 60 miles, 24,000 feet of total gain and loss

John Clarke on the *Tahumming Traverse*. PHOTO BY JOHN BALDWIN.

CHAPTER 14

The Biggest Arena: Alpine Style

For leading-edge alpinists, the big alpine-style ascents of the 1970s and '80s required that they learn to manage new levels of deprivation and suffering. In 1988, the great Polish Himalayan climber Voytek Kurtyka wrote an internationally published article reminding alpinists that their game is often called "The Art of Suffering." Extreme alpinists strive to wring out their ultimate potential by exploring the limits of duress while rationing just enough physical and emotional succor to keep the muscles working and the resolve intact. Each climber had to find just where and how hard he could push.

Kurtyka wrote, "Whenever a climber leaves the known paths, he enters an area without rules or routines to rely on. The only advice comes from deep inside the self, and hopefully the motivation is true."

Few North Americans followed or yet understood the track of extreme mountaineering in the Himalaya, but in Alaska and the Yukon climbers forged a parallel path. By the 1980s, dozens flew every spring to the Kahiltna Glacier landing site, and while most

aimed for the top of Denali via the west buttress, visionaries eyed the super-high surroundings for new levels of challenge.

Modern Alaska

The 10,000-foot east face of Mt. Foraker is the biggest sweep in view from the Kahiltna, but most climbers saw it only as a source of gargantuan avalanches, and as the grave of some Japanese climbers who had tempted fate there. In 1984, though, Mugs Stump alerted three Québecois climbers that the left side of the face was safe from seracs and that a potential route waited there. Australian Graham Sanders had hooked up with the French-Canadians, and, after contemplating the face from the basecamp latrine, he convinced his new partners that this was what they had come to Alaska for.

Climbers were starting to understand the wisdom of pre-acclimatization for hard routes on these big peaks, and Daniel Vachon, Julien Dery and Jean-Francois Gagnon had already ventured high on Denali's west buttress. With this advantage, there was by now no question that they should attempt a new route like this in alpine style. The route started up a long, S-shaped couloir, and after two days of sustained but relatively secure climbing they were a third of the way up the face. By the

↺ Steve House starting the crux pitch on the south face of King Peak. PHOTO BY JOE JOSEPHSON.

Jack Tackle starts one of the hardest pitches on Mt. Hunter's *Diamond Arête*. PHOTO BY JIM DONINI, COURTESY JACK TACKLE.

fourth day, however, Alaskan-style steep, rotten snow and ice-coated rock slowed their progress. Two difficult days later, they reached moderate ground on the southeast ridge. The three Canadians continued to the top while Sanders (who had not pre-acclimatized) waited to descend with them.

During this same May of 1984, a Slovakian team came to Denali to try a route on the right flank of the Cassin Ridge. The Czechoslovakian government strictly controlled travel by its climbers, and only teams that proposed a major new route that would bring recognition to the country would gain permission to travel. A return without success meant no chance to travel again. This was the context when Blazej Adam, Tono Krizö and Frantisek Körl, on their first visit to Alaska, climbed one of the steepest routes on Denali.

The Slovaks went capsule style, with 800 feet of fixed rope. Excellent granite and varieties of ice made for fine and demanding climbing. It took them three days to string their ropes over the rock cliffs above 13,500 feet. On the last and steepest pitch of this section, Adam took a 50-foot leader fall. They had not pre-acclimatized, and although the terrain eased above this point they did not move quickly. They reached the top 10 days after they started.

In June of this year, Yves Tedeschi and Benoit Grison climbed the conspicuous couloir on the left edge of the north buttress of Mt. Hunter. Yosemite-influenced Americans had not taken much interest in this obvious avenue along the lower part of the buttress, partly because it funnels avalanches during any snowfall. But these alpine-savvy Frenchmen raced up the couloir between storms and then veered directly up the eastern flank of the north buttress, reaching Hunter's summit after just four days of hard mixed climbing, having completed the most logical route up the wall.

From his *Isis Face* on Denali, Jack Tackle had gotten a rare good view of the east face of Hunter, and he saw a rock wall similar in scale and structure to the Diamond of Longs Peak. On top of that "Diamond" rose another 4,000 feet of moderately difficult Alaskan ridge to Hunter's higher summit. In 1985, Tackle recruited Patagonia veteran Jim Donini for his first climb in Alaska. The two took on the route with Yosemite-like alpine tactics—hauling packs and the second following with ascenders—using only two ropes. Along the left edge of "the Diamond," they endured numerous trials, including failing anchors, snow-choked chimneys, fracturing ice, a leader fall and avalanches pouring over their camp—and then they dropped their utility rope. They stayed on top of the situation, though, and after a week they reached a campsite near the summit, just as a storm came in. Howling wind turned them back, and they retreated through heavy snowfall and avalanches onto the northeast ridge. Many desperate rappels with their remaining rope and every last piece of hardware got them past a number of near-miss avalanches and down to the Kahiltna Glacier.

The big granite walls around the Ruth Glacier also attracted new attention in the late 1980s. Among a variety of routes on satellites of the Moose's Tooth and walls on the gorge's west flank, the biggest and maybe the best climb began when Austrian Andreas Orgler came with young Tyrolean Tommi Bonapace for a second attempt on a prominent pillar on the east face of Mt. Dickey. Mugs Stump had labeled this gem the *Wine Bottle*. Over six days, Orgler and Bonapace savored a smorgasbord of free climbing spiced with icy-wet chimneys, aid sections and perched snow patches. Each lead ended with a strenuous load haul. The route is one of the biggest Yosemite-like climbs anywhere, gaining 5,250 feet.

In 1991, Seattle buddies Mark Bebie and Bill Pilling took a helicopter ride past the approach hassles to Devils Thumb and promptly climbed the northeast face, the mixed route where Jon Krakauer had tempted fate years before. With belays and better ice, they found the climbing more amenable. Inspired by the firm, knobby granite, Bebie then convinced Pilling to circle around to the tower's prominent south pillar, an intimidating buttress to the right of the 1973 Lowe-Jones-Tejada-Flores wall. Although neither Bebie nor Pilling were masters on stone, they worked up dry and wonderfully knobby rock for 2,000 feet, requiring only a few pieces of aid. They spent their third night on the climb right below the summit, and the next day completed a route that many now view as a model for friendly climbing—when conditions are dry—on an Alaskan peak.

The Thunderbird

Dave Nettle is a hard-driving climber who likes to add uncertainty and strain to ascents by making long and sleepless drive-and-climb pushes from his Lake Tahoe home, even to objectives as distant as Mt. Robson. He looks at such endurance epics partly as training for expedition-scale stress, and among his loftier goals the *Hummingbird*

Ridge on Mt. Logan preyed on his mind. He convinced Tahoe-based Canadian Geoff Creighton to join him in the Yukon in late April 1990. They plotted a direct route to the highest arm of the ridge, aiming to bypass most of the *Hummingbird* and its infamous cornice chain. The two packed only basic bivouac gear, one thin rope, a handful of anchors and seven days of food. "The plan," wrote Nettle, "was to move fast, descend the route and most likely lose some weight." The last aspect of this triad would prove to be the most accurate.

In three days (including one resting in storm), Nettle and Creighton climbed some

Devils Thumb from the northeast. The 1977 Stutzman-Plumb ascent climbed the prominent prow facing the camera and angling up and left. The first Bebie-Pilling ascent climbed the ramps on the central face. The north face, to the right, remains an unclimbed and ultra-hazardous enigma. PHOTO BY BILL PILLING.

Bill Pilling below the south pillar of Devils Thumb. He and Bebie climbed the left skyline. PHOTO BY MARK BEBIE, COURTESY BILL PILLING.

Bill Pilling on the south pillar of Devils Thumb. PHOTO BY MARK BEBIE, COURTESY BILL PILLING.

5,000 feet of snow and ice. As they gained the narrow ridgecrest at 14,000 feet, storm winds rose again. After pressing on toward midnight, they chopped a sitting spot from a cornice, tied themselves to an anchor, and pulled their tent around them. Before long, part of the cornice gave way under Nettle. He fought his way out of the tent to huddle outside. Then the wind blew Creighton off the perch, and for the rest of the night he hung from the rope inside the tent "like a sack of potatoes."

In the morning the blizzard eased and they regrouped. However, they now realized the folly of trying to descend so much steep terrain with their meager gear. Thus they pushed upward and committed themselves to descending Logan's east ridge. Though the weather improved and the terrain eased, they had to take short days in order to keep their altitude headaches from deteriorating into serious illness. On their eighth day they made the summit. There, Nettle wrote, "I saw a desolate wilderness that seemed to mock our success and promise only hardship." Indeed, they found little comfort as they marched across three miles of summit plateau and down the snowy upper east ridge. At 14,000 feet, they paused to get the energy from their last remnants of food and fuel.

The two men were dismayed to see that the east ridge was much steeper and more complex than they had imagined. They struggled for hours and hours to get down safely, and as they reached the Hubbard Glacier their reward was to lose visibility in

Paul Teare starting a crux pitch on the *Phantom Wall*, Mt. Huntington. PHOTO BY JAY SMITH.

Alaskan Triumphs and Tragedies

In 1987, Nettle and Jim Quirk had made the first complete ascent of the west face couloir route on Mt. Huntington, and a couple of years later Nettle showed a Washburn photo of this face to his Tahoe neighbor, Jay Smith. By this time, Mt. Huntington had more routes per acre of terrain than any peak in Alaska, but Smith instantly noticed that the tallest aspect of this spectacular peak, on the right side of Nettle's photo, had not even been tried. He recruited another Tahoe-based climber, Canadian Paul Teare, and laid plans to attempt the 6,000-foot southerly aspect of the west face, which they called the *Phantom Wall*.

When the two men first looked at this wall in person, from the lower tip of the Harvard spur, they saw that in storm or direct sun the narrow basin below the wall was hammered with avalanches and rockfall. They labeled this approach corridor "Death Valley." On the face itself, however, they traced classic steep terrain. The approach gauntlet and inspiring face above encouraged them to head up the climb super-light, without bivouac gear. With minuscule packs and an early-morning start, they reached the face well ahead of any after-noon releases. That evening, they settled into a brief, shivering bivouac, but as they dozed a storm swept in, initiating appalling avalanch-es throughout the basin. They escaped as fast as possible onto the Harvard spur. The face had given them a taste of terror and of bril-liant climbing, and they both felt that with some better luck they could take the bril-liance to its conclusion.

They returned a year later, in 1991, and waited patiently while a week of fine weather shed loose material from the face. Then they packed as before, except for carrying sleeping bags for a better midroute rest. The plan worked perfectly, and with just one bivouac two of the finest alpinists on the continent threaded a narrow line of relatively moderate climbing up the steep face. In the middle of the route, five pitches on exquisite and icy granite—up to 5.10 and a few steps of aid—gave the spice of technical challenge.

Later that year, Wyoming NOLS instructors Greg Collins, Phil Powers and Tom Walter

the area's typical fog. Into the whiteness they slogged by compass bearing to round the east end of Mt. Logan. Though they were running gravely past empty, they kept their navigation straight. As they gasped up to the pass above the Seward Glacier, still 18 miles from basecamp, they spotted a bit of color. They dug and found a cache from Pete Schoening's 1952 expedition, with kerosene that got their stove sputtering enough to melt snow, and packages of Jell-O, gum and dried fruit. Nettle marveled, "Five years before I was born, someone carefully packed this food and hauled it into the middle of nowhere, where it had sat for 37 years before bailing our dehydrated and starving butts out of trouble." They named their route the *Thunderbird* variation, after the collapsing seracs that roared almost continuously off neighboring walls.

took light-and-fast tactics to Denali to attempt another hidden wall, the 7,000-foot-high northwest face of Denali's west buttress. Walter had scouted the wall the previous May, but was repelled by bitter temperatures and extensive blue ice. At the end of June of '91, though, he and his fellow guides found temperatures warm enough to climb without gloves, and the ice was nicely pliable. Most of the way they moved rapidly by simul-climbing with an occasional ice screw between them, stopping to belay only six mixed pitches. After 20 hours of climbing they had to take a break and chopped a ledge to steal some sleep. In the morning they continued to the easy ground atop the west buttress, which they'd planned to make their high point. They proposed that this wall be named the *Washburn Face.*

The following season, heavy May storms helped create hazardous conditions all over the Alaska Range, and that season a record 11 climbers didn't make it back. Among them was Mugs Stump, who perished when a huge crevasse lip gave way under him. A couple of weeks later, Colby Coombs, Ritt Kellogg and Tom Walter were climbing the final couple of hundred feet of Foraker's Québecois (*Pink Panther*) route when a small avalanche swept them down 1,500 feet. Walter and Kellogg were killed. Coombs sustained a broken back, but in one of North America's great survival epics he was somehow able to gain the southeast ridge and crawl down it and across the glacier to Kahiltna basecamp.

The Grandest Enigma
Among the great northern peaks, Mt. St. Elias was the first to be climbed, but, ironically, it had become the most enigmatic challenge. Climatic warming has thinned the upper Newton Glacier of the 1897 route into a maze of almost impassable, avalanche-threatened crevasses, and the peak's western routes are too difficult to be considered "regular" routes. In addition, St. Elias presents an acclimatization challenge for alpine-style ascents, for there is no way to get high without taking on a serious route. In 1975, a Seattle team sieged the exciting east ridge,

but cornices and avalanche slopes have not inspired repeats of this route. However, advanced climbers had long eyed two other extreme possibilities, the long southeast ridge and the staggering south face.

St. Elias's 15,000-foot south face is the only uplift in North America comparable to Denali's Wickersham Wall, and St. Elias' wall is steeper. Only eight miles from tidewater, the face is an enormous pylon in the continent's wettest storm track, collecting untold fathoms of snowfall and sloughing it off in constant, thundering cataclysms. Across the face runs a continuous band of super-active ice cliffs split by only one dividing spur. A few parties had approached the face, but all had turned tail. Southeast Alaska veteran Walter Gove believed the one cleaver would allow reasonably safe passage, and in 1984 he teamed up with young tiger and Mt. Rainier guide Andy Politz to try it.

Gove and Politz cramponed up most of the face in four days, waiting for one additional day in storm. They dug in their highest camp just below the crest of the southeast ridge, at 14,400 feet. After another rest day, they moved for the summit, but Gove fell behind. Politz continued to the top and when he returned to Gove just 45 minutes later, the 45-year-old could barely walk. He had suddenly developed severe altitude illness, and his hands and feet were half-frozen.

Politz revved into a heroic escape effort, leading the way as Gove crawled down the crevassed face. They descended as far as possible, to a campsite at 12,400 feet, after 41 hours on the move. After a night there, Gove had barely improved, and it was another 28 hours before they reached the bottom of the face. Gove would need a helicopter to get out, but two days of trying to hail planes for a rescue proved futile, so Politz began a long march alone across very treacherous glaciers. At a peninsula beyond Icy Bay, 44 hours after leaving Gove, he lit a flare to attract a crab boat, and when they answered his shouts he broke down and wept with relief. The next day a Coast Guard helicopter picked up Gove, who would lose five toes and parts of four fingers. He had learned as thoroughly as one could that "serious alpine [style] ascents are for the physically elite, and even then one is treading a fine line."

In 1993, a team of five Swiss and Czechs used intensive air access to solve the St. Elias acclimatization enigma. They got used to the thin air by first climbing three peaks in the Wrangells. The morning after they summited Mt. Blackburn, pilot Paul Claus picked them up, and after a night repacking at Claus' lodge, they flew to about 10,000 feet on the Columbus Glacier below Mt. St. Elias. They worked through an icefall to camp below the west face, where a 1978 Japanese team had climbed with fixed ropes. First, Ruedi Homberger, his son Urs, and Reto Rüesch climbed the fairly steep snow and ice face without putting on the rope. After climbing through the night they continued along the ridge to top out at 11 a.m. and returned without a bivouac. The next day, Miroslav Smid and Ueli Bula climbed the same face farther left, and then bivouacked in a tent atop the ridge. They summited the next morning.

Super-Alpine Ridges

Alpine-style attempts in Alaska and the Yukon naturally gravitated toward routes with direct ascent and retreat potential—that is, faces and walls—and few alpine-style climbers have been willing to take on the extra challenge of Alaska's big catenary ridges. Exceptions started in 1984, when the great Italian soloist Renatto Casarotto came to Talkeetna.

As he perused park-service photos of Denali, Casarotto saw the huge arabesque gable that Glenn Randall and Peter Metcalf had backed off, which they dubbed the *Ridge of No Return*. Casarotto made this his objective, and he went to climb it alone, with only two light ropes. Over 11 days, he belayed himself with friction knots as he traversed under and over cornices, above unpredictable hollows and across occasional rock. After each pitch he fixed the ropes to snow anchors, returned to his pack, and reclimbed the pitch. At the final headwall, he abandoned his ropes and made a 3,000-foot push to the top of the south buttress, where he

The south face of Mt. St. Elias. Gove and Politz climbed the rib above and slightly left of the tent. PHOTO TAKEN DURING A 1979 ATTEMPT BY WALT GOVE.

pitched his tent in a gale atop a 15,000-foot knob, his intended summit. The next morning he witnessed a climber fall and get injured, and on the way to initiate a rescue Casarotto fell into a crevasse himself. All emerged unscathed, but this accident foreshadowed Casarotto's death two years later on K2.

In 1986, NOLS instructors Dave Auble and Charlie Townsend made an alpine-style ascent of Mt. Foraker's *Talkeetna Ridge*. The early-May effort required 10 days of sustained climbing over corniced fins, granite knobs and icy chutes.

A year later, an alpine-style attempt on the *Hummingbird Ridge* claimed two of the top climbers on the continent. Dave Cheesmond was undoubtedly among the best alpinists in the world, and Catherine Freer was a rare light and certainly the strongest woman mountaineer in North America. Their ambition to make the first alpine-style ascent of the *Hummingbird* embraced their dreams of tackling profound challenges regardless of fame.

In May 1987, a pilot searching for the overdue climbers discovered Cheesmond and Freer's empty tent hanging off a broken cornice on the *Hummingbird*. They probably had been dumped out of the tent when the cornice broke. A year later, Seattle climber Carla Firey wrote in an obituary for her friend Freer, "We know that you and Dave Cheesmond chose the Hummingbird Ridge on Mount Logan in part out of dismay at the glamour antics associated with expeditions these days. It speaks of a determination, choosing climbs for the inherent difficulties rather than the popularity or public visibility." For many climbers, their deaths peeled away a layer of denial that says, if you're good enough mountaineering is essentially safe. When climbers this good are killed, the core of the game is laid open, and we see all-too-mortal hearts perhaps playing the odds too many times.

Midsummer of 1988, three Montana chums—Randy Waitman, Chuck Maffei and Jim Cancroft—plus their Australian friend Rowan Laver, climbed the complete north ridge of Denali's north peak. Canadians had climbed the upper half of this ridge in 1961, but despite the passing of 78 years since the Sourdoughs followed the final stretch of this ridge to the north peak, the elegant complete spine had never been traveled. The Montanans climbed in late June and found relatively firm conditions. They first skied up the Muldrow Glacier and put a cache halfway along the ridge. Then they returned and started the route from Gunsight Pass. In all, it took them 16 days to complete the *Pioneer Ridge* to the top.

Two years after this, Mark Bebie and Bill Pilling pioneered the long and classic-looking south ridge of Mt. Augusta. This stepped spine gains over 10,000 feet, and the pair climbed it in pure alpine style. From corniced arêtes to short steps of variable-quality rock

The south ridge of Mt. Augusta. PHOTO BY BILL PILLING.

(up to 5.8) and ice traverses, the route presented a kaleidoscope of challenge for six days, in remarkably perfect weather.

In 1993, Pilling was back in the Icefield Ranges with Carl Diedrich for another big ridge: the south spur of Good Neighbor Peak, Mt. Vancouver's 15,979-foot south summit. This ridge gains 8,000 feet in a steady, architectural rise. They waited for clear, cool weather and then climbed the ridge in four days, finding a variety of terrain, from firm granite to rotten shale and an array of snow and ice types. At the top of the peak, they decided to carry on with the tempting skyline traverse north to Vancouver's main peak. Unfortunately, Pilling started gasping with signs of pulmonary edema just as a storm came in. They bypassed the main summit and raced down as far as they could to weather the storm. When they resumed the descent, Pilling plunged through a crevasse bridge and tore his Achilles tendon and calf muscles. Pilling crawled behind Diedrich as they continued the descent, occasionally lowering down

Bill Pilling on good granite during the first ascent of the south spur of Good Neighbor Peak. PHOTO BY CARL DIEDRICH, COURTESY BILL PILLING.

Carl Diedrich high on the first ascent of the south spur of Good Neighbor Peak. PHOTO BY BILL PILLING.

steep sections. After four very long and painful days, they made it down the original 1949 northwest ridge route and back around the mountain to their basecamp.

Moonflower and Beyond

The north buttress of Mt. Hunter had come to epitomize the terrain sought by America's technical alpinists: sustained, edgy climbing on steep ice and sound granite. For many leading climbers, this buttress defined Alaskan climbing the way El Capitan defined rock climbing in the 1960s. In 1984, Seattle climber Pat McNerthney had set a new standard on the *Moonflower*, brilliantly leading "The Shaft" and most of the other toughest pitches without aid. (He needed only a pendulum over blank rock on "The Vision" section.) The focus on Hunter intensified in the 1994 season, as elite aspirants gathered at the Kahiltna basecamp.

A variety lined up for the *Moonflower*, although only Bill Belcourt and Randy Rackliff would complete it that year. Among those gunning for new routes were Scott Backes and Mark Twight, who had become

Mark Twight on Denali. PHOTO BY STEVE HOUSE.

proudly infamous for shoving his punkish, new-generation anger into the climbing spotlight. During much of the 1980s, Twight lived and climbed in Chamonix, and he took American climbers to task for being afraid of death and not embracing alpinism in its extremes. "American alpinists," he would say, "are the Jamaican bobsledders of world mountaineering." He also criticized American equipment manufacturers for not following the European trend and sponsoring leading alpinists. Yvon Chouinard, whose clothing company had grown to a fine position to sponsor climbers, countered that sponsorship would distort the incentives for mountaineering, and in a public letter he retorted that, if Twight needed money, he should "get a job."

By 1994, Twight had garnered sponsorships, worked with a coach on a training regimen, and refined his media image. He and Backes sought what he called "total alpinism," climbing that is technical, nervy, committing and fast. Any goal worth working for, he believed, would include suffering. He and Backes tried twice to push a new route up the steepest, most resistant facet of Hunter's north buttress, but came to the conclusion that less-steep terrain would allow them to move more swiftly. They shifted to the western edge of the buttress, a challenging but less sustained flank more suited to their style. Twight and Backes carefully packed fewer than 30 pounds each, including what they figured was enough hardware to retreat from very high on the route. They planned a measured gamble to return to the base just 72 hours after starting.

The two quickly climbed thin, steep ice, sometimes with marginal protection, through the first two granite bands, and by the end of the first day they bivouacked halfway up the 4,500-foot lower wall. The next morning they began a no-bivouac push up mixed ground through the upper two rock bands. They kept climbing through the night, and in the morning they reached the cornice at the crest of the buttress. There they paused to rest and rehydrate, while portentous clouds began sailing in from the

Scott Backes leading mixed ground through the highest rock band on *Deprivation*. PHOTO BY MARK TWIGHT.

west. They chugged toward the top, but with the approaching storm they concluded the summit was a goal set by others—and thus not worth more suffering or risk to their lives—and they veered onto their descent route. With radio contact helping to guide them through the dangerous and complex lower part of the west ridge, they raced the storm and reached the glacier exactly 72 hours after starting.

Twight pronounced that their "ethic was to climb between storms rather than counting on being hit by one and sitting it out." They called the route *Deprivation*, and Twight declared that its style represented "the future of Alaskan climbing." Over the next few years, Twight refined his theories about training, climbing and attitude, and published them in an excellent book, *Extreme Alpinism*.

About a week after greeting Twight and Backes with skis and hot drinks at the base of the west ridge, Australian-American Greg Child and Coloradan Michael Kennedy—both worldwide veterans—went to the

Mark Twight placing an ice screw while leading through the first rock band on *Deprivation* on Mt. Hunter. PHOTO BY SCOTT BACKES, COURTESY MARK TWIGHT.

Scott Backes at late-night sunset, at the top of the steep climbing on *Deprivation*. PHOTO BY MARK TWIGHT.

steepest part of Hunter's north buttress, where Backes and Twight had retreated. Child and Kennedy's Yosemite-style plan included extensive aid, hauling and a portaledge. Their complementary strengths mandated that Kennedy would lead the steep ice and Child would take the aid pitches. With a week of very technical climbing and persistence, they overcame the complex variety of steep terrain. At the top of the wall, they left their portaledge and wall gear hanging, pushed to the summit, and then carefully made their way down the west ridge, feeling vulnerable and exhausted. Kennedy said the *Wall of Shadows* was "the hardest route we'd done in our combined half-century of climbing."

A year later, Jack Tackle and Jack Roberts teamed up to try a similarly inspired route on the northwest face of the Yukon's Mt. Kennedy, a wall they named *Arctic Discipline*. They found steep and continuous thin ice, but no pockets of snow in which to dig a bivouac. They retreated and then came back in May 1996, equipped for hanging bivouacs. Although a lean winter had left even thinner ice, they went up and found climbing that Roberts described as

"pitch after pitch of hooking and scratching," with scant protection. With poise and creative gymnastics, they made steady progress without aid. But while readying for their last day of the steepest terrain, Tackle snapped on a crampon improperly, and it popped off and tumbled away. They kept going anyway, trading leads with three crampons between them and forcing the second to hop up with help from the rope. In this way they made it to the end of the steepest climbing, still a couple of thousand feet below the summit. They continued up a few pitches to join the last, easier stretch of the north buttress route, but when a storm blew in and snow began pouring off the mountain by the ton, they knew it was time to retreat. Working through lulls in the storm, with waves of snow washing over them, they made it to the glacier after two days of rappelling.

During this period, many climbers came to claim a successful ascent even though the summit waited higher. Christian Beckwith, then editor of the *AAJ*, eventually defined what seemed to be a growing consensus, that an effort on a new route could be considered successful if it connected to an existing route.

Jack Tackle leads a thin ice pitch on *Pair of Jacks* on the *Arctic Discipline* wall of Mt. Kennedy. PHOTO BY JACK ROBERTS.

Jack Tackle leading on *Pair of Jacks,* on Mt. Kennedy. PHOTO BY JACK ROBERTS.

In contrast, Jack Roberts said that on Mt. Kennedy, "We failed." He wrote:

> While most other games that climbers play...do not have to reach a summit...I feel that climbs on mountains are different. They deserve better.... The last few rope lengths to the summit are often the most difficult because the temptation to begin the descent early is so strong and the climbers may be at their most weary.... When one stands on top with nothing else above, the feeling is immense and so different from when one turns back.... It isn't so much that the summit offers success, it's that the feeling of that success is so special that nothing else in this world comes close. And that truth needs to be kept special.

Pure and Unencumbered

In 1995, guides Steve House and Eli Helmuth laid super-light plans for the 5,500-foot, south-facing wall above Denali's Peters Glacier to the crest of the northwest buttress. Starting from the Kahiltna Glacier, they took only a stove, a rope, a few anchors, bivouac sacks and a bit of food—a total of 20 pounds each. With no intention of completing the long, cold hike to either summit of Denali, they counted on a swift return once they capped the wall. Key to their strategy was to rest in the warmth of mid-day, when a sleeping bag and tent wouldn't be necessary. Going "night naked" like this was an idea made famous in 1986 by Erhardt Loretan and Jean Troillet on Mt. Everest. House and Helmuth were the first to use this strategy on a big, technical route in Alaska, where summer's nearly 24-hour visibility makes daytime resting even more sensible.

From early morning until afternoon, the pair climbed half the face, on a variety of thin ice, rock and easier terrain, to a resting spot. After a few hours, they resumed their climb and completed the plan perfectly. They traversed over to the west buttress and descended back to their camp at the 14,000-foot bench in a total of just 33 hours.

House had started serious alpine climbing in the late 1980s, as an exchange student visiting Slovenia. He had ambled into the acme of probably the world's most intense alpine climbing culture, where newspapers keep track of climbers' annual ratings, and where winter ascents of big buttresses in the Julian Alps carrying just snacks and a jacket are a matter of course. The Slovenian community fostered the boldest generation of climbers the Himalaya had ever seen. When House began visiting Alaska a few years later, the subarctic peaks looked to him like astounding but comprehensible possibilities for extended day-climbs—skilled, unburdened and continuous movement would be the challenge, the delight and, with no bivouac gear, the only way home.

House guided Denali again in 1996, and as he descended with his group he realized that unusually favorable conditions had settled on the mountain. A warm storm had given way to a solid freeze, and firm snow and ice lay everywhere. He walked down to the Peters Glacier again, this time alone. House aimed for a new route facing the previous year's, on the 7,000-foot northwest face of the west buttress. As he hiked left past the 1991 NOLS route, he came to a beautiful stream of "smooth, tan water ice." He followed this call upward and found more channels of firm but pliable ice, sometimes rearing to vertical but so friendly to ice tools that House soon found himself way above the glacier. Besides his fitness and anxious confidence, he carried only ice tools, two liters of water, three energy bars and a spare pair of gloves. As an emotional hedge against the fear of unroped climbing, he promised himself, "I won't climb up anything that I can't climb down and I will always listen to my intuition."

House continued into the extreme soloist's realm, where every hand is played with all the cards on the table, every bet is for the whole pot, and suppressed corners of the mind break through to remind the climber of life's true purpose. As the terrain turned mixed and strenuous, House found that "fear finds a hold.... I consider my life, needing to see the value it has. I'm surprised that now, in my most selfish moment, my need to live is defined in terms of other people. I see my sister in her wedding dress, I see my wife linking perfect powder turns. My friends are grouped around a picnic table in Yosemite.... I see myself in terms of the people I've known and I understand that I will be safe."

Corners and chutes led him into some near-vertical thin ice. Then he came to a traverse with crumbly rock and backed away. A second possibility turned bad when rocks screamed down near it. A third option was too thin. House began to consider down-climbing the whole face. Finally he turned a corner into "a beautiful green groove" that led to a snowy rock traverse, which he realized he wouldn't reverse. From there, however, friendlier ground eased the way to the top of the west buttress, and when he told the story of his 14-hour circuit, the alpine world began to rethink Alaskan climbing.

In June 1998, House teamed up with Canadian Rockies and Mt. Logan veteran Joe Josephson to try a "night-naked" ascent of King Peak's intimidating north face. However,

Steve House during a brief rest near the top of the south face of King Peak. PHOTO BY JOE JOSEPHSON.

after looking over this super-alpine Eigerwand, they circled to a less-steep face they could climb in ultra-swift style: the 7,500-foot southwest face, also unclimbed. The pair acclimatized by going up the King Trench. When their blood was ready and the weather seemed as stable as it would get, they packed a stove, one rope and some anchors, some water and food, light belay jackets and—their single concession to uncertainty—a shovel blade.

With their combined packs weighing less than 30 pounds, House and Josephson moved quickly up the bulk of the face, climbing 4,000 feet of fairly steep snow and ice. At the face's headwall they entered a narrow chute snaking through wild icicles and a variety of strange rock. House led a dire pitch through overhangs of icicle spears and rock roofs, with frighteningly scant protection. After this the couloir eased, the ice became thick, and they continued to the upper west ridge. However, they had climbed right through the warm part of the day, and now, at 9 p.m., they needed a rest. They dug in and got some food down, but gathering clouds

and wind forced them to get back up and keep going. They worked their way to the summit by 11:30 p.m., and in a thick cloud they descended with difficulty via Thayer's 1952 west ridge route. Poor rock allowed no rappel anchors, and they wove among ghostly seracs and drop-offs, reversed wrong turns, and finally found their way to skis cached in the King Trench. The experience prompted Josephson to call King Peak "the most difficult summit in North America."

What happened to "the Alaska Factor," the maxim of slower, heavier climbing in the far north? How was it that House and others could just step over the struggles and limitations of several generations of strong and talented climbers? For one, with speed as their goal, they carefully assessed their routes and conditions to avoid the deep snow, long ridges, extreme cold and/or super-sustained technical terrain of many Alaskan ascents. Second, these guys were extremely fit and finely attuned to their body's condition. Third, they were technically proficient on "mountaineering ground," able to move confidently across moderately difficult and

The south face of King Peak, on the left. House and Josephson climbed the obvious ice face and then the narrow ice chute angling up and left to the top. PHOTO BY JOE JOSEPHSON.

exposed terrain with minimal or no belay. Finally, their simple but profound ultra-commitment—the confidence to leave security out of the rucksack—itself made going fast more reasonable. Fred Beckey once wrote, "On McKinley, impatience is a sin," and his words still apply. These ascents are the result of a lot of patient preparation, training and care.

In his 1988 article "The Art of Suffering," Voytek Kurtyka concluded that modern Himalayan climbers had moved beyond suffering to "extreme lightness, the ease of action and the natural relationship with the mountain environment…. Suffering has been replaced by composure" as the faculty most at play. The North American elite were discovering that level.

Always More Mountains

The amazing power of the late '90s single-push ascents brought some to believe that this was the definition of the future—that new routes, in and of themselves, were no longer interesting. However, plenty of substantial, untraveled faces and buttresses still offered a great challenge with any sort of alpine-style tactics.

In 1997, world traveler Carlos Buhler and Alaskan Charlie Sassara hooked up to try a new route on 14,800-foot University Peak. Their whole enterprise evolved from the enthusiastic eye of mountaineer and pilot Paul Claus, who had been looking at University for years. First, Claus whetted Sassara's palate with a flight past the 8,500-foot east buttress. Then, in April of '97, he made the peak's second ascent by the original 1955 north ridge, finding he could land his Supercub in a basin at 10,000 feet, bypassing the awful icefall approach to the ridge. With Claus' info and a promise to be picked up in that basin, Sassara and Buhler headed for the east buttress.

Carrying five lean days of supplies, they started up a 45-degree chute, climbed another 1,000 feet up the face's 60-degree apron, and then chopped a place for their bivouac tent. When they woke to poor visibility and blowing snow, it seemed obvious they would

retreat and start anew with better weather. While they waited for the cool safety of evening to descend, they ate heartily from their food bag. As the sun lowered, though, the clouds parted, encouraging them to wait. When the morning dawned perfectly clear, they knew they had the weather, but they also had 7,000 feet of steep new route to climb with less food than they might need. They decided to go for it.

Classic alpine ice climbing took them around the crest of the rib, just under a long section of rocky cliffs. They were able to skirt most of this on the south side of the rib, and then follow a chute to tackle a few pitches of exciting mixed climbing. One memorable pitch had Sassara stemming a rock corner right on the prow of the rib. They broke onto steep ice and snow again, and the way was clear to the haunting serac cliffs near the summit. It was their sixth day on the face and their food was pretty much gone when they tackled those seracs. Four pitches of complicated and nervous climbing on hard ice and airy snow got them through. They reached the top, and as they warily surveyed the descent Claus flew past and dropped them a sack with three dinners.

In 1999, New England partners Joe TerraVecchia and Steve Larson eyed a 3,500-foot-high, diamond-shaped headwall perched on the 10,000-foot south face of Mt. Foraker, just right of the *Infinite Spur*. Starting in early June, they found that oppressive midday heat on this south face turned snow and ice to mush, so they took rests in sheltered nooks until the sun passed to the west. They climbed pitch after pitch of mixed terrain, and they were 30 leads up when they came to the intimidating headwall. Much of their lightweight gear was worn to breaking, and they had to spend some time repairing their packs and taping and even knotting the wear spots in their ropes. Luckily they were able to find ice and mixed ground threading most of the way through the steepest granite, and after 10 days they reached the final spine of the *Infinite Spur*. Small storms made it tough to finish, but they rationed food to complete one of the biggest, steepest faces in Alaska.

Mt. Foraker from the south. The *Talkeetna Ridge* (1968) faces the camera. In the ampitheater immediately to the right is the *Infinite Spur*. Just right of that is the wall that TerraVecchia and Larson climbed in 1999. Farther right are the *French Ridge* and the southeast spur. PHOTO #8049 © BRADFORD WASHBURN. COURTESY PANOPTICON GALLERY, WALTHAM, MA.

Single Push Forward

Leading North American climbers appraising the 1984 *Slovak Route* on the east flank of Denali's *Cassin Ridge* realized that this was a steep and challenging line, safe from falling masses, and worthy of a second ascent. In 2000, House, Twight and Backes decided an ascent of this route could be the next level of alpine-style climbing in Alaska. However, guides Kevin Mahoney and Ben Gilmore beat them to it. With little information about the Slovak ascent, the two persevered through seven days of harsh cold to make the first alpine-style ascent of the route.

Backes, House and Twight, though disappointed with this news, recharged their enthusiasm with the notion that a bivouac-free single push would be the statement they wanted to make. For nourishment they would take only a measured but ample supply of carbohydrate syrup packets. They'd stop for rehydration every 12 hours and speed these stops by carrying two stoves. Each climber would lead four pitches at a time, and during belays one of the three could doze off. When

Ben Gilmore leading a crux pitch on the first alpine-style ascent of the *Slovak Route* on Denali. PHOTO BY KEVIN MAHONEY.

they got to the easier, upper part of the route, they planned to abandon their technical gear and whatever else no longer served them. Twight scoffed at complaints about littering by asserting, "Honor means winning, which requires surviving."

Helped by a handwritten route description from the Slovaks and by ice ledges left from Mahoney and Gilmore's camps, the trio blitzed much of the route's hardest climbing in under 24 hours. House again found himself in "the zone" of poised intensity on steep and unprotected mixed climbing. After an hour's rest at over 14,000 feet, they continued with a couple of more hard pitches into the 3 a.m. dawn. Their energy began to wane and clouds obscured the way to connect with the upper *Cassin Ridge* (veering away from the Slovaks' original snow-basin finish). As they struggled to find a route, their pace and confidence withered, and it was a very spent trio that struggled to the crest of the *Cassin* at 17,400 feet, after more than two almost sleepless days. They had found the brutal

Steve House leading a difficult mixed pitch on the *Slovak Direct.* PHOTO BY MARK TWIGHT.

Scott Backes and Steve House following an ice runnel on the *Slovak Direct.* PHOTO BY MARK TWIGHT.

Steve House and Scott Backes climbing the last slope to gain the *Cassin Ridge*. PHOTO BY MARK TWIGHT.

test they sought, for with no bivouac gear and no fuel they had no choice but to keep going. The packed track of a previous party on the ridge eased the way toward the summit, but in some delirium House insisted after a while that they angle left through unbroken snow toward the west buttress. With this detour their amazing endurance came up short, and they gave up on the summit to gasp down to the 14,300-foot camp on the west buttress route, after being on the go for 63 nearly continuous hours.

Going ultra-light on big Alaska Range faces became the vogue in 2001. On a new route on the *Father and Son's Wall*, the face that House and Helmuth climbed below Denali's northwest buttress, Britons Ian Parnell and Kenton Cool found plenty of challenge in less than ideal conditions. After many turns of uncertain routefinding, cruxes of snowy rock climbing, deep-snow trail breaking and just one four-hour "lunch stop," they topped out on the northwest buttress hoping to take a long break in the sun. But typical Denali wind and cloud forced them to keep going. After a 46-hour roundtrip, they struggled back to Denali's 14,000-foot bench.

Steve House teamed with Argentine-American super-climber Rolando Garibotti this season for an ultra-light ascent of Foraker's *Infinite Spur*. This route presents at least as serious a prospect as the more technical *Slovak Direct* on Denali, because of the longer and more complex descent. They started up it with just one rope, a minimal rack, a stove, a gallon of water, ample carbohydrate packets and a bit of other food, a good weather forecast and a radio, jackets but no sleeping bags, and astounding confidence that they could get to the top in one long day.

Wearing his light pack, Garibotti led the block of lower mixed pitches. Then they simul-climbed up the snowy bulk of the route, roped but placing only an occasional snow anchor. At the crux upper headwall, House led directly up ice chutes, and after just 13 hours on the go they had put all the hard climbing and two-thirds of the elevation below them.

They found a flat spot under a serac, and here they melted snow and dozed for almost four hours. As dusk deepened they headed for the top, fairly exhausted. It took them almost eight hours to cover the last 2,500 feet of moderate ground before they could look north over central Alaska. The weather held nicely as they plugged down the Sultana Ridge and over Mt. Crosson for another 20 hours.

Garibotti reflected on this accomplishment with a detached gaze. He emphasized that their ultra-light packs made the climb easier, not harder. But he also figured that after 15 to 20 hours their plan for deprivation had become inefficient. "One mug of 'real food' and a sleeping bag to share—just five to seven hours of sleep would have made the overall trip faster, I think." He also regretted that "with our lack of equipment we could not spare the time to contemplate our surroundings."

The most comprehensive single-push ascent yet in Alaska came when Teton guide Stephen Koch paired with Slovenian Marko Prezelj—a Himalayan super-alpinist who has a knack for bringing out the best in many partners. In late June of 2001, they aimed for a new route on the south face of Denali, left of the *Cassin*. No one had visited this face since the 1983 Becker ascent. Prezelj and Koch first got used to the area and to the altitude with a variety of preliminary climbs, including an all-free ascent of the *Moonflower Buttress* on Mt. Hunter.

With daypacks and no bivouac gear, they set off for their new route from the west buttress' 14,000-foot plateau, starting with a tricky descent of the 1972 *West Rib* route, a stressful five-hour tour over bergschrunds and under seracs. They started their route up clean, steep granite choked with ice—a pitch that Prezelj said was his hardest lead ever in the mountains. The pair climbed in "blocks," with each climber leading three pitches or more in a row—a strategy that many had come to credit for a noticeable gain in efficiency compared with switching leads at each belay. Koch spoke of Prezelj's capacity: "Saying that Marko looks comfortable in the mountain environment is an understatement. He eats up vertical terrain like it is candy."

Koch and Prezelj made it almost a point of honor to lead as much as possible while still wearing their light packs. Pitch after pitch of mixed climbing unfolded, and Koch marveled at how "the rock was made for dry-tooling." As afternoon came, water ran down the rock, dangerously wetting them but also

Steve House leading a difficult ramp pitch on the *Slovak Direct*. PHOTO BY MARK TWIGHT.

The lower southwest face of Denali, showing the line of *Light Traveler*. PHOTO BY MARKO PREZELJ.

delivering needed fluids. As the sun set toward midnight, they desperately wanted a cooking break but no ledge appeared, and as the Denali night turned bitter they knew they had too little insulation to stop. Finally, after 27 hours on the go, Koch led over the last steep climbing, and as the sun came onto them again he found a boulder with a flat top.

After about 25 long, hard pitches they could finally sit, sleep, eat, drink and dry their clothes. In the afternoon they started again, finding the terrain easier but still requiring occasional anchors for 3,000 feet.

Soft snow made for hard work, and as their bodies started to wobble they hoped for another stove stop, but Koch discovered that

Stephen Koch high on *Light Traveler*. PHOTO BY MARKO PREZELJ.

their remaining fuel had leaked out. Later, Koch would write that their "commitment was complete. If something went wrong we had only ourselves to save us. Our margin of safety was small, but we would have had it no other way." They reached the upper *Cassin Ridge*, where they abandoned the weight of

their rope. Into another night too cold to stop they plowed upward, and, "It seemed like forever had come and gone." Forty-eight hours after they started, they arrived on the summit—their gamble of light and fast had played out just right, and they named the route *Light Traveler*.

Marko Prezelj leading a wet mixed pitch on *Light Traveler*. PHOTO BY STEPHEN KOCH, COURTESY MARKO PREZELJ.

Stephen Koch and Marko Prezelj on the summit of Denali, after completing Light Traveler. PHOTO COURTESY MARKO PREZELJ.

SUGGESTED ROUTES
FROM THIS PERIOD

Most of the ascents portrayed in this chapter fall outside the realm of anything this book can recommend. Less than a handful of elite climbers are familiar with these climbs, and for now they remain inspirational and experimental. Nevertheless, these "experiments" were carried out by climbers with an eye toward quality as well as difficulty, and it's impossible not to notice that many of them look worthy of pursuit.

The Slovak route on Denali, the three routes on Denali's south face left of the *Cassin* and the 1999 Foraker south face route take on the steepest and most solid rock and ice faces on two of the continent's most important peaks, and elite climbers must be eyeing them carefully. Huntington's *Phantom Wall* has been generating some talk too. And the '91 and '96 ascents of the northwest face of Denali's west buttress let us know that unusually good conditions for technical climbing form there, and it's only a matter of time until solid climbers seek them out again.

Mountaineers looking for grand, moderately difficult challenges in an astounding setting eventually will look more carefully at the routes opened up on the secondary giants of the Icefield Ranges. Kennan Harvey and Seth Shaw repeated the south spur of Good Neighbor Peak, and the Pilling routes on Mt. Augusta and Mt. Alverstone are so obvious that they have the potential to be labeled as classics. Finally, the Pilling-Bebie south pillar of Devils Thumb has generated a quiet buzz about a possible all-free second ascent.

Epilogue
The Wild Card

WHEN WE COMPARE mountaineering legacies among the continents, Europe carries the banner of alpinism's birthplace and core arena, Asia is the realm of ultimate peaks almost beyond the mountaineering concept, and South America, Africa and Antarctica have their diverse and exotic great ranges. In North America, mountaineering came of age bearing aspects of all these elements, but what's unique in our heritage is the context of wilderness. Mountaineering in North America started with ventures into wilderness; as we grew familiar with certain ranges we went farther afield; when wilderness seemed to be running out we acted to preserve it. In North America, mountains *mean* wilderness.

Mountaineering's strongest quality is to write great terrain into our souls; this is the fruit of engagement. When climbs inscribe their essays into us, wilderness adds another dimension to the text. Most of our notable ascents have been a long way from roads or easy viewpoints to scout conditions, with no fixed anchors, no huts, no rescue potential and no neighboring parties—conditions that demand a deeper commitment and broader competence than ascents in well-tracked mountains.

Accepting the logistical and emotional challenge of wilderness seems to have made us more cautious. Compared with the classic alpine legacy, North American mountaineering collected a reputation for heavier packs and lower technical standards. Sometimes, indeed, we have carried burdens for imaginary battles, but more often we have simply prepared appropriately for broader uncertainty. While we might speak of a love-hate relationship with the wilds—loving the sense of discovery while bemoaning the extra challenge—our instincts almost always have told us to keep the mountains wild. For North

Americans, the drive for great climbs has mixed with a desire to discover a world apart.

To many European historians, North America's mountaineering heritage has merited little more than a few side notes that help fill the gaps between alpine and Himalayan breakthroughs. This perspective neglects the breadth of the world's mountaineering legacy, and it overlooks how Europe's own climbers—often some of their best—have come to North America both for specific routes and to experience climbing where the mountains are practically undiscovered. From William Spotswood Green in 1888 to J. Norman Collie at the turn of the 20th century, from Fritz Wiessner in the 1930s to Doug Scott in the 1970s and Simon Richardson at the turn of the 21st century, almost every generation has seen European climbers come here when their own mountains began to seem too familiar. Enthusiasm for meeting mountains still in a state of nature played a role in the opening and occupation of our continent, and it has been a fulfillment of myth—our wilderness mountaineering has given added form to the Euro-American dream of renewal, and the engagement of our mountains has opened new doors to, in the words of author Antoine de Saint Exupéry, "that new vision of the world won through hardship."

Of course mountaineering's own progress takes wilderness and maps it, takes remoteness and makes it familiar, and takes mountaineering itself and packages it. Into the 1990s, mountaineering in North America was still an obscure sort of cult, and climbers expected to be hounded with the question "Why?" Now a fairly wide range of people accepts mountaineering as a positive activity. A sitting U.S. vice president has climbed Mt. Rainier, international diplomats meet in the Rockies, successful guides and sponsored climbers number in the hundreds, and Banff is only the most committed and sophisticated of the many towns that build their identities and economies around mountains and mountain adventures. By no coincidence, the best North American climbers now hold their own among the most capable mountaineers in the world. As dozens of people crowd popular routes on prime weekends, long gone are the days when we could automatically attach the label "wilderness" to a North American mountain ascent. Yet, compared with Europe, even our most popular mountains are undeveloped and our general culture is still unfamiliar with mountaineering ascents.

As some of the newest generation of mountaineers look to our mountains with neither the North American sense of wilderness nor the European legacy of alpinism, they get lost, figuratively and literally. Nothing exhibits this better than the cellular phone calls that rangers from Mt. Rainier to the Tetons and Mt. Washington get nowadays from dismayed would-be climbers asking for help simply because it's getting dark and they don't know where they are—fools who don't understand they are venturing way off the municipal grid.

For climbers more at home in the mountains around North America, the wilderness legacy lingers in our spirit, keeping us committed to self-sufficiency and maintaining an expectation of engagement with great hunks of terrain above and beyond the norms of civilized life. In that old interplay between accomplishment and experience, our wilderness mountains have given us a legacy weighted toward personal experiences. Public discourse focuses on accomplishments we can measure, yet can we assume that accomplishments are more important? The late Alex Lowe, one of history's most amazing climbing athletes, wrote in 1997:

> I think it's the nature of alpine climbs and alpine climbers that the most incredible stories are often guarded within the memories of the participants. Perhaps there is a reticence to publicize ascents in which the people involved knew that humility before the mountains was fundamental to success. These constitute the climbs on which no one was confused about having "conquered" mountains—the climbs on which success was more a function of grappling with the frail human spirit than grappling with the mountain. Mountains acknowledge and reward sufficient humility and allow the truly committed to tread their elusive summits.

The mountaineering heritage worldwide shows that we expect mountaineering to give us both accomplishments and experiences. Accomplishments establish the standards and make the celebrities, while experiences generate the stories and shape our characters. While we sometimes focus on one or the other, the honest truth is that the best climbs bring us home with profound experiences and great accomplishments, raised together in high balance. In this way, mountaineering is an avenue of growth and intensity that's rare in modern society.

Before the World War I era, mountaineering was seen as a character-building enterprise of exploration. After that, it became an endeavor into technical and topographic difficulty. The technical and topographic approaches gradually played out, and mountaineering became a search for greater personal engagement. Today, all these collected legacies are at play. We have climbers exploring new ground, ascending technically difficult terrain, and using strategies that require profound personal engagement—sometimes all in the same ascent. This evolution reveals a powerful desire to meet the challenges of great terrain, and eventually to arrive at something that sounds very similar to the joy, humility and renewal that our forerunners wrote about.

In the future, athletic accomplishments will certainly exceed the amazing standards we see today. Adventurous experiences also will continue to be part of our culture. But adventure needs uncertainty, and in North

America, where mountaineers have fought off *téléphériques* and highways, where whole subregions still have not seen a climber, discovery still deepens our experiences. Our mountains, more in their natural state than those in Europe, help keep the potential for experience young and our humility strong. Whatever the myths that future society will act out in the mountains, our great, wild places will continue to be a forum for both accomplishment and experience. With both these forces at play, the exact flavor and direction of mountaineering in the future remains deliciously uncertain.

If the broad goal of mountaineering is to lift both experience and accomplishment, is there a way to write the sense of experience into the standards of the game? Might there be a parameter to show not only that a summit was won but also that it was won with that classic mix of joy and humility?

In 1939, Coloradan Elizabeth Cowles proposed something like this in her essay for the *American Alpine Journal*, "Singing on the Summit." Cowles wrote: "With all the writing that has been done about the joys of mountaineering, it has always seemed strange to me that so little mention is made of music in the mountains. *For my part, I have never considered a summit really won until a song has been sung upon it*" (emphasis added).

Were summit songs accepted as a parameter for success, imagine how many peaks would still await their first ascent. Just as in any other measure of mountaineering success, weather, altitude, fatigue or other complaints would be no excuse for failing to fulfill the choral requirement. On a climb of Europe's Dent Blanche, Cowles took inspiration from her guide, Josef Georges, who did all the hard leading and yet, when they all reached the top and others "shivered in a cold and swirling mist," struck up with *La-haute sur la Montagne*.

Cowles' favorite summit chorales were Swiss, for the native folk melodies "seem to catch the very spirit of the mountains.... I have always felt that these words, *de tout notre coeur et tout simplement* ["simply and from the whole heart"], say more about the true love of hills than any others I know of." Perhaps the songs of her day no longer convey the same innocent glory, but certainly the modern climber could call out some contemporary hip-hop or classical aria to express and prove that the summit was won with wonder.

Alas, maybe the era is gone when we might welcome another's *karaoke* practice shattering the silence of mountain summits. Imagine topping out on the *Sunshine-Peewee Route* of Mt. Whitney only to hear 14 different teams caterwauling their claim. And there's probably good reason not to contaminate joy by making it a requirement. Yet Cowles' call is a good reminder that the mountaineering game might be at its best when it's played with light hearts:

> So let the mountain climber use as best he can such vocal chords as nature gave him. Let him sing when he climbs to forget his weariness, or to keep his courage up in extremis, but above all let him sing for the joy of singing on the mountaintop he has earned by his own efforts. How could it be possible, to paraphrase a remark of R. L. G. Irving, for anyone to receive so much and remain silent?

Appendices

Guidebooks to North American Mountains

Alaska

Alaska: A Climbing Guide, by Michael Wood and Colby Coombs. Seattle: The Mountaineers Books, 2001.

Denali: A Climbing Guide, by R. J. Secor. Mechanicsburg, Penn.: Stackpole Books, 1998.

High Alaska: A Historical Guide to Denali, Mount Foraker & Mount Hunter, by Jonathan Waterman. New York: The American Alpine Club, 1988.

British Columbia and Alberta

Alpine Select, by Kevin McLane. Squamish, B.C.: Elaho Publishing Corporation, 2001.

Bugaboo Rock: A Climber's Guide, by Randall Green and Joe Bensen. Seattle: The Mountaineers Books, 2003.

Bugaboos, The, by Chris Atkinson and Mark Piché. Squamish, B.C.: Elaho Publishing Corporation, 2003.

Selected Alpine Climbs in the Canadian Rockies, by Sean Dougherty. Calgary: Rocky Mountain Books, 1996.

Selkirks North, by David P. Jones. Squamish, B.C.: Elaho Publishing Corporation, 2004.

Selkirks South, by David P. Jones. Squamish, B.C.: Elaho Publishing Corporation, 2001.

The Waddington Guide, by Don Serl. Squamish, B.C.: Elaho Publishing Corporation, 2003.

Cascades

Cascade Alpine Guide, by Fred Beckey. Vol. 1, *Columbia River to Stevens Pass.* Seattle: The Mountaineers Books, 2000.

————. Vol. 2. *Stevens Pass to Rainy Pass.* Seattle: The Mountaineers Books, 2003.

————. Vol. 3. *Rainy Pass to Fraser River.* Seattle: The Mountaineers Books, 1995.

Climber's Guide to the Olympic Mountains, by Olympic Mountain Rescue. Seattle: The Mountaineers Books, 1999.

Climbing Mount Rainier: The Essentials Guide, by Fred Beckey and Alex Van Steen. Mukilteo, Wash.: AlpenBooks, 1999.

Mount Rainier: A Climbing Guide, by Mike Gauthier. Seattle: The Mountaineers Books, 1999.

Oregon High: A Climbing Guide to Nine Cascade Volcanoes, by Jeff Thomas. Portland, Ore.: Keep Climbing Press, 1991.

Selected Climbs in the Cascades, by Jim Nelson and Peter Potterfield. Seattle: The Mountaineers Books, 2003.

Sierra Nevada

Climbing California's Fourteeners, by Stephen F. Porcella and Cameron M. Burns. Seattle: The Mountaineers Books, 1998.

Climbing California's High Sierra, by Claude Fiddler and John Moynier. Gilford, Conn.: Globe-Pequot Press, 2002.

The Good, The Great, and The Awesome: The Top 40 High Sierra Rock Climbs, by Peter Croft. Mammoth Lakes, Calif.: Maximus Press, 2002.

The High Sierra: Peaks, Passes and Trails, by R. J. Secor. Seattle: The Mountaineers Books, 1999.

Colorado and Wyoming

A Climber's Guide to the Teton Range, by Leigh N. Ortenburger and Reynold G. Jackson. Seattle: The Mountaineers Books, 1996.

Climbing and Hiking in the Wind River Mountains, by Joe Kelsey. Evergreen, Colo.: Chockstone Press, 1994.

The High Peaks: Rocky Mountain National Park Rock & Ice Climbing, by Richard Rossiter. Evergreen, Colo.: Chockstone Press, 1997.

New England

AMC White Mountain Guide. Edited by Gene Daniell and Steven D. Smith. 27th ed. Boston: Appalachian Mountain Club Books, 2003.

An Ice Climber's Guide to Northern New England, by S. Peter Lewis and Rick Wilcox. Conway, N.H.: TMC Books, 2002.

Mexico

Mexico's Volcanoes: A Climbing Guide, by R. J. Secor. Seattle: The Mountaineers Books, 1993.

Parque Nacional San Pedro Mártir: Topographic Map and Visitor's Guide to Baja's Highest Mountains, by Jerry Schad. San Diego: Centra Publications, 1988.

General

Fifty Classic Climbs of North America, by Steve Roper and Allen Steck. San Francisco: Sierra Club Books, 1996.

Alpine Grades

This book is the first in the United States to apply the French system of overall alpine grades to the routes described. It's time North Americans began rating alpine challenges, just as they do essentially all other forms of climbing.

While North Americans have employed the National Climbing Classification System since the 1960s (see Chapter 11), this system has held strong to its roots in American rock climbing, and its most archetypal routes are in Yosemite Valley. The NCCS grades are widely understood as time-based measures of the degree and scale of technical climbing on rock faces and buttresses. For rock routes in such ranges as the High Sierra, American Rockies and Bugaboos, these I–VI grades assign well-understood values to overall challenge, and their use should continue. However, from ridgelines to ice faces, from Rainier to Robson and Deborah, the NCCS grades have been applied either awkwardly or, for the most part, not at all.

Starting in the 1990s, some widely traveled climbers began to advocate that North Americans adopt the French alpine grades, for this is a system rooted in alpine terrain and it is already popular around the world, including in South America. The French grades are adjectives, running from F (*facile*, or "easy") to ED (*extrêmement difficile*, or "extremely difficult"). French climbers developed this system after World War II as a general appraisal of overall difficulty among various mountain routes. In 2001 and 2003, Canadian authors David Jones, Kevin McLane and Don Serl assigned French alpine grades to routes in British Columbia. They and I have interpreted this system as a subjective measure of overall engagement challenge, taking into account everything from rock quality, steep snow, remoteness and technical ice to the degree and scale of technical difficulties, chance of escape, prevailing climate and descent complexities. The system also accounts for the compounding of such factors.

The ratings assigned by Jones, McLane, Serl and this book were made after fairly extensive discussions with well-traveled climbers who are familiar with both the French ratings and North American mountains. We sorted many North American routes into a progression of overall difficulty, compared them to routes internationally rated, and came up with some results. While some specific ratings applied in this book may need adjustment, they at least start to bring to North America a conceptual structure based not just on technical difficulty but also on broader alpine challenges.

In recent years, French guideauthors have added a "seriousness grade" (using Roman numerals I–VII) to impart more information on how risky, sustained and committing a route is. Thus a route might be rated D III. Ironically, this leaves the original adjective more as a measure of overall technical difficulty. It remains to be seen if this additional system will catch on, and how North Americans might make use of it.

Climbs in Alaska and the Yukon have been rated with a separate overall rating system initiated in the 1960s by Boyd Everett (see Chapter 9). Today, however, Alaska and the Yukon seem less like a separate realm than simply an especially demanding part of the mountain world at large. There are climbers who have experience in both classic alpine terrain and these northern ranges who are capable of comparing these routes to international standards.

Below is the progression of the French grades, with some interpretation of the typical character of the routes in each grade and some examples of routes at each level (including both routes described within this book and other examples).

F Easy (*Facile*)

Routes where reasonable endurance may be required but in normal conditions there is little risk of a serious fall. The climate is temperate and the altitude moderate.

Mt. Whitney, Trail Route; Mt. St. Helens; Mt. Temple, Southwest Ridge

PD Somewhat Difficult (*Peu Difficile*)

Routes with some exposure and modest technical difficulty, up to low fifth-class rock and/or snow slopes up to 45 degrees. Can also refer to long, technically easy routes in a harsher climate or at higher altitude, or with complex glaciers.

Mont Blanc, Standard Route; Pigeon Spire, West Ridge; Mt. Whitney, *Mountaineers (Muir) Route;* Mt. Hood, *Cooper Spur;* Citlaltépetl, Jamapa Glacier; Mt. Baker, Original Route

AD Fairly Difficult (*Assez Difficile*)

Routes that often include some mid-level fifth-class rock and/or snow and ice pitches up to about 50 degrees. Strong alpine climbers sometimes characterize AD routes as those that are reasonable for descent with few or no rappels. Can also apply to somewhat difficult routes in harsher or more inaccessible environments.

Bugaboo Spire, *Kain Route;* Gannett Peak, North Face; Mt. Goode, Southeast Couloir; Grand Teton, East Ridge (AD+)

D Difficult (*Difficile*)

Routes that have sustained technical difficulties or short sections of severe difficulties, or technically easy routes with substantial scale and climatic challenges.

Mt. Sir Donald, Northwest Buttress (D-); Denali, West Buttress; Snowpatch Spire, Southeast (Bedayan) Route; Temple Crag, *Sun Ribbon Arête;* Mt. Rainier, *Liberty Ridge;* Mt. Butters, Northeast Ridge; Mt. Stuart, Complete North Ridge (D+ by direct finish); Grand Teton, North Face (D+); Mt. Alberta, Original Route (D+)

TD Very Difficult (*Très Difficile*)

Routes with a full spectrum of severe challenges, usually including scale, sustained and hard fifth-class climbing and/or steep ice and snow, objective hazards and difficult climate.

South Howser Tower, West Buttress; Mt. Edith Cavell, North Face; Serra Five, Original Route; Slesse Mountain, Northeast Buttress; Denali, West Rib; Mt. Huntington, West Face Couloir; Keeler Needle, *Harding Route*; Mt. Waddington, South Face (TD+ by original route)

ED Extremely Difficult (*Extrêmement Difficile*)

Routes near or at the extremes of compounding difficulties. Challenges include large scale, sustained and very difficult climbing (probably on both ice and rock) and possibly objective hazards. Climbs more demanding than ED are problematic to gauge because so few people have climbed them, but the system expands by adding numerals.

ED

Mt. Combatant, *Skywalk* (complete); Mt. Andromeda, *Andromeda Strain*; Denali, *Reality Ridge*; Denali, *Cassin Ridge*; Eiger, North Face (original route)

ED2

Denali, *Slovak Direct*; Denali, *McCartney-Roberts*; Mt. Geikie, North Face *(Lowe-Hannibal)*

ED3

Mt. Logan, *Hummingbird Ridge*; Mt. Combatant, *Belligerence* ; North Twin, North Face

Index

Italicized numbers indicate pages with illustrations.